YOU
COULD
LOOK
IT UP

YOU COULD LOOK IT UP

THE REFERENCE SHELF FROM ANCIENT BABYLON TO WIKIPEDIA

JACK LYNCH

BLOOMSBURY PRESS

NEW YORK · LONDON · OXFORD · NEW DELHI · SYDNEY

Bloomsbury Press
An imprint of Bloomsbury Publishing Plc

1385 Broadway   50 Bedford Square
New York   London
NY 10018   WC1B 3DP
USA   UK

www.bloomsbury.com

BLOOMSBURY and the Diana logo are trademarks of Bloomsbury Publishing Plc

First published 2016

ISBN: HB: 978-0-8027-7752-2
ePub: 978-0-8027-7794-2

LIBRARY OF CONGRESS CATALOGING-IN-PUBLICATION DATA HAS BEEN APPLIED FOR.

2 4 6 8 10 9 7 5 3 1

Typeset by RefineCatch Limited, Bungay, Suffolk
Printed and bound in USA by Berryville Graphics Inc., Berryville, Virginia

To find out more about our authors and books visit www.bloomsbury.com. Here you will find extracts, author interviews, details of forthcoming events and the option to sign up for our newsletters.

Bloomsbury books may be purchased for business or promotional use. For information on bulk purchases please contact Macmillan Corporate and Premium Sales Department at specialmarkets@macmillan.com.

For Dan Traister
Prince of Librarians

CONTENTS

CHAPTER 0: *Prologue: Looking It Up*　　　3

CHAPTER 1: *Justice in the Earth: Laws of the Ancient World*　　　11

  CHAPTER 1½: *Of Making Many Books: Information Overload*　　　22

CHAPTER 2: *In the Beginning Was the Word: The First Dictionaries*　　　24

  CHAPTER 2½: *A Fraction of the Total: Counting Reference Books*　　　34

CHAPTER 3: *The History of Nature: Science in Antiquity*　　　37

  CHAPTER 3½: *Easy as ABC: The Rise (and Fall?) of Alphabetical Order*　　　48

CHAPTER 4: *Round Earth's Imagined Corners: Mapping the World*　　　52

  CHAPTER 4½: *The Invention of the Codex*　　　64

CHAPTER 5: *The Circle of the Sciences: Ancient Encyclopedias*　　　67

  CHAPTER 5½: *The Dictionary Gets Its Day in Court*　　　78

CHAPTER 6: *Leechcraft: Medieval Medicine*　　　82

  CHAPTER 6½: *Plagiarism: The Crime of Literary Theft*　　　91

CHAPTER 7: *New Worlds: Cartography in an Age of Discovery*　　　94

  CHAPTER 7½: *Tell Me How You Organize Your Books*　　　104

CHAPTER 8: *Admirable Artifice: Computers before Computers*　　　107

  CHAPTER 8½: *To Bring People Together: Societies*　　　119

CHAPTER 9: *The Infirmity of Human Nature: Guides to Error*　　　122

  CHAPTER 9½: *Ignorance, Pure Ignorance: Of Omissions, Ambiguities, and Plain Old Blunders*　　　133

CHAPTER 10: *Guarding the Avenues of Language: Dictionaries in the Eighteenth Century*　　　137

  CHAPTER 10½: *Of Ghosts and Mountweazels*　　　152

CHAPTER 11: *The Way of Faith: Guidelines for Believers*　　　155

  CHAPTER 11½: *Who's Who and What's What: Making the Cut*　　　167

CHAPTER 12: *Erotic Recreations: Sex Manuals* 170

CHAPTER 12½: *The Boys' Club* 181

CHAPTER 13: *Collecting Knowledge into the Smallest Areas:*

The Great Encyclopedias 185

CHAPTER 13½: *Dictionary or Encyclopedia?* 197

CHAPTER 14: *Of Redheads and Babus: Dictionaries and Empire* 200

CHAPTER 14½: *A Small Army: Collaborative Endeavors* 211

CHAPTER 15: *Killing Time: Games and Sports* 214

CHAPTER 15½: *Out of Print* 225

CHAPTER 16: *Monuments of Erudition: The Great National Dictionaries* 228

CHAPTER 16½: *Counting Editions* 242

CHAPTER 17: *Grecian Glory, Roman Grandeur: Victorian Eyes on the*

Ancient World 244

CHAPTER 17½: *Lost Projects: What Might Have Been* 257

CHAPTER 18: *Words Telling Their Own Stories: The Historical Dictionaries* 260

CHAPTER 18½: *Overlong and Overdue* 273

CHAPTER 19: *An Alms-Basket of Words: The Reference Book as Salvation* 278

CHAPTER 19½: *Reading the Dictionary* 290

CHAPTER 20: *Modern Materia Medica: Staying Healthy* 294

CHAPTER 20½: *Incomplete and Abandoned Projects* 307

CHAPTER 21: *The Foundation Stone: Library Catalogs* 311

CHAPTER 21½: *Index Learning* 323

CHAPTER 22: *The Good Life: The Arts and High Society* 326

CHAPTER 22½: *Some Unlikely Reference Books* 337

CHAPTER 23: *Presumed Purity: Science in a Scientific Age* 342

CHAPTER 23½: *At No Extra Cost! The Business of Reference Books* 352

CHAPTER 24: *Full and Authoritative Information: Doctrine for the*

Modern World 356

CHAPTER 24½: *Unpersons: Damnatio Memoriae* 368

CHAPTER 25: *Nothing Special: Books for Browsers* 371

EPILOGUE: *The World's Information: The Encyclopedic Dream*   382

A Brief Etymological Glossary   391

Acknowledgments   399

Bibliography   401

Notes   425

Index   443

YOU
COULD
LOOK
IT UP

PROLOGUE: LOOKING IT UP

T ALL BEGINS with the *written* word.

"Reference" means nothing without writing. "In a primary oral culture," wrote Walter J. Ong, the twentieth century's greatest theorist of orality, "the expression 'to look up something' is an empty phrase: it would have no conceivable meaning. Without writing, words as such have no visual presence. . . . You might 'call' them back—'recall' them. But there is nowhere to 'look' for them."[1] But because we live in a bookish and data-rich culture, we all know what it means to "look" for information. *You Could Look It Up* is an account of fifty great reference books, from the third millennium B.C.E. to the present, all of them ambitious attempts to collect a vast amount of knowledge and to present it to the world in a usable form.

For some, the reference book is the emblem of pedantry, sterility, dead facts rather than living wisdom. Charles Dickens gave us Thomas Gradgrind, the dry-as-dust pedant whose mantra is *"Fact, fact, fact!"* Sadly, the word *knowledge* is often paired with *rote*, as if a knowledge of facts necessarily precludes a deeper understanding or an imaginative engagement.

"Dictionaries do not spring into being," Sidney Landau wrote. "People must plan them, collect information, and write them. . . . No other form of writing is at once so quixotic and so intensely practical."[2] But when the public thinks about the people who write reference books—if the public ever thinks about them—they probably call to mind what Samuel Johnson called "harmless drudges." Howard Hawks's 1941 screwball comedy *Ball of Fire* sparkles with a script co-written by Billy Wilder. It features a team of socially inept professors, modeled on Snow White's seven dwarfs, who live together in a big house and work on an encyclopedia containing all the world's knowledge. Gary

Cooper, brilliantly cast against type as Professor Bertram Potts, stands at the head of this sorry crew of encyclopedists, lexicographers, and grammarians including Professors Gurkakoff, Magenbruch, Oddley, and Peagram. They are all utterly stymied when confronted with the va-va-voom burlesque-queen heroine, Katherine "Sugarpuss" O'Shea, played by Barbara Stanwyck.

But the actual world of reference books, overflowing with *fact, fact, fact*, is positively exuberant, passionate, bursting with knowledge, and their authors are not always sexless cartoon characters but include quirky geniuses, revolutionary firebrands, and impassioned culture warriors, many of them with the unflagging intellectual energy of a whirling dervish. *You Could Look It Up* tells the story of two emperors, a Roman naturalist who sailed his ship toward an erupting volcano and died in the falling ash, the inventor of the decimal point, the philosophers who were blamed for starting the French Revolution, the German folklorists whose gory tales still frighten children, and an Oxford classicist whose daughter Alice went down the rabbit hole to Wonderland.

You Could Look It Up is partly a call to read, or at least read *in*, these books, and to get to know the people who wrote them. A reference book collects a civilization's memoranda to itself. When we turn an ancient dictionary's pages, we read something never meant for our eyes, and we get to overhear the dead talking among themselves. That is why reference books have much to teach us, even when they are obsolete—especially when they are obsolete. Of course we can learn all sorts of trivia from old dictionaries and encyclopedias, but also much more than trivia. In looking at these old books we get the chance to look *through* them, at the people who created them and at the worlds they inhabited. When we discover that human beings were divided into five groups in the first *Encyclopædia Britannica*—American, European, Asiatic, African, and "monstrous"—we get a glimpse of early "scientific" race theory coming into being. An old atlas is worthless if we want to locate events in today's news, but it tells us plenty about how the world looked to another culture. An encyclopedia written before Columbus crossed the Atlantic says nothing useful about the smartphone, but it is one culture's way of describing the entirety of their physical, intellectual, and spiritual worlds. Even a book filled with numerical tables can end up telling a story about the incipient Industrial Revolution.

The dictionary, the encyclopedia, the atlas, the legal code—all act to distill knowledge. Distillation is the right metaphor. As any decent encyclopedia will explain, distillation removes impurities and gives us a concentrated essence. A solution goes into the alembic, where it is heated to boiling; the volatile spirits separate from the water and are captured, then allowed to condense on the other side. Out comes a purer form of the spirit—in our case, knowledge. The reference book is concentrated wisdom.

Even when concentrated, the information can still be overwhelming. A reference book is the product of a society trying to deal with more knowledge than even the most committed sage can hope to hold in memory. Reference books are big, because no one needs an encyclopedia with ten entries. Only when the body of information becomes too large to keep in our heads do we decide to offload it to paper and expand our memories into offsite storage.

And the more virtual memory a reference promises us, the more enthusiastic we are about its contents. At the heart of the reference genre is the Renaissance ideal of *copia*, Latin for "copiousness" or "fullness." Desiderius Erasmus, the very model of the Renaissance man and one of the most expansive minds the world has ever known, devoted a whole book to *copia*, the ebullient overflowing of words and ideas. He loved books that were crammed with knowledge, so much so that they were almost bursting at the seams, and everyone who has ever fallen in love with a dictionary or an encyclopedia has the same passion. This book tries to capture some of the copiousness that marks the great reference books.

Reference books shape the world. Encyclopedists and lexicographers rarely discover new facts, but by organizing and categorizing the old ones they can influence whole fields of knowledge. They determine what kinds of questions a civilization can ask about itself. Those who work under the imprimatur of some prestigious organization—*The Catholic Encyclopedia*, *The Great Soviet Encyclopedia*—proclaim unquestionable doctrine to the masses. Lexicographers may have no ambitions beyond telling an accurate story about a word, but they have determined the outcome in decisions of the Supreme Court. The compilers of the *Diagnostic and Statistical Manual of Mental Disorders* can, by declaring a given condition to be a psychiatric illness, save a criminal from the gallows or exclude a qualified person from government service. And yet, even though these books have all been compiled by fallible human beings, much of the world looks on them as unimpeachable. I'll argue—with only a small bit of exaggeration—that the reference book is responsible for the spread of empires, the scientific revolution, the French Revolution, and the invention of the computer.

⁂

What, exactly, is a reference book? In 1911, the librarian Gilbert Ward offered a succinct explanation: "Definition of a reference book.—A reference book is a book which is used for looking up particular points rather than for reading through."[3] Most books get their worth from their entirety, and it makes no sense to read just chapter 37 of *Don Quixote* or book 11, chapter 5 of *The Brothers Karamazov*. Reference works, on the other hand, are meant to be useful in pieces. Information is extracted from its original context, sliced, and rearranged, with the important level of organization being not the book or the chapter but the "entry," which is expected to make sense on its own. These entries are usually organized arbitrarily, designed to be conveniently located in answering questions that users might ask. That word "users" is a significant one: most books have readers, but reference books have users. Still, it is not always easy to draw a line between reference works and others. Is a cookbook a reference book? An anthology? Almost any compilation could count. In fact, any book in the world can become a reference book if we read in it to find a specific piece of information. But a proper reference book is designed to facilitate consultation rather than reading through.

Of course, a reference book need not even be a book. The works I discuss here include many garden-variety books, but there are also four-ton slabs of basalt and globally interconnected networks of semiconductors. Reference works have taken the form of stone tablets, papyrus scrolls, and numerical tables. They can be as grand as multivolume encyclopedias prepared by learned academies or as homely as stock reports and racing forms on cheap newsprint. Even *TV Guide*, issued for more than half a century as a weekly magazine, is a kind of reference work. And of course the most important reference works of the last few decades have been in electronic form, first on diskettes, then on CD-ROMs, and now on the Internet. "Book" is a more elegant word than "text," so I'll use it in this work, but usually in this expanded sense.

୬ঌ

You Could Look It Up does not pretend to be comprehensive, touching on all the world's important reference works—no book could do that. Instead, it contains accounts of fifty great works I find interesting, maybe because they are the first of their kind, maybe the biggest, or the most learned, or the most controversial, or the most influential, or maybe just the most eccentric or quixotic. I have borrowed my method from the ancient biographer Plutarch: each of the twenty-five chapters focuses on an exemplary pair of major reference works. Plutarch's *Parallel Lives* put important Greeks next to important Romans (Theseus and Romulus, Alexander the Great and Julius Caesar, Demosthenes and Mark Antony) and then explored the similarities and differences between them to highlight what was distinct about each figure. In my pairings I choose two more or less contemporary works on related subjects and set them in their historical context. Limiting my main discussion to just fifty books means many things are neglected. The reference house has many mansions, and I have had to omit too many important works, even whole genres: almanacs, timelines, biographical dictionaries, price guides, gazetteers, calendars, bibliographies, dictionaries of slang and regionalisms, faux reference books such as Ambrose Bierce's *Devil's Dictionary*, compendia of proverbs, and thesauruses did not make the cut. But I do get to discuss some of the most famous reference works—the dictionaries of Johnson, Webster, and the Grimms, Diderot's *Encyclopédie* and the *Encyclopædia Britannica*, Gray's *Anatomy*—with attention to what made them so noteworthy and, whenever it can be known, the personalities behind the books. Besides the central pair, each chapter touches on other relevant works, setting the major books in a longer historical context—sometimes looking back centuries to the origins of the form, sometimes looking ahead to the present day. Tucked between the chapters are shorter interludes that introduce stories that would otherwise go untold in a strictly linear history. In telling fifty little stories, I hope one big story emerges, as well as histories of some of the major reference genres—dictionary, encyclopedia, atlas, and so on.

I repeatedly ask a few questions: What need prompted someone to bring all this information together in one place? Who decided to rise to the challenge? What made them the right people for the job—or, at least, what made them think they were qualified? How did they go about their work? What carried them through the years, even decades, of work it took to compile these often million-word-plus compendia? What is in these books, and what is omitted? What did the world make of them? Finally, and most important, what do they tell us about the mentalities of the ages that produced and used them?

⁂

You Could Look It Up is both a history of and a love letter to the great dictionaries, encyclopedias, and atlases. It is also, I fear, something of a eulogy: we may be approaching the end of the era of the reference book. That is not to say reference is dead—in the information age it is more essential than ever. But the references of the future almost certainly will not be books in the traditional sense. Every technological revolution has shaken up the organization of information. Advances such as alphabetical order, page numbers, tables of contents, and indexes made it possible to organize old information for new purposes—and, as a side effect, revealed the limitations of the old technologies. As we begin thinking about new ways we might use an old book, we discover new things we would like to do with it, new ways of searching it.

The change we are living through now, in which hard-copy dictionaries and encyclopedias are becoming harder and harder to sell and publishers are scrambling to figure out what will work online, makes it all the more urgent that we understand the history of the genre. "As the information banks available on our computers expand vertiginously in the present," writes Anthony Grafton, "we have realized that we do not understand the ways in which information was created and transmitted in the past. New forms of cultural history are taking shape to fill this gap: histories that emphasize not the formal content of ideas but the institutions and practices that enabled them to be created and transmitted."[4]

⁂

Whenever I quote works in English I follow original spellings, including those of foreign names and titles, except when they require special characters and diacritical marks that are not available in most typefaces—there I have used the closest equivalents available to me. Outside quotations, I give names and titles in the most familiar forms. I provide the sources of all quotations in the endnotes, though when the source is obvious from context—when I quote the definition for *apron* in John Kersey's *New English Dictionary*, for example—I do not bother with notes. A handful of uncited quotations from living writers came from personal communication, and uncited translations from French, Italian, Spanish, German, Latin, and Greek are my own.

I've scattered some "vital statistics" about the major titles throughout the book: boxes give the full title of each reference work, the person primarily responsible for it, the principle on which it is organized, and the date of publication of the first edition. To give some idea of relative sizes, I give the number of volumes, pages, and entries, and, whenever I can manage, the physical size and even the weight of the book, along with the total surface area of all the pages, counting both front and back. (It's usually impossible to give measurements for books from before the age of print, and even printed books can be bound or trimmed differently, so consider the numbers approximations.) Word count is the total number of words, not merely the number of entries. (This book is around 140,000 words; the *Encyclopédie* would fill about 142 volumes this size, and Pauly-Wissowa is about 392 times longer than this book.) If the book had an afterlife, I give the latest edition. Round numbers are my best estimates; precise figures mean someone has counted, usually with the aid of a computer.

CHAPTER 1

JUSTICE IN THE EARTH

Laws of the Ancient World

The Code of	Justinian
Hammurabi	*Corpus juris civilis*
c. 1754 B.C.E.	529–34 C.E.

A LIST AS PITHY as the Ten Commandments fits comfortably in the memory. It can be learned quickly and passed on by oral tradition. As a society grows increasingly complex, though, a short list of thou-shalt-nots is insufficient.

It is easy to forbid murder, for instance, even to guarantee an eye for an eye. But how to settle the terms of a no-fault divorce, or establish a fair price for caulking a boat, or adjudicate rival claims about agricultural fees after a storm destroys much of a crop? As legal precedents multiply, as finer and finer distinctions arise, as more and more circumstances have to be accounted for, it becomes impossible for even the wisest sage to keep everything in his head. The most capacious memory eventually breaks down.

Laws, therefore, were among the first things to be written down in every literate society—and eventually those written laws grew long and complex enough to demand a reference book to make sense of them. Legal compendia are among the foundational reference works in nearly every civilization, and they take us back to some of the earliest known writing in the world. This chapter focuses on two important ancient legal codes, Hammurabi's *Code* of Babylonian law and the greatest attempt to codify the laws of ancient Rome. Together the codes of these long-gone societies give us insights into daily life that we cannot get through any other channels.

It is one of the oldest legal works in the world. The ancient story goes
back thousands of years, but the modern story begins in the nineteenth
century, when the French government began a series of exploratory digs
in Iran. Modern Khuzestan—known in antiquity as Susa or Shushan,
the city of the Persian kings—first attracted archaeologists' attention in
1810, when John MacDonald Kinneir believed he had identified Susa.
The ruins, Kinneir wrote, "consist of hillocks of earth and rubbish,
covered with broken pieces of brick and coloured tile. . . . These mounds
bear some resemblance to the pyramids of *Babylon*."[1] But nineteenth-
century Persia was a dangerous place, and several attempts to explore
the site ended badly.

After a series of failed expeditions, Jacques de Morgan took over what
the French government was calling the Délegation en Perse in 1897.
De Morgan had trained as a mining engineer and worked in Transylvanian
gold mines and Caucasian copper mines. His real passions, though, were
geology and paleontology. When he was thirty-four he was named
director of Egypt's Service des Antiquités, and he did pathbreaking work
on Egypt's prehistory. When he arrived in Persia, de Morgan put another
enthusiast for ancient Egypt, Gustave Jéquier, in charge of the daily
operations, and the dig began on December 18, 1897, nearly ninety years
after the site was identified. It was worth the wait: the location proved
richer than anyone expected.

In late December 1901, on a dig led by Jéquier, a shovel hit a large
piece of diorite. In the next few days more pieces turned up, and the
workers were able to assemble the fragments into a large round pillar
7' 4" (225 cm) high and between 5' 4" (164 cm) and 6' 2" (190 cm) in
diameter.[2] And though to all appearances it was an architectural rather
than a bibliographical find, it turned out to be a reference book of
sorts—one of the oldest known in the world.

On the stele, written in the cuneiform characters used throughout
ancient Mesopotamia, were 282 laws. Ancient monuments are often
badly degraded by the time they are excavated, but the stone on which
these laws had been carved was uncommonly hard, and the inscription
was still clear. Although the stele was broken into three pieces, they fit
together almost perfectly, with no significant gaps. It is not in perfect
shape—a substantial part of the text is missing—but the damage was

TITLE: *Hammurabi's Code*
COMPILER: Hammurabi, Emperor of Babylon
    (d. *c.* 1750 B.C.E.)
ORGANIZATION: Entries 1–5, introduction; entries 6–126,
    property; entries 127–282, persons
PUBLISHED: *c.* 1754 B.C.E.
ENTRIES: 282 laws
TOTAL WORDS: 5,500
SIZE: 7' 5" × 2' 2" (225 × 65 cm)
AREA: 15.7 ft^2 (1.5 m^2)
WEIGHT: 4 tons

caused not by time but by intentional human action. On the front, the last five columns have been erased; that part of the monument probably contained around thirty-five laws, some of which can be supplied from other sources, but others are now irretrievably lost. The surviving 282 paragraphs, though, are the most complete collection of laws we know of from the ancient Middle East, and they were compiled at the command of Hammurabi, the sixth king of Babylon and the first Babylonian emperor, who ruled for more than forty years in the early eighteenth century B.C.E. When he assumed power—in 1792 B.C.E., according to the usual calculation—Babylon was a small city-state. His father, who ruled before him, began to build it up, but Hammurabi turned Babylon from a minor outpost into the administrative center of an enormous Mesopotamian empire. He did it largely by codifying the legal system, and he did that largely by creating a work of reference.

At first the discoverers were not sure what to make of the pillar. It prominently bore the name Hammurabi, king of Babylon, but the find was in Susa, in the rival kingdom of Elam, about 230 miles (370 km) from Babylon. The German scholar Friedrich Delitzsch finally solved the puzzle. Even before the stele was discovered, he had published a learned article, *"Zur juristischen Litteratur Babyloniens"* ("On Babylonian Legal Writing"),[3] in which he suggested that such a sophisticated empire, with uniform laws across the whole of Mesopotamia, could not have functioned without a thorough legal code—and he hinted that it might yet survive somewhere. Thinking about the name Code Napoléon, he began calling this strictly hypothetical legal compendium the Code Hammurabi. And now de Morgan's team had found the very thing Delitszch had predicted. As James Pritchard notes, "Rarely in the annals of archaeology has the excavator been able to oblige his colleague the philologist by producing from the earth the very monument which the latter had suspected to have been in existence."[4] Eventually the mystery of the origin was solved. The Code did not originally come from Susa or anywhere else in Elam. It probably came from Sippar, about 19 miles (30 km) from Baghdad. In the year 1168 B.C.E., many hundreds of years after Hammurabi's death, it was carried to Susa by the Elamite king Shutruk-Nahhunte.[5]

Word of the discovery spread quickly. De Morgan settled on Jean Vincent Scheil, a member of his team, to make the work public, and in just three months Scheil translated and published the *Code*—blazingly fast by scholarly standards.[6] By 1902, every archaeologist and historian of the ancient world was paying attention.

The *Code* falls into three sections: an introduction (entries 1–5), laws regarding property (6–126), and laws regarding persons (127–282). The sections on property and persons are each subdivided into three groups.[7] The introduction opens with an invocation of the gods and an assertion of the emperor's authority:

> When Anu, the supreme, the king of the Anunnaki, and Bel, the lord of heaven and earth, who fixes the destiny of the universe, had allotted the multitudes of mankind to Merodach, the first-born of Ea, the divine master of Law, they made him great among the Igigi. . . . Then Anu and Bel delighted the flesh of mankind by calling me, the renowned prince, the god-fearing Hammurabi, to establish justice in the earth, to destroy the base and the wicked, and to hold back the strong from oppressing the feeble.[8]

The *Code* laid out the source of justice itself, the powers granted to the great Hammurabi, and the reason he was spelling out the laws. Then it introduced more specific laws. The laws themselves were not original with Hammurabi, and many of them had been in circulation for centuries. The contract law, for instance, goes back at least to the time of Ur, and some of the laws were originally written in Akkadian, in use centuries earlier. Plenty of legal situations must have arisen in real life that are not addressed at all. This means we are dealing not with a new system of laws, nor with a comprehensive code of all the laws of Babylon, but a digest of earlier legal writing, edited and reorganized to make it more suitable for finding what the reader needs. In other words, a reference work.

The *Code of Hammurabi* spelled out guidelines for dealing with matters of civil law, including relations between landowners and tenants, between buyers and sellers, and between masters and slaves. Laissez-faire economics was not the goal: commerce was strictly regulated. Hammurabi sets the fees for ox drivers and the liability for shoddy contracting in new houses. The interest charged on both money and grain was 20 percent. Doctors' fees varied for different social classes: for a major operation, the ratio of fees was 10 for the rich, 5 for the middle classes, and 2 for the poor.[9] Even very specific situations are covered in detail, as in law 48:

> If a man is liable for interest, and the god Adad has flooded his field, or the harvest has been destroyed, or the corn has not grown through lack of water; then in that year he shall not pay corn to his creditor. He shall dip his tablet in water, and the interest of that year he shall not pay.[10]

Or, even more strangely, law 108:

> If a (female) wine-seller has not accepted corn as the price of drink, but silver by the grand weight has accepted, and the price of drink is below the price of corn; then that wine-seller shall be prosecuted, and thrown into the water.[11]

A long section covered the criminal law. There were rules for people who cast wicked magic spells and for those who bore false witness in court. Those who stole from temples, or even received the stolen property, were condemned to death. Death was also the penalty for doing business with a child or a slave without the consent of a parent or master. One who stole an ox or a sheep had to repay thirty times its value, unless he was poor, in which case he had to repay ten times its value—or if he was really poor, and could not afford the fee, in which case he faced the death penalty. There were even rules for judges who reached the wrong conclusion in convicting someone.

Most notorious is the *lex talionis*, usually summed up as "an eye for an eye." The Latin *talio* refers to a punishment that is identical to the offense, so the *lex talionis* is a law of retribution. It appears most famously in Exodus 21:23–25: "And if any mischief follow, then thou shalt give life for life, eye for eye, tooth for tooth, hand for hand, foot for foot, burning for burning, wound for wound, stripe for stripe." (Exodus has many similarities with ancient Babylonian law, leading to extensive investigation of whether there was any direct influence.) The *Code of Hammurabi* has a series of laws that enact retribution on criminals:

195. If a son has struck his father, his hands shall be cut off.

196. If a man has destroyed the eye of a free man, his own eye shall be destroyed.

197. If he has broken the bone of a free man, his bone shall be broken.[12]

The *Code*, though, was hardly a model of enlightened social thinking— these were the penalties for blinding or breaking the bones of free men. Poke out a poor man's eye or break a poor man's bone, and there was merely a hefty fee; do it to a slave, and the penalty required only part of the cost. Retribution is not always directed at the guilty party:

209. If a man strike the daughter of a free man, and cause her fœtus to fall; he shall pay ten shekels of silver for her fœtus.

210. If that woman die, his daughter shall be slain.[13]

Passages like this are a reminder of why the study of ancient law can be so rewarding: nowhere else are the mores of a society on display more clearly. Legal codes do not set out to reveal the deep unconscious of a society; they are concerned only with regulating real-life legal conflicts. But they tell stories whether they want to or not. Here we see the world as the Babylonians saw it: some lives are worth more than others; all life is cheap; and if one life is not available for forfeit, another will do just as well.

܀

Another legal code is among the oldest written documents in Western civilization, but still more than a thousand years younger than the *Code of Hammurabi*. Historians confidently attribute a legal code to an ancient Athenian named Draco, and they say his laws were established in 622 or 621 B.C.E., but when pressed, they admit they are not even sure whether Draco existed, so intertwined are the historical figure and the legend.[14] The stories tell us that Athens at the time had no written laws, and Draco—who may have been an Athenian official already, or who may have been appointed specifically for this job—was charged with crafting a set of laws to govern the polis.

The result was a set of laws to cover various responses to both just and unjust killings. Manslaughter was to be punished with exile. In cases of homicide, kings were charged with judging whether the planner or the actual killer should face punishment. If some in a family were in favor of reconciliation, anyone who objected was able to veto the proposed penalty and call for retribution.[15] The actual law was a sophisticated piece of legislation, with several sections covering twenty or more provisions. What is remembered about Draco's laws, though, is not their complexity but their brutality. An Athenian named Demades said "Draco's laws were written in blood" rather than ink, because the penalties for almost all violations were so harsh.[16] "The distinguishing Character of *Draco's* Laws," wrote an eighteenth-century historian, "was *Severity*, or rather *Cruelty*; for every little Offence, and even Indolence itself, was by him punished with Death, for which he assign'd this Reason; *Small Faults seem to me worthy of Death, and for the most flagrant Offences I can find no higher Punishment*."[17] Legend held that Draco would carry out punishments even against inanimate objects: a statue that toppled and killed a man was put on trial and banished. (History does not record the statue's defense.) Though they were called "the noblest and most hallowed

> TITLE: *Corpus juris civilis*
>
> COMPILER: Tribonian (*c.* 485–542) on behalf of Justinian
>   I (*c.* 482–565)
>
> ORGANIZATION: 4 parts: the *Codex*, containing imperial
>   pronouncements; the *Digest*, a compendium of
>   Roman law; the *Institutes*, a textbook; and the *Novellae*
>   *constitutiones*, supplements to the original
>
> PUBLISHED: 529–34 C.E.
>
> VOLUMES: 66
>
> TOTAL WORDS: 1.35 million

[laws] of all . . . forever unaltered,"[18] they became unpopular, though they managed to last three centuries almost unchanged.

Draco's laws, though, were limited—they introduced written law to the Athenian polis, but it was a manageable body of law. Things were very different a few centuries later in Rome, by that time not a city-state but an empire that stretched from southern Spain to Jerusalem. It comprised a great many cultures, traditions, religions, and belief systems. To turn them into a coherent political entity required a substantial administrative machinery, and the Romans obliged. Rome was always a more regulated society than Greece. The Roman emperors believed in reorganizing, codifying, and structuring. "Their legal system," wrote Andrew Riggsby, "was vastly larger, more encompassing, more systematic, and more general than anything else that existed at the time."[19] Their most enduring gift to humanity, if we can call it a gift, may be bureaucracy.

By the sixth century C.E., though, the Empire had split in two, the Western Roman Empire centered on Rome and the Eastern Roman Empire centered on Constantinople. The Italian peninsula was nominally part of the Empire, but in practice it had become an Ostrogoth kingdom. The old order seemed to be breaking down.

This seeming chaos prompted Flavius Petrus Sabbatius Iustinianus Augustus, better known as Justinian the Great, to try to reassert the authority of the Empire. Unlike most of the emperors before him, Justinian came not from aristocratic stock but from a peasant family, and he was born not in Rome or Constantinople but in what is today part of Macedonia. His rise came when his uncle, Justin, adopted him as a son and took him to Constantinople. In 518, Justin was named emperor, and Justinian's influence on his uncle was considerable. Justin welcomed the input and took him on as a high-ranking adviser—in 527, he became a kind of co-ruler of the empire.

Not many months later, Justin died, and Justinian was his obvious successor. One of his first concerns was to put Roman law in order. The legal system was a mess, with extensive collections of statutes, precedents, and commentaries on the laws having piled up over the centuries; by this point they were filled with redundancies and even contradictions. Legal proceedings were getting bogged down in need-less complexity. Modern law, Justinian was convinced, was decadent.[20]

Early in 528, therefore, he established a commission of ten legal experts, including his chief aide Tribonian and a Constantinopolitan law professor named Theophilus, and ordered them to come up with a new catalog of laws (mostly civil, but also constitutional) based on the three major legal codes of the empire. Their job was not mere compila-tion: they were to reject everything that was out of date, and to adjust some provisions to make them more suitable to modern conditions. This work took fourteen months.

The next step was to compile the writings of the jurists, the legal scholars, who had been commenting on the laws for generations. Tribonian was placed in charge of that process, and he charged a committee of sixteen members, including Theophilus and his colleague Dorotheus, "to make excerpts from the ancient writers of authority." Obsolete commen-taries and those that duplicated or contradicted something already in the code were eliminated. The result was the *Digest*, a compilation of fifty books, each subdivided into titles. The work displays good scholarly habits: all the excerpts came with the names of their sources, the titles from which the extracts were taken, and the volume number of the quotation.[21]

While the *Digest* was still under construction, Justinian ordered the third part of his great project, a work called the *Institutes*, to serve as an introduction to the whole legal system. Tribonian, Theophilus, and Dorotheus were once again involved, and they were ordered to stick close to the writings of the classical jurists.

The resulting three-part *Corpus* had its failings: "Instead of a smooth, unified legal code, we have a document that shows its origins in cut-and-paste."[22] But it also had many virtues. It collected and reconciled countless scattered sources and ejected obsolete and useless provisions. Most important, though, everything was structured to help the reader find what he needed to know.[23] A sequence of entries gives the flavor of the whole, as an authority is cited and the relevant provisions in the original law are presented concisely:

54. Paulus, On the Edict of the Curule Ædiles, Book I.
Where property is sold in good faith, the sale should not be annulled for a trifling reason.

55. The Same, On the Edict of the Curule Ædiles, Book II.
A sale without consideration and imaginary, is considered not to be made at all, and therefore the alienation of the property is not taken into consideration.

56. The Same, On the Edict, Book L.
Where anyone sells a female slave under the condition that she shall not be prostituted, and if this is violated he shall have a right to take her back; he will have power to do so, even if the slave has passed through the hands of several purchasers.

Once the *Corpus juris civilis* appeared, Justinian prohibited any further references to the old commentaries: the new *Corpus* contained all that everyone needed to know. To make the point more emphatically, Justinian ordered many of the older writings burned. There were also to be no further commentaries: all the laws had been systematically surveyed, and everything a jurist needed to know was now in the *Digest*. It was a bold act, wiping out all the laws of the past and prohibiting commentaries in the future. The latter was a failure, since even during Justinian's life, legal scholars discovered they needed to write new commentaries.

The *Corpus* had a long afterlife. Although the ultimate collapse of the Empire's administrative structure led to the abandonment of Roman law for centuries, Justinian's brainchild was eventually revisited. There was a revival of interest in Justinian's legal code in the ninth century in the Byzantine Empire, the successor of the Eastern Roman Empire; legal scholars published a new version of the text in Greek, known as the *Basilica*, which informed Greek legal practice into the twentieth century. And in the eleventh century, in Bologna, scholars began to rediscover the Roman law in the West again. An important manuscript of the *Digest* turned up in 1070, leading to many new copies and further study. Here the influence was even more important than in Greece. The Bolognese legal scholars, who thought of themselves as citizens of an ancient Holy Roman Empire, came together to study the ancient texts. These legal students eventually joined with readers of medicine and theology and began to develop policies to govern themselves. The various groups of students and scholars decided to band together, and in 1088 established a group they called a *universitas* 'totality'. It was the first university in Europe, and it had Justinian's *Corpus* at its heart.[24] In many ways the university as we know it had its origins in study groups that sought to make sense of a reference book.

⁂

These two reference "books"—one of them actually a monument, the other a collection of many scrolls—had major real-world significance. In making laws public and accessible, the *Code* of Hammurabi and the *Corpus* of Justinian made the law itself a public affair, and even though the laws may have been brutal and arbitrary, at least they were known. Both Hammurabi and Justinian lived in worlds where few people were literate, and their law codes likely had little influence on the lives of the overwhelming majority of people at the time. But works like Hammurabi's *Code* and Justinian's *Corpus* provide evidence that works of reference— whether they take the form of manuscripts, printed books, or slabs of diorite—can empower their readers. The fact that a legal code exists is an indication that the law is more than the whim of an individual tyrant, that everyone is answerable to the principles embodied in the texts.

OF MAKING MANY BOOKS

Information Overload

DROWNING IN INFORMATION, being overwhelmed with more knowledge than we can ever know, is the modern condition. And yet it's not unique to our time. As soon as there was writing, some were convinced there was too much writing. "By these, my son, be admonished," said the preacher in Ecclesiastes somewhere between 450 and 200 B.C.E.: "of making many books there is no end; and much study is a weariness of the flesh" (Eccl. 12:12). Reference books are an attempt to make these "many books" manageable; they're also a testimony to just how unmanageable they remain.

The critic Harald Weinrich identified different modes of reading. Through most of history, people practiced "intensive" reading, focusing on a few books, since a few were all they had. Pliny the Younger advised this sort of reading: "Aiunt enim *multum* legendum esse, *non multa*," a pun on "reading a lot": "They say you should read *much*, not *many*" things. He meant that it was better to read a few sources intensively than to flit from book to book. But the era of print enabled "extensive" reading, where we have access to many books. And starting in the twentieth century, Weinrich found evidence of "defensive" reading, when "All readers have to defend themselves against too many books and avoid reading as often as possible."[1]

Gutenberg's development of printing with movable type made possible a new kind of extensive reading. In the manuscript age every book was expensive, since someone had to copy it by hand. Even the devout and literate could not hope to own a Bible unless they were wealthy. But printing knocked the prices down to the point where a new middle class could hope to own a few volumes, and the market responded by making volumes available. According to one estimate, about 5 million copies of books had been made in Europe between about 450 and 1450 C.E.[2] But in the half century after Gutenberg developed printing with movable type around 1450, somewhere between 8 and 20 million copies of the new printed books were circulating—more in fifty years than in the previous thousand. And in another hundred years, the number had topped 200 million.[3] The trend kept accelerating. Nobody knows how many new books appear these days, but the global figure is probably more than a million new titles annually, most of them in thousands of copies, for billions of new copies every year. The number is too large for precise counts, but by some estimates, the English-speaking world alone generates somewhere in the neighborhood of half a million titles and editions a year. On the conservative assumption that each is around 250 pages, and each page contains around 340 words, that's more than forty billion words of English text every year—116 million words a day, nearly 5 million an hour, 80,680 a minute, or 1,347 a second.

The idiom *information fatigue* is first attested in 1991, defined by the *Oxford English Dictionary* as "Apathy, indifference, or mental exhaustion arising from exposure to too much information, *esp.* (in later use) stress induced by the attempt to assimilate excessive amounts of information from the media, the Internet, or at work."[4] The term is new, but the idea is ancient. Ecclesiastes says that "in much wisdom is much grief: and he that increaseth knowledge increaseth sorrow" (Eccl. 1:18). Writing in 1621, Robert Burton included a section in his monumental *Anatomy of Melancholy*, an account of the causes of what we would call depression, on "Loue of Learning, or overmuch study. With a Digression of the misery of Schollers." He quoted Niccolò Machiavelli to the effect that "study weakens their bodies, dulls their spirits, abates their strength and courage, and good Schollers are never good souldiers."[5]

Enter the reference book, an attempt to cure the disease of overmuch study and to alleviate the misery of scholars. The atlas promises to take the world's maps and put them in a handy form; the encyclopedia promises to take an entire library and deliver only the parts you need and only when you need them. The degree to which they succeed will be one of the recurring themes of this book.

CHAPTER 2

IN THE BEGINNING WAS THE WORD

The First Dictionaries

Erya	Amarasimha
third century	*Amarakosha*
B.C.E.?	*c.* third century C.E.?

NO ONE KNOWS what the first dictionary was or when it was compiled, but we can reasonably assume that dictionary-like works appeared not long after the dawn of writing. The dictionary as we know it—a book containing an alphabetical list of words with etymologies, pronunciations, and a series of definitions, all in one language—was long in coming, and some of the earliest dictionaries seem unfamiliar to us. But dictionaries come in many varieties. Some of the earliest and most rudimentary are simply lists of words—lists with no definitions, etymologies, or notes of any sort—but still useful, because they might list all the words in some particular category.

The story begins in the ancient Middle East. He was called *Šarru-kinu*—the true king—though sources in other languages usually represent *Šarru-kinu* as *Sargon*. This is not the Sargon mentioned in the Bible—"In the year that Tartan came unto Ashdod, (when Sargon the king of Assyria sent him)"—but another king who lived more than fifteen hundred years earlier and came to prominence by conquering Sumer and establishing the Akkadian Empire.

Sumerian seems to have died out, more or less, as a spoken language around 1800 B.C.E., though that history is notoriously murky. Still, it did not disappear completely, and it remained the language of religious rituals and works of literature for another fifteen hundred years. This left the Akkadians in a difficult position. The Sumerian civilization had reached heights to which the Akkadians aspired, and they wanted to emulate the erudition of their predecessors. But that meant mastering their language, and the Sumerian language was a challenge. Written Akkadian borrowed the cuneiform characters of the Sumerians, but a shared writing system is not the same as a shared language. Akkadian scribes were obliged to learn to read and write Sumerian, but Sumerian struck Akkadian speakers as thoroughly alien.

The Akkadian language—sometimes called Assyro-Babylonian—is a Semitic language, part of the large family of languages including modern Arabic, Hebrew, Aramaic, Amharic, and Ge'ez. Sumerian, on the other hand, is not part of the Semitic family, and scholars to this day are unsure where it fits in the family tree of human languages. (Some propose that it is a "language isolate" with no known relatives.) It goes back at least to 3350 B.C.E., making it one of the earliest languages for which we have any evidence. The differences between Sumerian and Akkadian were more than a matter of vocabulary. Sumerian verb forms depended on roots along with prefixes and suffixes; Akkadian, like other Semitic languages, changed its verb forms by altering the vowels inside the words. Akkadian even had a different sound system from Sumerian. It was this difference that needed to be bridged. And so some of the earliest known word lists were born.

The first surviving glossary goes by the clumsy name of *Urra=hubullu*, compiled sometime in the second millennium B.C.E. (The title is sometimes presented, even more clumsily but more precisely, as UR$_5$-RA=*hubullu* or HAR-ra=*hubullu*.) The work gets its name from the first line, which gives an equivalent for "debt; interest-bearing loan; interest": *urra* in Sumerian means the same as *hubullu* in Akkadian.[1] It is a collection of twenty-four stone tablets containing a total of around 9,700 word pairs in Sumerian and Akkadian. Cuneiform writing had no alphabetical order, so the entries are arranged thematically: the first two tablets are devoted to legal and administrative matters, the rest to the material world. Trees and things made of wood appear in tablets 3 through 7, for instance; pottery is discussed on tablet 10; tablet 13 contains the names of domesticated animals; tablet 14 contains the names of 410 animals, including 120 insects; tablet 15 catalogs parts of the body; and so on.

The compilers of *Urra=hubullu*, concerned only with making life easier for scribes, had no grand thoughts of describing their universe. They were bureaucrats, not philosophers or poets. And yet they inadvertently left a picture of the universe as they understood it. As one writer puts it, "the work comprises a comprehensive survey of the animate and inanimate world, geography, and stars, as well as artificially produced objects, victuals, and many other things."[2] The most important version survives in the Louvre in Paris, though other copies, including students' copies (glossaries were often assigned as scribal exercises for students), can be found in other museums. The text was apparently used by students—and, if the clues provided by the text are to be believed, by beginning students.[3]

Lexicography became more sophisticated in ancient Greece. Even our word *lexicography* is Greek, from *lexikos* 'of words' and *graphia* 'writing'. The Greeks were fascinated by language, both their own and language in general. In the fourth century B.C.E., Philitas of Cos—an Alexandrian Greek scholar and poet, famous in his day as an early type of the absent-minded professor—pulled together the *Átaktoi glôssai*, or "Miscellaneous Glosses," and a few centuries later, Apollonius the Sophist compiled the *Lexeis Homerikai*, the first comprehensive dictionary of words found in Homer. Aristophanes of Byzantium, the librarian at Alexandria starting around 195 B.C.E., created a major lexicon, and the fifth-century-C.E. lexicon by Hesychius is valuable for containing the only surviving evidence of some Greek words.[4]

☙

Some of the most interesting early dictionaries, though, are not from Babylon or Greece but from China. A work called *Shizhou* existed as early as the ninth century B.C.E., but it does not survive, and little is known of it beyond the title. The *Erya* or *Erh-ya*, though, written in China probably in the third century B.C.E., is the oldest surviving dictionary of the Chinese language, containing glosses on just over 4,300 words drawn from early Chinese literature. The title means something like "approaching what is correct, proper, refined," and it is sometimes called *Approaching Elegance*, sometimes *The Ready Guide*. Heming Yong and Jing Peng describe its "remarkable position in the history of philological and linguistic studies in China":

It is the first work of exegetic studies conducted on a systematic basis and the first thesaurus dictionary of an encyclopedic nature. It aims to explain the meaning of ancient words and a great variety of object names and serves as the starting point from which other classic works can be justifiably interpreted. That partly explains why [Erya] has always been placed into the category of ancient Chinese classics rather than ancient Chinese dictionaries.[5]

Its background is murky; the identity of the writer or writers is unknown, as is even the century in which he, she, or they worked. (Tradition says the author was the Duke of Zhou, but so many things are attributed to this semilegendary figure, including the *I Ching* and the earliest Chinese classical music, that we should be skeptical of all such attributions.) Most experts agree, though, that it was written by a Confucian scholar sometime between the eighth and second centuries B.C.E.[6]

The *Erya* set out to explain the words in old Chinese literature—old even when the dictionary was compiled. The Qin Dynasty, which began in 221 B.C.E., was the first of the imperial dynasties in China. But the literature of the long Zhou Dynasty (1046 to 256 B.C.E.), from before the unification of China, was of particular interest. In the Confucian bureaucracy, the way to climb through the ranks of both the government and the larger society was to pass examinations on classic works of literature. Aspiring civil servants knew that their promotion depended on access to good dictionaries. Dictionaries were classified among the *hsiao-hsüeh* 'minor learning' rather than *ta-hsüeh* 'major learning', and major learning, as they understood it, had moral implications. But even the minor learning, which covered more or less the same territory as the modern word "linguistics," remained an essential step on the way to the better life. And so the *Erya* became an important work, sitting on the boundary between high culture and official culture.

The Chinese language lacks an alphabet, and the logographical system does not have any obvious equivalent to alphabetical order. For a long time Chinese dictionaries have been ordered according to either the "radicals" (basic strokes) of the Chinese characters or the tones and final sounds of the spoken words. Around 100 C.E., for instance,

TITLE: *Erya*
COMPILER: Unknown
ORGANIZATION: Primarily topical
PUBLISHED: third century B.C.E.?
ENTRIES: 2,094
TOTAL WORDS: 13,113

Xu Shen composed his *Shuowen jiezi*, a collection of 10,516 characters organized under 540 headers, one for each "radical" or basis to a written word. It deserves to be called the first systematic dictionary of Chinese, and its classification of words by radical would be used in Chinese dictionaries for a millennium and a half. But when the *Erya* was compiled, those systems had not yet been developed, so the anonymous creator of the *Erya* organized the work by subject. This places the work in a middle ground between dictionary, thesaurus, and encyclopedia: it gave not only definitions but clusters of thematically related words, and therefore gestures out to the larger world.

The book came in two parts: the first, chapters 1–3, focuses on common words, especially verbs and particles; the second, chapters 4–19, on specialized terms, mostly nouns. The nouns were divided into sixteen sections, grouped by topic: kinship, implements, architecture, geography, and so on.[7] The approach to defining was distinctive. "In the first section," one critic observes, "entries are defined by combining words of the same or similar meaning and then explaining them in terms of a word more commonly used at that time. If one of the words had an additional meaning, there would be an additional explanation."[8] A typical entry shows the associative logic that structures the whole work:

EXPLAINING THE HEAVEN

Round-hollow and very blue, this is Heaven. In springtime, Heaven is blue; in summertime, bright; in autumn, clear; in wintertime, Heaven is wide up. These are the four seasons.

In springtime, there is a greening sun-warmth; in summer, a reddish enlightening; in autumn a blank storing; and in winter a dark blossom. If all these expressions are harmonious, [the year] is called "jade candle." The spring gives birth; the autumn grows the adult; in autumn the harvest is completed; and in winter there is a peaceful tranquillity. If the harmony of the four seasons is thorough and correct, [the year] is called "illustrious wind." If the sweet rain comes down to the right time, the many things are at their best, it is called "sweet spring." This means luck.

As we might expect for an early work in any genre, *Erya* has its weaknesses. The definitions are short, and they often do little to explain the meanings of the words. The organization of words into thematic clusters is an interesting effort to make sense of the universe, but later eras have found it counterintuitive and hard to consult. But it was groundbreaking in its day, and it remains illuminating even long after it was superseded by other dictionaries. Moderns find *Erya* a valuable source for identifying the animals and plants, for instance, that appear in older Chinese literature. Even more important, it reveals how early Chinese writers organized their understanding of the social world, the natural world, and the divine world.

The original *Erya* led to a wide array of editions and annotations. The earliest is the *Hsiao erya*, or *Abbreviated Approaching Elegance*. There was also a *Kuang-ya*, or *Expanded Elegance*. In the third century C.E. came *Guangya*, or *Extension of Erya*, by Zhang Yi, with 2,345 entries. Early in the fourth century, Go Pu wrote *Erya zhu*, or *Annotations on Erya*, and around the year 1000, Xing Bing turned out *Erya shu, Explanations of Annotations on Erya*. As late as 1775, Chinese scholars were working on new versions of and annotations on the *Erya*, including Hao Yixing's *Erya zhengyi*, or *Meaning Verification of Erya*, and Wang Niansun's *Guangya Shuzheng*, or *Annotations and Textual Criticism of Guangya*.[9]

The *Erya* also prompted imitations, new dictionaries that attempted the task of defining words from scratch rather than extending the original work. Probably in the early third century C.E., Liu Xi wrote his *Shiming*, or *Explanation of Names*, a collection of 1,502 definitions in eight volumes and twenty-seven chapters. As Xue Shiqui explains, "its special feature is its use of phonetic explanations. It explains the meanings of words in terms of other characters of the same or similar sound, and makes assumptions about etymology based on the sound of a character"—or, as some have described it, semantics based on puns, or connections between the sounds of words. "At times," Xue goes on, "this method is misleading and far-fetched, but it did motivate scholars to analyze the meaning of a word from the viewpoint of the spoken language."[10]

In the year 837, *Erya* was named one of the Thirteen Confucian Classics, joining the *Book of Changes* (or *I Ching*), the *Classic of Poetry* (or *Shijing*), and the *Analects* of Confucius. As the Sinologist Endymion Wilkinson wrote, "This greatly enhanced the influence of the *Erya* on the interpretation of the classics, and no doubt also on the development of the language itself since generations of scholars memorized it."[11]

✵

Several centuries after the greatest early dictionary of China came the greatest early dictionary of India, the *Amarakosha*—probably compiled around the fourth century C.E., though some favor a later date. It had to be before the early ninth century, since other writers were referring to it by that period.[12] As with the *Erya*, little is known of the author, Amarasimha, but tradition says he was named one of the Navaratnas or "nine gems," the most extraordinary people in the court of king Chandragupta II.

The *Amarakosha*, also known as the *Nâmalingânusâsana*, is the "Immortal Treasure" that organizes the entire Sanskrit vocabulary into a logical order. It has remained an important work in the ancient literature of India ever since. It is not the earliest Sanskrit dictionary—that honor belongs to the *Nighantu*, a collection of words drawn from the Vedas. We have the names of other Sanskrit lexicographers, including Katya, Brihaspati, Vyadi, Bhaguri, Amara, Mankala, Sahasanka (Vikramaditya), Mahesa, and Jina. These early lexicons tend to fall into two categories, the dictionaries of synonyms and the dictionaries of homonyms. The synonymous dictionaries, organized topically, give clusters of words that stand for related ideas. The homonymous lexicons collect multiple meanings for a single written form, and they are usually organized not thematically but by letter, sometimes the first but often the last letter of a word.[13]

Amarasimha himself acknowledged that the *Amarakosha* resulted from his work of codifying, adapting, and abridging the works of

TITLE: *Amarakosha* or *Nâmalingânusâsana*
COMPILER: Amarasimha? (*fl. c.* 375 B.C.E.)
ORGANIZATION: Topical
PUBLISHED: *c.* third century B.C.E.
ENTRIES: 10,000
TOTAL WORDS: 15,000

those who came before him. The organization, though, seems to be original with him. The whole work is in poetry rather than prose, around fifteen hundred lines. It is organized into three *khandas* or books— *Svargadikhanda*, treating the gods and the heavens; *Bhuvagardikhanda*, on earthly things like animals and towns; and *Samanyadikhanda*, treating common words, especially on grammar—each of which is further divided into *vargas*, or sections.

It is not an easy book to use, as this entry makes clear:

Blood. Flesh used in sacrifice. Heart. Marrow, fat. Diaphragm. The tendon forming the nape of the neck. Any tubular organ of the body, as an artery, vein, intestine, etc. Kidneys. Brain. Any bodily excretion. Entrail. Spleen. Tendon, muscle. Liver. Saliva. Concretion on the eyes. Excretion of the nose. Wax of the ear. Urine. Feces, dung. Glene. Bone. Skeleton. Spine, backbone. Skull. Rib.

Where the entries end and the interpretations begin is far from obvious, and the book is useful only for nouns. But in combining the two common methods of organizing a dictionary, the homonyms and the synonyms, and in surveying the best literature in the Sanskrit language, Amarasimha developed a reference tool that served not only his own age but every succeeding generation that has worked through the literary tradition of the Subcontinent. As late as 1808, an English author could refer to "The celebrated Amara Kosha, or Vocabulary of Sanskrit by Amara Sinha," praising it as "by the unanimous suffrage of the learned, the best guide to the acceptations of nouns in Sanskrit."[14] Its influence extended even further, for another nineteenth-century reader influenced by the *Amarakosha* was Peter Mark Roget. The grouping of words in thematic clusters inspired his approach to classifying synonyms in the famous *Thesaurus* of 1852.

❧

Erya and *Amarakosha* were entirely independent works—there is no evidence of one influencing the other—but they are remarkably similar. Both are concerned with only a selection of the entire vocabulary of their respective languages; both are concerned with making sense of the great literary classics of their traditions; both are organized thematically, giving us a glimpse of how their authors classified the world's knowledge. Both also inspired long traditions. *Erya* is only the first in a long line of premodern Chinese dictionaries, culminating perhaps in *Peiwen yunfu*, put together by a team with support of the emperor in 1711, which contains 700,000 words—more than any other Chinese dictionary, even those created today—arranged by rhyme by their last character. Though there are no definitions, words and phrases are shown in use, providing a contextual clue to their meanings.[15] And the *Amarakosha* led to the *Anekarthasamuchchaya* of Shashvata, the *Trikandashesha* of Purushottamadeva, the *Haravali* of Purushottama, and others—not merely useful tools in making sense of older literature, but important works of literature in their own right.[16]

The West has its own major premodern dictionaries. For centuries, no Greek lexicographer rivaled the great Suidas, who lived in the late tenth century: everyone who worked with ancient Greek texts found his dictionary essential. The only problem is that Suidas never existed. The book known as "the dictionary of Suidas" was not actually a book by an author named Suidas, but a dictionary called *Suda*, a late Latin word for "fortress." Only in the twentieth century was its origin sorted out, but for a millennium this book, the high point of Byzantine scholarship, has been indispensable for students of Greek literature. It contains thirty thousand articles—some lexical, some encyclopedic, some somewhere in between—on language, literature, and history. The information is strangely miscellaneous. Some entries on important topics are short; some entries on trivial topics are long. The entire entry for Aaron, the brother of Moses and the first high priest of the Israelites, reads, "Aaron, a proper name." ("A proper name" is a favorite non-entry entry: "Abdiou [i.e. Obadiah], a proper name," "Abeiron, a proper name," "Aberothaeus, a proper name," "Abim, a proper name" . . .) The *Suda* remains valuable for its extensive quotations of Greek writers whose works have been lost—sometimes our only evidence about a Greek writer's style is the quotations in the *Suda*.

Advertisements for modern dictionaries always boast about all the new words that have been included since the previous edition, as if the sole virtue of a dictionary is its up-to-the-minute treatment of words like *locavore* and *hashtag*. But dictionaries can be valuable precisely for being old, for giving us a glance at the way a language was organized, and a world was understood, centuries or even millennia ago.

A FRACTION OF THE TOTAL

Counting Reference Books

"TOUTS LES GENS de Lettres sont d'accord," lexicographer Antoine Furetière wrote in 1684, "qu'il n'y sçauroit avoir trop de Dictionnaires"—"Men of letters agree that you can't have too many dictionaries."[1] But is there such a thing as too many?

Even in antiquity, reference books were supposed to fix the problems of information fatigue, serving as life preservers in a sea of information. In the end, though, they may just contribute to the flood. It didn't take long for even the reference books to start overwhelming their readers. The cultural commentator Ilan Stavans reports on his own explorations in the card catalog: "Today there are dictionaries of Aramaic, ballet, gerontology, hip-hop, knighthood, Napoleon's wars, proteins, Russian slang, and TV."[2]

What, then, is the total? Counting reference books is like counting the stars in the sky—something, incidentally, that reference books help us do. No one knows the answer, but the number is immense. Major research libraries devote large rooms to reference books, where they may number in the tens of thousands. Even that is a tiny fraction of the total. The Library of Congress Online Catalog, when asked to display all its holdings with the word *dictionary* in the title, comes back with an error message: "Your search retrieved more records than can be displayed. Only the first 10,000 will be shown." The same thing happens in a search for *encyclopedia*.

But we can get an idea of the magnitude of the task by searching a few major library catalogs. The General Catalogue of the British Library, one of the world's great collections, lists 38,904 titles that contain the word *dictionary*;[3] the Catalogue Général of the Bibliothèque Nationale de France contains 42,162 works with *dictionnaire* in their titles; the Deutsche National Bibliothek in Leipzig features 41,892 titles with the word *Wörterbuch*; the Rossiiskaia Gosudarstvennaia Biblioteka in Moscow has 16,124 titles with словарь (*slovar'*); Spain's Biblioteca Nacional de España has 12,563 titles with *diccionario*; the Italian Biblioteca Nazionale Centrale di Firenze has 7,760 titles with the word *dizionario*. The figures are similar for *encyclopaedia* (18,482 in the British Library), *encyclopédie* (24,273 titles in the Bibliothèque Nationale), and *Enzyklopädie* (8,549 in the Deutsche National Bibliothek).

In WorldCat, the combined electronic catalogs of 71,000 libraries from 112 countries, a search for *dictionary* comes up with 311,602 books, 35,756 separately cataloged articles, 15,051 Internet resources, 2,637 computer programs, 1,859 periodicals, 824 sound recordings, 659 visual materials, 239 maps, 238 musical scores, 154 archival records, and 19 "updated resources," for a total of 369,071 titles and editions. Throw in the words for *dictionary* in the other major European languages, and the total swells to 727,930. Another 259,724 records for *encyclopedia* in the major European languages brings the total number of dictionaries and encyclopedias to nearly a million. If it were possible to broaden the search further—covering every library; including Chinese, Japanese, Korean, Arabic, Hindi, Urdu, Bengali, Russian, and other languages whose speakers number in the hundreds of millions; and searching not only for dictionaries and encyclopedias, but also atlases, thesauruses, legal references, and so on—the number would be much higher.

So the answer is certainly in the millions, and a little time browsing library catalogs reveals just how various these books are. The Library of Congress, for instance, holds fifty-two dictionaries of metallurgy, as well as an *Encyclopedia of R.F.D. Cancels* (281 pages on the postmarks used on Rural Free Deliveries), an *Encyclopedia of Knots and Fancy Rope Work*, and a *Dictionary of Jewish Surnames from the Kingdom of Poland*. In the Bibliothèque Nationale de France is *Le Dictionnaire du rire: 4 000 histoires drôles* (The dictionary of the joke: 4,000 funny stories). German railway dictionaries number in the dozens. Robert O. Campbell's *Barriers: An Encyclopedia of United States Barbed Fence Patents* covers both the history of wire fencing and the patents on different varieties of barbed wire in 460 pages.

Pick any area of human endeavor—for that matter, pick almost any noun—and there will be at least one reference book about it. Cocker spaniel aficionados will want to get their hands on John F. Gordon's *Spaniel Owner's Encyclopaedia* (1967), while those who love tools can consult Mark Duginske's *Tools: A Complete Illustrated Encyclopedia* (2001). Even sewage treatment is covered in Clinton Bogert's *Glossary: Water and Sewage Control Engineering* (1950), Fritz Meinck's *Dictionary of Water and Sewage Engineering* (1963), W. Bischofsberger's *Lexikon der Abwassertechnik* (1974), the Swedish Tekniska Nomenklaturcentralen's *Avfallsordlista: Nordiska termer med motsvarighteter på engelska, franska och tyska samt defioniter på svenska och engelska* (1977), Hu Mingcao's *Ying Han shui ran kopng zhi ci hui* (1986), Shan Peihua's *Shui wu ran ming ci ci dian* (1987), Günay Kocasoy's *Kati atik termileri açiklamali sözlügü* (in Turkish, English, German, and French, 1994), Carmen Campbell's *Vocabulaire de la production d'eau potable et du traitement des eaux usées* (French and English, 1997), Krzysztof Czekierda's *Slownik gospodarki wodnosciekowej* (English and Polish, 2011), and dozens of others.

CHAPTER 3

THE HISTORY OF NATURE

Science in Antiquity

Theophrastus	Pliny
Historia plantarum	*Historia naturalis*
350–287 B.C.E.	*c.* 77–79 C.E.

OUR WORD *SCIENCE* comes from Latin *scientia*, which is in turn derived from the verb *scio* 'I know'. When it first showed up in the modern languages, it had the same broad range of meaning as Latin *scientia*, knowledge of any sort. As late as the nineteenth century, the word covered not only geology and astronomy but also poetry and history. No word corresponded perfectly to our modern sense of science. When people in the Renaissance wanted to refer to biology, chemistry, and physics, they used terms like "natural philosophy" and "natural history."

But lexical history is not the same as conceptual history, and long before there was a word for what we call science, people were energetically collecting information about the natural world—animal, vegetable, mineral, and beyond. Eventually it was necessary to collect new discoveries in a manageable compass. "Scientific" reference books have been with us for more than two millennia, and they have only grown in importance in our technological age. This chapter has at its heart two ancient works of natural history, one Greek, one Roman.

❧

We know more about Theophrastus than we do about most ancient Greek authors. He was born around 371 B.C.E. in Eresos, Lesbos. As a young man he headed to Athens, which was then at the height of its intellectual powers and the center of the philosophical world.

37

Theophrastus missed his chance to meet Socrates, who swallowed the hemlock in 399 B.C.E., but he did study at the Academy, where Plato was one of his teachers and Aristotle a friend and mentor.

Theophrastus went on to write widely. He was probably the author of an influential book on character types (the braggart, the flatterer, the ironist), another on metaphysics, and yet another on geology. One book, lost now and known only through a later paraphrase, explained the senses. His most important reference work, written in Greek as Περὶ φυτῶν ἱστορία (*Peri phytôn historia*), is better known by its Latin title, *Historia plantarum* (*The History of Plants*), though *A Treatise on Plants* captures the spirit better. It earned him the title "the father of botany." Greeks had written about plants before him, including his friend Aristotle. But in the words of one botanical historian, "no one before him had recorded a philosophic thought or suggestion about the plant world separately considered."[1] Robert Sharples goes further: "he so far surpassed his predecessors that the history of the subject in the west can be said effectively to begin with him."[2]

Like Aristotle, Theophrastus begins with first principles, including a philosophical attempt to distinguish the vegetable, animal, and mineral kingdoms. What seems like an easy problem quickly becomes entangled in philosophical complexity: it is easier to define plants in terms of what they are not than what they are. Many seeming plants differ enough from the familiar ones to leave us unsure what to do with them—things like fungi, lichens, and algae. Theophrastus lumped them all in with the plants—not the way modern taxonomy proceeds, but defensible in his day.

Theophrastus' greatest advance on previous botanical writers was the way he organized his material. Every science has to wrestle with classifying all the specimens that come under its purview, determining which qualities are what Aristotle called "essential," and which merely "accidental"; it is only fitting that one of Aristotle's schoolmates should be engaged in the effort. The key to a useful taxonomy consists of identifying the features that let us group like with like. For the geologist, which features—color, texture, hardness—make this rock like or unlike that rock? Should the meteorologist treat all the dark clouds as similar in kind, or all the fluffy clouds, or all the high clouds? The problems are

> **TITLE:** Περὶ φυτῶν ἱστορία (On the history of plants)
> **COMPILER:** Theophrastus (*c.* 371–*c.* 287 B.C.E.)
> **ORGANIZATION:** Topical: book 1, plant anatomy; book 2,
> growth; book 3, wild trees; book 4, foreign plants; book
> 5, woody plants; book 6, shrubs; book 7, small herbs;
> book 8, cereals; book 9, medicinal plants
> **PUBLISHED:** Between 350 and 287 B.C.E.
> **ENTRIES:** More than 500 species
> **TOTAL WORDS:** 100,000

especially challenging in the life sciences. Charles Darwin utterly rewrote plant and animal taxonomy by showing how variety in the natural world emerged from descent with variation, and modern scientists are able to use genetic analysis to confirm evolutionary descent. We can now put every living species into its proper kingdom, phylum, class, order, family, genus, and species. But without genetic tests, we run the risk of being misled by apparent similarities. If, for instance, we start by dividing animals into flying and nonflying, we end up with one group including most birds, many insects, flying fish, and flying squirrels, while chickens, ostriches, most fishes, and most squirrels are in the other group—somehow unsatisfying, because it also feels natural to keep the feathered animals together, all the fishes together, and so on. Flying, it seems, is an Aristotelian accident: most birds fly and most mammals do not, but the power of flight is not essential to being either bird or mammal.

Theophrastus had no conception of evolution or genetics, and he had to depend on naked-eye observation to see the deep connections. His task was even more difficult than classifying animals, because the features and behaviors of plants are less obvious to the untrained eye. The fact that some flowers are white, some pink, and some blue is merely accidental—they could just as easily be other colors—so a biological taxonomist should not make flower color an essential part of classification. Which qualities, though, do make each plant species what it really is? Should we put all the flowering plants in one group, the nonflowering plants in another? Keep the woody stems together? Are the grasses a distinct kind, or do many essentially different plants happen to look grassy?

Before Theophrastus, most plant classifications were based on human needs: plants were grouped based on their use as food or medicine, whether they were wild or cultivated, and so on. Theophrastus took a different approach and based his taxonomy on morphology or form. He used physical structure to define his four broadest categories: tree, shrub, half-shrub, and herb. He then went on to divide species all into flowering and nonflowering species—still an important distinction in botany. He went even further, dividing the flowering species into those with leafy flowers and those with capillary flowers, laying the groundwork for much later breakthroughs in petaliferous and apetalous flowers. He made important discoveries in the structure of flowers, though he did not understand that flowers were plants' reproductive organs. A master of close observation, Theophrastus described the minute structures of small seeds at a time when even the magnifying glass was unknown. Still he described plant morphology, from root to fruit, in more detail than anyone before him, distinguishing permanent from transient features of plant biology.

The structure of *Historia plantarum* reflects this taxonomic understanding. Book 1 covered the anatomy of plants, including roots, fruits, seeds, leaves, flowers, and other parts. It lays out his four broad categories, while acknowledging there were complex cases that would test his boundaries. Book 2 moves on to the growth of plants from seeds, bulbs, or roots. Book 3, on wild trees, corrects conventional wisdom by insisting that trees do not emerge from spontaneous generation. In book 4, Theophrastus examines foreign trees and shrubs, with attention to the wider Mediterranean world. Wood in its many varieties is the subject of book 5, shrubs of book 6, small herbs of book 7, and cereals, beans, and peas of book 8. In his discussion of woods he describes which ones are best suited to timber and which ones work well in a lathe. Book 9 is devoted entirely to the use of plants as medicines, making it one of the oldest surviving herbals. Theophrastus did his best to sort reliable fact from superstition, and the result is a magisterial survey of the entire plant kingdom as it was known in fourth-century-B.C.E. Greece. It touches on more than five hundred plant species, the large majority of which are cultivated rather than wild plants—he says that most wild plants cannot be discussed because they have been neither identified nor named. Still, he was the first to recognize the existence of aerial roots, which are common in orchids, mangroves, banyan trees, and other species.

Scholars believe Theophrastus intended his work as a set of lecture notes, but before long it was being employed as a reference book. The entries are curt and include quick lists of related plants or features, designed for easy consultation. Almost any ancient investigator into the plant kingdom would begin with Theophrastus, navigating through his taxonomy and finding a specimen's place in the larger scheme. And this decision to reduce the botanical world to a work of reference had lasting consequences. Because he devoted so much effort to a logical organization, one that was structured around the plants themselves rather than around human needs, his reference book served to turn attention outward to the natural world. He made the gathering of further information possible, because his collection revealed clearly where the gaps in knowledge were and signaled to the world where research might profitably proceed. Though Theophrastus' work was lost and forgotten through most of the Middle Ages, its rediscovery at the beginning of the fifteenth century led to a series of editions and translations at just the time the West was beginning its scientific revolution.[3]

Theophrastus' knowledge was daunting, but his most important successor in the ancient world makes even his polymathic range seem limited.

Gaius Plinius Secundus, better known as Pliny the Elder, was born in 23 C.E. at Como in the Italian Alps. He was schooled in Rome, by then as much the center of the intellectual world as Athens had been three and a half centuries earlier. Christianity was in its very earliest phases, and there is no evidence that it made any impression on Pliny. But Rome in the thirties and forties C.E. was a literary hot spot. Roman politics in the era was notoriously messy: the emperor Tiberius, who had effectively walked away from his duties after a coup, died in the year 37, leaving his great-nephew Caligula to become emperor; he was in turn assassinated after just four years. His uncle, Claudius, would take over until his own death in 54, when he was succeeded by his adopted son Nero.

This was the background to Pliny's life, and the political turmoil was more relevant to his career than such things usually are for scientists. Pliny was above all a man of the world. He commanded a cavalry squadron in Germany, Gaul, and Spain. He was a friend and confidant of generals, politicians, even emperors. He was at the center of political and military power in the early Empire. Still he found time to write. Only one of his works survives, but we are lucky to have a reliable list of all the others, because he cataloged his life's work in a letter to a friend: seven works, coming to a total of 102 scrolls (*libri* in Latin). He wrote on military matters, on grammar, and on Roman history, and he was an amazingly disciplined writer. Pliny's nephew, also called Pliny, preserved this account of his uncle at work, describing his "keen intelligence, incredible devotion to study, and a remarkable capacity for dispensing with sleep." The uncle would get up "long before daybreak" and work until two o'clock the next morning, pausing in his studies only to pay a visit to the emperor Vespasian. That devotion to his work was evident in everything he did: his only downtime was while he was in the bath, and even then he would have someone read to him. The same regime was in place at the dinner table:

> Over his dinner a book was read aloud to him and notes were made, and that at a rapid pace. I remember that one of his friends, when the reader had rendered a passage badly, called him back and had it repeated; but my uncle said to him, "Surely you got the sense?" and on his nodding assent continued, "Then what did you call him back for? This interruption of yours has cost us ten more lines!" Such was his economy of time.

A traveling secretary read to him on the road, and he even chided his nephew for walking anywhere in Rome: had he taken a sedan chair, he could have used the time to do more reading. As his nephew summarized his guiding philosophy, "He thought all time not spent in study wasted."[4]

Though Pliny read and wrote widely, he seems to have had scientific interests throughout his life. *Historia naturalis* means "natural history,"

TITLE: *Naturalis historia*

COMPILER: Gaius Plinius Secundus (Pliny the Elder)
(23–79 C.E.)

ORGANIZATION: Topical: book 1, introduction; book 2,
cosmology and meteorology; books 3–6, geography;
book 7, anthropology; books 8–11, zoology; books 12–27,
botany; books 28–32, medical zoology; books 33–37,
medicinal minerals

PUBLISHED: *c.* 77–79 C.E.

ENTRIES: 2,493

VOLUMES: 37

TOTAL WORDS: 395,000

though the phrase usually means what we would think of as the observational sciences generally. As Tom McArthur wrote, *Historia naturalis*
"could just as easily be interpreted in modern terms as *General
Knowledge.*"[5] Pliny and his readers would not have understood the fields
he covered as part of some broader enterprise called "science"; they
would have been more comfortable with the idea of "nature." As a
twentieth-century translator puts it, the *Historia* is "an encyclopaedia of
astronomy, meteorology, geography, mineralogy, zoology, and botany,
i.e. a systematic account of all the material objects that are not the
product of man's manufacture."[6]

Pliny's introduction delimits his scope: the "sacred, eternal, immea-
surable" is beyond our knowledge. "It is madness," he wrote, "downright
madness, to go out of that world, and to investigate what lies outside
it just as if the whole of what is within it were already clearly known."[7]
But everything else—*everything*—was fair game. He started with the
elements, understood to be four: earth, air, fire, and water. He also
gave not only astronomical observations but inferences and precise
measurements:

It is unquestionable that the moon's horns are always turned away
from the sun, and that when waxing she faces east and when

waning west; and that the moon shines 47½ minutes longer daily from the day after the new moon to full and 47½ minutes less daily to her wane, while within 14 degrees of the sun she is always invisible. This fact proves that the planets are of greater magnitude than the moon.[8]

Pliny was especially drawn to questions that were not yet settled. "There has been a great deal of minute enquiry among the learned," he observed, "as to the manner in which bees reproduce their species; for sexual intercourse among them has never been observed." He was even acute enough to notice evidence of seemingly vanished species, at a time when extinction was barely considered even as a possibility: "There is one thing at which I cannot sufficiently wonder—that of some trees the very memory has perished, and even the names recorded by authors have passed out of knowledge."[9]

Unlike Theophrastus, who aspired to keep humankind out of his book, Pliny has a particular interest in the parts of the natural world with a bearing on human existence. In the historian and scholar Foster Stockwell's account of Pliny, "nature serves humankind. Natural objects are invariably described in their relation to humans and not by themselves."[10] Some of his most energetic and detailed investigation into botany, for instance, deals with the grapevine, because wine was central to the Roman economy. From an attempt to reckon the number of varieties of grapes, he goes on to discuss the quality of the wines made from them—"some kinds of wine are more agreeable than others"—and from there to a discussion of the effects of alcohol on the body ("Wine has the property of heating the parts of the body when it is drunk and of cooling them when poured on them outside"), and then to a meditation on drunkenness ("Think of the drinking matches! think of the vessels engraved with scenes of adultery, as though tippling were not enough by itself to give lessons in licentiousness!").[11] There is even an account of the effects of temperature on already-fermented wine, a lesson that many liquor shops could stand to learn today.[12]

How much made it into the *Historia naturalis*? The eighteenth-century historian Edward Gibbon is not exaggerating when he calls it "that immense register, where Pliny has deposited the discoveries, the arts, and the errors of mankind."[13] Pliny claims to have covered twenty thousand "noteworthy facts" or "things of importance," drawn from 473 authors and two thousand volumes—and a modern scholar calls this tally "a severe underestimate."[14] His compilation is one of the longest works to survive intact from the ancient world. Critics have noted faults, particularly that Pliny is too credulous of his sources.[15] But the complaint is not entirely fair. The scientific method we take for granted was simply not a going concern in first-century Rome: no one was testing claims against reality. The job of a writer in antiquity was not to perform experiments but to weigh his sources, and here Pliny is exemplary. He was also unusually scrupulous about citing his sources, most of them Greek. He was genuinely interested in the claims of authority made by his sources, and he noticed that many facts related by "the most professedly reliable and modern writers" were actually copied verbatim from older writers.[16]

Pliny is in fact more scrupulous in testing his claims than most of his predecessors and contemporaries. Having disavowed any intention to talk about the spiritual, for instance, he occasionally paused to reclaim some phenomena for the natural world. "The common occurrences that we call rainbows," he says, "have nothing miraculous or portentous about them, for they do not reliably portend even rain or fine weather. The obvious explanation of them is that a ray of the sun striking a hollow cloud has its point repelled and is reflected back to the sun, and that the diversified colouring is due to the mixture of clouds, fires and air." The science is imperfect; the principles of the refraction of light would not be understood for more than sixteen hundred years. But the claim that rainbows are simply "common occurrences" is a milestone in the scientific understanding of the world. And even when he was at his least skeptical, he made it possible for later natural historians to supplement and correct his work. In this sense, even the credulous aping of superstition can contribute to the advancement of knowledge, because compilation on Pliny's grand scale made it easier to know which claims need to be tested and which refuted. He knew perfectly well that much remained to be done: his book was the beginning of a process, not the end. "Nor do we doubt," he wrote in his preface, "that there are many things that have escaped us also; for we are but human, and beset with duties, and we pursue this sort of interest in our spare moments."[17]

His devotion to research eventually did him in. On August 20, 79 C.E., when Pliny was in command of a Roman fleet, the first in a series of earthquakes shook the Naples area. Pliny, ever the curious naturalist, felt obliged to investigate. On August 22, around noon, the earth shook again—this time accompanied by a formidable explosion. The top of Mount Vesuvius had blown off, and the emerging smoke took the form of a pine tree, with a vertical "trunk" and "branches" coming out at right angles. Pliny watched with his nephew from Misenum, far enough from Vesuvius to ensure his safety. But the scientific spirit made him long for a closer look. As soon as the volcano erupted, he did what few would have the courage to do: instead of running away, he sailed directly toward it. As stones and ash came raining down on the ships, the sailors were terrified, but Pliny—as certain as ever that all time not spent in study was wasted—continued calmly dictating his latest work to a secretary by his side. He died in the shower of ash, a martyr to his scientific curiosity.

Pliny himself was asphyxiated, but the *Historia naturalis* lived on. Most of the other great natural historians of antiquity (such as Theophrastus) had written in Greek, a language almost unknown in medieval Europe before the fifteenth century.[18] Even though most of his sources were Greek, Pliny's decision to write in Latin made him one of the most widely read ancient "scientists" for more than a thousand years. Even after the Middle Ages, Pliny remained a vital presence. The *Historia naturalis* was put into print very shortly after Gutenberg's invention of movable type: the first printed edition appeared in Venice in 1469, with another in 1476. This shows that there was real demand for a fifteen-hundred-year-old book at just the moment that modern scientific epistemology was developing. But in 1492, Niccolò Leoniceno, an Italian scholar and physician, published *De Plinii et aliorum in medicina erroribus* (On the medical mistakes of Pliny and others), which set off a debate among the scholars of Ferrara at the end of the fifteenth century. It took another two hundred years for most investigators to abandon Pliny as a serious primary source.

❦

The volume of scientific information has increased by many orders of magnitude since Theophrastus and Pliny; the Roman's twenty thousand "things of importance," once a lifetime's work, are now collected in seconds in many scientific experiments. And reference books have worked to stay current with the increases in knowledge. We'll see scientific and medical encyclopedias scattered throughout this book. But the principles established by these classical writers—one focusing on the morphological features of his plant specimens, the other examining the relationships between the natural and the human worlds—established the pattern that scientific encyclopedists are still following.

EASY AS ABC

The Rise (and Fall?) of Alphabetical Order

SAMUEL JOHNSON'S FIRST definition of *dictionary* is "A book containing the words of any language in alphabetical order, with explanations of their meaning." But many early dictionaries were not alphabetical because there was not yet an alphabet.

Writing is more than five thousand years old. Mesopotamians were using their cuneiform script around 3300 B.C.E., and Egyptian hieroglyphs followed about a century later. But these systems were not alphabets. A symbol in either system could stand for an entire word, or sometimes a syllable, but not for a single sound. The Sumerians used around a thousand different cuneiform symbols, the Egyptians around five thousand hieroglyphs. Because there were so many, there was no order to them. The modern Chinese language works the same way: with nearly fifty thousand characters, no one could be expected to memorize them in any arbitrary order.

Reference books from the ancient world therefore cannot count on any obvious order. *Urra=hubullu* is, by some accounts, the oldest dictionary in the world. But it has no handy thumb tabs bearing the letters of the alphabet; instead it is organized thematically, and the divisions strike moderns as distinctly eccentric. Trees appear on tablet 3, but other plants on tablet 17; most animals are on tablets 13–14, but birds and fish show up on tablet 18.[1] It must have made sense to its original users, and it serves as a reminder that our familiar ways of looking at the universe are not the only ways.

Although both cuneiform and hieroglyphics eventually assumed some of the features of alphabets, most historians say the first true alphabet arose among the Semitic peoples of central Egypt around 2000 B.C.E. It was adapted from Egyptian hieroglyphs, and we can still

make out increasingly stylized versions of the original forms in some of
the letters. But the system took on a new logic: a symbol represented
not a word, not a syllable, but an individual phoneme. By the time the
system reached Phoenicia (modern Lebanon) around 1050 B.C.E., there
was no longer any obvious resemblance between the letter forms and
the pictures from which they evolved, and all pretense to being picto-
graphic was abandoned. Symbols now represented not things but
sounds. They had become an alphabet, achieving both economy and
flexibility.

Phoenicians were the great traders of the ancient Mediterranean.
Their ships could be found everywhere, and their alphabet came along
for the ride. From the Phoenician alphabet came the Aramaic alphabet,
which in turn spawned modern Hebrew and Arabic. Phoenician also
produced the Greek alphabet, which gave birth to the Latin alphabet,
which in turn is the basis of the Western European languages (as well
as many languages outside Europe). The Cyrillic alphabet, too, came
(much later) out of the Greek.

Some of the alphabet's advantages must have been immediately
obvious—it is much easier to learn to read with an alphabet than with a
logographic system. But one benefit came only much later—alphabetical
order. The alphabet need not be in any particular order: there is no reason
alpha should come before beta. We could arrange the letters as *QWERTY*
or *FUTHORC* or *PYFGCRL* or *MARESIDOT*, but for a still-
unknown reason we settled on *ABCDEFG*.

It was a long time before anyone used this order for practical purposes.
Ancient Greeks and Romans had ordered alphabets, but they hardly
ever used that order in reference books. Alphabetical order started to
appear in reference books in Europe in the thirteenth or fourteenth
centuries,[2] but readers still needed to have it explained to them. In 1286,
Johannes Balbus wrote in his *Catholicon*, "I will discuss *amo* before *bibo*
because *a* is the first letter of *amo* and *b* is the first letter of *bibo* and *a* is
before *b* in the alphabet."[3] More than three hundred years later, in 1604,
alphabetical order was still so alien to English readers that Robert
Cawdrey had to explain its use. "If thou be desirous (gentle Reader)
rightly and readily to vnderstand, and to profit by this Table," he
patiently advised, "then thou must learn the Alphabet, to wit, the order

of the Letters as they stand." The reader should learn the alphabet "perfectly without booke"—by heart—"where euery Letter standeth: as (b) neere the beginning, (n) about the middest, and (t) towards the end."[4] Shakespeare's contemporaries needed to be taught their ABCs.

Even after alphabetical order was familiar, many reference books were arranged topically or thematically, using the alphabet only within sections—so an encyclopedia's section on trees might put *ash* before *beech*, but the trees were kept together. Only in the seventeenth and eighteenth century did people realize how difficult it was to come up with a taxonomy of knowledge more intuitive than the alphabet. Alphabetical order still had enemies, who hated the thought of subjecting all human knowledge—a field that was supposed to be rationally structured—to the tyranny of an arbitrary order. It felt like failure. As the historian Peter Burke says, complete alphabetization "appears to have been adopted, originally at least, out of a sense of defeat by the forces of intellectual entropy at a time when new knowledge was coming into the system too fast to be digested or methodized."[5]

Given the hardiness of alphabetical order for so many thousands of years, it will likely remain in use for a long time to come, and parents will continue to beam proudly at their children as they learn to recite the letters in order—something they have been doing to music in the Anglophone world since 1835, when Charles Bradlee published Louis Le Maire's sheet music to "The A.B.C., a German Air with Variations for the Flute with an Easy Accompaniment for the Piano Forte." (The "German Air" was actually lifted from an eighteenth-century French folksong, which had been adapted by Mozart and had already shown up in English in 1806 as "Twinkle, Twinkle, Little Star.")

Still, alphabetical order occupies a less prominent place in our lives, especially in reference works, than it once did. Printed reference works need order because their information is spread through space—through pages and through volumes—and readers need help to navigate that space. In the electronic world, though, information takes up only a few molecules on a silicon chip or a few magnetized particles on a hard drive. There is an internal structure of the terabytes of information stored on Google's servers—information must be structured if it's to be found—but it's not as if all the information related to aardvarks and abacuses is stored on one part of their servers and the information on zydeco and zygotes on another. The user has no reason to care how that information is organized on the hard drives, as long as a query turns up the appropriate information when it is needed. As electronic reference works continue to displace print, and as searches continue to displace browsing, the world may have less reason to care about their ABCs.

CHAPTER 4

ROUND EARTH'S IMAGINED CORNERS

Mapping the World

Claudius Ptolemy	*The Domesday Book*
Geographike hyphegesis	1086
c. 150 C.E.	

S OME SAY THE cave walls at Lascaux, France, painted around 16,500 C.E., include star charts. If they are right, cartography has been an obsession of our species since we lived in caves. But even if the dots on Lascaux's walls amount to nothing, maps go back an almost unimaginably long way—more than eight thousand years, long before the first word was written down.

The earliest maps must have involved a truly dazzling act of imagination. For eons, when human beings saw the landscape, they saw it more or less from ground level. They must have climbed trees, hills, even mountains for a better view from time to time. But they always looked *out over* a landscape, never *down on* it. Maps demanded an imaginative leap: the viewer assumes a position no human being had ever actually occupied. Maps show the world as it had been seen only by birds— and the gods. They made it possible to think about physical space in new ways.

We know nothing about these earliest human attempts to capture the contours of their environment on a manageable scale. It is easy to suppose maps were drawn in the sand with a stick or etched in bark, but without evidence, all we have is speculation. Starting in the late seventh millennium B.C.E., though, we have unambiguous examples of cartography. In Catal Hüyük, Anatolia (modern Turkey), archaeologist James Mellaart discovered a map from around 6200 B.C.E. The nine-foot-long (277-cm) painting on the wall of a shrine, perhaps part of an even larger map, clearly represents the position of roughly eighty buildings, arranged in terraces, each higher than the one before it. A two-coned volcano, corresponding to the mountain Hasan Dag, appears in the distance, in mideruption, with fire running down its slopes. The locals knew the volcano well, because it was the source of the obsidian they used to make jewelry, tools, and weapons.[1]

Over the succeeding eight millennia there have been countless attempts to draw some part of the world, and these graphical "mediators between an inner mental world and an outer physical world" are milestones in our species' intellectual evolution.[2] Maps described faraway coastlines for adventurers and dreamers; they recorded conquests of foreign territory for rulers who needed to keep track of boundaries, whether to police their borders with troops or to collect taxes from the inhabitants. This last is especially important: cartographic advancement was often a byproduct of imperial conquest. Sometime around 324 B.C.E., for example, scholars in the employ of Alexander the Great compiled the *Satrapies*, a list of places Alexander had conquered as he expanded his empire. The *Satrapies* began with a strictly administrative purpose but later became guides to geography throughout what was then the known world.

☙

Long before Columbus, people knew the world was spherical. Eighteen hundred years before the *Niña*, *Pinta*, and *Santa María* left Spain, Greek geographers made impressively accurate estimates of the size of the globe. Eratosthenes, for instance, the chief librarian at the Library of Alexandria in the late third century B.C.E., started with the distance between two cities on the same latitude, Swenet and Alexandria: 5,000 stadia. He then performed an ingenious calculation, observing the elevation of the sun in these two cities by measuring shadows, which showed that Swenet and Alexandria were 7° 12' apart—one fiftieth of 360°, and therefore one fiftieth of the way around the earth. The rest of the computation was simple. If 5,000 stadia goes one fiftieth of the way around the earth, then the entire circumference should be 5,000 × 50 = 250,000 stadia. He then adjusted his estimate (for various technical reasons) to 252,000 stadia, the first scientific estimate of the distance around the whole earth. We don't know for certain how accurate it was, because we don't know exactly how long a stade was. An Attic stade, the Greek standard, was 185 meters, but an Egyptian stade was shorter, about 157.5 meters, and it is unclear which he was using. If he used the Greek measurement, his circumference of the earth came out to 46,620 kilometers—about 16 percent high, not bad for premodern measurement. If he used the Egyptian unit, then his answer was 39,690 km, less than one percent from the actual figure of 40,075 km.

Eratosthenes put all this knowledge to use in his book *Geographike*, an important bridge to modern maps. He divided the earth into zones based on their latitudes: a tropical zone around the equator, a pair of temperate zones to the north and the south of the equator, and a pair of freezing zones at the north and south poles. He then imagined a system of lines running in a grid across the surface of the earth, parallels and meridians, the functional equivalent of the latitude and longitude system that would be used two millennia later, and he used these lines to locate cities on the earth. It was the beginning of systematic geography.

A major development came at the beginning of the common era. The man Klaudios Ptolemaios (or Claudius Ptolemy) is a mystery, and we know neither where nor when he was born or died. He probably began his work in Alexandria, Upper Egypt, in the mid-120s C.E., and he refers to cities founded around 130 C.E., so the best guess is that he was born around the year 100. But though we know depressingly little about him, his works on astronomy, astrology, trigonometry, optics, harmonics, and chronology reveal a wide-ranging mind. And his modern translators are to the point: "On any list of ancient scientific works, Ptolemy's *Geography* will occupy a distinguished place."[3] His *Geography* (also known as *Geographica* or the Greek *Geographike hyphegesis*) was one of the West's first systematic attempts to collect all of the ancient world's cartographic knowledge in one place. Ptolemy was interested in both globes and two-dimensional maps, and he recognized the differences between them, because the three dimensions of the earth can never be represented on a flat surface without distortion.

Although he made observations of astronomical phenomena when he was in Alexandria, Ptolemy was no sextant-toting field cartographer.

TITLE: Γεωγραφικὴ ὑφήγησις (A guide to geography)

COMPILER: Claudius Ptolemaios (*c.* 100–*c.* 170 C.E.)

ORGANIZATION: Book 1, introduction; book 2, Ireland through Dalmatia; book 3, Italy, Greece, and the lower Danube; book 4, North Africa; book 5, Asia Minor through Babylonia; book 6, former Persian Empire; book 7, India and world map; book 8, overview of the regional maps

PUBLISHED: *c.* 150 C.E.

ENTRIES: 8,000

VOLUMES: 8

TOTAL WORDS: 83,000

Instead, he drew on the combined experience of generations of Greek and Roman cartographers, synthesized it, and made the results available to the world. His *Geographike hyphegesis* is not a map, exactly; rather it is an instruction book for a map, a list of coordinates—thousands of them, from the British Isles to India, China, and Sri Lanka—that, when plotted on a grid, describe a map of the inhabited world. Since it is much easier to copy text (digital information) than images (analog information), Ptolemy's decision to give coordinates gave his book a longevity that no actual map would ever have.[4] Even so, the manuscripts that survive are messy, fragmentary, and sometimes contradictory, so it is no easy feat to put together the text.

The *Geographike hyphegesis* is in eight books. The first serves as an introduction, and it features a substantial critique of the maps of one of Ptolemy's predecessors, Marinos of Tyre. We know nothing about Marinos beyond what we can gather from Ptolemy's text, which called him "the latest [author] in our time to have undertaken this subject,"[5] so he probably lived not long before Ptolemy himself. Ptolemy criticized his shortcomings, such as his inaccurate estimates of the size of the earth and his technical problems with his understanding of the projection of latitude and longitude onto the spherical surface of the earth. But still he borrowed from Marinos at length.

With book 2, Ptolemy introduced the coordinates that occupy most of his work, starting in the far west: Ireland, Britain, Hispania, Gaul, Germany, and the upper Danube. Book 3 covers the Italian and Greek peninsulas and the islands around them, as well as the lower Danube. Book 4 crosses the Mediterranean into northern Africa, and Ptolemy progressed from west to east, from Egypt to Ethiopia. Book 5 starts in Asia Minor—modern Turkey—and covers Armenia, Cyprus, Syria, and most of the Middle East. Book 6 is devoted to the regions that had once formed the Persian Empire. Book 7 is devoted to the Indian subcontinent, and included a description of a complete world map. Book 8—which some critics believe may include material not written by Ptolemy—surveys more than two dozen regional maps.[6]

A typical section shows Ptolemy's method:

In Hispania, known by the Greeks as Iberia, there are three provinces, Baetica and Lusitania and Tarraconensis. And the west and north borders of Baetica are determined by Lusitania and part of Tarraconensis respectively, a description of which is made as follows:

To the east the mouth of the river Ana	4	⅓ 37	½
Before the river turns east	6	⅓ 39	
Where the river touches the Lusitanian border	9	39	
And the line drawn from there along the border of Tarraconensis to the end of the Balearic sea	12	37	¼
Where the well springs of the river overflow	14	40	

Ptolemy measured his coordinates in degrees, with 360 to a circle, as we do today; he also provided fractions of a degree to approximate minutes: 4⅓ is 4 degrees 20 minutes. Coordinates, of course, have meaning only in relation to some known point. The equator provided him with a natural reference for latitude. The prime meridian is nothing natural, only a social convention, and at that time none was recognized. Greenwich was not used even by British cartographers until the late eighteenth century, and it was not adopted internationally until 1884.

Ptolemy picked the "Fortunate Isles," probably what we call the Canary Islands, for his starting point. There are of course plenty of inaccuracies in his reports; he was least reliable in reporting the east–west dimensions of the Mediterranean and in believing that some sort of land bridge connected Africa to China. But his was the most complete and most accurate picture of the world that could be had at the time.

With the collapse of the Western Roman Empire in the fifth century, the European field of vision narrowed considerably, and cartography suffered. Not so in the Muslim world: at the end of the first millennium, Islam's maps were more accurate than anything Europe had to offer. And in Muslim hands, Ptolemy's *Geography* took on new prominence, thanks to one of the most learned figures in the world. All we have are *probably*s for most of the basic facts of his life: he was probably born around the year 780 in or near Baghdad, was probably of Persian origin, and was probably based at Baghdad's Bayt al-Hikma, or House of Wisdom, during the Abbasid Caliphate. We can be certain, though, that Muhammad ibn Musa al-Khwarizmi was a polymath. He gave us two words whose importance has only grown in the centuries since he lived: the title of his book *Kitab al-muktasar fi hisab al-jabr wal-muqabala*, or *The Concise Book on Calculation by Restoration and Compensation*, is the source of the word *algebra* (*al-jabr* means "compensation"), and his name, al-Khwarizmi, once Latinized and then passed around through the modern languages, gave us the *algorithm*. Every high-tech computer calculation pays tribute to the ninth-century Islamic genius.

Al-Khwarizmi's *Kitab surat al-Ard* (*Book on the Appearance of the Earth*) is the expression of his lifelong interest in geography. It is the hardest of his books to date; many scholars guess 816–17 C.E., but some place it as late as 833 C.E. Al-Khwarizmi borrowed many of Ptolemy's coordinates and often used his reference points, though he also reorganized the material and checked the facts against the latest and best geographical information available to him. For nearly a millennium and a half, Ptolemy's *Geography*—in its Greek, Latin, and Arabic versions, updated by generations of cartographers in Europe and the Middle East—was the most important set of maps in the world, providing "the strongest link the chain between the knowledge of mapping in the ancient and early modern worlds."[7]

❦

As al-Khwarizmi proved, during Europe's so-called Dark Ages the serious intellectual work was going on far away. But that is not to say nothing was going on in Europe between the fall of the Roman Empire and the Renaissance. Cartography was too important to be neglected entirely. Even England—part of a small, cold, rainy island off the north-west coast of Europe, marginally significant in Western Europe, utterly irrelevant in the rest of the world—created a geographical survey in the eleventh century that would be unequaled in its extent for another eight hundred years.

Guillaume II, Duc de Normandie, turned his eyes across the Channel to the land of the Angles and the Saxons, and in 1066 he led an invasion that would prove to be one of the most consequential in Europe's long history. After leading his forces to a town on England's southern coast, Hastings, and defeating Harold Godwinson, Guillaume earned a new title: no longer merely the duke of Normandy, he was William the Conqueror. Anglo-Saxon England now had French-speaking rulers.

Nineteen years after the Norman Invasion, William was concerned about security. The Danes had their eyes on his country, and he needed money for soldiers to keep the Vikings away. The obvious source of revenue was taxation, but William had no idea how much his new country was worth. The Anglo-Saxon kings had neither the interest nor the administrative structure to compute the population and wealth of every village, but William was determined to find out. During the Christmas celebrations in 1085, therefore, he ordered a comprehensive survey of England in order to establish the basis for taxing his people. It was also a means of asserting his control over his still-new country, and of determining who among his subjects might be expected to fight on his side.

William charged seven or eight panels of commissioners with performing the great survey, and each was assigned a set of counties. These hundreds of commissioners and aides then fanned out across the country collecting information: the name of every hamlet, village, town, and city; the population; the number of people at each social rank and of each profession; the value of the buildings; even the amount of livestock. The *Anglo-Saxon Chronicle*, the most important year-by-year account of early English history, recorded the process:

> He had a record made of how much land his archbishops had, and his bishops and his abbots and his earls—and though I relate it at too great length—what or how much everybody had who was occupying land in England, in land or in cattle, and how much money it was worth. So very narrowly did he have it investigated that there was no single virgate of land, nor indeed (it is a shame to relate but it seemed no shame to him to do) one ox nor one cow nor one pig which there was left out, and not put down in his record.[8]

A book called the *Inquisitio comitatus Cantabrigensis*, or *Investigation of the County of Cambridge*, survives as a working draft of the material for Cambridgeshire, and it reveals how the commissioners proceeded, collecting information first by shires, then by hundreds, then by villages. Some facts came from written records, but most from in-person inspections and interviews. In each county town they organized sworn inquests of sheriffs, barons, and other representatives of each village, giving them questionnaires demanding precise answers to specific questions. Much of the public was unhappy, not yet reconciled to a French-speaking king whose agents were snooping around. Everyone knew this was a means of increasing tax revenues, and property owners tried to play down the value of their property, pointing out problems to the agents. To verify the accuracy of what they were told, the commissioners ordered special sittings of the county courts all over the country, where their sources were to give their testimony and jurors—half English, half French—worked to keep people honest.

When the commissioners had collected all the information, they reorganized it to account for the new feudal arrangements that followed the conquest of 1066, emphasizing the role of the barons in order to change the strictly geographical organization into something more informed by social hierarchies. For each county, the commissioners produced a list of landholders, from the king at the top to the poorest tenant at the bottom. They described all their fiefs, with the names of holders of manors from both 1066, right before William took over the country, and 1085, when the survey began. They provided the dimensions of plots of land, the number of workers on each estate, and the value of the land:

Land of the Bp. of Coutance

The Bp. of Coutance holds half a hide in FILVNGELEI, and Lewin of him. The arable employs ii ploughs. One is in the demesne; with ii bondmen. There are v villeins, and ii borders; they have i plough. There are ii acres of meadow. Wood ii furlongs long, and one furling broad. It was worth x *s.* Now xxx *s.* Alwin held it freely.

The collection of information took a total of eight months—astonishingly quick, considering how much they had to accomplish and how slowly both people and information moved—after which a second team of commissioners checked their work. Several monks were then set to work transcribing 2 million words of text.

The result was *The Description of England*, better known as *The Domesday Book*—a name that comes from the assumption that what appeared there was as authoritative as what God had written in the book of judgment for the end of time. In fact it was two books, with *Great Domesday* covering most of the country and *Little Domesday* giving the raw data on Essex, Norfolk, and Suffolk. Even in the combined work there were omissions. *Domesday* did not cover all of the north of England. London and Winchester were omitted altogether, though there are gaps in the manuscript, suggesting that there were plans to include other information at some point. Even so, the work occupies more than sixteen hundred large pages of parchment, collecting the names of 13,418 places and 109,230 "villeins" out of a population of around 2 million. It established a value for all the surveyed English land of £73,000. *The Domesday Book* served William well: with his new comprehensive reference book in hand, he determined his tax policies. He never got to make much use of the information, though, for he died in 1087, some say from illness and others from injury. But he left a powerful administrative machine in place for his son, William Rufus, and for a long line of Norman kings of England.

TITLE: *Book of Winchester* or *Liber de Wintonia*
COMPILER: William the Conqueror (*c.* 1028–1087)
ORGANIZATION: Geographical and by social rank
PUBLISHED: 1086
VOLUMES: 2, "Great Domesday" and "Little Domesday";
    now bound in 5 vols.
PAGES: 1,668
ENTRIES: 13,418 places
TOTAL WORDS: 2 million
SIZE: Great Domesday, 15" × 11" (38 × 28 cm); Little
    Domesday, 11" × 8" (28 × 20 cm)
AREA: 1,400 ft² (131 m²)

Even more important, though, may be the use subsequent researchers have been able to make of this great work of reference. *The Domesday Book* offers an unparalleled record of social life in eleventh-century England—the kind of snapshot we have nowhere else in medieval Europe. It shows us what happened in the first twenty years of William's reign: whereas once virtually the entire country was owned by native English, by 1086 just 4 percent of the land was under English control, with around 20 percent now under the personal control of William himself and the rest by his fellow Normans. Over the same period, we see women diminishing from owning 6 percent of the land to just 2 percent—fully two thirds of the land owned by women had been transferred to male control. It may surprise some to hear that England, long proud of its ancient heritage of liberty, had 28,235 slaves in 1085. Most of the peasants, though, were freemen, owning at least a garden plot. It was hardly a time of equality; fully a quarter of the country was owned by just a dozen barons, and much of the political power was in the hands of the nation's 1,027 priests.

The *Domesday* compilers had no intention to produce a work of social history, but they did so despite themselves. Windsor, now the home of Queen Elizabeth, was then a tiny village with one plow, one slave, and a fishery. Throughout England the principal meat was pork.

Cow's milk was available, but only to the rich. Honey, on the other hand, was abundant, and was used both as a medicine and to make mead. *Domesday*'s degree of detail is impressive: "In Louth, the Bishop of Lincoln had 12 ploughlands taxable. The bishop now has in lordship three ploughs, 80 burgesses. One market at 29 shillings, 40 freemen and two villagers. Two knights have two ploughs and meadow, 21 acres. Woodland, pasture in places, 400 acres."

Domesday also gives us insights into less popular professions: there were sixteen beekeepers in England, for instance, and one *joculatrix*, or female jester. We learn about local customs: in Chester, the book records, "If a widow have unlawful intercourse with a man, a fine of 20 shillings. If a girl, a fine of 10 shillings." There is even a glimpse of a private amour: *Little Domesday* related the story of a Breton soldier who fell in love with a woman in Norfolk and married her, one of the very few real-life accounts of everyday people in love in the whole of the Middle Ages.[9] This gazetteer cum census cum geological survey is the oldest surviving public record in the English-speaking world and one of the largest administrative efforts in the whole of the European Middle Ages. Nothing even approached its comprehensiveness until the Victorian era, when the 1841 census produced an even more detailed picture of the country. Not until the age of the railway and telegram could this survey completed at the beginning of the millennium be superseded.

The original *Domesday* has been an unusually peripatetic book. It was moved from the Anglo-Saxon capital, Winchester, to the new capital, Westminster, and eventually to Chancery Lane, the heart of England's legal profession. The Great Fire of London forced it to move again, to Nonsuch Palace, near Epsom, in 1666, before coming back to London. In the late eighteenth century, the British government spent £38,000—a staggering amount then—producing a type facsimile, but by this time it was recognized as a national treasure. New threats in the twentieth century once again took the book away from danger: during the First World War, it was protected at Bodmin Prison, and during the Second at Shepton Mallet Prison.

The original *Domesday Book* is now in the National Archives at Kew, in London's Richmond borough, where it remains the oldest public record in England. The book is coming up on a thousand years of age, and in that millennium it has suffered some serious indignities. Some of the worst assaults came from those who thought they were caring for it. Clumsy "restorations" and rebindings have caused irreversible damage. In the mid-1980s, a more careful team of three conservation specialists gave it the most thorough and careful refurbishment in its thousand-year history. The result was bound in five volumes, and the whole survey was digitized in August 2006.

⬥

That we have been mapping longer than we have been reading and writing is an indication of just how important the cartographic enter-prise is. Writings about place, whether as wide-ranging as Ptolemy's *Geographica* or as focused as *Domesday*, have been essential to our survival. They led our ancestors toward food and water and away from danger: think of the old "Here be Dragons" legend on sixteenth-century globes. And assembling extensive information about places has remained one of the most urgent tasks of reference publishing. Today the infor-mation is provided by satellites and served up in real time, and GPS may mean the end of most printed road maps. But both the need for accounts of distant places and the methods for compiling and presenting them have not changed much since Ptolemy and William sought to give a portrait of the worlds they inhabited.

THE INVENTION OF THE CODEX

B OOKS HAVE BEEN around a long time—more than five thousand years—but for most of that time they have not looked very bookish. The term *book* refers to any physical incarnation of a text, beginning with our earliest surviving writings, pressed into clay tablets or carved into architectural stone. The ancient Hebrews, Greeks, and Romans also had things they called books, but they were scrolls of papyrus, the form in which books circulated in much of the ancient world. A typical sheet of papyrus was between 12 and 16 inches (30 and 40 cm) long; twenty or so would be glued together to form a long strip of around 20 to 25 feet (6 to 8 m), which would then be wrapped around a wooden rod and rolled up.

Scrolls had real advantages over earlier forms of writing. They were lighter than clay tablets, longer lasting than wax tablets, and cheaper than either. They were good enough to serve literate cultures for many centuries. But scrolls also had disadvantages. You read a scroll by unrolling one side of the text and rolling it up on the other, keeping a few columns visible at any time. This was more convenient than switching from one clay tablet to another, but the only way to find a passage in the middle of a text is to start at the beginning and roll it out, column by column. Access is always sequential. To make matters worse, most early scrolls were written in "majuscule *scriptio continua*"—ALLCAPITALLETTERS WITHNOSPACESORPUNCTUATIONBETWEENTHEMMAKINGITALMOST IMPOSSIBLETOFINDAPASSAGEYOURELOOKINGFORESPECIALLYIN SOMETHINGASLONGASAWHOLEBOOK.

Things were shaken up when a novel way of arranging writing surfaces was invented. Instead of a stream of text on a long, continuous scroll, "A book made from hinged leaves" was developed[1]—that is, a series of sheets, written on both sides and bound together along one edge, usually either sewn or glued to a spine. This new format, known as a *codex*, made it possible to turn pages, and not just one at a time: one can flip quickly to the middle of a book.

It's unclear exactly when this new technology was developed. A set of six sheets of 24-karat gold, bound together with hoops and engraved in the Etruscan language, was discovered in Bulgaria in the 1940s. Scholars debate its authenticity, but the best guess is that it dates from roughly 600 B.C.E. While technically a codex, it seems to have been one of a kind. More influential was the Roman tradition of binding wooden tablets together with leather thongs. Eventually tablets gave way to sheets of parchment, very thin sheets of animal skin. In the first century B.C.E., bound collections of these sheets were used as notebooks, and a century later, they began to be used to distribute texts. By the third century, this new form of book had become widespread. The scroll did not die out altogether, at least not at once, but the codex became ever more popular as a medium for publishing.

Christians were early adopters of the new technology. Already in the second century, when the canon of the Christian Bible was being formed, most of the holy Scriptures were being distributed in codex form, while Roman and Hebrew literature was still circulating in scrolls.[2] The popularity of the newfangled reading technology among early Christians helped Christianity become a religion of the Word. Codices offered what the computer age has taught us to call *random-access memory*—the ability to go to any position in the text without reading through the entire work in sequence. And in works specifically designed to be consulted in short bursts rather than read from cover to cover, the ability to turn pages makes all the difference.

The codex made possible a number of related technologies. One was the page number—not unheard of in scrolls, but much more common when pages were clearly demarcated in the codex. And the page number enabled both the table of contents and the index. The latter is especially relevant, because an index turns any book into a reference book, if only for a moment. Even books written for sequential reading lend themselves to quick lookups when there is a list of topics in the back keyed to pages.

The codex made the modern reference book possible. Many things have changed, of course, over the last fifteen hundred years, starting with the material: at first papyrus, made from reeds; then vellum, made from calfskin; then paper, made first from rags and later from wood pulp. Bindings and title pages have changed radically, and decorations such as dust jackets and deckled edges were introduced over time. And Gutenberg's development of movable type changed the method by which words were put on pages. But these changes were motivated by concerns about cost, availability, durability, and advertising; they did not change the basic function of the book. A modern reader is immediately at home with even a fifth-century codex, and a fifth-century reader would know at once how to operate a hot-off-the-presses book today.

Our own era may finally be witnessing the form that will take over from the codex: the electronic book, whether it will be on the large screens of desktop computers, on dedicated devices, on tablets, or on some platform yet to be invented. Still, it would be foolish to bet against the codex. After nearly two millennia as the dominant form of distributing longish texts, it has a good track record.

CHAPTER 5

THE CIRCLE OF THE SCIENCES

Ancient Encyclopedias

Cassiodorus	Isidore
Institutiones	*Etymologies*
543–55 C.E.?	636 C.E.

*E*NCYCLOPEDIA BOTH IS and is not an ancient word. There was a phrase, *enkuklios paideia*, in ancient Greek, but (a) it did not mean *encyclopedia*, and (b) no one is entirely sure what it did mean. It appeared only a few times in ancient literature, and what it refers to is not always clear from context. The roots mean *circle* and *learning*, and for a long time, modern writers thought *encyclopedia* meant "the circle of the sciences," the organization of all knowledge in a tight bundle. The ancients, however, meant something like "well-rounded education." Aristotle, for instance, used the phrase *enkulia philosophemata* to refer to the foundations of philosophy, the things a student should study before getting into the complexities of real philosophy.[1]

Whatever the word signified in the ancient world, it did not mean a reference book—that was a post-Renaissance development. Encyclopedic works existed, however, aspiring to provide systematic coverage of all knowledge, at least all knowledge in one field or set of fields. Amenemope, an Egyptian in the late second millennium B.C.E., composed a wisdom text called the *Instruction*, or sometimes *A Text to Dispel Ignorance about Everything That Exists*. In thirty chapters it covered the known universe, both natural and supernatural, and offered advice on how to live a worthwhile life. Some have called it encyclopedic.[2]

The Greeks and Romans certainly had works that aspired to be comprehensive. Titles like Pliny's *Natural History* had an encyclopedic character, but many writers contend for the title of "first encyclopedist."

Some historians award the laurel to the Greek sage Speusippus, Plato's nephew, who died in 339 or 338 B.C.E. His work supposedly collected Platonic and Aristotelian ideas about philosophy, mathematics, the sciences, and so on—but we can only speculate, because only a few scraps of the text survive, not enough to tell us anything useful.[3]

The earliest Latin encyclopedias are equally mysterious. Around 158 B.C.E., Cato the Censor put together a Latin book often called an encyclopedia, though it does not survive. Another lost Latin encyclopedia came from Marcus Terentius Varro (116–27 B.C.E.), a soldier, senator, real estate investor, and wide-ranging writer. Quintilian, who knew something about learned Romans, called Varro "the most learned of the Romans." Saint Augustine later praised Cicero for appealing to the lover of words, and Varro for appealing to the lover of facts.[4] One scholar argues that Varro deserves to be called the real founder of the encyclopedia: "Marcus Terentius Varro was not the first Roman to write educationally, but he may reasonably be described as the first one to try to do it encyclopedically."[5]

Three of Varro's seventy-four known works are interesting to readers of reference books. One is the *Imagines*—*Images* or *Portraits*—collecting seven hundred biographical sketches on prominent Greek and Roman figures. Another is *Antiquitates rerum humanarum et divinarum libri XLI*, or *Human and Divine Antiquities in Forty-One Books*, which opens with six books on human affairs, six more on locations throughout the Italian peninsula, another six covering the history of Rome, and six on things, with the rest of the work devoted to divine subjects. Most of what we know about the lost *Antiquitates* comes from Augustine's attacks on it in his *City of God*.[6] And Varro's most encyclopedic work of all was *Disciplinarum libri IX*, or *Nine Books of Disciplines*,[7] one for each of the seven liberal arts, with additions for medicine and architecture. Not enough of this book survives for us to say much about it, but we can gather from the surviving fragments what sort of writer Varro was. Some scholars are exasperated by "his interest in minute details."[8] But Varro certainly had a passion for classifying, for covering a field systematically and drawing up a thorough outline of all the topics he was going to touch on, and he collected as many citations to earlier writers as he could, which puts him squarely in the encyclopedic tradition.

Other important and wide-ranging works of Latin late antiquity are Nonius Marcellus' *Compendious Doctrine*, written early in the fourth century, an early example of alphabetical order, and Martianus Capella's *Liber de nuptiis Mercurii et Philologiae*, or *Marriage of Mercury and Philology*, probably written early in the fifth century. The *Marriage* is a bizarre book, a complicated allegorical work mixing prose and verse, in which each of the seven liberal arts is figured as a bridesmaid at the mythological nuptials. It has few devotees today; one modern reader calls it "a fantastically boring mélange."[9]

※

In the first major reference book of the Christian era, *Institutiones divinarum et sæcularium litterarum*, the sixth-century polymath Flavius Marcus Aurelius Cassiodorus Senator sought to reconcile pagan learning with the new divine revelation.

Cassiodorus was born to an aristocratic family in Italy, perhaps of Syrian descent, and as a very young man he began a legal career. He worked with the Germanic conquerors—the so-called "barbarians"—who effectively ran sixth-century Italy. Theoderic the Great, an Ostrogoth, employed the twenty-year-old Cassiodorus as a secretary. From 507 to 511 he held the post of *quaestor*; in 514 he was named *consul*; in 526, *magister officiorum*, or chief of the civil service; and in 533, he was finally named *praetorian prefect*, a position that amounted almost to prime minister.[10]

After some years in this position, Cassiodorus went to Constantinople, the center of the Eastern Roman Empire, and passed almost two decades there. But eventually he decided to retire, and he returned to Italy. He applied to Pope Agapetus for permission to open an academy of Christian learning in Rome, modeled on the pagan academies in Antioch and Alexandria but with a new Christian focus. Agapetus was unpersuaded. Cassiodorus therefore retired from Rome at the age of seventy-one, after five decades near the center of power, and headed for the south of Italy. Though a layman, he established a monastery he called the Vivarium, where he encouraged the monks to copy old manuscripts, including those of the pagan literature of pre-Christian Rome. The scriptorium in a monastery, with tonsured, brown-robed monks hunched over desks as they copied old texts, is now such a familiar image that we assume it was

> **TITLE:** *Institutiones divinarum et saecularium litterarum*
> **COMPILER:** Flavius Magnus Aurelius Cassiodorus Senator
>   (*c.* 490–*c.* 585)
> **ORGANIZATION:** Book 1, religious practice and reading the
>   Bible; book 2, the seven liberal arts
> **PUBLISHED:** 543–55 C.E.?
> **VOLUMES:** 2
> **TOTAL WORDS:** 28,000

somehow inevitable. But the idea, if not original with Cassiodorus, was promoted more energetically by him than by anyone else, and he deserves much of the credit for literary monasticism.[11]

He wrote his two-volume *Institutiones divinarum et sæcularium litterarum* (*Institutes of Divine and Secular Literature*) for the monks at the Vivarium. The work "covered everything from commentaries on the Holy Scriptures to geometry and astronomy. He even explained book-binding, lighting, and timekeeping."[12] The book is largely a reading list, a systematic annotated bibliography for readers of the Bible:

> St. Jerome, who enriched the Latin language remarkably, also attended to our interests by his usual admirable translation of the two sermons of Origen on the Canticle of Canticles. And this Rufinus, too, an eloquent translator, expounded more fully in three books by adding some sections up to that precept "Catch us the foxes, the little foxes that damage the vineyards" (Song of Songs 2:15). After those men, Epiphanius, bishop of Cyprus, treated the whole book in one brief volume in Greek. We have had this book and others translated into Latin with the Lord's aid by our learned friend Epiphanius. I have, therefore, included these most careful commentators on this book in a single volume to offer the reader all extant writers on this work in one place.

The book also includes information about scribal practices. In ancient handwriting, for instance, it was easy to confuse the letters *V* and *B*, so Cassiodorus advised his monks, eager "to avoid mixing the great good with faulty words by altering letters," to read up on "the ancient orthographers."[13]

Book 1 is a detailed handbook on religion, the Church, and interpreting both the Bible and secular texts. Each of the first nine chapters is devoted to a book of the Bible, after which comes a chapter on methodology, and then a series of miscellaneous chapters: discussions of the synods that established authoritative doctrine for Christianity; the biblical canon as it appeared in various writers; even a list of books at the Vivarium. Cassiodorus offered advice on reading Scripture, on understanding history in Christian rather than classical terms, and the greatest teachers in the Christian tradition, from the earliest church fathers to his own contemporaries. His favorites are obvious, including "Blessed Hilary, blessed Ambrose, and blessed Jerome," as well as "Blessed Augustine, that excellent teacher, warrior against the heretics, defender of the faithful." The total in book 1 came to thirty-three chapters, "a number acknowledged to correspond with the age of the Lord when he offered eternal life to a world laid low by sin."[14]

Book 2, much shorter than the first, covered the seven liberal arts, with four chapters on the quadrivium and three on the trivium. Cassiodorus feels a need to justify this secular learning in a Christian context—the liberal arts were the heart of a pagan education, not a Christian one. But Cassiodorus reminds his readers that "the holy Fathers have not decreed that the study of secular letters should be rejected," because secular learning is ancillary to religion. Still, it is hard to miss the defensiveness in his tone when he justifies secular knowledge. The personal, even intimate, character of the first book is gone, and the long list of readings is replaced by more specific information.

Here is where the book looks most like an encyclopedia, as Cassiodorus ranges across the liberal arts: "There are six parts in a rhetorical speech: introduction, statement of the facts, division, proof, refutation, conclusion"; "There are six harmonies: (1) the diatessaron; (2) the diapente; (3) the diapason; (4) the diapason and diatessaron; (5) the diapeson and diapente; (6) the disdiapason"; "The backward motion or regression of the stars is what the Greeks call *hypopadismon* or *anapodismon*, i.e. when the star in carrying out its motion seems to be moving backward at the same time"—all of this is the stuff of classical Greek and Roman learning. Cassiodorus seems to have seen his mission as translating and transmitting the classical world to the Christian "barbarians" in the West.

Despite Cassiodorus' profound knowledge and his determination to collect and disseminate information, he reminded the brothers at the Vivarium that "knowledge is not found in letters alone, but that God gives complete wisdom 'to everyone according as he will' (1 Corinthians 12:11)." He knew perfectly well that "many illiterate men come to true knowledge and grasp the right faith"; the learned, conversely, are too apt to be misled: "Therefore let the mind be ever intent on the general meanings of the books, and let us set our minds on that contemplation which does not merely make a sound in the ears but lights the interior eye." The *Institutiones* is a profoundly learned work, and yet it has a complex, even ambivalent, attitude toward learning—learning is useless if it does not contribute to piety. Cassiodorus is concerned with the differences and relationships between sacred and profane learning, and his book is ultimately about knowledge itself—what we should know and what we need to know. Historian Arnaldo Momigliano calls it "one of the most formative books of the Middle Ages."[15]

He has been called the last wise man of the ancient world, and the man on the boundary between the ancient and medieval worlds. His *Etymologiæ*, also known as *Origines*, became the most popular reference work of the Middle Ages, being copied by hand countless times and even surviving into the age of print, nearly a thousand years after he wrote.

His name was Isidore—now Saint Isidore—and he came from Spain, where he was born around 560. The Roman Empire still had an official existence at this point, but its administrative powers were only a pale shadow of what they had once been, and in Spain in particular the Empire was in retreat. Isidore's family came from Cartagena, on Spain's Mediterranean coast, but in the middle of the sixth century the Byzantine Empire assumed control of the region, forcing the family to relocate to Seville. Isidore's parents died when he was still a child, and he was raised by his brother Leander, an abbot with access to a fine

TITLE: *Etymologiarum libri XX*

COMPILER: Isidorus Hispalensis (Isidore of Seville)
  (*c.* 560–636)

ORGANIZATION: 20 books: (1) grammar, (2) rhetoric,
  (3) mathematics (including music, geometry, and
  astronomy), (4) medicine, (5) law, (6) order of Scripture,
  (7) God and angels, (8) faith and the church,
  (9) languages, civics, family relations, (10)
  miscellaneous terms in alphabetical order, (11) human
  beings, (12) animals, (13) the four elements, (14) the
  earth, (15) cities, fields, and roads, (16) minerals, (17)
  agriculture, (18) war and games, (19) ships and trades,
  (20) food and domestic implements

PUBLISHED: 636 C.E.

VOLUMES: 20

ENTRIES: 463 numbered or lettered chapters, often
  subdivided

TOTAL WORDS: 191,000

school. Leander had an impressive career before him: around the year 580, he would become bishop of Seville, a position from which he would exercise considerable influence over Church policy. Other members of the family were active in the Church as well: Isidore's sister Florentina became a nun, and his brother Fulgentius became bishop of Ecija. But Isidore himself had a more distinguished career than any of them. He was learned, with some knowledge of both Greek and Hebrew— probably not much, but this was at a time when very few in the West had any knowledge of either language. He knew not only the major Christian authors but also the works of the great pagan writers, including Pliny's *Historia naturalis*. Around the year 600, he succeeded his brother as bishop of Seville.

He probably began his *Etymologiae* sometime around the year 617, and he was certainly at work on it by 622. Isidore kept at it until his death in 636, when it was completed, edited, and published by his student Braulion. The Latin is simple, making the book accessible even to those who were not well educated, and the range of subjects it covered is positively dizzying. It collects useful knowledge from 154 authors and assembles it into a twenty-book compendium covering grammar, mathematics, medicine, languages, geography, zoology, agriculture, and, above all, religious life. Isidore has been called "a bright light in an age which for a number of reasons has been called dark."[16]

Working from the assumption that knowledge of words leads to knowledge of things, Isidore explored the world by looking deep into the origins of words. This approach is visible in the opening section of the *Etymologies*, where he discusses the words *discipline* and *art*, relating them to the words for *learning*, *full*, *knowledge*, *strict*, and *virtue*:

> Discipline and art (De disciplina et arte) 1. A discipline (*disciplina*) takes its name from "learning" (*discere*), whence it can also be called "knowledge" (*scientia*). Now "know" (*scire*) is named from "learn" (*discere*), because none of us knows unless we have learned. A discipline is so named in another way, because "the full thing is learned" (*discitur plena*). 2. And an art (*ars*, gen. *artis*) is so called because it consists of strict (*artus*) precepts and rules. Others say this word is derived by the Greeks from the word ἀρετή [*arete*], that is, "virtue," as they termed knowledge.[17]

As it happens, *art* does not come from *arete*, and even if it did, the etymology would not fix the meaning of anything. This is an example of what linguists call the "etymological fallacy," the idea that the "true" meaning of a word is somehow lurking in its origins rather than in the way it is used by people in the real world. As Isidore himself put it, "The knowledge of a word's etymology often has an indispensable usefulness for interpreting the word, for when you have seen whence a word has originated, you understand its force more quickly. Indeed, one's insight into anything is clearer when its etymology is known." For Isidore, though, etymologies were the key to hidden knowledge. So, for instance, the word *medicina* (medicine) was supposed by Isidore to come from *modus* (moderation), because "nature grieves at excess and rejoices at restraint. Hence those who drink potions and remedies copiously and unceasingly are troubled. Anything that is immoderate brings not health but danger."[18] The word *medicine* itself therefore teaches us a valuable medical lesson.

This etymology, alas, is bunk. Although both *medicine* and *moderation* come ultimately from the same Indo-European root, **med-* 'to take appropriate measures', they took very different routes to get there, changing their meanings over the millennia, and neither comes from the other. Besides, **med-* is also the root of *modest, meditate, mode, modern,* and *gamete.* No one today would make the argument that modernity, modesty, and meditation have some secret connection. But for Isidore, this is where wisdom was to be found. It led him to speculate about words' histories, with superficial similarities between words serving to link them together. In his discussion of "tiny flying animals," for instance, he explained that "Bees (*apis*) are so named either because they cling to each other with their feet (*pes*), or because they are born without feet (cf. *a-,* 'without'), for they develop feet and wings afterwards."[19] The effect is a text richly stocked with seeming puns, but the puns are more than casual wordplay; they are intended to give us a profound insight into the truth—a poet's understanding of the universe.

Even when Isidore's facts are not supported by modern scholarship, the *Etymologies* offers a fascinating glimpse of the way people saw the world in the seventh century. Isidore loved classification, as with warfare: "There are four kinds of war: just, unjust, civil, and more than civil," or literary works: "There are three genres of 'literary works' (*opusculum*). The first kind are extracts (*excerptum*), which in Greek are called *scholia* . . . The second kind are homilies (*homilia*), which Latin speakers call 'talks' (*verbum*) . . . Third are tomes (*tomus*), which we call books or volumes."[20] Sometimes his taxonomic urge got out of hand, as in this riot of Latin kinship terms:

> The originator of my birth is my father, and I am his son or daughter. The father of my father is my grandfather (*avis*), and I am his grandson (*nepos*) or granddaughter (*neptis*). The grandfather of my father is my great-grandfather (*proavus*), and I am his great-grandson (*pronepos*) or -daughter (*proneptis*). The great-grandfather of my

father is my great-great-grandfather (*abavus*) and I am his great-great-grandson (*abnepos*) or -daughter (*abneptis*). The great-great-grandfather of my father is my great-great-great-grandfather (*atavus*), and I am his great-great-great-grandson (*adnepos*) or -daughter (*adneptis*). The great-great-great-grandfather of my father is my great-great-great-great-grandfather (*tritavus*), and I am his great-great-great-great-grandson (*trinepos*) or -daughter (*trineptis*).[21]

Little original research informs the *Etymologies*. As the modern editors put it, Isidore's "aims were not novelty but authority, not originality but accessibility, not augmenting but preserving and transmitting knowledge"; the work as a whole is "complacently derivative." He drew extensively on the greatest Latin stylists, including Virgil, Cicero, and Lucan, as well as the Bible, which he cites more than two hundred times. But evidence suggests he did not even read all the authors he cited, copying them instead at second hand. Still, few books had anything like Isidore's influence on the intellectual life of the Middle Ages: "It would be hard to overestimate the influence of the *Etymologies* on medieval European culture," write his modern editors, "and impossible to describe it fully. Nearly a thousand manuscript copies survive, a truly huge number."[22] Every medieval library with any intellectual pretensions owned a copy, and the greatest authors of the Middle Ages—Bede, John Gower, William Langland, Geoffrey Chaucer—quoted him. Even as the manuscript age came to an end, the *Etymologies* remained a central text. It was printed as early as 1472, in the very dawn of movable type, and went through ten more printings before 1500.

Isidore was canonized as a saint in 1598 and named a Doctor of the Church in 1722. He remains an inspirational force today, and in a way that would make the encyclopedist proud. In 1997, Pope John Paul II proposed Isidore as the patron saint of the Internet, and the Order of Saint Isidore of Seville is working to make it official.

❦

Even before the development of a type of book called an encyclopedia, there were writings that were unambiguously encyclopedic—concerned with capturing all the essential knowledge in the world and collecting it in one place. Cassiodorus and Isidore were engaged in comparable projects around the same time, as the old pagan intellectual order was collapsing and a new Christian one coming into being. As late antiquity shaded into the period later called the Dark Ages, these reference books did their part to keep the lights on.

THE DICTIONARY GETS ITS DAY IN COURT

W E CALL BOOKS "influential" all the time. To see real influence exerted by a book, though, look to the reference shelf. Reference books may well have saved some lives and sent others to the gallows.

The United States has a long history of deferring to dictionaries in interpreting the U.S. Constitution. A federal "Dictionary Act"—1 U.S. Code §1—governs the interpretation of statutes ("words importing the singular include and apply to several persons, parties, or things; words importing the plural include the singular; words importing the masculine gender include the feminine as well . . ."), and legal theorists who espouse originalism and textualism are especially quick to turn to dictionaries. Because the Constitution was written in the 1780s, two dictionaries have been favorites for those who would argue over troublesome terms: Samuel Johnson's *Dictionary*, published in 1755 and revised in 1773 (see chapter 10), and Noah Webster's *American Dictionary*, published in 1828 (see chapter 16).

As early as 1785 the U.S. Supreme Court referred to Johnson's *Dictionary*, and it keeps coming back to it, including in some high-profile cases. The committee responsible for drawing up impeachment charges against Richard Nixon turned to Johnson for a definition of *crime*, and Johnson's definition of *war* was introduced into the proceedings of a suit challenging Bill Clinton's authority to order air strikes in Yugoslavia. When the Court argued over whether the Constitution mandates the census takers to count every individual or allows them to use a combination of sampling and statistical methods, the Justices looked up the Constitution's word *enumerate* in Johnson. In *Eldred v. Ashcroft*, on the constitutionality of the Copyright Term Extension Act, a plaintiff argued that the extension of copyright terms went beyond the "limited" terms called for in the Constitution. Justice Ginsburg ruled against him, writing for the majority, "The word 'limited' . . . does not convey a meaning so constricted. At the time of the Framing, that word meant what it means today," and she attributed her definitions to one "S. Johnson."

But the recourse to dictionaries is not limited to Johnson and Webster. Definitions of *confinement* from *Webster's Third New International* and the *Oxford English Dictionary* featured in legal arguments over John Hinckley's request to leave a mental hospital in 1999 after his attempted assassination of Ronald Reagan,[1] and words like *prevent, delay,* and *report* in statutes routinely send lawyers, judges, and scholars to dictionaries. Chief Justice John Roberts cited five dictionaries in one legal opinion, including the definition of the word *of.*[2] An opinion by Justice Breyer in 2013 lets loose a tsunami of dictionary citations:

> On the one hand, a law dictionary in use in 1867 defines the word "defalcation" as "the act of a defaulter." . . . 1 J. Bouvier, Law Dictionary 387, 388 (4th ed. 1852). See also 4 Oxford English Dictionary 369 (2d ed. 1989). . . . Black's Law Dictionary . . . defines "defalcation" first as "EMBEZZLEMENT," but, second, as "[l]oosely, the failure to meet an obligation; a nonfraudulent default." Black's Law Dictionary 479 (9th ed. 2009) (hereinafter Black's). See also American Heritage Dictionary 474 (5th ed. 2011) . . . 4 Oxford English Dictionary, *supra,* at 369 . . . Webster's New International Dictionary 686 (2d ed. 1954) . . . Webster's Third New International Dictionary 590 (1986). . . . Modern dictionaries often accompany their broad definitions with illustrative terms such as "embezzle," American Heritage Dictionary, *supra,* at 474, or "fraudulent deficiency," 4 Oxford English Dictionary, *supra,* at 369.[3]

The habit of citing dictionaries has grown markedly in the last twenty years. The *Marquette Law Review* found dictionaries cited in 225 Supreme Court opinions between 2000 and 2010, a fourteenfold increase over the 1960s, and those citations came from a staggering 120 different dictionaries. Not everyone is happy with this development.

The lexicographer Jesse Sheidlower argues that "it's probably wrong, in almost all situations, to use a dictionary in the courtroom. . . . Dictionary definitions are written with a lot of things in mind, but rigorously circumscribing the exact meanings and connotations of terms is not usually one of them." Besides, when justices are able to cite more than a hundred dictionaries at will, Sheidlower notes, "It's easy to stack the deck by finding a definition that does or does not highlight a nuance that you're interested in."[4]

Reference works other than dictionaries also occasionally get their chance to testify as expert witnesses. The U.S. *Federal Rules of Evidence* specifies that "the party offering a publication must establish it as a 'reliable authority.' . . . The requirement may be satisfied by judicial notice of the reliability of the treatise. Widely accepted publications such as the Merck Index, The Encyclopedia Britannica and the Physician's Desk Reference are examples."[5] Even works of classical scholarship have had their day in court. In the 1993 *Evans v. Romer*, on Colorado's constitutional amendment barring protected status for same-sex couples, part of the case hinged on whether Western attitudes toward homosexuality have always been negative. Someone introduced a passage from Plato's *Laws* as evidence, which describes homosexual intercourse with the word τόλμημα (*tolmêma*)—but what did the word mean when Plato used it? It came from a root meaning *dare* or *have courage*, and one expert witness testified that it meant a "shameless" act or "abomination," while another insisted Plato was referring to a "daring" deed. The court found itself getting a lesson on the history of the revisions of the Liddell-Scott-Jones *Greek–English Lexicon* in its various editions from 1843 to 1968.[6] And the stakes can be high. In 1994, an American plaintiff who'd had his rights limited because of his homosexuality won a case partly on the basis of the revision of the *Diagnostic and Statistical Manual*: the pre-sentence report, according to a federal court, "improperly included Donaghe's 1968 diagnosis as a homosexual deviant as a factor for departure. Homosexuality is no longer categorized as a psychiatric disorder. Diagnostic and Statistical Manual of Mental Disorders (1987) (DSM-III-R)."[7]

American lawyers and judges are especially drawn to reference books, but it happens elsewhere, too. In England, the *Domesday Book* has been introduced into evidence for centuries (see chapter 4): it's still useful in disputes over historic boundaries. In 1838, two legal scholars advised lawyers that "Domesday-book is the ultimate criterion for determining, what lands are ancient demesne of the crown; a question of practical importance in the present day, especially in regard to the validity of fines, which have been levied of those lands,"[8] and the nine-hundred-year-old book has been cited in an English court as recently as 1982.

LEECHCRAFT

Medieval Medicine

Bald	Avicenna
Leechbook	*Kitab al–Qanun fi al–tibb*
c. 950 C.E.	1025 C.E.

M EDICINE FEATURES IN a number of reference works, but medical references constitute their own substantial and specific genre. A rich and international library of these books goes back to antiquity, and they provide invaluable evidence for historians. In India, the *Sushruta Samhita*, probably written in the sixth century B.C.E., became one of the founding works of Ayurveda, or Indian medicine; its collection of more than a thousand diseases and nearly a thousand treatments was rediscovered in the eighth century C.E. when it was translated into Arabic. Pedanius Dioscorides wrote a five-volume *Peri hyles iatrikes* (*On Medicine*) in the first century C.E.. It lists the healing properties of around six hundred plants and almost a thousand drugs, and it earned the praise of the encyclopedist Cassiodorus. Marcellus Empiricus wrote *De medicamentis* (*On Medicines*) in the fourth or fifth century, and the work was read for a millennium. This chapter focuses on two pioneering works in the field we would classify as medicine, one from Anglo-Saxon England, the other from Persia.

❧

We are not even sure a physician named Bald existed. The sum total of the information we have on him comes from a note in Latin hexameters on sole surviving manuscript: "Bald owns this book, which he ordered Cild to write." Perhaps that means Cild was the author, and Bald hired him to write the text. Or it may mean that Bald composed the text and got Cild to work as a scribe, making a clean copy. Or perhaps it was all a fiction. The book mentions two other doctors, Dun and Oxa, who offered advice, but we have no record of them, either. Still, the author, whatever his name, was active in the ninth or tenth century, and the only early surviving copy of his work, the *Læceboc*—*Leechbook*, or *Book of Healing*—is from around the year 950. The name invokes barbarism, though it helps to know that the Old English word *læce*, pronounced something like "*latch*-uh," meant "physician" before it meant "blood-sucking worm." In fact, nowhere in Old English medical literature are the annelids mentioned explicitly.[1] The book is a systematic handbook on Old English medical recipes and cures—all part of the field known as *læcedom* 'leechdom' or *læcecræft* 'leechcraft'.

The ninth century is right in the middle of what have been called the Dark Ages, though things were not quite so dark as they are sometimes made out to be. King Alfred, who died in 899, had worked to build an intellectual culture in England, and Bald may have been part of that movement—though medical historian Malcolm Cameron warns that "we have not enough information to do other than guess." The *Leechbook* is the oldest medical book we have from England, but most historians believe early medieval English medicine was insular. English authorities quoted only other English authorities, and very little knowledge was coming into England from the Continent. There was also no indication that Anglo-Saxon physicians were familiar with Galen or any of the other major medical writers of ancient Greece or Rome. The *Leechbook* helped to change that. The book had an English audience in mind: it is written in Old English, not in Latin, so the author had no ambition to be read abroad. But while plenty of homespun English remedies appear in it, interspersed among them are treatments proposed by Greek, Roman, and other sources. Some of Bald's prescriptions are translated directly from Latin works. As Cameron points out, "From the contents of his book it appears that Bald had available to him in one form or another much of the best of Byzantine and Roman medicine from the third to the ninth centuries, either in Latin or in English translation." The book "shows a conscious effort to transfer to Anglo-Saxon practice what one physician considered most useful in native and Mediterranean medicine."[2]

TITLE: *Læceboc,* or *Medicinale anglicum*

COMPILER: Bald (*fl.* ninth c.)

ORGANIZATION: Book 1 on external diseases, book 2 on
internal diseases, each arranged from head to foot

PUBLISHED: *c.* 950

PAGES: 256

ENTRIES: 155 chapters

TOTAL WORDS: 32,000

SIZE: 10½" × 7" (27 × 19 cm)

AREA: 131 ft^2 (12 m^2)

The book's two main divisions treat of external and internal maladies, and it may be the only medieval text to start with this fundamental
distinction.[3] Within each section, the organization is *a capite ad calcem*—
from the patient's head down to his shoes. There are sixty-six chapters,
containing remedies that cover a wide range of conditions from hiccups
to "rotten lung." One proposed cure for a headache is to take a stalk of
crosswort (a flowering plant in the family *Rubiaceae*) and bind it to the
head with a long piece of warm red flannel. Bald men were encouraged
to follow a prescription from Pliny: prepare an ointment out of linseed
oil and the ashes of burned bees and apply the result to the scalp overnight. Someone suffering from pain in the lower back was advised to set
goat hair on fire and allow the smoke to waft to the afflicted part. There
were treatments for both overactive and sluggish libidos (agrimony
boiled in ale for the former, agrimony boiled in milk for the latter),
inflamed spleen (peas and bread in hot water), and bellyache (take
apples, pears, peas, and the flesh of small birds and boil them in water,
vinegar, and wine). For a painful spleen, shellfish, half-grown pigs, the
meat of goats, and the juice of peas were prescribed, and for diarrhea,
cabbage juice soup or, for more serious cases, old cheese boiled in goat's
milk with goat's grease. A run-of-the-mill lung problem was said to
respond to beets simmered in butter, but a case of the dreaded "rotten
lungs" called for something fancier: a drink made from bog myrtle, a
flowering shrub known to scientists today as *Myrica gale*, boiled with

malt in water, replaced after a while by fresh yeast, mixed with worm-wood (a plant in the genus *Artemisia*), woundwort (a plant in the genus *Stachys*, also known as betony), and daisies.

Some of the "cures" have less to do with medicine than with magic—the agate, for instance, is a powerful talisman. As medical historian Debby Banham points out, "Early medieval medicine was not that effective in actually curing anyone." All of this was long before the advent of evidence-based medicine. Still, that does not mean the prescriptions were useless. Many of the "medicines" probably provided at least some liquid to help the dehydrated, and some calories to give strength to those who had been weakened by some ailment. As historian Audrey Meaney argues, the *Leechbook* "is by far the most comprehensive and best organized of all the Old English medical compilations. . . . The system used to sort and classify all this material must have been extensive and was usually also very efficient."[4]

These are all things Bald related directly; he also managed to speak indirectly, revealing things about Old English medical practice. As Cameron observes, "we find phrases which give an idea of what was expected of a practising physician. There are recipes which contain remarks such as 'as physicians know how' and 'add a sufficient amount of honey,' rather than detailing the whole of the preparation of a medicine"—evidence of the expectations of his audience. The book also reveals that Bald was no "slavish copier of the masters of medicine," as is evident in the book: "he often omitted parts of his sources or added to them, he rearranged, he expressed opinions, he selected with an eye to what was important to his society, he offered substitutes for exotic drugs."[5]

Bald opened up English medicine to the wider world, but his success was limited, and England remained intellectually insular. Bald's work must have been considered important at one time, because the only surviving manuscript we have was written well after the author's death—someone thought the old book was valuable enough to copy. But that attitude eventually changed, and Bald exerted hardly any influence on posterity.

There was, however, a center of medical inquiry that was much more vigorous and influential. Just as early medieval Europe lagged behind Islam in its knowledge of geography, it paled in comparison with Muslim knowledge of the natural world. Bald's book, however seminal, looks unsophisticated when put next to a work published not long afterward.

The Persian polymath Abu 'Ali al-Husayn ibn 'Abd Allah ibn Sina Balkhi', better known in the West as Avicenna, lived at the end of the tenth century and beginning of the eleventh and was one of the most wide-ranging minds of the Islamic world. A physician, poet, musician, astronomer, and politician, he has 450 books to his credit, with demonstrated expertise in a dozen fields of knowledge—among them astronomy, chemistry, mathematics, philosophy, and physics. Of all of his areas of knowledge, though, medicine was the one for which he was most renowned. He was therefore ideally suited to compile the *Qanun*, a compendium of cutting-edge knowledge not only on medicine but on hygiene, on mental well-being, and on humanity's place in the natural world.

We know more about Avicenna than about most other early compilers of reference books thanks, first, to an autobiography he wrote covering his first thirty years, and then to a biographical sketch written shortly after his death by his friend and disciple al-Juzjani. We know, for instance, that he was born in Afshana, the son of a high-ranking civil servant. Afshana was near the Persian region of Bukhara, the capital of the Persian Samanid dynasty and a great center of learning in the Islamic world. We know, too, that he was mostly self-educated. His father provided him with tutors, but he soon left them behind. By the time he was ten he had memorized the Qur'an; by the age of sixteen, he had learned everything his tutors had to teach him.

Having finished with the course of instruction his teachers had for him, he turned his attention to natural science, metaphysics, and medical theory. He studied Greek logic and mathematics with particular interest. He read Plato, Galen, the Stoics, Ptolemy's *Almagest*, and Euclid's *Elements*, as well as Arabic philosophers such as al-Farabi and Abu Abdallah al-Natili. Most of all, though, he read Aristotle, and especially the *Metaphysics*. At last he found something that challenged him.

TITLE: *Kitab al-Qanun fi al-tibb*

COMPILER: Abu 'Ali al-Husayn ibn 'Abd Allah ibn
  Al-Hasan ibn Ali ibn Sina (*c.* 980–1037)

ORGANIZATION: Book 1, humoral theory; book 2, "simples"
  and method; books 3–4, pathology; book 5,
  compounding medicines

PUBLISHED: 1025

VOLUMES: 14

TOTAL WORDS: 1 million

Having learned the Greek language, he read the original text, trying to make sense of it by reading an Arabic commentary by al-Farabi. He read the book forty times, attempting over and over to plumb its depths. In the words of philosophy professor Coeli Fitzpatrick, "Avicenna's persistence and self-discipline in learning were legendary."[6]

Writings on medicine were always among those he read most attentively. Even as a teenager he claimed to have read every medical book available in late tenth-century Persia. From theory he turned to practice. Avicenna began treating the ill, and he rapidly developed a reputation as a physician. This reputation reached the very top of the social hierarchy in 997, when Nuh ibn Mansur, Sultan of Bukhara, appointed him one of his personal physicians. Avicenna was just sixteen or seventeen. The time in Mansur's service was a revelation: Avicenna now had access to the whole of the sultan's library. The voracious reader made his way through the entire collection by the time he was eighteen. Later in life he reflected, "I now know the same amount as then but more maturely and deeply; otherwise the truth of learning and knowledge is the same."[7] In his own writings, he combined Greek and Islamic thought, and he organized classical knowledge into a system that made sense in a Muslim context.

Avicenna wrote two major books on medicine. One, the *Kitab al-Shifa*, or *Book of Healing*, is a wide-ranging meditation on the health of the mind. The other, *Kitab al-Qanun fi al-tibb*, or *The Canon of Medicine*, is much more encyclopedic in its organization. Its fourteen volumes and more than a million words, densely packed with information, were compiled at Isfahan. It is an avowedly eclectic book, combining Galenic medicine, from second-century Greece, with older Aristotelian science and modern Islamic medicine. Avicenna's interest in reconciling Greek and Arabic thought shows up even in his title: the Arabic word *qanun* is borrowed from the Greek *kanon* 'measuring rod', meaning "rule" or "standard." But Avicenna drew from even more distant sources, including Indian medical theory and the *Zhubing Yuanhuo Lun*, an early seventh-century Chinese medical work. He has been praised for his clarity, his arrangement of information for maximal usefulness, and his ability to express complicated matters in the most concise way possible.

"Medicine," Avicenna wrote in his preface, "is a science from which one learns the status of the human body with respect to what is healthy and what is not, in order to preserve good health when it exists and restore it when it is lacking."[8] The first book brings Greek medicine to bear on the basic principles of anatomy, health, and illness. The four humors—blood, phlegm, yellow bile, and black bile—were introduced and linked to the four elements—earth, air, fire, and water. Disease emerges from an imbalance of the humors, usually because of some obstruction. To bring them into balance, he prescribed "emetics, cathartics, enemas, sedatives, and other drugs, bleeding, blistering, and cauterization."[9]

The second book moves on to "simples," the basic medicines that are not compounded of multiple ingredients, and it spells out Avicenna's conception of what we have come to call the scientific method. Book 3 explores pathology, with a systematic overview of twenty-one bodily organs or systems, while book 4 looks at other sorts of pathologies that span the entire body. This is the part that also introduces the rudiments of surgery. Finally, book 5 provides advice on compounding simples into more sophisticated medicines. Some have called it "the first pharmacopeia," with its discussion of more than 760 medicines.[10]

A medical historian writes of the book's "practical tenor": "Ibn Sina's intent, all too successful, was to give practitioners ready guidelines for immediate application, without too much worry over theory, and with a minimum of skeptical doubt or radical experimentation."[11] Another describes how the book works as a reference source:

If one wishes to use the *Canon* as a reference tool, the arrangement ... works well for some subjects.... One can, for example, relatively easily find an answer to any of the following questions: When and in what conditions is bleeding an appropriate treatment? What are the medicinal powers of cinnamon? What treatments are recommended for deafness? For various kinds of fevers? How is theriac compounded?[12]

The *Qanun* is less useful, though, in its anatomical discussions, which are scattered throughout the book and therefore ill-suited to quick reference.

Expectations about medical knowledge were very different a thousand years ago. We now demand our medical textbooks be as up-to-date as possible, but Avicenna, like most writers of his time, demanded ancient authority. "The *Qanun*," one scholar explains, "remains a compendium largely of traditional material."[13] Avicenna, for instance, leaned heavily on Galen, whose work was eight centuries old when Avicenna wrote—and even Galen was mostly backward-looking at the time he wrote. Still, Avicenna made some conceptual breakthroughs that are now a standard part of medical thinking. Medicines, for instance, Avicenna argued, should be tested before they are tried—"The experiment must be done on a single, not a composite, condition. In the latter case, if the condition consists of two opposite diseases and the drug is tried and found beneficial in both, we cannot infer the real cause of the cure"—an anticipation of what would become the clinical trial. Predating later medical thought, he suggested that tiny organisms might be responsible for illnesses centuries before science offered a germ theory. He called for explicit attention to observation and experimentation, and he believed in treating the whole patient, integrating body and mind into one concern, making him a forerunner of modern medical practice, including the field of psychiatry.

In fact Avicenna is a forerunner of much later medical thinking. He wrote in Arabic, but the *Qanun* eventually made its way into many of the world's languages, including Persian, Latin (Gerard of Cremona rendered it as *Canon medicinæ*), Chinese (*Huihui yaofang*, or *Prescriptions of the Hui Nationality*), and Hebrew, as well as most of the major

languages of Europe. It continued to be used—not as a work of antiquarian interest, but as a real medical reference—even into the seventeenth and early eighteenth centuries in Europe. Even today, some
practitioners of alternative traditional medicine in the Middle East turn
to Avicenna for practical guidance. The *Qanun*, in the words of one
historian, "might be called the most famous medical textbook ever
written, and it was retranslated and reprinted in Europe down to the
middle of the seventeenth century. . . . Of all the great characters of
history Avicenna has an especial interest to medical men."[14]

Bald and Avicenna probably lived within a few decades of each other,
but they never knew of each other's existence. England and Persia were,
for all practical purposes, on opposite sides of the world. But they were
engaging in the same enterprise, trying to incorporate the best thinking
about medical practice from ancient and foreign sources into their own
domestic system. For Bald that meant Latin and Byzantine prescriptions; for Avicenna it meant ancient Greek medical theory. And both
chose the form of the reference book in which to advance their syncretic
conception of medicine, because it was the most reliable way to translate
theory into practice. It is a valuable reminder that encyclopedias can be
the site of important cross-cultural dialogue.

CHAPTER 6 ½

PLAGIARISM

The Crime of Literary Theft

THOMAS COOPER'S *THESAURUS linguæ Romanæ & Britannicæ* (*Treasure-House of the Roman and British Tongue*), a Latin–English dictionary, appeared in 1573. Shortly afterward, the Puritan pamphleteer known as Martin Marprelate turned his guns on Cooper, accusing him of plagiarism—of lifting entries without acknowledgment from Thomas Elyot's Latin dictionary, Robert Estienne's French dictionary, and John Frisius's German dictionary. And he was right: Cooper had resorted to the pastiche for which teachers castigate dishonest students who think "research" means cutting and pasting from the World Wide Web.

Cooper might have defended himself by pointing out that dictionaries *always* "borrow" from one another. It has been going on from the beginning: as Sidney Landau puts it, "The history of English lexicography"—and it is just as true of other languages and other reference genres—"consists of a recital of successive and often successful acts of piracy."[1] Even the first monolingual English dictionary, Robert Cawdrey's *Table Alphabeticall* (1604), has been accused of plagiarism. It is hard to imagine how a work that is the first of its kind can steal from predecessors when it has no predecessors, but around half the headwords in Cawdrey's book were taken from a table of difficult words in *The Englishe Schole-Maister*, published by Edmund Coote eight years earlier. Cawdrey got his comeuppance when another lexicographer, John Bullokar, copied many of Cawdrey's entries for his *English Expositor*. Cawdrey's son then revised his father's dictionary, stealing entries back from Bullokar.

One of England's more bloodthirsty lexicographical rivalries began in 1656, when Thomas Blount published the biggest English dictionary to date, *Glossographia*. Two years later a dictionary called *A New World of English Words* appeared, compiled by Edward Phillips, nephew of the great poet John Milton. Phillips's title picks up on some of the excitement surrounding the discovery of the real New World, which was still a comparatively novel subject in 1658. But Phillips found himself in trouble because his *New World of English Words* was not actually all that new—many of the entries were lifted straight out of *Glossographia*. Blount, unamused, responded with a deliciously nasty pamphlet, *A World of Errors Discovered in the New World of Words*. "Must this then be suffered?" Blount asked.

> A Gentleman ... writes a Book, and the Book happens to be acceptable to the World and sell; a Book-seller ... instantly employs some Mercenary to jumble up another like Book out of this, with some Alterations and Additions, and give it a new Title.... Thus it fared with my *Glossographia*, the fruit of above Twenty years spare hours.[2]

Blount insisted that Phillips's dictionary was "extracted almost wholly out of mine" and claimed that wherever Phillips added original material, he made it worse. It recalls a putdown often attributed to Samuel Johnson, but not actually spoken by him: "Sir, your book is both good and original. But the parts that are good are not original, and the parts that are original are not good." Phillips must have smarted when he was smacked by Blount, but he was not improved by the scolding: in later editions he continued to pillage other dictionaries, including some that had criticized his first edition.

Such pilfering was not limited to England. In 1607, for instance, the Frenchman César Oudin published his *Trésor des deux langues françoise et espagnole*, a French–Spanish dictionary. Two years later the French section was lifted by Hierosme Victor, who used it in his *Tesoro de las tres lenguas, francesa, italiana y española*.[3] And in the nineteenth century, the two most important American lexicographers—Noah Webster and Joseph Emerson Worcester—spent years accusing each other of thievery.

What seems strangest to moderns is that some reference book compilers were happy to confess their plagiarisms. When Robert James published the proposals for his *Medicinal Dictionary* in 1741, he gave would-be subscribers a quick overview of the competition, then: "Their Attempts were indeed useful, and are therefore to be mentioned with Gratitude." The authors of other medical reference works "have succeeded so well," he wrote, "that often nothing can be added to the Accuracy of their Expositions; and such Passages we have carefully translated"—*translated* in its etymological sense of "carried over"—without even any "unnecessary Variations" in the prose. Having lifted all the good parts from the earlier medical dictionaries, James believed his book "will probably make them less necessary to future Students," and "what is not to be found in *this* Dictionary, it will be generally in vain to seek in *any other*."[4]

Although the word "plagiarism" is ancient—it comes from Latin *plagiarius* 'kidnapper'—the idea that lifting someone else's words might be wrong is modern. Medieval writers would not have understood the charge: for centuries, writers (and painters and sculptors and composers) were encouraged to copy the masters as closely as possible. Only in the seventeenth and eighteenth centuries did a notion of intellectual property become current, so that Samuel Johnson could define *plagiary* in 1755 as "A thief in literature; one who steals the thoughts or writings of another" and "The crime of literary theft."

Today, getting caught brandishing scissors and paste can be enough to ruin a career. And yet every reference book writer spends a lot of time looking over rivals' shoulders. As lexicologist Sidney Landau points out in one of the best overviews of dictionaries, that is almost certainly a good thing:

> Some of the eighteenth- and nineteenth-century lexicographers publicly acknowledged their indebtedness to specific predecessors. Sad to say, very few twentieth-century lexicographers have done so. The pressures of the marketplace dictate that every dictionary be "new." A really new dictionary would be a dreadful piece of work, missing innumerable basic words and senses, replete with absurdities and unspeakable errors, studded with biases and interlarded with irrelevant provincialisms.[5]

CHAPTER 7

NEW WORLDS

Cartography in an Age of Discovery

Abraham Ortelius	Johann Bayer
Theatrum orbis terrarum	*Uranometria*
1570	1603

S CIENTIFIC CARTOGRAPHY TOOK a great step backward in the early Christian world. The Greeks had done sophisticated scientific calculations on the size and shape of the earth, and Islamic geographers were mapping the extremities of the known world. In Christendom, though, the cartographic enterprise was much less energetic. People who believed that all the answers could be found in the Bible also believed that calculation and observation were unnecessary. Cosmas Indicopleustes, a merchant and traveler, published a map in his *Aigyptiou Manachou Christianike Topographia* (*Christian Topography*, around 540 C.E.) that rendered a flat earth with far more attention to the position of Eden than the position of the Scilly Isles. All his evidence was from the Bible. He had no truck with "the miserable Pagan belief that earth and heaven are spherical." "What can be more absurd," he asked, "than the Pagan doctrine? . . . The Pagans are at war with divine Scripture."[1] Not until 1410 did one of the ancient works of geography reenter European consciousness, when a Latin version of Ptolemy's *Geographike hyphegesis* turned up. For the next century, Europeans were busy both rediscovering ancient knowledge about the world and discovering other things for the first time.

Beginning in the sixteenth century, as Europe underwent the cultural changes known collectively as the Renaissance, both the intellectual and the physical world got bigger. It was the great age of exploration, when European powers set out across the oceans and discovered that the world was many times larger than their predecessors had imagined. Abraham Ortelius's *Theatre of the World* described the globe early in the age of European expansion, while Johann Bayer's catalog of the stars was the result of a different kind of exploration taking place around the same time.

⛢

After being neglected for centuries, the best cartographic works of antiquity were resurrected in the fifteenth century and discovered to be compatible with Christian understandings of the world. Ptolemy's *Geography* was a newfound favorite; even Pope Pius II wrote a commentary on it, and his successor Julius II commissioned wall maps in the Loggia del Cosmografia in the Vatican.[2] The *Geography* was first printed in 1475, and six editions appeared across Europe in the next quarter century, many of them supplemented with new maps of regions the ancient geographer never dreamed of.

The fifteenth century was also the beginning of Europe's great age of exploration. Diego de Silves discovered the Azores in 1427, Portuguese explorers found Cape Verde in 1446, Bartolomeu Dias rounded the Cape of Good Hope in 1488, Christopher Columbus spied land in 1492, John Cabot landed in Newfoundland in 1497, and Amerigo Vespucci identified the Amazon in 1499. All of their discoveries were added to the best maps of the ancients, and brand-new maps were constantly being drawn. One of the greatest cartographers of the early sixteenth century was Gerardus Mercator, known as the "Ptolemy of his time." He was born in Rupelmonde, in modern Belgium, and educated in Brabant. Mercator earned a living producing scientific and mathematical instruments, and in the mid-1530s he and some associates produced a globe. Mercator was involved because of his talent as an engraver, but he soon demonstrated a cartographic knack, and he began making his own maps in 1537, starting with views of the Holy Land and moving on a year later to a world map. As a friend of Mercator put it, his European map "attracted more praise from scholars everywhere than any similar geographical work which has ever been brought out."[3] It was a new era for cartography.

Even more important than Mercator, though, was one of his friends. Abraham Ortelius—known in his native Dutch as Ortels—was born in

Antwerp in 1528, and although he traveled throughout Europe, he always returned to the city of his birth. Antwerp was a perfect base for a sixteenth-century geographer. Now in Belgium, it was then part of the Seventeen Provinces, ruled by Habsburg Spain. When Ortelius was born it was a city of ninety thousand people and an intellectual hub, with the Plantijn printing house based there and the great humanist scholar Desiderius Erasmus in nearby Rotterdam. It was an artistic as well as an intellectual center, and some of the greatest artists of the day—Titian, Tintoretto, Bruegel—were active in the area. Most important for Ortelius, though, was Antwerp's place at the center of the administration of a great commercial empire. Some of the biggest businesses in sixteenth-century Antwerp were the trade in sugar, pepper, and cinnamon, with imports coming from the Portuguese and Spanish colonies in the New World. Every day hundreds of oceangoing vessels docked in Antwerp. The trade in luxury goods from the empire poured money into the city, which became one of the largest in Europe, and one of the richest—according to historian Fernand Braudel, "the centre of the *entire* international economy."[4]

This is the vantage point from which the great mapmaker saw the world. Ortelius took a job around 1547 as an engraver, reproducing others' maps in print, and then as a map illuminator, hand-coloring engraved maps and mounting them on linen backing. Cartography was getting a boost from a new technology, as the old carved woodblocks were giving way to engraved copperplates, producing at least three benefits: maps could show much more detail; the plates could be kept and revised as necessary; and they could make many more impressions, leading to more copies at a lower price.

Like Mercator, Ortelius began strictly as an engraver, but cartography appealed to him as well. He traveled widely—to Italy, to Frankfurt, to Paris, to England—sometimes with Mercator. He drew on this firsthand knowledge of the world when he moved from engraving others' work to making his own around 1564, when his first map—*Typus orbis terrarum*, a world map—appeared. He followed it up a year later with a map of Egypt and went on to produce important maps of Asia and Spain.

Ortelius was more than a craftsman: he was a serious thinker about geography and cartography. Christophe Plantijn published his *Synonymia*

TITLE: *Theatrum orbis terrarum*

COMPILER: Abraham Ortelius (1527–98)

ORGANIZATION: Geographical

PUBLISHED: Antwerp: Gilles Coppens de Dienst, May 20, 1570

PAGES: 38 leaves, 53 double-columned maps

SIZE: 16" × 10½" (40 × 26.5 cm)

AREA: 147 ft² (13.6 m²)

PRICE: 5 florins 10 stuivers for a small-paper copy, 7 florins 10 stuivers for a large-paper copy, and 16 florins for a hand-colored large-paper copy

geographica in 1578, a sophisticated theoretical consideration of the value of ancient sources of geographical information. Ortelius would revise the *Synonymia* several times, using the title *Thesaurus geographicus* for the later editions. The final edition, published in 1596, seems to have been the first work to propose a theory that would be demonstrated by science only in the twentieth century. Ortelius noticed that the contours of continents thousands of miles apart are curiously complementary, as if they had once been joined: the eastern coast of South America, for instance, seems as if it was meant to interlock with the western coast of Africa. Ortelius imagined that catastrophic forces—earthquakes, floods—might have somehow torn the continents apart. No one took this eccentric thought seriously for centuries, but the idea was revived in the early twentieth century, and in 1926 someone coined the term *continental drift*. The phenomenon was finally demonstrated convincingly in the 1960s—a third of a millennium after Ortelius had the initial brainstorm.

Ortelius the cartographer did not go it alone. He benefited from Mercator's friendship, and he made good use of all the best cartographers in Europe. Ortelius's achievement was not producing original maps, but collecting the best and most up-to-date maps in one place and in one uniform edition. There had been world maps before, and of course there were countless maps of specific regions. No one, though, had ever prepared a single printed source that collected maps, all in the same format, that covered the entire globe. Ortelius's suite of fifty-three maps and accompanying explanatory text was published in Antwerp in May 1570, bearing the title *Theatrum orbis terrarum* (*Theater of the Globe of the World*).

The *Theatrum* offered what is now standard in every atlas but was then a novel way of organizing a collection of maps. It opened with a world map, then moves on to more detailed maps of the continents. Ortelius covered the old world of Europe, Africa, and Asia, and even included the latest information from the new world of North and South America, but he missed two entire continents—Australia and Antarctica would not be known to Europeans for generations. He also inexplicably threw in an extra one, occupying nearly the whole of the South Pacific, perhaps influenced by legends of the Incans. And his western coast of South America looks nothing like the real world. To his credit, though, Europeans had encountered North America just a few decades earlier, but Ortelius captured it, labeling it AMERICA SIVE INDIA NOVA, with California depicted accurately as a peninsula.[5] Vast stretches of Africa and the Americas were blank, awaiting word from explorers, but the bigger story is how much Ortelius knew at that early period.

The reaction to the *Theatrum* was fast and overwhelmingly positive. As Mercator wrote to Ortelius on November 22, 1570:

> I have examined your Theatrum and compliment you on the care and elegance with which you have embellished the labours of the authors, and the faithfulness with which you have preserved the production of each individual, which is essential in order to bring out the geographical truth, which is so corrupted by mapmakers. . . . You deserve great praise for having selected the best descriptions of each region and collected them into one manual, which can be bought at small cost, kept in a small space and even carried about wherever we please.[6]

Mercator was not quite right about the "small cost." The *Theatrum* was not cheap when it first came out, and subsequent editions—especially when they were hand-colored—became even more expensive.

One source even calls the hand-colored large-paper edition "the most expensive book of its time."[7] Despite the expense, though, it was a hit, and both the success and the expense of the *Theatrum* led to imitators, such as Gerard de Jode's *Hemispherium ab aequinoctiali linea, ad circulum poli arctici* (1578). But Ortelius was shrewd, keeping for himself the legal rights to the text, the images, and even the channels of distribution.[8] He issued revised versions of the *Theatrum*, dozens of editions that grew larger over time. The edition of 1612 had grown to 167 maps, with information from nearly two hundred documented sources and always the most *au courant* knowledge about the world. Translations of the text from the original Latin into Dutch, German, Italian, Spanish, French, and English followed quickly. Only in 1624 was the *Theatrum* overtaken by a more thorough and accurate atlas.

Ortelius produced what most scholars consider the first atlas, but the term was not his. Mercator first used the name of the ancient Greek Titan for his own book, based largely on Ortelius's *Theatrum*: he called it *Atlas, sive cosmographicae meditationes de fabrica mundi* (*Atlas, or Cosmographic Meditations on the Structure of the World*, 1578). As Mercator put it, this collection of fifty-one maps was published "to honor the Titan King Atlas, King of Mauritania, a learned philosopher, mathematician and astronomer."[9]

☙

Ortelius and Mercator were looking around, but some cartographers were busy looking up. "Space," says that ever-reliable reference work *The Hitchhiker's Guide to the Galaxy,* "is big. Really big. You just won't believe how vastly hugely mindbogglingly big it is. I mean you may think it's a long way down the road to the chemist, but that's just peanuts to space."[10]

Astronomers are charged with dealing with that mind-boggling bigness. There had been many ancient efforts to map the heavens. Some interpreters view the dots on the cave walls at Lascaux from 16,500 B.C.E. as a very early star chart. The Farnese Atlas, which may date from as early as the first century B.C.E., is a sculpted white marble depiction of Atlas supporting the celestial sphere on his shoulder. It shows the constellations, though not the stars that make them up. A Roman manuscript from the second century C.E., the *Planisphere of Geruvigus*, maps the stars from an earthly point of view. Around the same time Claudius Ptolemy borrowed a star catalog from Hipparchus and depicted 1,022 stars gathered into forty-eight constellations. Ptolemy's list became the canonical list for a millennium and a half. As late as 1536, a star chart by Peter Bienewitz—also known by the Latin form of his name, Petrus Apianus—showed Ptolemy's forty-eight constellations and the stars that make them up.

"No greater problem is presented to the human mind," said the path-breaking Harvard astronomer Annie Jump Cannon, than classifying the stars.[11] To Johann Bayer, that problem was merely an encouragement. The German lawyer and astronomer is best known for *Uranometria*, which reduced the colossal amount of new information flooding in from observational astronomers to some systematic order. Bayer's great atlas of the heavens was the first to try to catalog every star in the universe. It could not have come close to its stated goal, but it did make the work of subsequent astronomers like Galileo and Isaac Newton possible.

Little is known of Bayer's life. He was born in Bavaria in 1572, and around the age of twenty he began his studies at the University of Ingolstadt, founded a century before and to this day one of the most prestigious universities in Europe. After Ingolstadt he moved to Augsburg, about eighty miles from his hometown, where he worked as a lawyer; there he developed an interest in astronomy, and particularly in *uranography*, the mapping of the stars and noting their relative magnitude (brightness).

When Bayer began his work, Ptolemy was still the unquestioned master, but new astronomical discoveries were forcing people to rethink conventional wisdom. Bayer did not need to start from scratch; he made use of Tycho Brahe's catalog of just over a thousand stars. But he revised Tycho's work, adjusting the magnitudes where Tycho got them wrong, and roughly doubling the length of the catalog. Bayer settled on the title *Uranometria: Omnium asterismorum continens schemata, nova methodo delineata, æreis laminis expressa.* The first word, *Uranometria*, was a neologism: it means "the measure of Uranus," the father of Kronos and the grandfather of Zeus; this made him the Greek god of the heavens.

TITLE: *Ioannis Bayeri Rhainani I.C. Vranometria:*
Omnium asterismorum continens schemata, nova methodo
delineata, aereis laminis expressa
COMPILER: Johann Bayer (1572–1625)
ORGANIZATION: By constellation
PUBLISHED: Augsburg, Germany: Christophorus Magnus,
1603
PAGES: 59
ENTRIES: 1,564 stars in 51 maps
SIZE: 13¾" × 9½" (35 × 24 cm)
AREA: 53 ft² (5 m²)

The subtitle explained what purchasers would find in the volume:
"containing plans of all the stars, displayed in a new method, and
engraved on copper."

The fifty-one maps in *Uranometria* were designed by Bayer, based
largely on the work of an earlier mapper of the stars, and engraved on
copperplate by Alexander Mair.[12] Each of Ptolemy's forty-eight constellations got its own map. Bayer took the classical constellations seriously,
and he included beautiful illustrations of mythological figures supposedly represented in the stars, not mere stick figures. But while the maps
were things of beauty, they were also prepared with great scientific care.
Bayer superimposed his maps over a grid in what cartographers call
trapezoidal projection and geocentric orientation, with the margins
calibrated for each degree.[13] He was also the first European astronomer
to offer a systematic account of the southern sky, and he added twelve
constellations—Apis, Avis Indica, Chameleon, Dorado, Grus, Hydrus,
Indus, Pavo, Phoenix, Piscis Volans, Toucan, and Triangulum Australe—
to the ancient Ptolemaic list. The observations constitute a significant
achievement, considering that Bayer was working in the age before telescopes were used in astronomy.

Bayer's most lasting contribution, though, and one that outlasted
his charts, was the system he worked out in *Uranometria* for naming
stars—the first Western attempt to do so on a scientific basis. People

had been assigning names to stars since the earliest days of astronomy, but there was no rhyme or reason to the naming: the brightest star in the night sky was called Sopdet ("the sharp one") by the ancient Egyptians and Sirius ("glowing") by the Greeks; the sixth-brightest star, at the left foot of the constellation of Orion, was named Seba-en-Sah ("toe star") by the Egyptians and Rigl Gawza al-Ysra ("left foot of the central one") by the Arabians, a name picked up by the Romans as Rigel. The names were colorful but unsystematic, and as the list grew, the traditional names came to seem increasingly inadequate for serious astronomical work.

Bayer, though, gave each star a name that provided useful scientific information: a star's name indicated the constellation in which it appeared and its relative brightness among all the stars in that constellation. He began each star's name with a Greek letter, usually putting the brightest stars in each constellation near the beginning of the alphabet, and then specified the constellation (using the genitive case of the Latin name). What had long been known as Sirius, for instance, became, in Bayer's system, α Canis Majoris, the brightest star in the constellation of Canis Major, the Great Dog. Rigel, one of the brighter stars in the constellation of Orion, became β Orionis (or β Ori for short). By the same logic, α Centauri, the star closest to our own sun, was the brightest in the constellation named for the Centaur.[14] (When the twenty-four letters of the Greek alphabet ran out in any given constellation, Bayer turned to the Latin alphabet, giving us star names like *d Centauri* and *G Scorpii*.)

Bayer's *Uranometria* caught on, and it "set the standard for future celestial atlases due to its beauty and accuracy."[15] After the first edition of 1603, later printings—with the charts, the accompanying text, or both—appeared in 1624 (twice), 1639, 1640, 1641, 1648, 1654, 1655, 1661, 1666, 1689, 1697, and 1723. Just as important, most of the new star catalogs of the early seventeenth century followed Bayer closely, spreading his work long beyond the era in which his own book was in print. Bayer's work would not be superseded for more than a century: while the posthumous publication of John Flamsteed's star atlas in 1729, *Atlas coelestis*, offered a more thorough catalog of the stars, even that is deeply indebted to Bayer's *Uranometria*.

The Renaissance marked an epoch for mapmaking, and Ortelius was one of the most important figures. In the words of one historian, "The period of cartographic incunabula, characterized by a slavish following of old doctrines and strongly influenced by Ptolemy, was closed. The new period trusted the knowledge of the earth to first hand exploration and scientific investigation rather than to ancient classics."[16] Historians of cartography sometimes refer to this period as the Dutch era, because maps from the Netherlands dominated the world trade in maps—but soon the maps would dominate the world. Kings and princes went on to use cartography to create a consciousness of the nation-state as a coherent entity, one that could be made visible on a wall.[17]

Bayer's work, meanwhile, has been continued by countless astronomers since, and today's biggest astronomical catalog, USNO-B1.0, contains just over a billion items. This is around 640,000 times as many as the 1,564 in *Uranometria*, and the catalog itself is about twice the size of the whole of the English Wikipedia. Even this, though, represents a tiny fraction of the stars that exist in the universe. No one knows an exact number, and astronomers argue about even the order of magnitude. One plausible guess of the number of stars, though, puts the figure at seventy sextillion—70,000,000,000,000,000,000,000, or 7×10^{22}. To put this in context, there are roughly a thousand stars in the sky for every grain of sand on the earth. Even the Brobdingnagian USNO-B1.0 has covered only around 0.0000000000015 percent of the estimated total. Astronomers therefore have a lot more work ahead of them. Even if all seven billion people on the planet were put to work around the clock, held to an assembly-line pace of cataloging one star per minute, it would take them about 19 million years to get through them all. What's more, a recent discovery suggests we might have to triple our best guess about the number of stars in the universe.[18] If that turns out to be true, the seven billion of us working on the problem will not get a breather for 38 million years more.

TELL ME HOW YOU ORGANIZE YOUR BOOKS

'VE DEFINED REFERENCE books in terms of how individual readers use them, but there's also an institutional definition: reference books are the ones that never leave the library.[1] That's good news for those inside the library, but it can be disconcerting to those outside. Dictionaries, encyclopedias, and all sorts of guides have their passionate devotees—Sean Pidgeon, a novelist and reference publisher, confesses, "I am addicted to looking things up"[2]—and for junkies like him, waiting until the next library trip to look up a pressing item is simply unthinkable. Reference addicts keep the books they need close at hand. Writers such as Jorge Luis Borges, Umberto Eco, and David Foster Wallace have spent their lives inside encyclopedias, dictionaries, concordances, and atlases. "I'm told that when Auden died," biographer Francis Steegmuller wrote in 1980, "they found his *OED* all but clawed to pieces. That is the way a poet and his dictionary should go out." Vladimir Nabokov, on the other hand, had little interest in the *OED*; he was a partisan of *Webster's Second New International Dictionary* (1934). After growing weary of using it only in the library, he bought a copy of the bulky volume and took it with him even when he traveled.[3]

Where to keep them? In his book-length ode to reference books, *Dictionary Days*, Ilan Stavans wrote, "An aphorism comes to mind: 'Tell me how you organize your books and I'll tell you who you are.' Thus said a teacher of mine years ago." Stavans confesses that his own shelves are a mess, with a significant exception: his dictionaries. "An entire wall is filled with them. These volumes seek perfection . . . they systematize knowledge."[4]

Princeton historian Anthony Grafton may win the contest for most interesting home reference section, thanks to a six-foot-tall "book wheel" or "reading wheel," modeled on a contraption designed by European scholars in the late sixteenth century. "Think of a small Ferris wheel," writes a reporter who has seen it, "with shelves instead of seats"; the shelves rotate, like the cars on a Ferris wheel, so that the books always remain upright. "From his seat he can rotate any one of eight shelves into view by spinning the wheel. With a tug, Grafton rotates past Greek, Latin, and Hebrew lexicons until a book on eclipses drops into view. 'Not everyone has *Eclipses for Humanists*,' he observes dryly."[5]

While I wait for the opportunity to get my own book wheel, I keep the bulk of my reference collection in the study, directly over the computer where I do most of my writing. The ones I use most often are on the lowest of the four shelves, so I can reach them without standing up. There I keep *The Oxford Companion to English Literature* in both the fifth and sixth editions; there, too, the *Oxford Classical Dictionary*, third edition (soon to be replaced by the fourth); *Merriam-Webster's Collegiate Dictionary*, eleventh edition; *Chambers Biographical Dictionary*; *The Chicago Manual of Style*, sixteenth edition; *Brewer's Dictionary of Phrase & Fable*, centenary edition; *The Oxford Dictionary of Quotations*; *The Oxford Companion to the Year*, *The Oxford Companion to the English Language*; and the major foreign language dictionaries: *Le nouveau petit Robert*, Duden's *Deutsches universal Wörterbuch*, and Zingarelli's *Vocabolario della lingua italiana*, along with a handful of bilingual dictionaries from Oxford, Webster, and Langenscheidt. The next two shelves contain works I need less often, maybe once a week—things I can reach simply by standing up. There I keep Bergen and Cornelia Evans's *Dictionary of Contemporary American Usage*; *The Concise Oxford English Dictionary*; the *MLA Handbook*; dictionaries of languages I need less often (*A Concise Hebrew and Aramaic Lexicon of the Old Testament*, *The Learner's Russian–English Dictionary*), the systematic reference grammars (Allen and Greenough's *New Latin Grammar*, the *Oxford English Grammar*, Zanichelli's *Lingua italiana*, *Sweet's Anglo-Saxon Primer*), the guides to usage and citation formats (Fowler and Fowler's *King's English*, Strunk and White's *Elements of Style*), specialized English dictionaries (Eric Partridge's *Dictionary of Slang and Unconventional English*), and miscellaneous references (Wellisch's *Indexing from A to Z*, the *NBC Handbook of Pronunciation*, Alberto

Manguel's *Dictionary of Imaginary Places*). The top shelf is too high to reach without a stepping stool; I use it for the reference books I consult every few months or less, such as the *Concise Encyclopedia of Heraldry*, the *English–Norwegian, Norwegian–English Dictionary*, and a grammar of Irish Gaelic. Some of these, truth be told, have acquired a layer of dust.

The latest *Chambers Dictionary* is just an inch too tall for my shelves, so it lies on its side. *Webster's Third New International* is far too tall to fit on a shelf, and its weight would make it dangerous for me to try to take it down from overhead. It sits on the floor to my left, blocking access to a filing cabinet and leaning up against a facsimile of Webster's *American Dictionary of the English Language* from 1828. My facsimile of Johnson's *Dictionary of the English Language* from 1755 is on the floor behind me, leaning on the bookcase devoted to Samuel Johnson's works. Other heavyweights—the *Historical Thesaurus of the Oxford English Dictionary*, the new *Oxford Latin Dictionary*, Liddell and Scott's *Greek–English Lexicon* in both the intermediate and full versions—have to go on top of a row of bookcases. The famous eleventh edition of the *Encyclopædia Britannica* (1911) would occupy too much space in the study; its twenty-nine volumes are downstairs. My old *Compact OED*, with its magnifying glass—now obsolete, but I've had it since I was a freshman and can't bear to part with it—and the fourth and fifth editions of *The American Heritage Dictionary* rest on top of a filing cabinet.

Of course I keep plenty of works on the computer. I had the third edition of the *American Heritage Dictionary* installed on my hard drive starting in the DOS days of the early 1990s, and now I have a number of important reference works bookmarked in my Web browser: the *Oxford English Dictionary*, Merriam-Webster, the *Oxford Dictionary of National Biography*, and the *English Short-Title Catalogue*, among many others. And of course Google and Wikipedia are perennially available. My iPhone also has the electronic versions of Merriam-Webster's *Collegiate, American Heritage, Chambers*, the *Larousse* for French, and versions of Liddell and Scott's Greek lexicon and Lewis and Short's Latin dictionary, as well as a smattering of less impressive bilingual dictionaries for quick lookups, and the Wikipedia app. I rarely go more than an hour or two without using one of them.

CHAPTER 8

ADMIRABLE ARTIFICE

Computers before Computers

Henry Briggs	Johannes Kepler
Arithmetica logarithmica	*Tabulæ Rudolphinæ*
1624	1627

"MATH CLASS IS tough!" So declared the Teen Talk Barbie doll in 1992, enraging a generation of feminists who despaired of finding children's toys that did not reinforce harmful gender stereotypes. But Barbie was right: math is hard.

If it is not quite so tough for us today, that is because we are spoiled by tiny computers that go with us everywhere. In the age of the feature-packed mobile phone, we need not even divide a restaurant bill by hand. A computer with more computing power than the entire Apollo program had at its disposal is there to give us an answer as quickly as we can press the buttons. But it has not always been so. For most of history, all calculations were done by hand, because there was no other way to do them.

Books containing page after page of digits may be the most referency of all reference books in their unsuitability for reading through. Dictionaries, encyclopedias, even the phone book can make for entertaining browsing: there is always the hope of coming across amusing names. But it is hard to read more than a few lines in a table of numbers without feeling one's energy waning, and even the most devoted reference book enthusiast will have trouble with this:

1201	3,07954,30074,0290	1234	3,09131,51596,9721
	36,14602,6382		35,17978,9847
1202	3,07990,44676,6672	1235	3,90166,69575,9568
	36,11596,7313		35,15131,5712

1203	3,08026,56273,3985	1236	3,09201,84707,5280
	36,08595,8196		35,12288,7632
1204	3,08062,64869,2181	1237	3,09236,96996,2912
	36,05599,8908		35,09450,5497

and so on, for 396 folio pages.[1] Hardly gripping reading. And yet such unreadable tables shaped the modern world.

The tables are designed as labor-saving devices: they take the place of long calculations done by hand, allowing us to look up the answers rather than arriving at them manually. In American restaurants, for instance, where a tip of 15 to 20 percent of the bill is customary, many people keep a small laminated card in their wallets on which are 15%, 18%, and 20% tips on various totals. These tip charts are descendants of old-fashioned "ready reckoners," printed tables that go back centuries and were especially common in countries without metric measurement or decimal coinage.[2] A mercer selling 8½ yards of cloth at 4s. 3d. a yard would be grateful for any shortcut in figuring that the total was £1 16s. 1½d. John Mayne's *Socius Mercatoris; or, The Merchant's Companion* (1674) was there to answer the question, as were almanacs and books like *Harris's Pocket Journal*.

❧

As handy as these were, though, they answer only very specific kinds of questions. Of course no book could provide tables to answer *every* calculation someone might need to perform, but with the discovery of the mathematical function known as the logarithm, one could compile tables to help with almost any calculation—huge tables, to be sure, but finite, and eminently useful.

Merriam-Webster's definition of *logarithm* is as good as any brief definition can be: "the exponent that indicates the power to which a base number is raised to produce a given number." Alexander John Thompson is more expansive in *Logarithmetica Britannica*, the standard modern work on the subject:[3]

The logarithm of a number *N*, to any base *a*, is defined here as the power *y* to which the base *a* must be raised to produce the number *N*; that is, if

$$N = a^y,$$

y is the logarithm of N to base a, or

$$y = \log_a N.$$

The mathphobic will welcome a clearer explanation still, which begins with exponents. Exponentiation is simply repeated multiplication. We use superscript numbers to indicate the number of times a number (called the *base*) is multiplied by itself: $2^3 = 2 \times 2 \times 2 = 8$; $6^4 = 6 \times 6 \times 6 \times 6 = 1,296$. More generally, a^n means $a \times a \times a \ldots$ with a appearing a total of n times.

Because our counting system is known as base 10, powers of 10 are especially significant, and 10 is the most common base for logarithms. The number 10 can also be written as 10^1. The number 100 can be written as 10×10, or 10^2; 1,000 can be written as $10 \times 10 \times 10$, or 10^3; and so on. A logarithm performs exponentiation in reverse.[4] Since $10^1 = 10$, it follows that $\log(10) = 1$. Since $10^2 = 100$, it follows that $\log(100) = 2$; since $10^3 = 1,000$, it follows that $\log(1,000) = 3$; and so on. Logarithms need not be whole numbers. It is easy to see that $\log(1,000) = 3$ because $10^3 = 1,000$, but it is less obvious that $\log(25)$ is 1.39794, because $10^{1.39794} = 25$, or $\log(2,000)$ is 3.30103, because $10^{3.30103} = 2,000$.

Logarithms fascinate mathematicians. They speed the calculation of compound interest and the half-lives of radioisotopes. They are linked in unexpected ways to prime numbers and trigonometrical functions. The constant e—the base of the "natural" log, roughly 2.71828—makes a surprise appearance in one of the most remarkable equations in history, $e^{\pi i} + 1 = 0$, which brings together the five most basic constants in mathematics. But logarithms might have remained little more than mathematical curiosities were it not for one further remarkable property: the logarithm of a product is the sum of the logarithm of the two factors—in a formula, $\log(a \times b) = \log(a) + \log(b)$. To put it another way, if $a \times b = c$, then $\log(a) + \log(b) = \log(c)$. We can check it with an example: since $10 \times 100 = 1,000$, it follows that $\log(10) + \log(100) = \log(1,000)$: $\log(10) = 1$; $\log(100) = 2$; $\log(1,000) = 3$.

This seemingly abstruse insight has a practical application: it lets us express multiplication in terms of addition, and division in terms of subtraction. Since addition is easier than multiplication, especially for large numbers, and subtraction is much easier than division, calculations can be speeded up by reducing complicated multiplications and divisions to much simpler additions and subtractions, with the help of a list of logarithms. To multiply any two numbers—say, *a* × *b*—look up log (*a*) and log (*b*) in a table; manually add those two numbers together; then look up that sum in another column of the table and find the number that has that sum as its logarithm—that gives the product. So, for instance, to multiply 2,384 by 1,635, look in the table for the logarithm of 2,384—it is 3.377306—and the logarithm of 1,653—it is 3.213517—and add them together: the sum is 6.590823. Turn to the table again and find the number that has for its logarithm 6.590823: it is 3,897,840, the product of the numbers. Division works in much the same way. It can be expressed in terms of subtraction: log (*a* ÷ *b*) = log (*a*) − log (*b*). To divide 9,910,233 by 4,387, look for the logarithm of 9,910,233—it is 6.996084—and the logarithm of 4,387—it is 3.642165—and subtract one from the other: the difference is 3.353919. Then find the number that has for its logarithm 3.353919: it is 2,259, the quotient of the numbers. Best of all, this requires no mathematical sophistication, because you can do it without knowing the first thing about logarithms and exponents. It is simply a procedure: look up *a*, look up *b*, add or subtract them, and look up the result.

Logarithms make many other mathematical operations simpler. If the concept sounds complicated, that is because we live in the computer age, when dividing 9,910,233 by 4,387 requires no more effort than typing the numbers into a spreadsheet, pocket calculator, or mobile phone. In the age of long division, though, it could take half an hour to perform a division like that, and with so many steps, error was always a possibility. How much easier it was when logarithms were introduced to look up two numbers in a table, perform one simple subtraction, and then look up another number in a table.[5]

These properties of logarithms were discovered in the early sixteenth century by a Scottish baron named John Napier. Born in 1550 in Merchiston Castle, not far from Edinburgh, Napier studied at St. Andrews University.[6] He was notoriously argumentative and a vindictive neighbor, but he also did much to improve society, such as developing new fertilizers and water pumps for coal pits. He worked on plans to repel a Spanish invasion of England with gigantic mirrors that could direct the sun's rays and set enemy ships on fire, and he drew up plans for new guns and even prototypes of twentieth-century tanks.[7] This master tinkerer also made a number of advances in mathematics; the decimal point was his invention.[8]

He was working on logarithms as early as 1594. Napier complained that "there is nothing that is so troublesome to mathematical practice, nor that doth more molest and hinder calculations, than the multiplications, divisions, square and cubical extractions of great numbers," and he "began therefore to consider in my mind by what certain and ready art I might remove those hindrances."[9] His book, *Mirifici logarithmorum canonis descriptio*, appeared in Latin in 1614, laying out the principles of logarithms. Early support from the astronomer Johannes Kepler gave Napier the cachet he needed. Soon logarithms were the talk of all the mathematicians in Europe, and people began discovering practical uses for them in navigation, making them of interest to commercial interests such as the East India Company.[10]

Calculating logarithms for individual applications is, however, unimaginably time-consuming. Long division is child's play next to calculating a logarithm by hand. What was needed was a table of logarithms to facilitate any real-world mathematical problem. Preparing that list required a preposterous effort, but that was the contribution of Henry Briggs. This English mathematician became interested in logarithms in 1615, and he wrote to a friend, "Naper [*sic*], lord of Markinston, hath set my head and hands a work with his new and admirable logarithms. I hope to see him this summer, if it please God, for I never saw book, which pleased me better, and made me more wonder."[11] After visiting Napier in 1616, Briggs resolved to calculate as many logarithms as possible, to allow his readers to perform all manner of calculations more easily.

The first fruits of his labor appeared right after Napier's death in 1617, a pamphlet called *Logarithmorum chilias prima*, the first printed table of logarithms. The preface explained the purpose:

Here is the first thousand logarithms which the author has had printed, not with the intention of becoming public property, but

TITLE: *Arithmetica logarithmica sive Logarithmorum chiliades triginta, pro numeris naturali serie crescentibus ab unitate ad 20,000: et a 90,000 ad 100,000 quorum ope multa perficiuntur arithmetica problemata et geometrica*

COMPILER: Henry Briggs (1561–1630)

ORGANIZATION: 88 pages on the principles of logarithms, then 300 pages of tables from 1 to 20,000 and 90,000 to 100,000.

PUBLISHED: London: William Jones, 1624

PAGES: 396

ENTRIES: 30,000

TOTAL WORDS: 29,000 words of discussion, 90,000 numbers in tables

SIZE: 13¼" × 8¼" (33.6 × 21 cm)

AREA: 300 ft² (28 m²)

partly to satisfy on a private basis the wish of some of his own intimate friends: partly so that with its help he might more conveniently solve not only several following thousands but also the integral table of Logarithms used for the calculation of all triangles. . . .

In a slight volume neither the enjoyment nor the toil has been slight.[12]

The pamphlet was a start, but Briggs's greatest work appeared in 1624 under the title *Arithmetica logarithmica*, a table of the base-10 logarithms of all the whole numbers from 1 to 20,000 and from 90,000 to 100,000.

His precision was formidable: fourteen decimal places for each of his thirty thousand entries. His second edition, published in 1628, was supplemented by the Dutch publisher Adriaan Vlacq, who covered 20,001–89,999, giving the world a complete set of the first hundred thousand base-10 logarithms. Complicated calculation would never be the same, and Briggs's book was the foundation of every table of logarithms published for centuries. No one bothered with new calculations until the end of the eighteenth century.

Chilias septima.

Num. absolu	Logarithmi.	Num. absolu	Logarithmi.
6701	3,82613,96179,3591	6707	3,82652,83063,4066
	6,48055,6334		6,47475,9338
6702	3,82620,44234,9925	6708	3,82659,30539,3404
	6,47958,9447		6,47379,4182
6703	3,82626,92193,9372	6709	3,82665,77919,7586
	6,47862,2849		6,47282,9313
6704	3,82633,40056,2221	6710	3,82672,25201,6899
	6,47765,6540		6,47186,4730
6705	3,82639,87821,8761	6711	3,82678,72388,1629
	6,47669,0520		6,47090,0436
6706	3,82646,35409,9281	6712	3,82685,19478,2065
	6,47572,4785		6,46993,6426

This work in many ways made the scientific revolution possible. The engineering projects of the Industrial Revolution could never have come to fruition without logarithms, and scientific astronomy would still be in its infancy. Pierre-Simon Laplace, the nineteenth-century French mathematician and astronomer, marveled at this "admirable artifice which, by reducing to a few days the labour of many months, doubles the life of the astronomer, and spares him the errors and disgust inseparable from long calculations."[13]

The logarithm made possible an ingenious invention, the slide rule—a convenient way of approximating logarithms without a table. The numbers on a ruler are spaced according to their logarithms, so the physical positioning of the rulers takes the place of looking up numbers in a book. The earliest slide rule was devised by Edmund Gunter around the year 1620, but a great leap forward came from William Oughtred in the 1620s and '30s. The result "would be the faithful companion of every scientist and engineer for the next 350 years, proudly given by parents to their sons and daughters upon graduation from college"[14]—a tradition brought to an end only by the invention of the pocket calculator in the

1970s. What had served the world as a calculator was actually a reference book reduced to a few notched sticks.

🙌

Logarithms have real-world applications, but they are generated according to the principles of pure mathematics. They tell us things about numbers, not about the world, and should therefore be true everywhere and always. A mathematician in another universe, charged with calculating base-10 logarithms, should come up with the same answers as ours. There is nothing empirical about them. Other tables of numbers, though, are dependent on real-world facts, and though expressed in the language of mathematics, they are not really mathematical tables. Astronomy, for instance, is an eminently empirical science, since the only way to tell the location of the stars is to look at them.

Monuments such as Stonehenge and the Goseck Circle tell us people have been keeping track of astronomical phenomena for at least seven thousand years. They got pretty good at it in ancient Babylon, Egypt, Greece, and India—much better than we might expect, since they had to rely on the naked eye to keep track of stars, comets, and planets. Claudius Ptolemy collected the best astronomical observations of his day in his *Prokheiroi kanones* (*Handy Tables*), which a modern historian calls "the first mass produced mathematical table."[15] Not until the early modern era did people fully appreciate that the natural world behaves according to laws that can be understood as mathematical relations. As Galileo famously put it, "Philosophy is written in this grand book, the universe, which stands continually open to our gaze. But the book cannot be understood unless one first learns to comprehend the language and read the letters in which it is composed. It is written in the language of mathematics."[16] It was one of the most important discoveries our species ever made.

The sixteenth and seventeenth centuries were a time of rapidly progressing knowledge. Astronomers now had telescopes; more and more observations and formulas were accumulating, and reference books were there to provide relief. Stars are relatively easy to track, because they are so far away that they seem immobile. For practical purposes, the stars are fixed. The astronomical bodies that are closer to us, though, really do seem to move; we can witness this over the course of hours rather than over centuries. Only complicated calculations can tell where the moon will be visible at any given time—likewise for all the planets.

The ancients in many cultures worked on simple tables, and in 1080 a group of astronomers from Toledo, Spain, compiled tables that allowed astronomers to predict the location of the sun, moon, and planets with unprecedented precision. In the thirteenth century a group assembled by Alfonso X of Castile worked to update the Toledan tables, and the result was named for the patron. The Alphonsine tables gave mathematical descriptions of the relations between the sun, the moon, and the planets relative to the fixed stars. After circulating in manuscript for decades, the tables were printed in 1483, and new versions appeared over the next three centuries.

But, while they were adequate for many purposes, the Toledan and Alphonsine tables had serious flaws, and others sought to improve on them. The Danish nobleman Tycho Brahe was the best observational astronomer of the sixteenth century, and his ability to collect data over decades was unmatched. While he was still a student, he realized that the older tables were inaccurate, and he published a series of works based on careful observation of the heavens. In 1592 he produced a catalog of 777 stars—not only the largest such catalog, but the first wholly original one to appear in the West since Ptolemy's a millennium and a half earlier. Tycho, however, never published most of his observations. He died in 1601, just fifty-four years old, and his *Astronomiæ instauratæ progymnasmata* appeared after his death.

Legend says Tycho's dying request to his assistant, Johannes Kepler, was to publish his observations, but twenty-three years passed between Tycho's death and the completion of the tables, and then another three years before the book appeared. Kepler disagreed with his predecessor on the geocentric or heliocentric model of the solar system, and he reworked many of Tycho's equations and observations to make them consistent with the brilliant system devised by Polish canon Nicolaus Copernicus almost a century earlier. At length Kepler produced in 1627 the *Tabulæ Rudolphinæ* (*Rudolphine Tables*), named for Holy Roman Emperor Rudolf II, Kepler's onetime patron, who had died in 1612.

The *Tables* were more accurate than any of their predecessors, both because of the careful observations made by both Brahe and Kepler and because they were built on a firmer foundation of Copernican astronomy. Simple to use, at least compared to other astronomical tables, they made it possible to determine the longitude of planets at any time, past, present, or future, and they provided answers that were an order of magnitude more precise than their predecessors. Readers could consult Kepler's formula by using the logarithms that had been discovered only a few years earlier. Napier's work had been published in 1614; Kepler was reading him by 1617, and he saw at once their potential.

⚘

The early numerical tables, like so many early examples of reference genres, were the works of individual scholars working without substantial assistance. But just as dictionaries and encyclopedias eventually grew too large for lone talents, so did numerical tables eventually require substantial teams.

At the end of the eighteenth century, the French engineer Gaspard Clair François Marie Riche de Prony oversaw one such workshop. Inspired by Adam Smith's recently published *Treatise on the Wealth of Nations* (1776), he assembled a team of some sixty unemployed hairdressers to do carry out his instructions. (In the wake of the French Revolution there was less call for high-end hairdressers, not least because, thanks to Citizen Joseph-Ignace Guillotin's eponymous invention, fewer aristocratic heads needed dressing.) The work was carried out on an industrial scale: in just two years, de Prony and his hairdressing computers calculated 10,000 sines to twenty-five decimal places, 2,000 logarithms of sines and tangents to fourteen decimal places, 10,000 logarithms of the proportions of sines and tangents, and the logarithms of numbers from 1 to 10,000 to nineteen decimal places and of numbers from 10,000 to 20,000 to fourteen places. The work filled seventeen folio volumes of manuscript, though they sat unpublished for ninety years.[17]

The production of tables achieved assembly-line efficiency in the late 1930s. The American Works Progress (later Projects) Administration, founded in 1935 to provide jobs for "employable workers" during the

TITLE: *Tabulæ Rudolphinæ, quibus astronomicæ scientiæ, temporum longinquitate collapsæ restauratio continetur; a Phœnice illo astronomorum Tychone, ex illustri & generosa Braheorum in regno Daniæ familiâ oriundo Equite, primum animo concepta et destinata anno Christi M D LXIV*

COMPILER: Johannes Kepler (1571–1630)

ORGANIZATION: Three sections: the Ptolemaic stars, the stars identified by Brahe, and the southern hemisphere's stars identified by Pieter Dircksz Keyser; thereafter by logarithmic sines of each minute of the quadrant

PUBLISHED: Ulm, Germany: Jonas Sauer, September 1627

PAGES: 247

ENTRIES: 1,440 stars and 75,000 pieces of information

SIZE: 13¾" × 9" (35 × 23 cm)

AREA: 213 ft² (19.9 m²)

WEIGHT: 3 lb. 3 oz. (1.45 kg)

Great Depression, established the Mathematical Tables Project in 1938 as one of its "small useful projects." Useful it was, but hardly small: it was one of the largest-scale computing operations in the pre-ENIAC age, headed by a Polish-born mathematician, Gertrude Blanch, who supervised 450 clerks.[18] Just as de Prony had learned a lesson from Adam Smith, Blanch took her cue from Henry Ford—she gave each group of workers a single task: some did only addition, some only subtraction. The best were trusted with long division. The resulting tables of logarithms and other functions were published in twenty-eight volumes; in some of them, no one to this day has discovered a single error.

But the work of Briggs, of Kepler, of de Prony, of Blanch was all rendered obsolete in the last third of the twentieth century, because of something no one could have foreseen in the 1940s, let alone in the 1620s—fast, plentiful, and cheap computers. When the newly invented electronic digital computers were first brought to bear on elaborate calculations, nearly everyone took it for granted that the computers' job would be to prepare accurate tables. The machines would tirelessly print long tables of logarithms, sines, and cosines, but the comparatively simple operations of adding and subtracting those numbers would continue to be done by hand. Computing time was far too expensive to waste on trivial calculations like adding 3.377306 to 3.213517. According to an often-repeated story, IBM president Thomas J. Watson declared in 1943, "I think there is a world market for maybe five computers." The remark is almost certainly apocryphal, but it reflects the assumptions of the early digital days: computers were large and expensive, and the mechanical task of manipulating those numbers should be entrusted to minimally skilled laborers. We are left with the strange paradox that mathematical tables were rendered entirely obsolete by the computer, although tables were the main reason computers were invented. The computer itself—the transformative technology of the last sixty years— is an unintentional byproduct of the reference book.

TO BRING PEOPLE TOGETHER

Societies

R EADING AND WRITING reference books is generally solitary work. Merriam-Webster's headquarters in Springfield, Massachusetts, has a famously quiet working environment, dating back to Philip Gove's editorship of the *Third New International*, where even whispers can earn dirty looks. It's one of the few remaining places where two honest-to-goodness phone booths can be found, to ensure that conversations don't disturb the lexicographers hard at work. What Peter Sokolowski of Merriam calls "a powerful culture of silence" keeps the place as hushed as a library.

Fortunately for those who thrive only in society, though, there are more companionable outlets for indulging in lexicography and even lexicophilia. The national academies that sponsored many of the great national dictionaries are, for the most part, still busy, centuries after their founding, and they can sometimes be positively rowdy compared to the Merriam offices. One of the oldest private organizations, unsupported by any state, is the Philological Society of London; the group, founded in 1842, called for a "new English dictionary" and set in motion the project that became the *Oxford English Dictionary*. Organizations like the Royal Geographical Society, the American Geographical Society, and the Société de Géographie have promoted cartographical projects. One of the largest scholarly groups for the study of dictionaries is EURALEX, the European Association for Lexicography, founded in 1983; it spawned a series of sibling organizations: AUSTRALEX, the Australasian Association (1990), AFRILEX, the African Association (1995), and ASIALEX, the Asian Association (1997).

The friendliest society of the lot, though, is the Dictionary Society of North America, a group founded "to bring together people interested in dictionary making, study, collection, and use." The DSNA was born in 1975 at a colloquium on the history of English dictionaries held at Indiana State University in Terre Haute, Indiana—still the home of one of the best collections of dictionaries in the world. After toying with a number of names—the Society for the Study of English Dictionaries, the Society for the Study of Dictionaries and Lexicography, the Lexic Society, and the Lexicographical Society of America—they settled on the Dictionary Society of North America. The society now boasts more than four hundred members from around the world, and while professional lexicographers and academics are well represented in the membership directory, so, too, are librarians, journalists, book collectors, and plain old enthusiasts.[1]

The group meets every other year for a gathering that is part scholarly conference and part egghead bacchanal. Meetings have been held sometimes in big cities (Philadelphia, Montreal, Las Vegas), sometimes in smaller university towns (Ann Arbor, Urbana, Durham). The 2011 meeting in Montreal attracted a diverse group of working lexicographers, educators, historians, literary scholars, even computer scientists from all over the world. There were representatives from the *Oxford English Dictionary* and from Merriam-Webster; others included graduate students and professors emeriti, some in shorts and sandals, others in natty tailored suits and bow ties. The presentations ranged from explorations of the typography of Robert Cawdrey's *Table Alphabeticall* to dictionaries of Caribbean creole, from debates over the layout of learner's dictionaries to the practical difficulties of transcribing hip-hop lyrics—sometimes the only evidence of the first occurrence of a new word or sense is a bad bootleg recording of a rap concert from the 1970s.

A reporter covering the event—mostly out of bemusement—went on to identify the lexicographer and language columnist Ben Zimmer, editor of the pathbreaking *Visual Thesaurus*, as "a major geek." In some circles that might have led to a libel suit, but most of the DSNA participants embraced the nerdiness of the event, even performing dictionary-related songs at the conference-ending banquet. Peter Sokolowski, editor at large for Merriam-Webster and editor of *Merriam-Webster's French–English Dictionary*, was excited by one of the more technical presentations and tweeted to his thousands of followers, "Just heard a talk on French verb classification. Geek out."

Anyone who has read this far in this book without being a member of the DSNA should head at once to http://www.dictionarysociety .com/. The subscription to the annual journal, *Dictionaries*, is worth the price of admission.

CHAPTER 9

THE INFIRMITY OF HUMAN NATURE

Guides to Error

Index librorum prohibitorum	Sir Thomas Browne
1559	*Pseudodoxia Epidemica*
	1646

T o care about truth is also to care about falsehood. Any system dedicated to the discovery and dissemination of truth will at some point need to deal with departures from that truth. A few antireference books, therefore, offer dutiful catalogs of the things we should not believe.

Nowhere is the quest for truth more urgent than in religion, and some of the bitterest struggles with error happen in the religious arena. Modern democratic states have tended toward a live-and-let-live policy, but through most of our history, authorities have been substantially less forgiving. Christianity, for example, has a long history of wrestling with, and often suppressing, error. Jesus was the way, the truth, and the life— but finding that way, knowing that truth, and living that life required first knowing what Jesus actually said. This gave the early figures in the Church the difficult task of figuring out which writings constituted the inspired Scripture. The Hebrew and the Christian Bibles are not unified books, but rather miscellaneous writings collected long after they were written. The pieces were written over more than a millennium, with the earliest dating from the eleventh or tenth century B.C.E. and the latest in the Christian Bible from the end of the first century C.E. But these few dozen books are not the only writings from that period to survive: many other candidates for inclusion were circulating. Identifying the divinely inspired ones was difficult.

The so-called Muratorian fragment, a list of books of the Bible, was written in the seventh century but seems to be a copy of something much earlier, perhaps from the late second century C.E., between about 170 and 200. This fragment gives the earliest known version of the Christian canon, which both codified the accepted books and rejected others. Churches were forbidden to use the latter in the liturgy. The canon, in other words, is both a list of sacred books and a list of banned books.

The bans continued with later writings on religious matters. Any books that promoted heresies such as Montanism and Marcionism in the second century and Arianism in the fourth were in due course proscribed by the Church. And once Christianity became the official religion of the Roman Empire, a series of ecumenical councils, beginning with the First Council of Nicaea in 325, went further in delineating the true and the false, with the concomitant banning of anything that did not make the cut. Pope Anastasius banned Origen's works in the late fourth century, and Pope Gelasius in 496 issued the Gelasian Decree, with a list of authentic Scripture, recommended reading, and heretical and apocryphal books. Early Christians found a justification for their exclusion of offensive doctrine in the Bible itself. Acts 19:19 reads, "Many of them also which used curious arts brought their books together, and burned them before all men." If the Apostles could burn books, surely the Church was within its rights in doing the same.

※

Christians had been registering and tabulating heresy since the earliest days of the Church, but two developments in fifteenth- and sixteenth-century Germany made the project much more urgent. The first was Gutenberg's invention of the printing press around 1450. The number of books, both the number of new titles and the number of copies of each title, boomed, and the authorities grew uncomfortable. In 1469, Pope Innocent VIII went so far as to decree that all books had to be approved by religious authorities before they could be read; François I of France went further and banned all printed books, with a death penalty for printers, in order to be certain that nothing slipped through. The second development was the Protestant Reformation, which began when Martin Luther nailed his famous ninety-five theses to the church door at Wittenberg in 1517. Now there was a huge new category of heresy, one that threatened a mortal wound to Holy Mother Church. That both of these revolutions, printing and Protestantism, happened in the same region and within a few decades of each other is one of the most significant conjunctions in the history of Europe.

This energetic propagation of heresies prompted one of the most influential but also paradoxical reference books in all of European history—a book in which everything is wrong. It was variously known as the *Index librorum prohibitorum* or the *Index expurgatorius*, but it was usually enough to call it simply the *Index*: books the Roman Catholic Church deemed heretical. Not all were related to Protestantism, but that was clearly the most important category of heresy in the sixteenth century. As historian Benedict Anderson puts it, the *Index* was "a novel catalogue made necessary by the sheer volume of printed subversion."[1]

Registers of problematic books had been published starting in the 1520s, but the first official printed list came in 1544, when the Faculty of Theology at the University of Paris issued a catalog of banned books. It proved both influential and in need of rapid updating, so new editions followed in 1545, 1547, 1549, 1551, and 1556. The theologians at the University of Leuven (in what is now Belgium) offered their own index in 1546, again with revised editions following in rapid succession. A Portuguese list appeared in 1547; the first Italian list—a Venetian index— appeared in 1549; and a Spanish list was printed in 1551.

The most influential of all the versions, though, came from Rome a few years later. In 1557, Pope Paul IV gave the Congregation of the Inquisition an urgent task: to come up with a complete list of banned books. One list was prepared quickly—probably too quickly, because the Church authorities found it unsatisfactory and declined to print it. In January 1559, though, a longer version appeared. It was the first one to come from Rome, and it was the first one actually to be called an *Index*. Because it was prepared under Paul IV, it has become known as the *Pauline Index*.

More than a thousand books appeared in it, all of them forbidden to the laity. There are three rubrics for each letter of the alphabet. The first group, "Auctores quorum libri & scripta omnia prohibentur" ("Authors all of whose writings are banned"), listed heretical authors, including

TITLE: *Index auctorum, et librorû, qui ab officio sanctæ Rom. et Vniuersalis Inquisitionis caueri ab omnibus et singulis in uniuersa Christiana Republica mandantur, sub censuris contra legentes, uel tenentes libros prohibitos in bulla, quæ lecta est in Cœna Dûi expressis, et sub alijs pænis in decreto eiusdem sacri officij contentis*

COMPILER: Office of the Roman Inquisition

ORGANIZATION: Alphabetical by first names and titles of anonymous works

PUBLISHED: Rome: Antonio Blado, January 1559

PAGES: 72

ENTRIES: 1,130, including some duplicates

TOTAL WORDS: 5,700

SIZE: 8" × 5" (20.5 × 13 cm)

AREA: 20.6 ft² (1.9 m²)

LATEST EDITION: *Index librorum prohibitorum, SS. mi D.N. Pii PP. XII iussu editus* (Vatican City: Typis Polyglottis Vaticanis, 1948)

John Calvin, Martin Luther, and William Tyndale. (Luther in fact was listed under both *L* for "Lutherus" and *M* for "Martinus Lutherus.") The second category was "Certorum auct. Libri prohibiti" ("Banned books of known authors"): works such as Girolamo Savonarola's first sermon on Exodus and his commentary on Job, Polydore Vergil's *De inventoribus rerum*, and commentaries on Ovid's *Metamorphoses*. The final category, "Incertorum auct. Libri prohibiti" ("Banned books by unknown authors"), listed anonymous books, such as *Brevis & compendiosa instructio de religione Christiana* (*Brief and Compendious Instruction in the Christian Religion*), *Germanicæ nationis lamentationes* (*Lamentations of the German Nation*), and *Cur ecclesia quattuor Evangelia acceptavit* (*Why the Church Has Four Evangelists*).

The most sweeping bans appeared against Protestantism, the most obvious threat to the Catholic Church. A prime example was. Henry VIII, once *defensor fidei*, "defender of the faith," who appeared on the list of forbidden authors as "Henricus viij Anglus." The other Abrahamic faiths were also viewed as enemies, and "Thalmud Hebræorum" (the Talmud) and "Alchoranus Mahometis" (the Qur'an) were both interdicted. Closer to home, Cornelius Agrippa and Rabelais were among the forbidden authors, and the twenty books of the Catalan theologian Ramon Lull that Pope Gregory XI had condemned in 1376 went on the list, even though Lull would eventually be beatified by one of Gregory's successors, Pius IX. The *Decameron* ("Ioannis Boccacij lib. inscrip. Cento nouelle," "The book written by Giovanni Boccaccio, *A Hundred Stories*") was excluded as too racy. It is surprising to see the Bible on the list, but there are dozens of them, most of which earned their way there with doctrinally dodgy commentary, as with "Nouum Testamentum apud Ioannem Crispinum 1555, Cum omnib. similibus libris Noui Testamenti" ("The New Testament published by Johan Crespin in 1555, with all similar books of the New Testament"). Toward the end of the book was a list of publishers whose works were banned—simply printing the works of heretical authors earned a spot on the *Index*.

But a single list was not sufficient. Another *Index* was prepared by a commission established by the Council of Trent in 1564, under Pius IV, known as the *Tridentine Index*. This one established ten general norms that influenced Catholic censorship for centuries. The first nine covered categories always automatically banned because of their heresy; the tenth reasserts the need for approval before publication. These Tridentine rules prohibited all books by heretical authors on matters of religion, all obscene works, and works on astrology, divination, and the occult. This council ruled that the Vulgate—the Latin translation of the Bible, prepared by Jerome in the fourth century—was the only "official" Bible, and that no religious books could be printed without the approval of the Church.

All the versions of the *Index* forbade not only the publishing but also the reading of these books, with the penalty for disobedience being excommunication from the Church. The *Index*, however, was never seen as a comprehensive catalog of forbidden books. Canon law allowed for both censorship in advance of publication and condemnation of books already published, and the Vatican made liberal use of both kinds of prohibition. Even Bible reading was permitted only by those licensed by a bishop or inquisitor.

For the first few decades, the process by which a new *Index* was compiled was strictly ad hoc. In 1571, though, Pope Pius V created a new organization within the Church: the Congregation of the Index, a permanent body charged with censoring new publications. It was busy. In 1588, Pope Sixtus V ordered a new and expanded *Index* in which the ten Tridentine rules would be replaced by twenty-two new rules, but Sixtus died before it was complete, and this *Index* would go unpublished. The version of the *Index* issued by Clement VIII in 1596 topped two thousand banned books, and by the middle of the eighteenth century, it had grown to more than four thousand writers and works. Each edition republished the previous one with new additions.

Several broad categories of offense were likely to get a book into trouble. Any theological text that contradicted Church doctrine was certain to wind up on the prohibited list: an attack on Trinitarianism, for instance. John Milton's writings were forbidden for their bitter attacks on the Roman Catholic Church: "The increase of Popery is at this day no small trouble and offence to the greatest part of the Nation."[2] Mysticism was not tolerated, nor was Gallicanism, which tried to give the civil authorities control over the Church. Neither were some books that had nothing to do with theology. The most famous examples appeared not long after the early versions of the *Index*: works that promoted the heliocentric theory of Copernicus, according to which the sun rather than the earth is the center of the universe, were proscribed. Books that ridiculed the clergy were of course candidates for banning, and their authors' protestations that the satire on abusive priests was really meant to strengthen the Church by drawing attention to abuses were ignored. The final category was smut: anything lascivious was quickly suppressed. The Marquis de Sade's *Juliette and Justine* was banned, as was Gustave Flaubert's *Madame Bovary*, which may seem comparatively tame today, but in the 1850s shocked the world with its sympathetic portrait of an adulteress.

Over its long history, the *Index* has included Francis Bacon, Pierre Bayle, Henri Bergson, George Berkeley, Auguste Comte, Jean d'Alembert, René Descartes, Denis Diderot, Dumas père & fils, Edward Gibbon, Thomas Hobbes, Victor Hugo, David Hume, Immanuel Kant, John Locke, Nicolas de Malebranche, Blaise Pascal, Ernest Renan,

Jean-Jacques Rousseau, Benedict Spinoza, Voltaire, and Émile Zola. Some names catch us unawares. The novel *Pamela* by Samuel Richardson seems a model of piety. The Dutch humanist Desiderius Erasmus remained a devout Catholic, even in the midst of the Protestant Reformation, but his satires on the abuses of the clergy were enough to put him on the first Roman *Index* in 1559. Books could also come off the list. Johannes Kepler's *Epitome astronomiae Copernicanae* was banned in 1621, but a mere 214 years later, in 1835, it was deemed safe. Copernicus and Galileo were removed in 1822.

From its origins in the 1520s through its last edition in 1948, the *Index* attempted to combat more than four hundred years of heresy. The First Vatican Council in 1870 considered reworking the whole system of censorship, but nothing came of it. Not long after that, Pope Leo XIII revised the legislation somewhat, with a new version—this time known as the *Leonine Index*—in early 1897. This *Index* was reissued and revised several times; it reached a twentieth edition in 1948, listing five thousand prohibited titles. Still, Leo's work was less about banning individual titles than about laying out principles to guide the faithful. Nonetheless, the *Index*'s days were numbered. The Second Vatican Council, convened by Pope John XXIII in 1962, called for a Church more open to modernity. The pastoral constitution known as *Gaudium et spes*—"Joy and Hope"—was officially promulgated on the last day of the council by Pope Paul VI. It included the provision "Let it be recognized that all the faithful, clerical and lay, possess a lawful freedom of inquiry and thought." The new openness to freedom of thought was followed shortly afterward by the official demise of the *Index*: on June 14, 1966, the practice of banning books was officially brought to an end.

❦

A very different attempt to patrol the borders of truth produced one of the strangest books ever published in any genre. It does not quite deserve to be called a reference book, but then, it does not really fit in any other category.

Thomas Browne's *Pseudodoxia Epidemica*—the title, made up of Latinized Greek roots, means something like "outbreak of false belief"—is an imposing compendium of error. Browne was a quirky

English polymath who studied at Oxford and became a physician, publishing a spiritual autobiography called *Religio Medici* (*The Religion of a Physician*) that became a wholly unexpected bestseller in 1643. Though Browne was devout, his main concern was not false Christian doctrine but folk beliefs without foundation. And his four-hundred-page *Pseudodoxia* is chock full of these misguided beliefs.[3]

We make mistakes, Browne explained, because we are human: "The first and father cause of common Error, is the common infirmity of humane nature; of whose deceptible condition, although perhaps there should not need any other eviction, then the frequent errors, we shall our selves commit, even in the expresse declarement hereof." In the Bible between the Fall and the Flood, he pointed out, "there is but one speech delivered by man, wherein there is not an erronious conception." Some errors were attributable to "an invisible Agent," who "playes in the darke upon us, and that is the first contriver of Error, and professed opposer of Truth, the Divell"—Satan himself. And Browne warned that youthful errors, however innocent, eventually turn into rigid dogma: "we are very sensible how hardly teaching yeares do learn; what roots old age contracteth into errours, and how such as are but twigges in younger dayes, grow Oaks in our elder heads, and become inflexible unto the powerfullest arme of reason." His book becomes an extended attack on credulity, or "an easie assent, to what is obtruded, or a believing at first eare what is delivered by others."[4]

Browne's approach is almost scientific, and it shows the influence of the Baconian project—Francis Bacon's idea that we arrive at truth by observing the natural world and testing our assumptions against reality. After each erroneous assertion, Browne lines up all the authorities on either side, often switching into Latin and Greek for sentences at a time. He then applies his own reason and experience, and sorts out the truth as he understands it. The range of subjects he addresses is overwhelming. To browse Browne's "Alphabetical Table," the subject index appended to the fourth edition, is to get a glimpse of the glorious miscellaneity of Browne's mind. A typical run of entries:

Aqueducts, why commonly adorned with Lyons heads
Arabian learning what

TITLE: *Pseudodoxia Epidemica; or, Enquiries into Very
Many Received Tenents and Commonly Presumed Truths:
By Thomas Brovvne Dr. of Physick*
COMPILER: Thomas Browne (1605–82)
ORGANIZATION: Book 1, error; book 2, plants and
minerals; book 3, animals; book 4, humans; book 5, the
arts; book 6, geography and history; book 7, astronomy
PUBLISHED: London: printed for Thomas Harper for
Edward Dod, 1646
PAGES: xx + 386
TOTAL WORDS: 187,000
SIZE: 10½" × 6¾" (27 × 17.5 cm)
AREA: 205 ft² (19.2 m²)
WEIGHT: 2 lb. 10 oz. (1.2 kg)

Arcadians, their antiquity. In what sense elder then the moon
Archimedes his burning glasses. His removing the earth
Areopagus, what
Argus
Aristotle. His arguing for the eternity of the world. Never disputed
the ebbing and flowing of the Sea. His Maxime touching felicity
Aristotle, a Proselyte of Moses law.[5]

Book 3 takes up false beliefs about animals, and the first creature
examined is the elephant: "There generally passeth an opinion it hath
no joynts; and . . . that being unable to lye downe, it sleepeth against a
tree, which the Hunters observing doe saw almost asunder; whereon the
beast relying, by the fall of the tree falls also down it selfe, and is able
to rise no more." Other animals are surrounded by their own legends.
Some claimed that the chameleon "liveth onely upon ayre, and is
sustained by no other aliment." But Browne found the claim "very questionable . . . there are found in this animall, the guts, the stomack, and
other parts officiall unto nutrition." If chameleons ate only air, then
"their provisions had beene superfluous." "That a Bever to escape the

Hunter, bites off his testicles or stones, is a tenent very ancient," but one should not believe it.[6]

Many of the claims Browne responded to came from Scripture: "That a man hath one rib lesse then a woman, is a common conceit derived from the history of Genesis, wherein it stands delivered, that Eve was framed out of a rib of Adam." Browne noted that simple "reason or inspection" will point out the error, "for if wee survey the Sceleton of both sexes and therein the compage of bones, wee shall readily discover that men and women have foure and twenty ribs, that is, twelve on each side."[7] He was careful never to disagree with Scripture itself, but he worked hard to stamp out misunderstandings of the Bible.

Some of his challenges to widespread beliefs were subtle, and they show that he cared about precision. What about the belief that "the heart of man is seated in the left side"? Browne found it "refutable by inspection," which may come as a surprise to anyone who has not studied medicine. But in fact "the base and centre thereof is in the midst of the chest." The "Mucro or point thereof inclineth unto the left," but for the most part the heart is in the center.[8]

Browne's style is as distinctive as his strange mission to catalog errors. A perfectly characteristic sentence:

> Although who shall indifferently perpend the exceeding difficulty, which either the obscurity of the subject, or unavoidable paradox-ologie must often put upon the Attemptor, will easily discerne, a worke of this nature is not to bee performed upon one legge, and should smell of oyle if duly and deservedly handled.[9]

Browne never met a sesquipedalian Latinism he didn't like. He adored making up words, most of them based on obscure Greek and Latin roots. The *Oxford English Dictionary* records *Pseudodoxia* as the first appearance of 589 words, including *alliciency* (attractiveness), *ambilevous* (the opposite of *ambidextrous*), *bombilation* (a humming sound), *cecutiency* (partial blindness), *deuteroscopy* (second view or ulterior meaning), *equicrural* (having legs of equal length), *exantlation* (the act of drawing out, as water from a well), *festucous* (like straw), *lithontriptic* (having the property of breaking up stones in the bladder), *ophiophagous* (feeding on

snakes), and *retromingent* (urinating backward). An improbable number
of his words have stood the test of time: he was the first to use *approximate*, *carnivorous*, *continuum*, *hallucinate*, *perspire*, *ulterior*, and *veteri-
narian*. He was also the first to take existing words and give them new
forms, turning *additional* into *additionally*, *electric* into *electricity*, *consistent* into *inconsistent*, *medicine* into *medical*, and *select* into *selection*.

The book at times verges on the unreadable, with the polysyllabic
words and the paragraph-long sentences conspiring to keep all but the
most learned and devoted readers from understanding a page. But,
contrary to expectation, *Pseudodoxia Epidemica* was a hit: there were
eight separate editions, several reprintings in Browne's collected works,
and Latin, Dutch, German, and Danish translations. Browne kept
revising the text with each new version, and a substantial public was
eager to join Browne in his reformation not of the Church but of
learning itself.

❦

The two books, the *Index* and the *Pseudodoxia*, seem superficially similar:
both are collections of things the faithful should not believe. The most
serious problem for the Protestant Browne, though, was exactly the
opposite of the one facing the Catholic Church: in his view, people
were too inclined to accept arguments on the basis of authority—or, to
translate this into Brownish, "the mortallest enemy unto knowledge, and
that which hath done the greatest execution upon truth, hath beene a
peremptory adhesion unto Authority." The "establishing of our beliefe
upon the dictates of Antiquities"[10] was the root of all evil: physicians still
looking back to Galen and physicists relying on Aristotle. The new epistemology that would eventually be labeled the scientific method was the
way out. For the Church, on the other hand, the problem was an outbreak
of freethinking—people taking stances on important matters they were
not qualified to consider. Thus the Church reasserted its authority to
keep contrary opinions out of circulation. The subtitle of the *Index* could
easily be *The Dangers of Skepticism and the Importance of Authority*; the
subtitle of *Pseudodoxia* could just as easily be *The Dangers of Authority
and the Importance of Skepticism*.

IGNORANCE, PURE IGNORANCE

Of Omissions, Ambiguities, and Plain Old Blunders

Reference works have a strange authority. Words are words because they are "in the dictionary," and angry debates are settled after a glance into an encyclopedia. But these books are not infallible—as their compilers will be the first to admit. There is never a question of whether they contain errors, just how many and how embarrassing those errors are.

Still, the notion that reference works are authoritative oracles dies hard. In 1954, one critic advised his readers to stop worshiping the dictionary—too many people "think that every word has a correct meaning, and that dictionaries and grammars are the supreme authority in matters of meaning and usage." (That was a not-so-subtle dig at the G. & C. Merriam Company, which had been using the phrase "supreme authority" in its advertisements for two decades.) "These people," the writer complained, "never inquire by what authority the writers of dictionaries and grammars say what they say. It is incredible to see teachers bow down to the dictionary. If a person says, 'The dictionary is wrong!' he is looked upon as out of his mind."[1]

Actually, dictionaries and encyclopedias are often wrong. Edward Phillips's *New World of Words* (1656) contains some glaring goofs: Phillips defined *gallon* as "a measure of two quarts" (it should be four), and the musical note called a quaver is "half of a crotchet, as a crotchet is the half of a quaver," which creates a challenging mathematical problem.[2] John Ash's dictionary of 1775 defined *esoteric* and *exoteric*—opposites— as two spellings of the same word. In 1728, Ephraim Chambers tried to anticipate criticism by declaring to the world that his *Cyclopædia* was probably teeming with mistakes: "For *Errors*, they cannot be very few, considering the Hands thro' which most Parts of our Knowledge have passed, and from whom we are obliged to take our Accounts." He could only plead that the offense was nearly universal: "What one Author, upon the most particular Subject, will you produce, that has not his share of 'em? and what *Argus* could possibly see, and correct the Errors in all the Authors he had to do with?"[3]

The first really great English lexicographer, Samuel Johnson, knew this better than most. Lexicographers, he explained, can never hope for actual praise; the most they can hope for is "to escape reproach"—but "even this negative recompence has been yet granted to very few."[4] His prediction was accurate: his own dictionary was widely criticized for its mistakes, the most famous of which concerned his definition of the word *pastern*. The pastern is actually the part of a horse's foot between the fetlock and the hoof, but Johnson's entry reads, "The knee of an horse." At least he was forthright about it. "A lady once asked him how he came to define Pastern" that way, recorded James Boswell. "Instead of making an elaborate defence, as she expected, he at once answered, 'Ignorance, Madam, pure ignorance.'"[5]

Ignorance led Johnson into some of his other errors. Although *windward* and *leeward* are antonyms, for instance, Johnson defined them identically, as "Towards the wind." But other failures in defining apparently came from his knowing too much. Readers informed that a *cough* is "A convulsion of the lungs, vellicated by some sharp serosity," or that a *network* is "Any thing reticulated or decussated, at equal distances, with interstices between the intersections," come away knowing little more than when they began.

Errors come in many varieties. Some entries are bad because they tell us nothing. John Kersey was a master of the non-definition definition: his *New English Dictionary* (1702) defined *fork* as "a well-known instrument," *cat* as "a well-known creature," and *dog* simply as "a beast." Here are two more entries in their entirety:

Ake, as, my head akes.
An *Apron*, for a Woman, &c.

And while Benedykt Chmielowski deserves full credit for writing the first Polish encyclopedia, *Nowe Ateny albo Akademia wszelkiej sciencyi pełna* (*New Athens; or, The Academy Full of All Science*), in 1745–46, his no-nonsense entry for *horse*—"Koń—jaki jest, każdy widzi" ("Horse: everyone can see what it is")—is still proverbial in Polish.

"I'd long wondered," writer Ammon Shea recently mused, "why it was that people seemingly felt an irresistible urge to write in with corrections for dictionaries—until I began reading the *OED* and realized what a powerful urge I have, when I find a mistake in the dictionary, to share it with someone.... When I find a simple typo, I get a feeling of minor triumph. When I find something more substantial, such as a misspelled word, I begin to think I should set about applying for a professorship somewhere."[6] A. J. Jacobs felt the same rush when he spotted a lapse in the most important English-language encyclopedia, as he did "maybe once every four hundred pages" when he read the *Britannica*: "I feel like the middling student with a C average who has somehow busted the smartest kid in the class as he was writing an equation on the black-board. I still remember fondly when I discovered that the entry on Dvur Kralove, a Czech city, had a backward quotation mark."[7]

Many are convinced that Wikipedia, prepared without the benefit of paid and carefully selected experts, is loaded with errors, though the evidence is mixed. Admittedly, "Wikipedia vandals" sometimes intentionally introduce errors out of a mischievous sense of fun: "On January 11, 2008," Nicholson Baker observes, "the entire fascinating entry on the aardvark was replaced with 'one ugly animal'; in February the aardvark was briefly described as a 'medium-sized inflatable banana.'"[8] When Wikipedia entries begin suffering from too many vandals, as when the late-night television comic Stephen Colbert puckishly urged his viewers to spread the misinformation that wild elephant populations were growing, administrators will "protect" them, and only trusted Wikipedians are permitted to revise them until the vandals have grown bored and turned their attention elsewhere.

Still, people are convinced that an encyclopedia prepared entirely by volunteers will be riddled with howlers. But a study carried out by the journal *Nature* compared Wikipedia to the most recent *Britannica* by surveying scientific articles and found no significant differences in the number of errors.[9] Britannica was not happy. "Almost everything about the journal's investigation," they said in a press release, "from the criteria for identifying inaccuracies to the discrepancy between the article text and its headline, was wrong and misleading. Dozens of inaccuracies attributed to the *Britannica* were not inaccuracies at all, and a number of the articles *Nature* examined were not even in the *Encyclopædia Britannica*. The study was so poorly carried out and its findings so error-laden that it was completely without merit." The debate continues.

CHAPTER 10

GUARDING THE AVENUES OF LANGUAGE

Dictionaries in the Eighteenth Century

Dictionnaire de	Samuel Johnson
l'Académie françoise	*A Dictionary of the English*
1694	*Language*
	1755

B Y THE EUROPEAN Middle Ages, there were dictionaries in great profusion—but hardly any of them addressed the languages people actually spoke. Medieval dictionaries were mostly in Latin, the language of the Church, the language of the law, and the language of scholarship. No one thought a dictionary of Spanish, Swedish, or Dutch worthwhile. By the sixteenth century, though, interest in vernacular languages had begun to grow. Not coincidentally, this was also a time when national identities were coming into focus and the modern nation-state was being invented. People who once thought of themselves as Bourguignons, Lyonnais, or Bordelais started thinking of themselves as French; Prussians, Saxons, and Westphalians were becoming German. These nations defined themselves linguistically: a nation was a group of people sharing a language.

Starting around the year 1500 a few lexicographers began to treat the modern languages, at least tentatively. The *Universal vocabulario en latín y en romance*—Latin entries, Spanish definitions—was published in Seville by Alfonso de Palencia in 1490, and two years later Antono de Nebrija's important *Diccionarium latinum–hispanum et hispanum–latinum* appeared in Salamanca, making possible translation in both directions between Spanish and Latin. It was a substantial work, with nearly twelve thousand entries. An even more significant work came in 1611, when Sebastián de Covarrubias y Orozco published his *Tesoro de la lengua castellana o española.*[1] Still, Covarrubias himself did not create a nationwide consciousness of the language; that had to wait until the Spanish Royal Academy published its *Diccionario de la lengua castellana*, better known as the *Diccionario de autoridades*, between 1726 and 1739. It drew its material from the greatest Spanish writers (the *autoridades*, or "authorities").[2]

The process was much the same in Italy. An Italian dictionary, *Memoriale della lingua*, published by Giacomo Pergamini in 1602, has been called "the very first dictionary of definitions dealing with a modern language to be published in Europe."[3] The most important early seventeenth-century dictionary in Europe, though, was the work of another academy, the Accademia della Crusca, which began work in Florence in 1583. The result of the academicians' efforts was the five-volume *Vocabolario degli Accademici della Crusca* in 1612. The *Vocabolario* is self-consciously literary in its orientation: the quotations are drawn from a canon of great Italian writers, especially Dante, Petrarch, and Boccaccio, all from Tuscany, the privileged center of Italianness. No longer a debased modern form of Latin, Italian was now a living language in its own right, capable of expressing everything the classical languages could. The *Vocabolario* became the basis of Italian lexicography for three centuries: new editions continued appearing as late as 1923, and even today the standard Italian dictionary traces its origins back to the Accademia.

❦

The most important academic dictionary of all time, though, was that of the Académie Française, the greatest of the national academies then and now. It had its birth in the informal Paris salons of the early seventeenth century. Some of the most famous were held at the fashionable Hôtel de Rambouillet, near the Louvre, where Mme de Rambouillet established a forum in which men and women could discuss books and politics rather than gossip and scandal. News of these gatherings made their way to Cardinal Richelieu, who thought that the French state should recognize linguistic excellence in some official capacity. In January 1635, therefore, the chancellor of France drew up the letters patent establishing the Académie as an official body. No longer merely a club of like-minded amateurs, it was now an official body sanctioned by the crown. It has remained in operation, interrupted only by the French Revolution, ever since.[4]

The early members had much in common. They were required by charter to be "of good manners, of good reputation, of good spirit, and suitable for academic functions."[5] Within a few years, the Académie established strict rules for membership. The number of members would be fixed at forty, and they would serve from the time of their appointment until their death—the lifetime term gave them the nickname *les Immortels*. Over the centuries the members of the Académie have been some of the most distinguished French intellectuals. Early members included some of the brightest lights of France. Although the *Immortels* have included a few political radicals, the organization itself has been deeply conservative in its operation. The fair sex were excluded: no woman was admitted as one of the forty *Immortels* until 1980, more than a third of a millennium after the founding of the Académie. Still, the list of members over the centuries is a who's-who of French cultural life: Pierre Corneille, Jean Racine, François Fénelon, Pierre-Simon Laplace, Alexandre Dumas fils, Victor Hugo, Alexis de Tocqueville, Prosper Mérimée, Louis Pasteur, Paul Valéry, Eugène Ionesco, Fernand Braudel, Claude Lévi-Strauss, Jean Cocteau, Jacques Cousteau, Marguerite Yourcenar, and Marc Fumaroli have numbered among the immortals.

Their founding document declared that "The first mission of the Academy shall be to work, with all possible care and diligence, to give certain rules to our language and to make it pure, eloquent, and more suitable for treating arts and sciences," and a dictionary was the way to accomplish that purpose. The members read their way through the best authors to produce both a chronicle and an idealized image of the French language. Once a week, a member presented a discourse on a subject the Académie chose, and together they worked to refine the French language of its impurities.

The first general editor was Claude Favre de Vaugelas, one of the original Academicians. Vaugelas had his virtues, but productivity was not among them. His obsession with correctness slowed progress on the dictionary to a crawl. He spent fifteen years working on *A* through *I*, but then died poor, his estate unable to cover his debts. Creditors seized his

TITLE: *Le Dictionnaire de l'Académie françoise: Dedié au Roy*

COMPILER: Académie française

ORGANIZATION: Alphabetical by root word, *a* to *zoophyte*

PUBLISHED: August 24, 1694

VOLUMES: 2

PAGES: 1,478

ENTRIES: 5,492 main entries, 13,269 subentries

TOTAL WORDS: 1.5 million

SIZE: 14½" × 9¼" (36.4 × 23.5 cm)

AREA: 1,360 ft^2 (126.4 m^2)

LATEST EDITION: *Dictionnaire de l'Académie française*, 8th ed. (Hachette, 1932–35); the 9th ed. is in preparation

papers, including the incomplete materials for the dictionary, forcing the other members to negotiate for their return. The dictionary took forty years to complete.

The Academy made a few eccentric decisions. They resolved to exclude all technical and scientific terms from the main dictionary, sponsoring a separate *Dictionnaire des arts et des sciences*, edited by Thomas Corneille, brother of the playwright. They also took a different approach to alphabetical order from that of most other lexicographers. They alphabetized not by word but by root—that is, all derived forms that share an etymological origin were put under the root word, so *invalider* 'to void, to invalidate' appeared not in the *I*'s, but under *V* for the root *valoir* 'to be worth,' and *canin* 'canine' was placed under *chien* 'dog'. There is something appealingly logical about having all related words in a cluster, and the standard Latin and Greek dictionaries by Robert and Henri Estienne were organized this way. But it posed real problems for casual users who are not already masters of etymology. As one critic writes, "It was easy . . . to find *devoir* [*must, ought*] in its alphabetical place, but an initial search for such related words as *indû* [*unjustified*], *endetté* [*indebted*], and *debiteur* [*debtor*] would lead only to a cross-reference."[6] The system, moreover, was not followed consistently: *atourner* 'to dress' comes from *tourner* 'to turn', but it appeared under *A*, not *T*.[7]

Another problem was a failure of execution rather than planning: the definitions were notoriously weak. The dictionary defined *homme* 'man' simply as "animal raisonnable"; *femme* 'woman' is "la femelle de l'homme." *Amour* 'love' is "sentimens de celuy qui aime" (feeling of one who loves).[8] Moreover, they did not draw their examples from actual literature, as the Accademia della Crusca had done, but invented them for the purpose:

> TASTE. n. m. One of the five natural senses by which we make out flavors. Having the right taste, a delicate taste, exquisite taste, depraved taste, tired taste. it pleases the taste, tickles the taste, flatters the taste. each has his own taste, different tastes, not all tastes agree, there's no arguing over taste.
>
> It also means, Flavor. Meat that tastes good, tastes bad. this has an excellent taste, a fine taste, a delicate taste, an exquisite taste, a noted taste. this bread has a taste of hazelnut, this wine has a taste of earth, this gives good taste to sauces.
>
> One says, that *A sauce is of high taste*, to say, It is salty, spicy, or vinegary.
>
> It is also used for, Appetite. The patient begins to have a taste for wine. he begins to get his taste back. he finds nothing to his taste.
>
> They say prov. of Something too expensive, *The cost makes you lose your appetite.*

This policy, decided on as early as 1638, was meant to guarantee that there would be no errors or lapses, but it had the strange side effect of suggesting that the work of even the greatest writers did not meet the Académie's standard of "correct" French.

The appearance of the *Dictionnaire de l'Académie françoise* in 1694 was something of a damp squib. The volumes were beautifully printed and headed by a grand frontispiece, prompting one commentator to call the book "sumptuous, unforgettable, worthy of a zenith of France."[9] But Vaugelas's pace was so sluggish that two rival dictionaries had come out before it,[10] and the Académie was embarrassed by the omission of so many words that had appeared in the works of their rivals. Louis XIV himself praised the competition, not the official dictionary. Within just six months of publication, therefore, the academicians decided that, instead of turning their attention to a French grammar, they would produce a revised edition to make up for the shortcomings of the first.

With this second edition, the *Dictionnaire* began to overcome its inauspicious beginnings. The new edition brought with it some changes in policy, most notably that it followed straightforward alphabetical order, making the work accessible to a broader audience. From that time to this, the Académie's dictionaries have gone from strength to strength. A *Nouveau dictionnaire de l'Académie françoise* appeared in 1718, a third edition in 1740, and a fourth in 1762. The international prestige of French culture in the eighteenth and nineteenth centuries turned the *Dictionnaire* into a model for dictionaries around the world, and the Académie's work was established by law as the official standard of the French language—a status never accorded to any dictionary in the English-speaking world. The eighth edition (1932–35) is the most recent complete *Dictionnaire*, and the Académie has been working since 1986 on a ninth edition.

❧

How different were events two hundred miles away from the Académie's Paris headquarters. The *Dictionnaire de l'Académie françoise*, prepared by an academy with official government sanction, was all about authority and propriety. But there was no Académie Anglaise, no Académie Britannique. Britain lagged behind the other European nations in establishing official regulatory bodies to assume control over the language.

Mythology has treated Samuel Johnson's *Dictionary of the English Language*, published in 1755, as "the first English dictionary"—but the mythology is as wrong as can be. There had been English dictionaries generations before Johnson's. The *Promptorium parvulorum, sive clericorum* (*Storehouse for Children or Clerics*), probably by Galfridus Grammaticus (Geoffrey the Grammarian), was written around 1440 and published in 1499; it was the first extended attempt to give Latin equivalents for an English vocabulary of about twelve thousand entries. English–Latin

dictionaries on the same plan continued to appear, including the anony-
mous *Catholicon Anglicum* in 1483, Richard Huloet's *Abcedarium Anglo-
Latinum* in 1552, John Withals's *Shorte Dictionarie* in 1553, John Baret's
Alvearie in 1573, and John Rider's *Bibliotheca Scholastica* in 1589. There were
also dictionaries going the other way. Sir Thomas Elyot wrote the first
English book with "dictionary" in its title, *The Dictionary of Syr Thomas
Eliot Knyght*, a Latin–English dictionary, in 1538, and Thomas Cooper's
Thesaurus linguae Romanae et Britannicae followed in 1565.[11]

These early dictionaries were bilingual; the first English–English
dictionary, Robert Cawdrey's *Table Alphabeticall*, appeared in 1604. On
its own merits it was mediocre at best. The definitions were skimpy, and
it covered just twenty-five hundred "difficult" words:

modell, measure,
moderate, temperate, or keeping a meane,
moderation, keeping due order and proportion:
§ moderne, of our time
modest, sober, demure
§ moitie, halfe.
molestation, troubling.

Once Cawdrey broke the ice, though, English dictionaries began to
appear regularly, and they grew over time. Henry Cockeram's *English
Dictionary; or, An Interpreter of Hard English Words*, appeared in London
in 1623. He had two separate alphabetical sequences. The first part
contains "the choisest words themselues now in vse, wherewith our
language is inriched and become so copious." Next to each of these hard
words "the common sense is annexed"—a translation into plain English.
Cockeram informed the curious that *soporate*, for example, means "To
bring asleepe." The second half went in the opposite direction, translating "common sense" into "choicest words." Someone who needed
to speak about *dung* but blushed at using such a low word could turn to
Cockeram and try out *ordure*; someone who feared *drawing near* was
too common might find *appropinquation* the better choice. *Mighty* was
good, but *armipotent* was better. And *rip*, *rowe*, and *rub out* were
upgraded by Cockeram to *dilorigate*, *remigate*, and *deterge*.

TITLE: *A Dictionary of the English Language: In Which the Words Are Deduced from Their Originals, and Illustrated in Their Different Significations by Examples from the Best Writers: To Which Are Prefixed, a History of the Language, and an English Grammar*

COMPILER: Samuel Johnson (1709–84)

ORGANIZATION: Alphabetical, *a* to *zootomy*

PUBLISHED: London: printed by W. Strahan for J. and P. Knapton; T. and T. Longman; C. Hitch and L. Hawes; A. Millar; and R. and J. Dodsley, 1755

VOLUMES: 2

PAGES: 2,300

ENTRIES: 42,773

TOTAL WORDS: 3.5 million

SIZE: $15\frac{1}{2}$" × $9\frac{1}{2}$" (39.4 × 24 cm)

AREA: 2,330 ft^2 (217 m^2)

WEIGHT: 12 lb. (5.6 kg)

PRICE: £4 10s.

These English dictionaries, though, lacked the authority of a national academy. English writers therefore started calling for an English academy.[12] A member of London's Royal Society, John Evelyn, encouraged that group to get to work on "a Lexicon or collection of all the pure English words." Jonathan Swift made waves with *A Proposal for Correcting, Improving and Ascertaining the English Tongue*, and Daniel Defoe called for an academy in his *Essay upon Projects* (1697). Between 1660 and 1730, in fact, England was riddled with proposals for an academy—but one after another they fizzled. And perhaps for this reason the great heap of dictionaries that had appeared between 1604 and 1749—twenty of them—did not seem authoritative to many people. John Dryden, writing in 1693, was direct: "we have yet no *English Prosodia*, not so much as a tolerable Dictionary." David Hume agreed in 1741: "The Elegance and Propriety of Stile have been very much neglected among us. We have no Dictionary of our Language, and scarce a tolerable Grammar." And in 1747, William Warburton noted that "the *English* tongue, at this Juncture, deserves and demands our particular regard." He lamented that "we have neither GRAMMAR nor DICTIONARY, neither Chart nor Compass, to guide us through this wide sea of Words."[13] Despite a considerable library of English dictionaries, the world still seemed convinced that none merited the name.

The answer came not from an academy, but from a group of publishers who set a lone scholar to work on the task. We do not know why a consortium of booksellers approached Samuel Johnson in 1746 with the idea of his writing a dictionary. He was an unlikely choice. Johnson came from the provinces, in Lichfield, not from London. He was prodigiously learned, but no academic—he spent just over a year at Oxford before a shortage of funds forced him to withdraw without even an undergraduate degree. He became a schoolmaster for a brief while, but no one could call him a success.

In 1737 he left the provinces to find fame in London as a scholar and playwright. He hoped his verse tragedy, *Irene*, though not quite ready, would be a hit when it appeared, and he planned to publish editions of neo-Latin poets. But the market for verse tragedy and neo-Latin poets was only slightly better in 1737 than it is today, and his dreams came to nothing. Miscellaneous journalism, with skimpy payments by the printed sheet, was all that was open to him. Johnson stuck at it for years, and he built a reputation as a decent scholar, but only among a knowing few. To top it off, he was a gawky bundle of nervous tics who twitched and spat as he talked (most likely he suffered from Tourette's syndrome).

And yet, if the choice of Johnson was unlikely, it was also inspired. His memory was prodigious, and few could match his reading. He promised to deliver a complete dictionary to rival the French *Dictionnaire* in just three years. Disbelievers scoffed: forty scholars had needed forty years to produce the *Dictionnaire*. Johnson was ready with a gloriously brassy riposte: "This is the proportion. Let me see; forty times forty is sixteen hundred. As three to sixteen hundred, so is the proportion of an Englishman to a Frenchman."[14]

He did, in fact, miss his deadline. From contract to publication took not three years but nine—still an impressive proportion next to the sixteen hundred man-years the French had taken. Johnson lived at that time on Gough Square in London (the only one of his London houses that still stands), and he worked nearly alone in his attic. He read through hundreds of books for his source material; when he saw a passage that illustrated a word, he underscored the appropriate word, wrote its initial letter in the margin, and drew vertical lines at the beginning and end of the relevant passage. A half dozen amanuenses took the books he marked and copied passages out by hand onto slips of paper, but he otherwise worked solo. These slips would become the raw material for his *Dictionary*, both the source of his quotations and the material that guided his definitions.

When the *Dictionary* finally appeared, several features made it a milestone. One has to do with the meanings. Although numbered senses had been used inconsistently in a few prior English dictionaries, Johnson took them further than anyone had before, and he was a master of distinguishing subtle shades of meaning:

PRIDE *n. s.* [*prit* or *pryd*, Saxon.]
1. Inordinate and unreasonable self-esteem.

I can see his pride
Peep through each part of him.   *Shakesp. Henry VIII.*

Pride hath no other glass
To shew itself, but pride; for supple knees
Feed arrogance, and are the proud man's fees.   *Shakesp.*

He his wonted pride soon recollects.   *Milton.*

Vain aims, inordinate desires
Blown up with high conceits engend'ring pride.   *Milton.*

2. Insolence; rude treatment of others; insolent exultation.

That witch
Hath wrought this hellish mischief unawares;
That hardly we escap'd the pride of France.   *Shakesp.*

They undergo
This annual humbling certain number'd days,
To dash their pride and joy for man seduc'd.   *Milton.*

Wantonness and pride
Raise out of friendship, hostile deeds in peace.   *Milton.*

3. Dignity of manner; loftiness of air.

4. Generous elation of heart.

The honest pride of conscious virtue.   *Smith.*

5. Elevation; dignity.

A falcon, tow'ring in her pride of place,
Was by a mousing owl hawkt at and kill'd.   *Shakesp.*

6. Ornament; show; decoration.

Whose lofty trees, yclad with summer's pride,
Did spread so broad, that heavens light did hide.   *F. Qu.*

He provided etymologies for every word, something the *Vocabolario* and *Dictionnaire* neglected, though he got many wrong, and sometimes confessed ignorance: *tatterdemalion* is from "*tatter* and *I know not what.*" At least as important, he backed up these definitions with quotations— somewhere in the neighborhood of 115,000 of them, drawn from English literature between the 1580s and his own time, with particular attention to Philip Sidney, Francis Bacon, Walter Raleigh, William Shakespeare, John Milton, John Dryden, John Locke, Joseph Addison, Jonathan Swift, Alexander Pope, and the King James Bible. Quotations like these could be found in classical lexicons and the Italian *Vocabolario*, but no English dictionary maker had ever used them half as systematically as Johnson.

This may be the most significant difference between Johnson and *les Immortels.* The French *Dictionnaire* provided examples of words in use, but they were all made up by the Academicians: they knew what the best usage was, even when it differed from what real writers had used. For Johnson, by contrast, the canon of great authors was his starting point, and this corpus-based approach was central to his conception of what makes a word a word: real words had to be found in actual litera-ture. On the very few occasions when he included a word he had not found "in the wild," as it were, he did it with reservation, clearly indi-cating that these words were provisional candidates by citing as an authority just "Dict.," for "Dictionary":

> Many words yet stand supported only by . . . *Dict.* . . . of these I am not always certain that they are seen in any book but the works of lexicographers. Of such I have omitted many, because I had never read them; and many I have inserted, because they may perhaps exist, though they have escaped my notice: they are, however, to be yet considered as resting only upon the credit of former dictionaries.[15]

The story of the composition of Johnson's *Dictionary* is one of progressive disillusionment. The initial proposal was revised into publishable form and became *The Plan of a Dictionary of the English Language*, issued in 1747. There Johnson expressed his intention to clean up the language—the same sort of thing would-be academicians had been calling for since the 1660s, and the sort of thing the Académie Française had done in the 1690s. He even viewed his task in quasimili-tary terms. "When I survey the Plan," he wrote,

> I am frighted at its extent, and, like the soldiers of Cæsar, look on Britain as a new world, which it is almost madness to invade. But I hope, that though I should not complete the conquest, I shall at least discover the coast, civilize part of the inhabitants, and make it easy for some other adventurer to proceed farther, to reduce them wholly to subjection, and settle them under laws.

The metaphors are suggestive. Johnson saw himself as a Roman legion-naire preparing to invade an unruly Britain and impose imperial order and regularity on it—to take the Germanic barbarians and civilize them with Latinate elegance and propriety. The language was a rebellious population: he would "civilize part of the inhabitants" and encourage someone else to "reduce them wholly to subjection." This is strange language coming from Johnson, who later in life became one of his age's most vocal opponents of colonial expansion.

Before long, though, he realized his intentions were misplaced. No one can hope to "civilize" a living language; it is pure foolishness to impose rules on it. He wrote of the way the academicians wanted to stop the language from changing: "With this hope ... academies have been instituted, to guard the avenues of their languages, to retain fugitives, and repulse intruders." His opinion of their success is telling: "their vigilance and activity have hitherto been vain; sounds are too volatile and subtile for legal restraints; to enchain syllables, and to lash the wind, are equally the undertakings of pride."[16]

This became much clearer as the *Dictionary* was approaching completion. Johnson had asked Philip Dormer Stanhope, the Fourth Earl of Chesterfield, to serve as his patron, but the distinguished nobleman brushed him off. Once the book was ready to appear, though, rumor said it was going to be a blockbuster, and Chesterfield decided he wanted credit for supporting it. He therefore published a review before the fact, right before the *Dictionary* came out, insisting that "The time for discrimination seems to be now come. Toleration, adoption and naturalization have run their lengths. Good order and authority are now necessary." He attributed this sad state of affairs specifically to the lack of an authoritative dictionary: "I had long lamented that we had no lawful standard of our language set up, for those to repair to, who might chuse to speak and write it grammatically and correctly." Johnson had provided the solution, and Chesterfield demanded that the world acknowledge his authority. "I will not only obey him," Chesterfield vowed, "like an old Roman, as my dictator, but, like a modern Roman, I will implicitly believe in him as my Pope, and hold him to be infallible while in the chair."[17] But Johnson, who might once have been flattered at the thought of being an emperor, almost certainly found the metaphor from the papacy too much to handle. He saw through Chesterfield's ploy and wrote one of the nastiest letters in the English language, telling his lordship that his assistance was not wanted. Part of the vitriol came from the shoddy treatment Johnson felt he had received: Chesterfield had refused to be bothered when Johnson needed the help. But part of it also came from Johnson's recent thinking about the state of the language. Only a fool would, he concluded, "imagine that his dictionary can embalm his language, and secure it from corruption and decay," and yet "With this hope . . . academies have been instituted." Johnson realized that no academy can change the fact of language evolution, and even if it could, it should not. Language, he realized, develops on its own, and a lexicographer must "not form, but register the language."[18]

The *Dictionary* appeared in two folio volumes on April 15, 1755, not merely the largest English dictionary yet published, but as long as the first seven monolingual English dictionaries put together. Early reviews were strong, and the actor David Garrick wrote a poem celebrating his friend's superiority to the French academicians and their dictionary, turning the *Dictionary's* publication into an event of national moment:

> *Talk of war with a Briton, he'll boldly advance,*
> *That one English soldier will beat ten of France;*
> *Would we alter the boast from the sword to the pen,*
> *Our odds are still greater, still greater our men . . .*
> *First Shakespeare and Milton, like Gods in the fight,*
> *Have put their whole drama and epic to flight;*
> *In satires, epistles, and odes, would they cope,*
> *Their numbers retreat before Dryden and Pope;*
> *And Johnson, well-arm'd like a hero of yore,*
> *Has beat forty French, and will beat forty more.*

Sales of the expensive volumes were slow at first, but low-cost abridged editions put Johnson's work within the reach of middle-class readers. Over the next few decades, the essential shelf of books in nearly every British home grew. At one time, every reader could have been expected to own at the very least a Bible, a *Book of Common Prayer*, and *The Pilgrim's Progress*. In the eighteenth century, Shakespeare's works were added to the list. And by century's end, a dictionary—Johnson's *Dictionary*—became a fixture in every literate household.

૨ઙ

There may be no more exemplary pair of reference books than the *Dictionnaire* and the *Dictionary*: they represent opposite poles on the dictionary continuum. On the one side is the authority imposed by academic prestige and government sanction, promoting clear notions of right and wrong—the French say *normatif,* the English *prescriptive.* On the other, Johnson's approach to language was almost laissez-faire, believing that the job of the lexicographer was merely to note what actual people said, and recognizing that trying to regulate a human institution as messy and as complicated as a language was impossible. The only hope was to let the language evolve on its own. These two notions of the language have been at war ever since. Lexicographers and grammarians have to declare an allegiance to one side or the other, and in doing so they are certain to disappoint much of their potential audience.

OF GHOSTS AND MOUNTWEAZELS

OOK UP THE word *foupe* in Samuel Johnson's *Dictionary*, and you'll discover that it means "To drive with a sudden impetuosity. A word out of use." But it was more "out of use" than even Johnson realized—in fact it is not a word at all. Johnson misread the long *s* of the rare word *soupe* 'to swoop' and inadvertently coined a new word. He also summoned the word *adventine* into existence, even though his source, Francis Bacon, had written *adventive* and a printer had accidentally set it as *adventine*. Another misprint in an early edition of Bacon led James Murray to enter the word *dentize* in the *OED*, meaning "to cut new teeth." But the word was *dentire*, misprinted in the 1626 edition of Bacon's *Sylvia*.

Instances like this abound in dictionaries, and W. W. Skeat, the great Victorian philologist, coined the term *ghost word* for these not-quite-existent words: "Like ghosts, we may seem to see them, or may fancy that they exist; but they have no real entity. We cannot grasp them; when we would do so, they disappear."[1] A typo in the *Edinburgh Review*—*kime* instead of *knife*—led to the appearance of *kime* in several dictionaries; since the original sentence referred to Hindus stabbing their hands with *kimes*, people assumed a kime must be some ghastly torture device.[2] And a printer's inability to read the verb *nurse* in Sir Walter Scott's novel *The Monastery* created a verb *to morse* appearing in collections of Scottish lowland dialect.

The most famous ghost of the twentieth century appeared in *Webster's Second New International*, published in 1934. *Webster's* included many abbreviations in its wordlist, and the compilers planned to include the abbreviation for *density*, usually *D*, though sometimes a lowercase *d* is used. In July 1931, one lexicographer—Austin M. Patterson, special editor for chemistry—typed a 3 × 5 card explaining the abbreviation: he headed it "D or d" and provided the explanation "density." But when it came time to transcribe the card, someone misread it and ran the letters together without spaces, producing "Dord, density." And then, because *Webster's* had a policy of beginning all words with a lowercase letter, the entry made it into the dictionary as "*dord*, density." It took five years for a Merriam editor to notice the strange entry, supported by neither etymology nor pronunciation. After investigating—no one could find any evidence for a word *dord*—he realized it was a mistake. He made an annotation: "plate change / imperative / urgent," and the printer removed *dord* from the next reprint, filling the otherwise empty line by adding a few letters to the entry for *doré furnace*.[3]

Some incorrect entries, though, are intentional, part of a long tradition of clever frauds in reference books. The German *Brockhaus Enzykopädie* has a tradition of including one prank entry in every edition—when a new edition is published, the old joke is removed and a new one inserted.[4] One of the best such larks is the last entry in Robert Hughes's *Music Lovers' Encyclopedia* of 1903, *zzxjoanw*, supposedly a Maori word, miraculously polysemous, that means "drum," "fife," and "conclusion." (Never mind that the Maori language does not have the letters *z*, *x*, or *j*.) The first edition of the *Collins COBUILD English Language Dictionary* (1987) sports an entry for *hink*: "If you hink, you think hopefully and unrealistically about something." And the *Neue Pauly Enzyklpädie* includes a learned entry on *apopudobalia*, an ancient game similar to football, which prompted a retort in a learned journal, pointing out six serious mistakes in the entry. The reviewer missed the fact that the entry was just a jeu d'esprit, with no basis in fact.[5] Other fakes are less jovial: in 1986 a laid-off editor from *Britannica* retaliated by vandalizing the encyclopedia's database, changing every occurrence of "Jesus" to "Allah." (His own boss became "Rambo.")[6]

An even more elaborate fake appeared in 1975, when the *New Columbia Encyclopedia* included a long entry on the distinguished American fountain designer Lillian Virginia Mountweazel, who had achieved some fame with *Flags Up!*, a collection of photographs of rural American mailboxes. Ms. Mountweazel, alas, met a premature end, dying in an explosion while she was researching an article for *Combustibles* magazine.

Although Mountweazel was nothing more than an inside joke among the encyclopedia's authors, she is said to have appeared in other encyclopedias and biographical dictionaries—proof that other editors have pilfered from the *New Columbia*. The term *mountweazel* is now used to refer to these mischievous entries inserted in reference books.

Mountweazels also seem to feature in some struggles over intellectual property. In 2001 the *New Oxford American Dictionary* included a made-up word, *esquivalience* ("the willful avoidance of one's official responsibilities"), designed to catch rivals who simply copied the *New Oxford American* in their electronic editions. When the word materialized in Dictionary.com, they knew something untoward had happened.[7] Cartographers are said to do the same thing—the *trap street* is a nonexistent road that appears on a map.

There are problems, though, with using fake entries to catch copyright violations. The first is that the number of unintentional errors will always be far greater than the number of intentional errors, whatever the reference work. All dictionaries, encyclopedias, chronologies, and atlases, even the best, have many errors. There is no legal benefit, moreover, to loading a dictionary, encyclopedia, or atlas with errors— copyright law gives no incentive. While reproducing someone else's entries verbatim is a violation of copyright law, it is a violation of copyright whether those entries are true or false. Lifting facts from another reference work, though, is not illegal, even if it may be shifty or lazy. A dictionary that contains *esquivalience* may deserve scorn for being a shoddy dictionary, content to let filching take the place of serious research. Unless it reproduces the wording of the *New Oxford American Dictionary*, though, it's not illegal. A legal ruling in the United States in 1992 confirmed this view: a federal court declared, "To treat 'false' facts interspersed among actual facts and represented as actual facts as fiction would mean that no one could ever reproduce or copy actual facts without risk of reproducing a false fact and thereby violating a copyright. . . . If such were the law, information could never be reproduced or widely disseminated."[8]

CHAPTER 11

THE WAY OF FAITH

Guidelines for Believers

Antoine Augustin Calmet	Alexander Cruden
Dictionnaire historique, critique,	*A Complete Concordance to the*
chronologique, géographique et	*Holy Scriptures of the Old and*
littéral de la Bible	*New Testament*
1720–21	1738

RELIGIONS ARE RARELY improvised. They represent a collective body of knowledge transmitted from one generation to another. And because most religions presume to address a tremendously wide range of subjects—the origin of the universe, the history of humanity, the underpinnings of morality, the nature of the afterlife—they tend to produce overwhelming amounts of text.

Every literate religious community accumulates a collection of scripture, narratives, laws, genealogies, wisdom literature, prophecies, and interpretations; before long, the sheer volume of text threatens to overwhelm even the most devoted believer. Reference works have therefore stepped in to distill the wisdom of the ages, to illuminate the path, and to justify righteous beliefs and behaviors. But these books do more than simply reflect already-existing beliefs. In compiling far-flung facts, the authors of reference books actively shape the religious practices and doctrine of the communities they chronicle. Though Marcus Terentius Varro's *Antiquitates rerum humanarum et divinarum*, completed in 47 B.C.E., survives only in fragments today, its summary of previous religious practices influenced the religious practice of his contemporaries, helping to constitute religion as a coherent field of inquiry. In a sense, Rome had no religion until it had an encyclopedia of religion.

Judaism is prominent among the religions of the book; it has a tradition of scholarly commentary going back as far as our records allow us to look. Already by 500 B.C.E., exegetes had extracted from the Hebrew Bible a set of 613 *mitzvot*, ethical principles that should direct the virtuous life. Later commentators added glosses, observations, and interpretations to these summaries of biblical wisdom, known collectively as the Mishnah and the Talmud. The result is the Halakhah, which means something like "the way." The collection has served Orthodox communities as a collection of essential principles for twenty-five centuries. The Halakhah is not so much a book as a library, and a growing one at that: every year there are dozens, if not hundreds, of new books interpreting the interpretations. It has even spun off mighty reference books in its own right, such as Jacob Neusner's *Halakhah: An Encyclopaedia of the Law of Judaism*, published in five volumes in 2000.

❧

Antoine Augustin Calmet of Lorraine, France, was educated by Benedictines at their abbey in Breuil. At the age of sixteen he joined the abbey of Saint-Mansuy in Toul, northeastern France, and he was ordained in 1696. His first post after his ordination was teaching philosophy and theology at Moyenmoutier Abbey in Lorraine. With his brother monks he began collecting material for an interpretation of the Bible. Earlier commentaries focused on the "allegorical" (mystical) and "tropological" (moral) meanings of the Bible, but Calmet wanted to emphasize the literal meanings: readers should master the basic facts of biblical history before moving on to the symbolic significance. He published the first part of his *Commentaire littéral sur tous les livres de l'Ancien et du Nouveau Testament* in 1707, a work that reached twenty-three quarto volumes in 1716. Even before the first edition was finished he was at work on a second, which appeared in twenty-six volumes between 1714 and 1720, and then a third, further enlarged edition from 1724 to 1726. A series of Latin translations of his commentaries appeared across Europe over the next seven decades.

Calmet's next major work continued this interest in the literal meaning of the scriptures. In fact it is also a kind of commentary, but instead of being structured by the biblical text, it arranges all the factual information alphabetically. The *Dictionnaire historique, critique,*

TITLE: *Dictionnaire historique, critique, chronologique, géographique et littéral de la Bible, enrichi d'un grand nombre de figures en taille-douce, qui représentent les antiquitez Judaïques*

COMPILER: Antoine Augustin Calmet (1672–1757)

ORGANIZATION: Alphabetical, *Aaron* to *Zuzim*

PUBLISHED: Paris: Emery, 1720–21

VOLUMES: 4

PAGES: 1,073

ENTRIES: 5,450

TOTAL WORDS: 1.3 million

SIZE: 15¾" × 11" (40 × 28 cm)

WEIGHT: 14 lb. 3 oz. (6.5 kg)

AREA: 1,290 ft² (120 m²)

---

chronologique, géographique, et littéral de la Bible appeared in four folio volumes in 1720–21, with an expanded edition appearing between 1722 and 1728. The dictionary opens with more than a hundred pages of front matter: a dedication to the prince royal, a preface explaining his purpose, a royal privilege, and a very long and detailed annotated bibliography of suitable works for learning about the Bible (including not only Latin and French, but also Syriac, Arabic, Persian, Armenian, Coptic, and Greek Bibles). The erudition is formidable, even daunting. Then comes a map of the ancient world, and a pair of "Carte[s] du Paradis Terrestre" ("Maps of the Earthly Paradise"), one following a map by Daniel-Pierre Huet, with Eden placed where modern Basrah in Iraq stands, the other Calmet's own, with Eden near Mount Ararat in Turkey. Another map shows the wandering of the Israelites in the desert, and yet another where the Apostles traveled. All of this front matter is complemented by lengthy back matter: a chronology of biblical events, guides to the weights and measures used in the Bible, a survey of ancient money, and so on.

The information presented in the dictionary proper is heterogeneous. Some entries are very short, hardly more than cross-references: the

whole of the entry for *Lahem* reads "Ce mot est mis pour *Bethléem*"—
"This word is used for *Bethlehem*." Others are long: the entry for *grace*
fills columns. There are also entries on classical mythology: Hercules,
for instance, is explicitly mentioned nowhere in the Bible, but Calmet
noticed the ways the scriptures invoke the Greek hero in their treatment
of Joshua, Samson, and Moses. Marginal notes provide the biblical citations and the Hebrew words.

Virtually all the personal names in the Bible were given an entry,
ranging from a few words for Sobab (*"fils de David & de Beth-sabée"*—
son of David and Bathsheba) to many pages for Adam (*"le premier
homme créé de Dieu,"* the first man created by God), Moses, David, Mary,
Jesus (*"fils de Dieu, vrai Messie, Sauveur du Monde,"* son of God, true
Messiah, savior of the world), John the Baptist (*"précurseur de nôtre
Seigneur* JESUS-CHRIST,*"* forerunner of our Lord Jesus), and the
Apostles. Locations, too, were covered in detail, with learned entries on
Sodom, Judea, and Bethlehem. Entries like *déluge* (flood) and *sabbathum*
go on for pages, often with elaborate calendrical calculations trying to
pin down when events occurred. The entry for *croix* (cross) covered
the ancient practice of crucifixion, with illustrations of various ways of
crucifying criminals and learned citations to John Chrysostom, Aelius
Lampridius, Cyprian, Gregory Nazianzus, Titus Livy, and a dozen
others. But not merely the central symbols of Christianity were
covered—anything in the lives of biblical figures was fair game. There
are entries on elephants and scorpions, synagogues and troglodytes,
athletes and fountains. Essays usefully illuminate practices like *simonie*
(simony) and viticulture, and even worthwhile articles on sandals and
trumpets are included. Calmet was careful, though, to avoid controversy. He was a devout Catholic, and his dictionary was therefore rigorously orthodox. The entry for *heresie* is loaded with contempt for those
who stray from Church teaching: it contains nothing but impeccable
Catholic doctrine, supported by dozens of marginal citations to provide
the scriptural authority for every assertion.

Like his commentary, the Bible dictionary went through a series of
expanded editions and translations, and it remained a standard work
of biblical investigation well into the nineteenth century. Calmet went
on to write a history of his native Lorraine, the *Histoire ecclésiastique*

et civile de la Lorraine (1728), and his learning and piety were rewarded
with a series of ecclesiastical postings. Pope Benedict XIII even
wanted to make him a bishop, but he rejected the offer. He died in Paris
in 1757.

⁂

Calmet's dictionary was outward looking: it moved from the religious
text to the world at large. Whether he was discussing Old Testament
juniper bushes or tracing the history of the Caliphate, he started with
the original Scripture and then looked to the real world beyond it.

Other religious reference books, though, are focused not on the real
world but strictly on the text itself. Dictionaries of the sacred languages,
such as Santes Pagninus's אוצר לשון הקדש *hoc est, Thesaurus linguæ sanctæ,
siue lexicon Hebraicum* (*Thesaurus of the Holy Language, or Hebrew
Lexicon*, 1575) and William Dugard's *Lexicon Græci Testamenti alphabe-
ticum* (*Alphabetical Lexicon of the Greek Testament*, 1660), are linguistic
rather than historical. And one of the great reference books, Alexander
Cruden's *Complete Concordance to the Holy Scriptures of the Old and New
Testament* (1738), points not from words to world, but squarely at the
words themselves.

Cruden's title page includes a motto from the Book of John, "Search
the Scriptures, for in them ye think ye have eternal life, and they are
they which testify of me," and his book really is about a new way of
searching the Scriptures. The work is titled a *Concordance*, and it opens
with a definition of this newfangled reference genre that he suspected
some of his readers might not understand: "A Concordance," Cruden
explained, "is a Dictionary, or an Index to the *Bible*, wherein all the
words, used thro' the Inspired Writings, are ranged alphabetically, and
the various places where they occur, are referred to, to assist us in finding
out passages, and comparing the several significations of the same
word." Such a book was certain to be useful, he wrote, because it "tends
so much to render the study of the holy Scriptures more easy to all
Christians."[1]

A concordance is an index—a comprehensive, or nearly comprehensive index—of words. A short passage from the Bible, Ecclesiastes 1:4–7,
shows how a concordance works:

4. One generation passeth away, and another generation cometh: but the earth abideth for ever. 5. The sun also ariseth, and the sun goeth down, and hasteth to his place where he arose. 6. The wind goeth toward the south, and turneth about unto the north; it whirleth about continually, and the wind returneth again according to his circuits. 7. All the rivers run into the sea; yet the sea is not full: unto the place from whence the rivers come, thither they return again.

TITLE: *A Complete Concordance to the Holy Scriptures of the Old and New Testament: In Two Parts: Containing, I. The Appellative or Common Words in So Full and Large a Manner, That Any Verse May Be Readily Found by Looking for Any Material Word in It . . . II. The Proper Names in the Scriptures . . . The Whole Digested in an Easy and Regular Method, Which, Together with the Various Significations and Other Improvements Now Added, Renders It More Useful than Any Book of this Kind Hitherto Published*

COMPILER: Alexander Cruden (1699 or 1701–70)

ORGANIZATION: Alphabetical, *abase* to *zealously*

PUBLISHED: London: Printed for D. Midwinter, A. Bettesworth and C. Hitch, J. and J. Pemberton, R. Ware, C. Rivington, R. Ford, F. Clay, A. Ward, J. and P. Knapton, J. Clarke, T. Longman, R. Hett, J. Oswald, J. Wood, A. Cruden, and J. Davidson, 1738 (first copies available in November 1737)

PAGES: 1,024

ENTRIES: 12,000 lemmas, 250,000 citations

TOTAL WORDS: 2.7 million

SIZE: 11" × 9" (28 × 23 cm)

AREA: 705 ft^2 (65.5 m^2)

PRICE: 17s.

The passage is eighty-one words long, but because some (*and*, *the*, *generation*, *rivers*) are repeated, there are just fifty-four different words:

> abideth, about, according, again, all, also, and, another, ariseth, arose, away, but, circuits, come, cometh, continually, down, earth, ever, for, from, full, generation, goeth, hasteth, he, his, into, is, it, north, not, one, passeth, place, return, returneth, rivers, run, sea, south, sun, the, they, thither, to, toward, turneth, unto, whence, where, whirleth, wind, yet

Some of these words are duplicates of a sort: *ariseth* and *arose* are both forms of *arise*; *come* and *cometh*, *return* and *returneth* have the same roots with different inflections. And a handful of words—*about, and, but, for, from, he, his, into, is, it, not, the, to, toward, unto*—are too common to be of any interest to most people, so many concordance-makers remove these so-called "noise words." That leaves this list of thirty-six unique substantive root words:

> abide, according, again, all, also, another, arise, away, circuit, come, continually, down, earth, ever, full, generation, go, haste, north, one, pass, place, return, river, run, sea, south, sun, they, thither, turn, whence, where, whirl, wind, yet

With the list established, a useful index can be generated. For each word in the list, there is a pointer to every place in the text where it appears. The simplest concordance gives each word along with its location:

> **go** Eccl. 1:5, 1:6
> **haste** Eccl. 1:5
> **north** Eccl. 1:6
> **one** Eccl. 1:4
> **pass** Eccl. 1:4
> **place** Eccl. 1:5, 1:7

But because this is not enough to be useful, concordances usually give readers a little context, producing a list like this:

go

Eccl. 1:5 . . . and the sun *goeth* down and hasteth to . . .

Eccl. 1:6 . . . The wind *goeth* toward the south . . .

haste

Eccl. 1:5 . . . goeth down, and *hasteth* to his place . . .

north

Eccl. 1:6 . . . and turneth about unto the *north* . . .

one

Eccl. 1:4 . . . *One* generation passeth away . . .

pass

Eccl. 1:4 . . . One generation *passeth* away . . .

place

Eccl. 1:5 . . . and hasteth to his *place* where he arose . . .

Eccl. 1:7 . . . not full: unto the *place* from whence . . .

And so on, through the entire list—and eventually through all 14,298 unique words of the Christian Bible. (This method of presentation has been known since 1959 as KWIC, or "keyword in context.")

The simplest use of a concordance is answering questions of the form "Where's the part where . . .?" A reader who remembers "manna from heaven" can turn to any Bible concordance and find nineteen references to *manna*, of which four are in Exodus 16 and three in John 6—one of those probably contains the passage the reader is seeking. But a concordance can do more than refresh hazy memories; it encourages questions that would otherwise be impossible to answer. A reader wanting to know about attitudes toward wine in the different parts of the Bible could turn to a concordance and quickly discover that the word *wine* appears in 248 verses in the King James translation of the Bible, spread out over 165 chapters. The earliest reference comes in Genesis 9, where Noah gets drunk and uncovers himself; in Genesis 19, Lot's daughters get him drunk "that we may preserve seed of our father." In Deuteronomy, though, wine is an agricultural staple. In Esther and the two books of Chronicles, it is a luxury item. For the prophets Isaiah and Jeremiah, wine is a metaphor as often as it is a beverage. The Gospel of Matthew also leans toward the metaphorical: in chapter 9, Jesus runs through a series of parables, including "Neither do men put new wine into old bottles: else the bottles break, and the wine runneth out, and the bottles perish: but they put new wine into new bottles, and both are preserved." And so on.

The earliest known Bible concordance appeared around the year 1230 or 1240: Hugh of Saint-Cher, a French friar, worked with his Dominican brothers to break down the Vulgate into the *Concordantiae Sacrorum Bibliorum*. The first Hebrew concordance was begun by Rabbi Isaac Nathan ben Kalonymus in 1438 and completed a decade later; it appeared in print in 1523. There was also a Greek concordance to the original text of the New Testament, published in Basel in 1546. Life got much easier for everyone after 1545, when Robert Estienne (Robertus Stephanus) introduced numbered verses into the text of the Bible, making it possible to cite chapter and verse with precision.

English concordances began appearing during the Reformation— Protestants have always been expected to read the Bible for themselves rather than relying on the interpretation of a priest. The first printed English Bible concordance appeared in 1535, when Thomas Gibson, or Gybson, published a concordance to the New Testament. The whole Bible had to await John Marbecke's *Concordance, That Is to Saie, a Worke Wherein by the Ordre of the Letters of the A.B.C. Ye Maie Redely Finde Any Worde Conteigned in the Whole Bible, So Often as It Is There Expressed or Mencioned*, published in 1550. Marbecke advertises the remarkable powers of this new kind of book to his royal patron: it makes it possible "that whatsoeuer sentence or worde were written in the moste sacred Bible, any man hauyng but competent learnyng, might easely turne to the originall place thereof, and that without study, although he remembred but one woorde of the sentence, whiche he desired to finde."[2]

Cruden knew Marbecke and the other concordances well enough to write a detailed history of the form,[3] but he was not impressed by his predecessors' work, and he resolved to produce his own concordance that would solve all the genre's problems. Cruden started every morning at seven and worked nearly without interruption until one o'clock the next morning—an eighteen-hour workday every day. At this pace he finished most of the manuscript in just a year, though proofreading took more time. As one of his biographers asks, "Was there ever . . . another enthusiast for whom it was no drudgery, but a sustained passion of delight, to creep conscientiously word by word through every chapter of the Bible, and that not once only, but again and again?"[4]

Cruden originally planned a small octavo edition and even printed up some sample pages to work on matters of page layout, but he realized that this format was too small and eventually settled on an arrangement of his material that fit well on a larger quarto page. His *Concordance* is in three alphabetical sequences. The first contains what he calls "the appellative or common words, which is the principal part. It is very full and large, and any text may be found by looking for any material word, whether it be substantive, adjective, verb, *&c.*" The second series covered proper names in both the Old and New Testaments, with "the various Significations of the principal words, which, I hope, will be esteemed a very useful improvement, there not being any thing of this kind in the other large *Concordances*." A reader can discover there that, for example, Abimelech means "father of the king," and Joshua means "the Lord, the saviour." Finally, Cruden compiled "a *Concordance* for those books that are called *Apocryphal*, which is only added that this work might not be deficient in any thing that is treated of in any other *Concordance*; those books not being of divine Inspiration, nor any part of the Canon of Scripture."[5]

Cruden's timing was bad. He dedicated his work to Queen Caroline, the wife of George III, and presented her with the first copy to come off the press, on November 3, 1737. He clearly had high expectations of a reward. But just six days later, perhaps before she had even looked at the book, Caroline took to her bed at St. James's Palace with intense abdominal pains. Physicians thought it was colic, but she had suffered a rupture of the womb. For eleven days she suffered tremendous pain before dying an exemplary death: her last word was simply "Pray." Cruden never got the royal recognition he desired. He did, however, live long enough to see his book reach a second edition in 1761 and a third in 1769. Three more editions would appear before the end of the century, and the *Concordance* has remained an essential reference work for English-speaking Christians to this day. New editions were appearing as recently as the 1990s.

As impressive as Cruden's *Concordance* is, later concordances are more sophisticated, distinguishing different senses of what seem to be the same words. The English word *bow*, for example, can be either a noun ("And Jehu drew a *bow* with his full strength, and smote Jehoram") or a verb ("thy father's children shall *bow* down before thee"). More to the point, the Christian Bible is a multilingual work, with most of the Old Testament in Hebrew (with bits in Aramaic) and the New Testament in Greek. But most concordances index the words in a translation, and many fine shadings of meaning are lost. The word *love*, for example, appears 310 times in the King James Version, but that single English word translates nine Hebrew and ten Greek words, some of which refer to erotic love ("Come, let us take our fill of *love* until the morning"), some to lust ("she was more corrupt in her inordinate *love* than she, and in her whoredoms more than her sister"), some to brotherly love ("be ye all of one mind . . . *love* as brethren"), some to self-preservation ("He that *loveth* his life shall lose it"), some to compassion ("Now God had brought Daniel into favour and tender *love*"), some to divine love ("For the Father *loveth* the Son"), some to greed ("For the *love* of money is the root of all evil"). James Strong's *Exhaustive Concordance of the Bible* (1890), probably the most sophisticated in a series of wordbooks that offer insights into the word of God, allows even those with no knowledge of Hebrew or Greek to make out the meanings of the original words by comparing all the instances of each kind of love.

And although concordances started with Scripture, the method can work with any body of text. Cruden himself applied his concordance-making technique to one of England's greatest poets in 1741 with *A Verbal Index to Milton's "Paradise Lost,"* the first time an English work other than Scripture got the concordance treatment. Others followed. Andrew Becket's *Concordance to Shakespeare: Suited to All the Editions, in Which the Distinguished and Parallel Passages in the Plays of that Justly Admired Writer Are Methodically Arranged* appeared in 1787, the first of a long series of Shakespeare concordances including Marvin Spevack's *Complete and Systematic Concordance to the Works of Shakespeare*, 6 vols., 1968–70, based on the Riverside Shakespeare. In the late nineteenth and early twentieth centuries, concordances to many authors were published, and by looking at the dates when they appeared we can construct a history of when modern writers became the subject of serious scholarly attention: Alfred, Lord Tennyson in 1869, Alexander Pope in 1875, Jean la Bruyère in 1878, Dante in 1888, Robert Burns in 1889, Percy Bysshe Shelley in 1892, Thomas Gray in 1908, both William Wordsworth and *Beowulf* in 1911, Edmund Spenser in 1915, Robert Browning in 1924, Geoffrey Chaucer in 1927, Ralph Waldo Emerson in 1932, Edgar Allan Poe in 1941. And in 1872, a different kind of holy scripture was analyzed in *A Concordance to the Constitution of the United States of America: With a Classified Index, and Questions for Educational Purposes* by Charles W. Stearns.

When computers were put on the job starting in the 1970s, dozens of automatically generated concordances were published, but computers also killed off the genre. Hard-copy concordances are little used today; one can search electronic texts and get faster results than are possible by flipping back and forth in heavy books of small print. But the conjunction of concordance and text searching is significant. Our new high-tech habits let us see the old books in new lights. What is a concordance but an attempt to perform every possible full-text search in advance and to collect the results between two covers?

WHO'S WHO AND WHAT'S WHAT

Making the Cut

W HAT DETERMINES THE contents of a reference book? For some, little discretion is involved. The compiler of a table of logarithms has to make a few early policy choices—what range of numbers, what interval between them, how many decimal places—but after that the decisions are largely set. An atlas declares its scope and its scale, and then it sets to work. Other books, though, present their editors with difficult decisions about what's in and what's out.

All dictionaries, for instance, are forced to be selective. "Almost every criticism made of dictionaries," Sidney Landau observes, "comes down at bottom to the lexicographer's need to save space."[1] There is no such thing as "unabridged": dictionaries sold with that label, even works as extensive as the *Oxford English Dictionary* and the Grimms' *Wörterbuch*, exclude more words than they admit. They all reject a huge technical vocabulary—millions of names of chemical compounds, biological species names, the specialized jargon of many professions—and most leave out nonce (ephemeral, single-use) words, slang that has its day and rapidly disappears, trademarks, and the like. Still, they are all interested in including new words, senses, and usages when they can actually be found "in the wild." Merriam-Webster explains that each day, its editors "devote an hour or two to reading a cross section of published material, including books, newspapers, magazines, and electronic publications; in our office this activity is called "reading and marking." The editors scour the texts in search of new words, new usages of existing words," and so on. When they find something new, an entry goes into their "citation files," now nearly 16 million words collected since the 1880s, and these citations are used as raw material for revised entries.

"Before a new word can be added to the dictionary," Merriam explains, "it must have enough citations to show that it is widely used. . . . A word may be rejected for entry into a general dictionary if all of its citations come from a single source or if they are all from highly specialized publications that reflect the jargon of experts within a single field."[2] Most dictionaries have policies on how long a new word has to be in circulation before it earns inclusion—five years, maybe ten, maybe more—to avoid flash-in-the-pan coinages that will be forgotten before the new edition goes to press. They do their best to resist pressure to include words coined by special interests, and they draw the line at made-up words. Every working lexicographer has had the experience of being offered new words. Kory Stamper captures the tone of these "helpful" messages from readers: "Hi, I noticed you don't have my coinage 'flabulous', which means 'tremendously fat', in your dictionary."[3] These are offered—sometimes for free, sometimes for a modest charge—but almost always turned down with a polite form letter.

The biggest determinant of selectivity is physical space. The decision to eliminate not only encyclopedic information but also tens of thousands of obsolete words from *Webster's Second* (1934) to make room for new ones in *Webster's Third* (1961) was motivated, above all, by the determination to keep the *Unabridged Dictionary* to a single volume. In encyclopedic works, including biographical dictionaries, that usually entails brainstorming a list of candidates for inclusion, ranking them in order of "importance"—undoubtedly subjective—and cutting those that fall below a line determined by the page count.

Even online sources have limits. Wikipedia could, at least in theory, have an entry for every person in the world. But the Wikipedia community is still trying to define the criteria for inclusion. When Jimmy Wales, one of Wikipedia's founders, visited Gugulethu, South Africa, in September 2007, he created a short entry for Mzoli's Meats, a butcher shop and restaurant. A nineteen-year-old administrator nixed it twenty-two minutes later, citing number 7 of the Criteria for Speedy Deletion: it contains "no assertion of importance/significance." This led to a dispute among the Wikipedian community, with "inclusionists" willing to tolerate any article, however trivial, that someone might find useful, and "deletionists" determined to prevent people from dumping unprocessed facts. Wales himself was taken aback by the "shockingly bad faith behavior" of those who should "find a new hobby."

EROTIC RECREATIONS
Sex Manuals

Aristotle's Master-Piece 1684	*Harris's List of Covent-Garden* *Ladies* 1761

ROTIC WRITING HAS a very long history—love poems, seduction narratives, tales of courtly love, and outright pornography can be found in many ancient literatures. Even the Bible contains a frankly erotic work, a poem variously known as the *Song of Songs*, the *Song of Solomon*, and the *Canticles*. For centuries, theologians scrambled to interpret the *Song* metaphorically or symbolically, eager to show that the eroticism is not *really* eroticism—the beloved has been turned into the Church, the lover into the believer. If a few of the comparisons seem far-fetched to modern sensibilities—"thou hast doves' eyes within thy locks: thy hair is as a flock of goats ... Thy teeth are like a flock of sheep ... Thy neck is like the tower of David builded for an armoury ... Thy two breasts are like two young roes that are twins, which feed among the lilies"[1]—well, they probably were racy in their original context.

Classical Western literature is also rich in eroticism, and sometimes it takes a form that gets strangely close to that of a reference book. The Roman poet Ovid wrote an *Ars amatoria*—usually translated as *The Art of Love*—an instructional poem that treats courtship and sex as an "art" in the Latin sense of a technique, even a craft. Ovid inspired a series of manuals of various sorts on love, such as Andreas Capellanus's *De arte honeste amandi* (*The Art of Courtly Love*) in the twelfth century. But the East was far ahead of the West in this respect. European literature after the fall of Rome can seem sexually frigid compared to what was going on in India and Persia. Probably the most famous, or infamous, sexy reference book of all time is the *Kama Sutra*, ancient India's guide to the erotic arts. Its origins are mysterious. Writer Vatsyayana Mallanaga has long been associated with it, though that attribution poses some chronological problems. The only thing we know about Vatsyayana is that he probably lived sometime between the fourth and sixth centuries c.e. But most scholars date the *Kama Sutra* between the fourth century B.C.E. and the late second century c.e., too early for Vatsyayana. Still the attribution sticks, for lack of a better candidate.

The *Kama Sutra* was probably composed in north or northwest India. It is written mostly in prose, though short bits of verse appear throughout. Although it is known as a sex book, only a small part of it deals directly with sex; it is really a book on virtuous living. A happy and virtuous life, though, included sexual pleasure. The Sanskrit word *kāma* means sensual desire or pleasure, which includes sexual pleasure. And *sutra*, one critic says, "means something like a thread or string of aphorisms, little bits of knowledge that are easily passed on. . . . I . . . see the sutras as kind of an early form of Wikipedia."[2]

Some of this erotic literature was accorded a position of great dignity in the culture that produced it; some was hidden, passed around in samizdat copies. Reference works, though, bring respectability to everything they touch. For a long time, these two worlds—the erotic and the encyclopedic, the sweaty wantonness and the dusty authority—seemed incompatible, at least in the West. Beginning in the seventeenth century, though, encyclopedias of sex began appearing. Some of them offered genuinely useful medical and scientific information about reproduction; others served no purpose other than titillation.

❧

Edward Phillips, a minor writer, is remembered by historians for two things: first, he was the nephew of the poet John Milton; second, he published a significant English dictionary, *The New World of Words*, in 1671. Earlier, in 1658, he wrote a book called *The Mysteries of Love & Eloquence*, with its preface dedicated to "the Youthful Gentry" and a dedicatory epistle "To those Cruel Fair ones, that triumph over the distresses of their loyal Lovers, the Author wisheth more Clemency; and to their afflicted Servants, more magnanimity and Roman Fortitude."[3] A reader not clued in to seventeenth-century London might find the title comparatively tame, as in the promise to discuss "The Arts of Wooing and Complementing; as They Are Manag'd in the Spring Garden, Hide Park; the New Exchange, and Other Eminent Places." But Spring Garden (later renamed Vauxhall), Hyde Park (a royal park, open to the public since 1637), and the New Exchange (a bazaar near the stock market on the Strand) were notorious haunts of prostitutes.

The most notorious seventeenth-century sex manual in the English-speaking world, though, bore the strange title *Aristotle's Master-Piece*. The supposed author's name is bogus—the Greek philosopher had nothing to do with it, and the work was credited to him only to lend it some scrap of respectability. The name game was not original; pseudo-Aristotelian books had been appearing in England since the late sixteenth century. And it didn't work this time, either: *Aristotle's Master-Piece* was banned in Britain until the 1960s. But the prohibition did not keep it from circulating; in fact its popularity makes it difficult to study today. We are not even certain when the first edition was printed; few copies of the early editions survive, since most of them were read (and otherwise used) until they fell apart.

Much of the information in the book was lifted from Jacob Rüff's *De conceptu et generatione hominis* (*On Conception and Generation*, 1554) and Levinus Lemnius's *Secret Miracles of Nature* (1564). *Aristotle's Master-Piece* promised to cover a wide range of subjects, and the subtitle insisted the whole thing was "Very Necessary for All Midwives, Nurses, and Young-Married Women." But the long title page gives little idea of the real contents. The promised "pictures of several monstruous births" did offer a prurient glance at gruesome birth defects, but the book was notorious for other reasons. In real life it was marketed neither to midwives nor to "nurses and young-married women." Much of the book was pornography, pure and simple.

To twenty-first-century sensibilities, seventeenth-century pornography does not seem very pornographic.[4] *Aristotle's Master-Piece* sometimes reads more like a sermon than a sex guide. "It plainly appears in Holy Writ," the book declared, "that this glorious Vniverse, bespangled with gaudy Fires, and every where adorned with wonderful objects, proclaiming the *Wisdom* and *Omnipotence* of the Great *Work-Master*,

TITLE: *Aristoteles Master-Piece; or, The Secrets of
   Generation Displayed in All the Parts Thereof... to
   Which Is Added a Word of Advice to Both Sexes in the Act
   of Copulation: And the Pictures of Several Monsterous
   Births Drawn to the Life*

COMPILER: Unknown

PUBLISHED: London: Printed for J. How, and are to be
   sold next door to the Anchor Tavern in Sweethings
   Rents in Cornhil, 1684

PAGES: ii + 190

TOTAL WORDS: 39,000

SIZE: 6" × 3¼" (15 × 8.5 cm)

WEIGHT: 5.7 oz. (160 g)

AREA: 26 ft² (2.4 m²)

who in Six Days Erected all Things for his Pleasure." Maybe *erected* is a
dirty pun, but the sentiment is wholesome enough, and the point is that
God created sex for humanity's pleasure—no heretical belief, but one
embraced by the Puritans themselves in seventeenth-century England.
"That Marriage is an Honourable State," wrote the author, "ordained by
God in Paradice, and since Confirmed by our Blessed Saviour, who
wrought his first Miracle at a Wedding, I hope none will deny; therefore
it is convenient that Parents well take care of their Daughters Chastity."[5]
No need to blush there.

Once the book gets going, though, there is little doubt that it should
be categorized as what Jean-Jacques Rousseau called a *"livre à lire d'une
seule main,"* a book to be read with one hand. It is telling that the
description of the female sex organs is far more expansive than that of
the male. The gynecological details are exceedingly frank for an age in
which such information was usually suppressed in print:

The parts that offer themselves to view, without any deduction, at
the bottom of the Belly, are the *Fissura Magna* or the Great Chink,
with its *Labia* or Lips, the *Mons Veneris* and the Hair, These parts

are called by the General Name of *Pudenda*, because when they are
bared they bring *Pudor* or Shame upon a woman. . . . The Clytoris
is a substance in the upper part of the Division, where the two
Wings concur and is the Seat of Venereal pleasure.[6]

And when, in the first few pages, the author promises "to Vnravel the
Mystery of Generation, and divers other Mysteries,"[7] we can assume
many readers' pulses raced.

The book stressed that the reason for sexuality is reproduction:
the author knew that "a young likely Couple" may well be "desirous of
Mutual Enjoyment," but he (she?) insisted that it was "for Generation-
sake, which is the chief End for which Wedlock was ordain'd." The
book offers no information about contraception, only pragmatic advice
for promoting pregnancy—warning, for instance, against withdrawal
too soon after "they have done what nature requires," so that they do
not lose "the fruit of the labour." There is a great deal of advice on
promoting fertility: be sure "to Copulate at distance of time, not too
often, nor yet too seldom, for both these hurt Fruitfulness alike; for
to eject immoderately, weakens a Man, and wastes his Spirits, and too
often causes the Seed by long continuance to be ineffectual, and not
manly enough." Sometimes, of course, the advice was distinctly presci-
entific: "Now the fittest time (they say) for the Procreation of Male
Children, is when the Sun is in *Leo*, and the Moons Sign is *Virgo*,
Scorpio, or *Sagitarius*."[8]

Still, even though procreation is the goal, a surprising amount is said
in favor of sexual pleasure—and, unusually for the age (or almost any
age), in favor of sexual pleasure for both men and women. Men, in the
author's opinion, are more strongly driven by lust—"GOD has firmly
impressed [sexual desire] in all Creatures . . . Male and Female; but
more especially on Man"—and this "unruly" energy requires constraint:
God "has thought it convenient to prescribe him Bounds, and confine
him to the Vse of the Matrimonial Bed; that so they might not defile
themselves with wandring Lust." But women, too, are sexual beings,
as the author revealed in the title to chapter 1: "Of Marriage, and at
what Age Virgins and Youths are Capable of the Marriage-Bed, and the
Reasons that prompts [*sic*] them to desire it."[9]

When nudged, female desire can be every bit as unruly as men's, particularly when, "the Spirits being brisk, and in a manner inflam'd when they arrive at this Age, if they eat salt sharp things, Spices, &c. whereby the Body becomes still more heated, then the irritation and proneness to Venereal Embraces, is very great, nay some times almost insuperable." While male and female desires have different motivations—"The Venereal Appetite . . . proceeds from different causes for in men it proceeds from a desire of Emission, and in women from a desire of Completion"—at least the author acknowledged female desire. Women needed to have sex, because prolonged virginity was bad for their health: "if a woman do not use Copulation to eject her Seed, she oftentimes falls into strange Diseases." Thus the grand anatomical analogy: "The Action of the *Clytoris* in women is like that of the *Penis* in men. . . . And as the *Glans* in man is the Seat of the greatest pleasure in Copulation, so is this in Women."[10] *Aristotle's Master-Piece* even suggested that pregnancy is impossible without the female orgasm—though this enlightened regard for women's pleasure tended to be removed from editions printed in the nineteenth century.[11]

Aristotle's Master-Piece had an astonishingly long afterlife. Bibliographers have counted more than 250 separate editions, but all of them survive only in tiny numbers of copies—libraries did not consider them worthy of preservation. Nonetheless, over the course of a full century, more than half the popular books on reproduction were versions of *Aristotle's Master-Piece*: "No other single text or group of texts came anywhere near such renown."[12] It was popular in colonial and republican America: in 1744, the preacher Jonathan Edwards scolded young men in Massachusetts for reading it.[13] Early in the nineteenth century it was mentioned in Sir Walter Scott's novel *Woodstock*, and it makes several appearances in James Joyce's *Ulysses*, where "Mr Bloom turned over idly pages of *The Awful Disclosures of Maria Monk*, then of Aristotle's *Masterpiece*. Crooked botched print. Plates: infants cuddled in a ball in bloodred wombs like livers of slaughtered cows. Lots of them like that at this moment all over the world. All butting with their skulls to get out of it. Child born every minute somewhere." Later in the book Molly Bloom gets the name wrong: "should we tell them even if its the truth they dont believe you then tucked up in bed like those babies in the

Aristocrats Masterpiece he brought me another time as if we hadnt enough of that in real life without some old Aristocrat or whatever his name is disgusting you more with those rotten pictures children with two heads and no legs thats the kind of villainy theyre always dreaming about."[14] Evelyn Waugh's *Vile Bodies* tips its cap to the book as well: a suspicious customs officer sorts through luggage and pulls out a printed list of books containing "Aristotle, Works of (Illustrated)." It could still be found in sex shops in Soho in the 1930s.[15]

⚮

Jack Harris (real name John Harrison), the "Pimp General of All England," was a waiter at the Shakespeare's Head tavern in Covent Garden, and although he held a respectable position as a justice of the peace, he was also a "procurer of lewd women for bawdy purposes." Harris apparently lent this modified form of his name—willingly or not—to Samuel Derrick, an Irish poet who was apparently responsible for at least the early editions, perhaps with his mistress.[16] Together they produced an eminently practical guide to London's strumpets, trulls, and doxies, along with useful information on their fees and the special services they would provide to those with sufficient funds.

There were sixteenth-century directories of prostitutes, such as the *Tariffa delle puttane di Venegia* (*Tariffs of Venetian Prostitutes*, 1535), and in the eighteenth century, English taverns typically kept handwritten lists of local prostitutes—just one of the services they provided to their customers. Prostitution was illegal, of course, but both the author and the users would have taken comfort in the fact that there was little organized law enforcement to do anything about it. And so the old guides were transformed into a new annual compendium on erotic gratification. The world depicted by *Harris's List* is one of hypercharged masculine sexual desire. As critic Elizabeth Denlinger puts it in one of the best accounts of the book, "What do men want? . . . [*Harris's List* says] that men want whores; that men want to read about whores; that men want to read about themselves successfully visiting whores."[17]

The earliest extant edition is from 1761, but an edition was advertised in April 1760, and there may have been a few before that. Annual publication was "timed to the Christmas season, when London was at its

TITLE: *Harris's List of Covent-Garden Ladies; or, New Atlantis for the Year 1761: To Which Is Annexed, The Ghost of Moll King; or A Night at Derry's*

COMPILER: Samuel Derrick? (1724–69)

PUBLISHED: London: Printed for H. Ranger, near Temple-Bar, 1761

PAGES: xxiv + 187

ENTRIES: 164

TOTAL WORDS: 38,000

SIZE: 6¼" × 3¾" (16 × 9.5 cm)

AREA: 33 ft² (3 m²)

PRICE: 2s. 6d. (apparently 1s. 6d. in 1760)

LATEST EDITION: *Harris's List of Covent-Garden Ladies; or, Man of Pleasure's Kalendar for the Year 1793* (London, 1793)

most crowded."[18] The 1761 edition contains 113 women in the main series, with 53 more tacked on in an appendix, and over the course of the *List*'s long history, the volumes were typically under 150 pages, covering somewhere between 120 and 190 prostitutes. It is possible that, at least in some of the later volumes, women paid to be included in the list—craigslist *avant la lettre*.[19]

The book was supposedly published by one H. Ranger, operating near Temple Bar on Fleet Street. But *ranger* was a term at the time for a womanizer, and the name is almost certainly a pseudonym. The early books seem to have actually been produced by a disreputable publisher named Joseph Burd. The prostitutes' names were technically concealed, but one need not have been a profound cryptographer to determine that "Miss L–w–s" is Miss Lewis, or "Mrs. H–m–lt–n" is Mrs. Hamilton. For each, the reader got a description of her appearance, an account of her prices, and a résumé of her particular charms: one prostitute was known for her "kisses fierce and fervent"; another "will *grasp* the *pointed weapon* with genuine female fortitude." Leering wordplay is common, sometimes verging on the pornographic. As Denlinger explains, the descriptions "combined appeals to the imagination of the sedentary reader and directions to the male walker of the streets ... names, addresses, and prices all point to their practical use, while the lush descriptions of women also function as soft-core pornography."[20] Not all the entries, though, were complimentary, as this one from 1773 shows:

Mrs. F–wl–r. To be found at C–rt–r's Bagnio, Bow-street.

"A Gorgon face, and serpent tongue."

This lady excels any we have mentioned—in ugliness. Her person coarse, her features the same, pock-marked, rude and uncouth in her behaviour; her skin we cannot say any thing about, as we are no judge of painting; and, notwithstanding, she is always well dressed: she married the son of a butcher in Bedford-street, whom she inveigled, and would have sent to the gallows, but, to his parents comfort, his death saved them from much sorrow.

She possesses every thing, in our opinion, that is disgustful; drinks, takes snuff, and swears like a trooper. She kept not long since a bawdy-house, and from that laudable profession turned out again. She is about 36, and the sooner we put an end to her character the better, as it is disagreeable to write, and we are sure must be so to read any more about her.

Sales of the book were brisk. One visitor to London said *Harris's List* sold eight thousand copies a year, though that seems unlikely. Even so, several volumes seem to have gone into second editions, and advertisements point out that copies sometimes sold so quickly as to become scarce. Of the thirty-six or so editions from 1760 to 1795, only seven appear in the standard bibliography of the period, and ten more have been tracked down in private collections.[21] This means roughly half the presumed editions are not known to exist anywhere, and most of the others are extremely scarce: a single copy survives of the 1761 edition, two of 1764, two of 1765, one of 1766, and none from 1767 through 1770.

Harris's List came to an ignominious ending in spring 1794, when the publishers were busted for releasing a certain "wicked, nasty, filthy, bawdy, and obscene" title.[22] They were victims of a new commitment to virtue. George III had issued a proclamation in 1787 "for the encouragement of piety and virtue," and the authorities responded by cracking down on both prostitution and pornography. In 1795, one of the *List*'s publishers was sent to Newgate prison for a year and ordered to post £150 security for three years.

※

Sex manuals gained a new prominence in the seventeenth and eighteenth centuries, and in the late nineteenth century, human sexuality began to be the subject of scientific rather than strictly moralistic inquiry. One of the most important results was *Psychopathia Sexualis: Eine klinisch-forensische Studie* (1886), by Richard Freiherr von Krafft-Ebing. It was one of the first modern, scientific surveys of sexual practice, though Krafft-Ebing still worried about appealing to the wrong crowd. "In order that unqualified persons should not become readers," he wrote, "the author saw himself compelled to choose a title understood only by the learned, and also, where possible, to express himself in *terminis techinicis*. It seemed necessary also to give particularly revolting portions in Latin rather than in German."[23]

By the middle of the twentieth century, sex research was beginning to attract attention among the larger public. Books like *Our Bodies, Ourselves*, published in 1973 by the Boston Women's Health Book Collective, broke new ground by bringing a feminist concern with women's health to the encyclopedia format. It was part of a movement in the 1970s that brought sex advice to the respectable middle-class world, above all with Alex Comfort's *The Joy of Sex: A Cordon Bleu Guide to Lovemaking* (1972). Comfort was an amazingly versatile writer. His first book, *The Silver River*, an account of his South Atlantic travels, appeared before he was eighteen, and three years later he published his first novel, *No Such Liberty*, while he was a student at Cambridge University. He got his bachelor's degree in 1943 and his M.A. in 1945, before earning a Ph.D. at the University of London in 1949. A year after taking his doctorate he published the anarchist tract *Authority and Delinquency in the Modern State*, as well as his first book on the subject for which he would be remembered, *Sexual Behaviour in Society*. From there it was on to the Royal College of Physicians and London Hospital, where he qualified in medicine and specialized in gerontology. That was the subject of a learned book, *The Biology of Senescence*, 1956, a subject he revisited for a popular audience in 1964 in *The Process of Aging*.

In *The Joy of Sex*, the author's name is rendered more respectable by the author's credentials—"Alex Comfort, M.B., Ph.D."—on the cover, a modern version of the attribution to the eminently respectable Aristotle. Comfort's title echoed *The Joy of Cooking*, one of the most popular American cookbooks since its first publication in 1936. And the subtitle, with its promise of *cordon bleu*–style sex, no doubt cashed in on the craze for gourmet cooking that had swept America starting with Julia Child's *Mastering the Art of French Cooking* (1961). Newly sophisticated palates, no longer content with tuna casseroles and Spam sandwiches, now wanted *foie de veau à la moutarde* and *filets de poisson à la Bretonne*. Comfort, or perhaps his publisher's marketing department, was shrewd in promising a similarly sophisticated set of recipes for *l'amour*. With its scandalously frank discussion of sex—including positions other than missionary, and even venturing into swinging and spanking—it has been credited with sparking the sexual revolution. But in the long perspective, we can see that what appeared so new on its publication was part of a tradition that goes back centuries.

T HE WRITERS DISCUSSED in this book range from harmless drudges to mighty emperors, from retiring scholars to revolutionary provocateurs. The reference shelf holds the works of child prodigies and wizened sages, profound linguists and mathematical geniuses. And yet one group is very poorly represented among the editors of reference books: women.

Men, of course, have been much more visible in public life through most of history, and any list of great public achievements is going to be disproportionately male. But the exclusion of women is rarely as complete as it is in reference publishing. It is not hard to come up with great women poets, novelists, mathematicians, scientists, philosophers, and artists from antiquity to the present. But female lexicographers or encyclopedists are in exceedingly short supply. Women must have been active among the compilers of information—wives and sisters of the named editors probably did much of the real work in books credited to men—but, if so, they have left few traces.

Though women have been hard to find on mastheads, they have long been imagined as part of a target audience. Robert Cawdrey's *Table Alphabeticall* (1604) was notoriously "gathered for the benefit & helpe of ladies, gentlewomen, or any other vnskilfull persons"; Henry Cockeram's *English Dictionarie* (1623) was pitched at "ladies and gentlewomen" as well as foreigners; and Thomas Blount's *Glossographia* "is chiefly intended for the more-knowing Women, and less-knowing Men."[1] *The British School-Master; or, The English Spelling-Book* included in its second edition (1722) a "vocabulary of most sorts of provisions, apparel, household furniture, &c. Very useful for all ladies, housekeepers, &c. who are defective in spelling." But even these books that claimed to enlighten women gave them shoddy treatment between their covers. The first edition of the *Encyclopædia Britannica* (1769–71), for instance, devoted all of one line to the entry "WOMAN, the female of man. See HOMO," and the *Encyclopédie* was just as dismissive. The first edition of Nathan Bailey's *Dictionarium Britannicum* (1730) did not even offer a definition, just an etymology (and an inaccurate one at that): "WO'MAN [wiman, prob. of wamb and man, *Sax.*]." The *Dictionnaire de l'Académie françoise* (1694) likewise defined *femme* as "La femelle de l'homme"—the female of man—and then offered some instructive sentences containing the word: "God took woman from Adam's side," "women are naturally timid," "that man is addicted to wine and women."

There have been a few reference books specifically for women, some—though not all—written by women as well. In 1694 *The Ladies Dictionary: Being a General Entertainment for the Fair-Sex: A Work Never Attempted Before in English* was published by "N.H.," who had grand plans for "such a Book, as might be a 𝕮𝖔𝖒𝖕𝖑𝖊𝖆𝖙 𝕯𝖎𝖗𝖊𝖈𝖙𝖔𝖗𝖞 to the *Female-Sex* in all *Relations, Companies, Conditions and States* of Life; even from CHILD HOOD down to *Old-Age*, and from the *Lady* at the Court, to the *Cook-maid* in the Country."[2] Some entries offered definitions—"𝕻𝖗𝖊𝖌𝖓𝖆𝖓𝖙, big with Child; also full, copious, ripe"—though not all are useful: "𝕺𝖑𝖎𝖛𝖊, from the Olive Tree" is unlikely to illuminate those who were in darkness. Others offered cultural literacy: "𝕻𝖍𝖎𝖑𝖔𝖒𝖊𝖑𝖆, flying from *Tereus*, who had ravish'd her, and cut her Tongue out," or "𝕾𝖆𝖕𝖕𝖍𝖔, stil'd for her curious Verse, the tenth Muse, but her wanton way of Writing hindered much of the Merit of them." More common, though, were the moral lectures:

> We find by lamentable, if I may not say, fatal Experience, that the world too much allows *nakedness* in Women; and 'tis now pass'd into a custom so general, that it is become common almost to all Women and Maids of all sorts of conditions. . . . Let us strive . . . to make these Women know how great their Fault is in coming to Church in such indecent Habit, and if I may presume to say, so as it were *half naked.*

There is much on sexual immorality: "𝕻𝖗𝖔𝖘𝖙𝖎𝖙𝖚𝖙𝖊, (*prostituta*) she that for many suffers her self to be abused by all that come, a common

Harlot," or "𝕻rostitute 𝕯oxies . . . will for good Victuals, or for a very small piece of Money, prostitute their Bodies . . . they are destructive Queans, and oftentimes secret Murtherers of the 𝕴nfants which are illegitimately begotten of their bodies." We know nothing of the author, but the word "your" in "The *Virtues and Accomplishments* of your *Sex*"[3] gives a a strong hint that N.H. was a man—as does the condescension throughout.

The M. U. Sears who wrote *The Female's Encyclopædia* (1830) identifies herself as a woman, but we have to trust her on that; the name appears on no other books. (Perhaps she was the wife or sister of the publisher W. J. Sears.) The book is hardly a model of feminist enlightenment. Though it offered useful information, some of the advice is hard for modern sensibilities to tolerate. A section on "Learned Ladies" advises that "A lady should appear to think well of books, rather than to speak well of them"[4]—a nineteenth-century precursor of the girls-who-wear-glasses tagline. The author was convinced that "not more than one woman in fifty has it in her power to marry the man whom she really would prefer to all others." "Women," Sears declared, "are to conceal their feelings, although they like any of the other sex, or they will appear bold, and become objects of ridicule; and a lady of delicacy would rather die, than first disclose her partiality."[5]

More heartening was Matilda Betham's *Biographical Dictionary of the Celebrated Women of Every Age and Country* (1804). Betham set out to write "a General Dictionary of Women, who had been distinguished by their actions or talents, . . . which had never been done in our language."[6] Not all her celebrated women were role models, and she backed away from then-controversial feminists like Mary Wollstonecraft. But she consistently tried to see things from women's point of view. Even Boadicea, usually depicted as a villainess of the first water, got a sympathetic three-page portrait. Eve, the source of all earthly evil in a long misogynist tradition, was "seduced by the evil spirit." Betham's dictionary is almost a precursor of *A Feminist Dictionary* by Cheris Kramarae, Paula A. Treichler, and Ann Russo, published in 1985 at the height of second-wave feminism.

In the long history of reference books, women have rarely received their due, and even more rarely have been in charge of the text. Yet there are a few honorable exceptions to the male-only rule. The late twelfth-century *Hortus deliciarum*, or *Garden of Delights*, was composed by Herrad of Landsberg, the abbess of Hohenburg, which may make it the oldest reference book by a woman. More recent is the work of Jacoba H. van Lessen, a lexicographer who joined the *Woordenboek der Nederlansche taal*—the greatest dictionary of the Dutch language, and one of the greatest dictionaries in the world—in 1929. Seventeen years later she was promoted to editor in chief, a position she held until her death in 1951. Susan Standring published the thirty-ninth edition of *Gray's Anatomy* in 2004, Marie-Hélène Corréard and Valerie Grundy edited the *Oxford–Hachette French Dictionary*, and Susan Ratcliffe is now editor of the *Oxford Dictionary of Quotations*. But they remain the distinguished exceptions.

Even in the twenty-first century, men still far outnumber women at the head of reference projects. Plenty of women work as lexicographers, but few have their name at the top of the masthead. And the brave new world of online reference does not seem much better. Jimmy Wales of Wikipedia estimates contributors are "80 percent male, more than 65 percent single, more than 85 percent without children, around 70 percent under the age of 30"[7]—and some think that 80 percent figure is an underestimate. The Wikimedia Foundation estimates just 13 percent of Wikipedia contributors are women.

CHAPTER 13

COLLECTING KNOWLEDGE INTO THE SMALLEST AREA

The Great Encyclopedias

Denis Diderot and	*Encyclopædia Britannica*
Jean le Rond d'Alembert	1768–71
L'Encyclopédie	
1751–72	

RANCE AND BRITAIN had incompatible ideas about the role of authority in their dictionaries, with the Académie Française calling for an officially enforced standard of linguistic propriety and the English taking a more laissez-faire approach to the language. More differences appear in their attitudes toward the encyclopedia. This time, though, the French were not the authoritarians. The *Encyclopédie* was a product of radical Enlightenment philosophy, and its authors sought to overturn conventional pieties. British encyclopedists, conversely, sought to consolidate the received learning of the ages and pass it on to the next generation.

Ambitiously wide-ranging books were all the rage in seventeenth-century Europe. In 1677, Johann Jacob Hofmann, a professor at the University of Basel, published two sizable folios and called the work a *Lexicon universale historico-geographico-chronologico-poetico-philologicum.* In case that list of disciplines was not grandiose enough, in 1701 Fra Vincenzo Coronelli published the beginning of his *Biblioteca Universale, o sia Gran Dizionario Storico, Geografico, Antico, Moderno, Naturale, Poetico, Cronologico, Genealogico, Matematico, Politico, Botanico, Medico, Chimico, Giuridico, Filosofico, Teologico, e Biblico.* It was supposed to reach forty-five volumes, but Coronelli died after producing just seven, and he took his erudition with him to the grave. But another monster of a work—sixty-four volumes and 64,309 pages—appeared between 1731 and 1750, when the publisher Johann Heinrich Zedler, supported by nine editors, produced the *Grosses vollständiges Universal-Lexicon aller Wissenschaften und Künste*, or *Complete Universal Lexicon of all Sciences and Arts*, described in one source as "the most colossal of German compilations."[1]

England had its own encyclopedias, foremost among them Ephraim Chambers's *Cyclopædia; or, A Universal Dictionary of Arts and Sciences*, 2 vols. (1727, with 1728 on the title page), an attempt to explicate the mysteries of hundreds of trades when Britain was gearing up for the Industrial Revolution. Chambers, the son of Presbyterian farmers from the northwest of England, had worked as the apprentice to a bookseller, engraver, and globe maker. When his apprenticeship was over, he settled at Gray's Inn and began a career as a journalist and translator.[2] His *Cyclopædia* was announced as the product of "*E. CHAMBERS* Gent."— no mere tradesman he. But to judge by the title, modesty was not among Chambers's gentlemanly virtues:

> *Cyclopædia; or, An Universal Dictionary of Arts and Sciences; Containing the Definitions of the Terms, and Accounts of the Things Signify'd Thereby, in the Several Arts, Both Liberal and Mechanical, and the Several Sciences, Human and Divine: The Figures, Kinds, Properties, Productions, Preparations, and Uses, of Things Natural and Artificial; the Rise, Progress, and State of Things Ecclesiastical, Civil, Military, and Commercial: With the Several Systems, Sects, Opinions, &c. among Philosophers, Divines, Mathematicians, Physicians, Antiquaries, Criticks, &c.: The Whole Intended as a Course of Antient and Modern Learning: Compiled from the Best Authors, Dictionaries, Journals, Memoirs, Transactions, Ephemerides, &c. in Several Languages.*

The book was priced at four guineas to subscribers—a huge amount, maybe two months' wages for an unskilled day laborer. But sales were good, and Chambers was rumored to have been given a £500 honorarium by his publishers as a token of their gratitude. After his death in 1740, his *Cyclopædia* continued to grow. The fourth edition appeared in 1741, followed in 1753 by a huge two-volume *Supplement*.

These are formidable books, but few of them can be described as works of genius. Not so the *Dictionnaire historique et critique* (1697), a gloriously eccentric exploration of people considered important by the philosophical and political revolutionary Pierre Bayle. Bayle's father and brothers were killed for their Protestantism, and Bayle himself, after concealing his faith, fled France for Protestant Rotterdam. There he worked on his oversized *Dictionnaire*—despite the title, more of an encyclopedia than a dictionary. Bayle was as driven as any scholar has ever been. "Plays, pleasure-parties, games, collations, excursions into the country, visiting, and the like recreations," he said, "necessary to many students, as they say, are not in my line. I waste no time in that way. Neither do I waste time in domestic cares, nor in trying for place or for favor, nor in any such matters."[3]

The *Dictionnaire* is an intensely quirky book. The main text is a biographical encyclopedia of major thinkers from Aaron to Zuylichem. But that main text occupies just a narrow band at the top—most of every page is occupied by long, discursive footnotes, even footnotes on footnotes, that question and subvert the main text by challenging conventional religious, philosophical, and moral beliefs. A revolutionary treatise emerges in the notes: what looks at first like a biographical dictionary is actually a fierce work of advocacy for religious toleration, and an equally fierce attack on conventional moral principles.[4] The *Dictionnaire* enjoyed the two sure signs of influence: rapid sales among the public, and rapid censorship by church and state. It was officially banned in France (not that the ban hurt sales), and the Reformed Church in Rotterdam summoned Bayle and quizzed him on his heresies.[5] But over the years the *Dictionnaire* numbered among its devoted readers Frederick the Great of Prussia, Voltaire, Edward Gibbon, and Lord Byron.[6]

❧

The encyclopedic background, then, is deep, but much greater was to come. The eighteenth century was Europe's greatest age of encyclopedias: more than fifty major general encyclopedias appeared in that period. And the greatest of them all so dominates the field that it is called simply *L'Encyclopédie*, as if all the others didn't matter. The *Encyclopédie, ou dictionnaire raisonné des sciences, des arts et des métiers*

(*The Encyclopedia, or Systematic Dictionary of Sciences, Arts, and Trades*) appeared between 1751 and 1766. It is not merely one of the world's great reference books but one of the towering monuments of European intellectual history—even one of the most influential works in world literature. The historian Hans Koning makes a bold but defensible claim: "Perhaps no other book, or set of books, has ever had the impact in its century of those twenty-eight volumes."[7]

The two guiding lights were Jean le Rond d'Alembert and Denis Diderot. D'Alembert, the illegitimate son of an aristocratic soldier and a renegade nun turned salonnière, was a scientific and mathematical prodigy.[8] When just twenty-six, he published a pathbreaking work on Newtonian mechanics, and he became a member of three of Europe's leading learned societies: the Académie des Sciences, the Königlich-Preußische Akademie der Wissenschaften, and the Royal Society. His partner seems, at least at first, as different from him as can be. Diderot is famous as one of the greatest conversationalists of all time, owing to a uniquely powerful mind. He dabbled in "philosophical writing" when "philosophical" was a euphemism for anything that threatened the power of the state. The range of his interests has rarely been matched: he wrote poetry, novels, plays, literary criticism, philosophy, music criticism, scientific works, translations, and more. Unlike d'Alembert, whose mathematical writings attracted little notice from the authorities, Diderot was arrested in 1749 for his writings.

The publishers' original plan for *L'Encyclopédie* was simply a French translation of Chambers's *Cyclopædia*. Diderot and d'Alembert were hired to supervise the translation, and d'Alembert in particular thought he was being invited only as an editor for the mathematical entries. "Borrowing" other nations' reference books was common; Diderot himself had just finished translating and adapting Robert James's medical dictionary. Once Diderot and d'Alembert got their hands on the project, though, they radically reconceived it. They were probably without revolutionary intentions at first—no one imagined an encyclopedia becoming the center of an intellectual firestorm. Eventually, though, they proposed a wholly new kind of book, "nothing less than the basic facts and the basic principles of all knowledge; it was to be a war machine of the thought and opinion of the Enlightenment."[9]

TITLE: *Encyclopédie, ou dictionnaire raisonné des sciences,*
des arts et des métiers, par une société de gens de lettres
COMPILER: Denis Diderot (1713–84) and Jean le Rond
d'Alembert (1717–83)
ORGANIZATION: Alphabetical, from *a* to *Zzuéné*
PUBLISHED: Paris, 1751–72; index 1780
VOLUMES: 28 (17 of text, 11 of illustrations) + 5 vols.
supplement
PAGES: 18,000
ENTRIES: 71,818
ILLUSTRATIONS: 2,885
TOTAL WORDS: 20 million
SIZE: 15½" × 9½" (39.5 × 24.5 cm)
AREA: 18,600 ft² (1,742 m²)
WEIGHT: 246 lb. (112 kg)
PRICE: 280 livres to subscribers

Two works lay out the principles: Diderot's *Proposals*, published separately before the rest of the book, and d'Alembert's *Preliminary Discourse*, published at the beginning of volume 1. Diderot grandly said the book would "serve all the purposes of a library for a professional man on any subject apart from his own,"[10] and d'Alembert justified the project as a whole. The *Preliminary Discourse* in particular is a manifesto—not merely for a reference book, but for the whole of the intellectual enterprise known as the Enlightenment. It is a discourse on method, "an adjustment of the rationalist spirit of Descartes to the empiricism of Locke and Newton—a fusion of traditions which lies at the foundation of the *Encyclopedia*."[11]

The *Preliminary Discourse* opens with humanity's instincts for self-preservation and natural desire for knowledge. D'Alembert distinguished the things we can know with certainty from the things we can know with probability, the things that must be true from the things that happen to be true. He then turned to what he called an "art"—"any system of knowledge which can be reduced to positive and invariable rules independent of caprice or opinion"[12]—and distinguished the "liberal" from the "mechanical" arts—those that can be performed by the mind and those that are performed by hand.

Having laid out the first principles on which the arts were founded, the encyclopedists began their survey of all of human knowledge. The *Encyclopédie's* seventy thousand articles were written by the leading figures of the Enlightenment: Rousseau, Voltaire, Montesquieu, and d'Holbach were all among the *encyclopédistes.* "The encyclopedic arrangement of our knowledge," they wrote, "consists of collecting knowledge into the smallest area possible and of placing the philosopher at a vantage point . . . high above the vast labyrinth, whence he can perceive the principal sciences and the arts simultaneously."[13]

The first two volumes appeared together in 1751, and the production was messy. Different sizes of capital letters are used for headwords, apparently without rhyme or reason. "In the typographical tangle of the *Encyclopédie*," wrote one critic, "titles occasionally appear italicized in upper case, italicized and in lower case, or in a combination of words in capital letters and lower case words, either italicized or not italicized." Some articles are signed with the names of their contributors, but many were not, and while it was once assumed that Diderot was responsible for all the unsigned articles, it now appears that there was nothing systematic about the practice.[14]

At first glance, there is nothing especially revolutionary about the articles. In volume 8, for instance, published in 1765, there are entries on the *hypotenuse* ("the longest side of a right triangle . . . The *word* is Greek, from ὑπὸ, under, and τείνω, extend"), *Janéiro* ("South American river on the coast of Brazil"), *Iliad* ("name of an epic poem, the first and most perfect of those that Homer wrote. See EPIC"), *imitation* ("It is the artistic representation of an object. Blind nature imitates nothing; it is art that imitates"), *immeubles* ("These are fixed goods that have a known location, and that cannot be transported to another place"), and so on. The very long entry *imprimerie* 'printing press' is typical of the focus on the skilled trades. It opens with a definition of printing before moving into a long discussion of the history of printing with movable type, an account of technical aspects such as justification, the roles of the compositor and proofreader, an account of the differences in printing folio, quarto, octavo, and duodecimo, and so on.

And yet a more careful look at that same volume reveals content that made the authorities nervous: as John Lough notes, "passages reflecting the outlook of the Enlightenment are hidden away in the most unlikely places."[15] The articles on *ignorance* and *illusion*, for instance, are illuminating glances into Enlightenment ideas about the source of knowledge. While a less heterodox work might explain ignorance and illusion in religious terms—becoming enlightened means approaching biblical truth—the *encyclopédistes* had a strictly secular conception of these matters. And it gets more explicit still. That same volume includes an article for *Jésuite*, and although it opens with a declaration that there is no original research here—"We say nothing here ourselves. This article is just a brief and faithful summary of accounts given in court"—in fact it is a devastating portrait of fanatical and bloodthirsty zealots. The entry on *Jésus-Christ* is less direct; the encyclopédistes could not blaspheme the Savior. They could, however, get in more subtle digs: "Jesus Christ, founder of the Christian religion. We can call this religion *the best philosophy*"—not that it *is* the best, only that we can *call* it that. The early Christians come across as narrow-minded: "I don't know why the early disciples of *Jesus* criticized Platonism ... Doesn't every system of philosophy have some truths?" The Church Fathers were also "sometimes embarrassed by logical fallacies, and their arguments were unsound"—and of course "They have contempt for reason and science."

The book's revolutionary project was noticed, and conservatives, especially in the Church, were alarmed. The authors went through the motions of disavowing heresy. D'Alembert's *Preliminary Discourse*, for instance, flirts with danger in speaking of "however absurd a religion might be"—but then tries to dodge responsibility with the parenthetical qualification "(a reproach which only impiety can make of ours)."[16] And while they insisted that priests should be telling us nothing about this world—that is the business of humanity—they were careful to acknowledge the existence of a creator, to avoid problems with the Church.

No one was fooled. Friends in high places staved off prosecution for a while, but when that protection was exhausted, the civil and ecclesiastical authorities were out for blood, and they took action against not only the contributors but the book itself. The police organized burnings of the manuscripts, and subscribers were ordered to surrender their copies to the nearest post office. Copies of the book were locked in the Bastille as if they were themselves criminals.[17] Nevertheless, the contributors continued working clandestinely. In fact, the scandal attracted kindred souls as contributors to the later volumes. But the whole project became much riskier. D'Alembert largely withdrew, remaining involved only on uncontroversial entries on mathematical subjects.

More than one critic has summarized the influence of the *Encyclopédie* on French thought. It promoted skepticism about traditional claims, willingness to question the authority of both the Church and the state, discontent with the status quo, and determination to make the world better through the application of reason. And soon these very qualities would shake the foundations of the French nation. Though it would be foolish to offer any monocausal explanation for an epochal event in world history, it is hard to overstate the significance of the *Encyclopédie* in turning society upside down in 1789. Entries such as *peuple* 'people', *droit naturel* 'natural right', and *autorité politique* 'political authority' offered new ways to think about statecraft. "Seventeen years after completion of publication," wrote Koning, "and as an unmistakable sequel, came the French Revolution."[18]

⬥

A work much less interesting in its first incarnation became the more successful franchise. The *Encyclopædia Britannica* (1768–71) was Britain's answer to the *Encyclopédie*.

The *Encyclopædia Britannica* was not the first Britannic encyclopedia, but the story in Great Britain is different from the story on the Continent. Although colossal works of profound erudition were all the rage in seventeenth-century Europe, the English got in on the act late, in 1704, when the clergyman John Harris published his *Lexicon Technicum; or, An Universal English Dictionary of Arts and Sciences Explaining Not Only the Terms of Art, but the Arts Themselves*. The alphabetical arrangement and the large scale (8,200 entries) were new in Britain, and the emphasis on science and technology was new anywhere. "Technical Harris," as he was called, may have begun the practice of tapping experts to contribute to encyclopedias, since one entry was written by Isaac Newton—though it is also possible that he simply plagiarized Newton without permission.[19] He and Ephraim Chambers satisfied British readers for much of the eighteenth century, but when the *Encyclopédie* appeared, the British knew at once that they were outclassed. They decided they needed a comparable work with systematic coverage of all areas of knowledge.

Like *L'Encyclopédie*, the project began as the brainchild of publishers, this time Colin Macfarquhar and Andrew Bell, based in Edinburgh. The location is important: coming out of Scotland, this was a *British* project, not an English one. The political entity called Great Britain was only a few decades old, and the *Britannica* embraced the Union and celebrated a British identity founded on liberty. Macfarquhar and Bell hired another Scot, William Smellie, to do the real work. The son of an architect, Smellie was born in 1740 in the suburbs of Edinburgh. He received a classical education at his grammar school, but had to leave school at the age of twelve. He was then put to work as the apprentice to a stay maker, constructing women's undergarments from whalebone. He found the work distasteful and was glad when he got a job as a proofreader. It was a good position for an autodidact, who had taught himself sciences and languages and even became a founding member of the Newtonian Society, an Edinburgh club that promoted literary and especially scientific learning. At the time he was "as devoted to whiskey as to scholarship,"[20] but he seems to have kept his drinking under control while he worked on the book.

On June 8, 1768, the publishers issued a prospectus seeking subscribers for a work of one hundred weekly installments, to begin in November of that year. Each twenty-four-page number would cost sixpence; the well-off could spend an extra twopence for high-grade paper.[21] (Those who paid the surcharge were probably disappointed, since the printing of the whole set was sloppy; the page numbering was often wrong, and at one point two hundred page numbers were skipped.)

Even Smellie's most ardent defenders had to admit that his was not a work of profound original research. His biographer wrote that he "used to say jocularly, that he had made a Dictionary of Arts and Sciences with a *pair of scissors*, clipping out from various books a *quantum suffcit* of matter for the printer." Far from denying his dependence on other sources, he advertised his wide reading in more than 150 books.

TITLE: *Encyclopædia Britannica; or, A Dictionary of Arts and Sciences, Compiled upon a New Plan: In Which the Different Sciences and Arts are Digested into Distinct Treatises or Systems; and the Various Technical Terms, &c. Are Explained*

COMPILER: William Smellie (1740–95)

ORGANIZATION: Alphabetical, *Aa* to *zygophyllum*, with eighteen very long "treatises" and many short entries

PUBLISHED: First in 100 weekly parts beginning in January 1768, then in three volumes, Edinburgh: Printed for A. Bell and C. Macfarquhar and sold by Colin Macfarquhar at this printing-office, Nicolson-street, 1771

VOLUMES: 3

PAGES: 2,382

ENTRIES: 18,600

TOTAL WORDS: 2.6 million

SIZE: 10" × 8" (25.4 × 20.3 cm)

AREA: 1,314 ft^2 (122.8m^2)

WEIGHT: 13¾ lb. (6.3kg)

PRICE: £2 10s. (£3 7s. on fine paper)

LATEST EDITION: 15th ed., 1974, 32 vols., approx. 40 million words

He claims to have "had recourse to the best books upon almost every subject, extracted the useful parts, and rejected whatever appeared trifling or less interesting." In fact he seems to have cited some books that he never actually read, relying on secondhand summaries.[22]

About a third of the Encyclopædia is taken up by eighteen long entries called "treatises": agriculture, algebra, anatomy, arithmetic, astronomy, bookkeeping, botany, chemistry, farriery (caring for horses), geometry, law, medicine, metaphysics, midwifery, moral philosophy, music, navigation, and surgery.[23] The rest of the entries were very brief, most no more than fifteen lines. Some subjects were omitted altogether:

there were no biographical entries at all. There was plenty about falconry but nothing about historical method. As Smellie put it in his preface, "Utility ought to be the principal intention of every publication. Wherever this intention does not plainly appear, neither the books nor their authors have the smallest claim to the approbation of mankind."[24] That is characteristic of the British approach to practicality, and Smellie's biographer explained that the Newtonian Society was named "in honour of the immortal NEWTON, the author, so to speak, of the true science of nature, as founded upon observation and rigid mathematical induction, in opposition to the wild theories of DESCARTES and others."[25] British common sense trumps airy-fairy French theorizing.

Unlike the *Encyclopédie*, the *Britannica* is conventional in its religious beliefs. And even though it was created by a Scot during the Scottish Enlightenment, the radical figures who played such a large role in that movement were absent from the *Britannica*. Unlike the freethinkers of the French Enlightenment, the Scots at the helm of *Britannica* had no interest in tearing down old structures of knowledge. That is not to say religious subjects were avoided entirely. Islam received a great deal of attention; the entry *Mahometans* is seventeen pages long, and the articles on *Alcoran* (that is, the Qur'an), *caliph, hegira,* and *mosque* are clear, thoughtful, and, by the standards of the age, reasonably impartial.[26] The only entry that seems to have stirred real controversy in its day was the long treatise on *midwifery*, with its associated illustrations. According to some sources, moralists were scandalized by the explicit gynecological details and urged readers to tear out the offending pages.

Considering the book's monumental importance over the next two and a half centuries, we know frustratingly little about what early readers made of it. None of the great writers of the day—James Boswell, David Hume, Adam Smith—left any comments on the first edition of the *Britannica*, and the few comments we do have by others are mostly negative. Sales, though, were apparently good enough to warrant London reprints in 1773 and 1775, for a total of maybe three thousand sets.[27]

※

The *Encyclopédie* was a one-off—no one has ever had the temerity to produce *Encyclopédie II*. The book's influence can be measured not in the number of subsequent editions but in terms of the skeptical, Enlightenment-friendly conception of the world that emerged from it, and it may well have contributed to the collapse of the Ancien Régime.

The compilers of the *Britannica*, on the other hand, had more modest ambitions than those of Diderot and d'Alembert, but their book has stayed alive. The first edition was seriously flawed by any measure, but its sales were enough to lead to a second edition, which introduced biography. It was so successful that it was promptly pirated in an American edition (with the offensive word *Britannica* and the dedication to the hated George III omitted). By the time of the third edition in eighteen volumes (1788–97), it was much larger than any other English-language encyclopedia, and it began to feature entries contributed by experts in various disciplines.[28] The book continued to grow. *Britannica* hit twenty-two volumes and 17,801 pages with the seventh edition of 1842. *Meliora*, a quarterly review, was rapturous about the eighth edition, calling it "the greatest collection of literary wealth ever compiled. . . . Three hundred and forty writers . . . have united their learning to make this gigantic store-house of knowledge. The possession of such a work is a library, for its matter is equal to one hundred ordinary octavo volumes. No library of English literature is complete without this Encyclopaedia."[29] *Britannica* connoisseurs are especially enamored of the eleventh edition (published November 1910), which continues to sell briskly on the secondhand market.

DICTIONARY OR ENCYCLOPEDIA?

T HIS BOOK USES terms like *dictionary, encyclopedia, thesaurus, atlas,* and so on, on the assumption that readers will be able to tell them apart. Usually it's easy. Two reference genres, though, are disconcertingly close to each other: the dictionary and the encyclopedia.

Dictionaries are traditionally about words and encyclopedias about things, but many works we would call encyclopedias were originally published as dictionaries or lexicons (such as John Harris's *Lexicon Technicum* of 1704, the *New Royal and Universal Dictionary of Arts and Sciences* of 1769–71, and, across the Channel, Bayle's *Dictionnaire historique et critique* of 1697), and many works called themselves by both names apparently interchangeably (such as Ephraim Chambers's *Cyclopædia; or, An Universal Dictionary of Arts and Sciences* and the *Encyclopædia Britannica; or, A Dictionary of Arts and Sciences* of 1771).

Still, we can make some generalizations. Entries in encyclopedias tend to be longer than those in dictionaries, and encyclopedias usually cover just nouns, while dictionaries cover all the parts of speech. Some say a dictionary cannot be translated into another language, whereas an encyclopedia can be. Whether or not that definition will hold up to serious scrutiny, it's not a bad test. Dictionaries also tend to exclude proper nouns (people, places), unless in appendixes.

As soon as we establish those rules, though, reality intrudes. Law dictionaries, biographical dictionaries, gardening dictionaries—all are really encyclopedias. And some encyclopedic information tends to find its way into even the general-purpose dictionaries: the proper names *Lothario* or *Einstein* have come to serve as synonyms for *lover* and *genius,* and in that sense they need to be defined rather than discussed. Some dictionaries offer other encyclopedic information, such as the altitudes of mountains, lists of kings and presidents, characters in famous works of literature, populations of cities, and so on. (American dictionaries have been more welcoming of encyclopedic information than dictionaries hailing from Britain.)

A dictionary explains that a *barometer* is a device for measuring atmospheric pressure, and an encyclopedia explains how a barometer is constructed, how it measures the atmosphere, and what the readings mean. But the two often run into each other. Most encyclopedias start out with a short dictionary definition, and many dictionaries will venture into encyclopedic information, whether they want to or not. Even *Webster's Eleventh Collegiate*, a dictionary that avowedly has no room for encyclopedic information, defines *barometer* as "an instrument for determining the pressure of the atmosphere and hence for assisting in forecasting weather and for determining altitude"—but the uses to which the instrument is put are really part of an encyclopedic understanding, not a linguistic one.

One of the great sources of frustration over the publication of *Webster's Third New International Dictionary* in 1961 was its abandonment of nearly all the encyclopedic information; many reviewers were emphatically not pleased. The *Second* (1934) was loaded with encyclopedic information—lists of presidents and popes, characters in Dickens and Shakespeare, hundreds of figures from mythology, thousands of places, and thirteen thousand "noteworthy persons." It aspired to be the only reference book an educated person needed on his or her shelves. Not so the *Third*: all that information was unceremoniously deleted. It was to be pure dictionary. Some critics were appalled: "Think if you can," wrote one reviewer, "of a dictionary from which you cannot learn who Mark Twain was ... or what were the names of the apostles."[1]

And yet even the resolutely lexical *Webster's Third* manages to sneak encyclopedic information in, though not in the obvious places. The etymologies sometimes contain digressions, and even some of the definitions struggle to draw the line between lexical and encyclopedic material. The notorious *Webster's Third* entry for *hotel* is practically an encyclopedia entry masquerading as a dictionary definition:

hotel: a building of many rooms chiefly for overnight accommodation of transients and several floors served by elevators, usually with a large open street-level lobby containing easy chairs, with a variety of compartments for eating, drinking, dancing, exhibitions, and group meetings (as of salesmen or convention attendants), with shops having both inside and street-side entrances and offering for sale items (as clothes, gifts, candy, theater tickets, travel tickets) of particular interest to a traveler, or providing personal services (as hairdressing, shoe shining), and with telephone booths, writing tables and washrooms freely available.

CHAPTER 14

OF REDHEADS AND BABUS

Dictionaries and Empire

Inamura Sampaku	Henry Yule and
Haruma-wage	Arthur C. Burnell
1796	*Hobson-Jobson*
	1886

THE EARLIEST DICTIONARIES in most traditions are not the monolingual volumes we most often use but bilingual works serving as a link between two linguistic communities. That makes sense: the need to communicate with others who do not understand you at all has often been more urgent than pinning down all the subtleties of a language. And some of those bilingual dictionaries played an essential role in a nation's imperial ambitions. The Spanish in early America, for instance, had to deal with native languages. An anonymous and unpublished eighteenth-century *Bocabularia en lengua Quiche y Castellana* (*K'iche'–Spanish Vocabulary*) was aimed at helping Spanish conquistadors communicate with their new Mayan conquests. The Spanish side of the vocabulary reveals the missionary function: *diablo* (devil), *disciplinado* (disciplined), *dicipulo* (disciple), *divinidad de Dios* (divinity of God). The same is clear in another K'iche'–Spanish dictionary from 1745, with native equivalents for Spanish terms such as *la santissima Trinidad* (the most holy Trinity) as well as a section of phrases on "Preguntas dela Doctrina Christiana" (Questions on Christian Doctrine): "Donde esta Dios—Apacatzih Coui Dios?," "Quien es Dios—Apachinal Dios?"[1]

A Dutch–Japanese dictionary was written two hundred years ago to keep Japan sealed off from the rest of the world. Today, though, it can be a way of opening that world up and looking in. For generations, the bridge between Japan and the West was seven inches wide—the width of a book published in Edo.

Japan has a long lexicographical history, though the earliest examples do not survive. A dictionary called *Niina*, or *New Characters*, was compiled in 682 C.E. and presented to the emperor—a list of Chinese characters with Japanese annotations. Around 835, Kukai's *Tenrei bansho meigi*, or *Myriad Things*, featured about a thousand Chinese characters. Shoju edited the *Shinsen Jikyo* around the year 900, with more than twenty thousand characters in Chinese and Japanese; the *Ruiju myogisho*, from around 1100, contained more than thirty thousand. The *Wamyo ruijusho*, by Minamoto no Shitago, was compiled in 938 on a different plan: instead of arranging words by "radicals," the basic strokes that make up the Chinese characters, it was arranged thematically, borrowing and adapting the categories of the ancient Chinese *Erya* (see chapter 2).

The *Nippo jisho*, or *Vocabulario da lingoa de Iapam*, was a milestone in the early modern period: a Japanese–Portuguese dictionary that appeared in 1603 with the aim of helping Portuguese missionaries learn the language. It contained 32,293 Japanese words rendered in the Latin alphabet, with Portuguese explanations for each. The dictionary was the work of Jesuits, with Father João Rodrigues, a missionary, credited for the compilation. It was immensely useful in its day, and it is still valuable for providing evidence on the pronunciation of Japanese at the beginning of the seventeenth century.

The *Nippo jisho* promised a new age of intercultural communication between East and West, but that was not to be. Europeans had been visiting Japan since 1543: first Portuguese traders, then Spanish, Dutch, and English vessels, trading in silk, cotton, and spices as well as spreading the Christian Gospel. But tensions began rising in the early seventeenth century. The Japanese authorities grew weary of the Christian missionaries and issued a series of decrees expelling them. The populace was divided over the actions of the shogunate. In 1637–38, forty thousand peasants, mostly Catholic converts, rose up against the shoguns in the Shimabara Rebellion, both for their anti-Christian policies and their high taxation. The Tokugawa shogunate would not tolerate the challenge to their authority, and they responded with more than a hundred thousand troops. The leader of the rebellion, Amakusa Shiro, a Catholic, was beheaded.

The Sakoku Edict, which followed in 1639, effectively closed Japan off from the rest of the world. It prevented egress: the Japanese were not allowed to leave the country, and anyone who somehow managed to get out and tried to return faced the death penalty. And while no Japanese could get out, no Europeans could get in. Japanese forces maintained an effective blockade on their own country. When Portuguese warships tried to land at Nagasaki, a Japanese fleet of nearly a thousand ships drove them away. Any foreigners who did manage to get to Japan were detained, and their ships were searched for missionaries.

The era is known as the *Sakoku* 'closed country' or 'chained country'. The closure was not absolute; some trade with China and with Korea remained. The only significant Western contact, though, was with the Vereenidge Oostindische Compagnie, or Dutch East India Company, which set up a trading post at Dejima—a small artificial island in the bay of Nagasaki, created in 1634 when a canal was built to separate a peninsula from the mainland. It was originally set aside for the Portuguese, but when they were expelled in 1639, the Dutch were moved from Hirado to Dejima. A heavily guarded bridge linked the island to the mainland, but the Dutch were not routinely permitted to cross to Nagasaki, nor most Japanese to cross to Dejima. For centuries, this Dutch enclave was the only tolerated European outpost in the country. All other Europeans, known as *komojin* 'redheads', were proscribed.

The Dutch were allowed because Holland valued Japanese trade enough to make concessions other nations were not willing to make. They agreed not to evangelize, and even to refrain from holding their own religious ceremonies in their host country. They also declared enmity to Portugal and Spain, the two sharpest thorns in Japan's side, partly on religious grounds (Dutch Protestants resented Iberian Catholics), but also because the Dutch were waging their own war for independence from the Spanish, who controlled the Netherlands until 1648.

This was a time of rapid technological advance in the West. In the seventeenth and eighteenth centuries, Europeans described the circulation of the blood, worked out the laws of planetary motion and gravitation, developed the calculus, and invented the microscope, telescope, and barometer. The Dutch were on the cutting edge. Throughout this period the Netherlands was the most economically and technically advanced country in Europe. The Japanese followed these developments from afar, getting news about European advancements only through Dutch channels, and they wanted what the West had to offer.[2] The Dutch brought scientific works, medical instruments, maps, and other tokens of Western modernity to Japan. This led to the development of the field of *Rangaku* 'Dutch studies' or 'Dutch learning', which became synonymous with "Western studies."

The Dutch were expected to conform to a strict set of rules for interacting with the Japanese. The chief of the trading post, the *opperhofd*, was regarded as the representative of a state owing allegiance to the Shogun. He would make presentations to the Shogun on annual trips to the capital, Edo (modern Tokyo), providing expensive and elaborate gifts. Only a very few Japanese had permission to interact with the Westerners. A small group of interpreters held their posts as hereditary translators, and they were trained from childhood under Dutch tutelage; a few samurai received permission to engage in *Rangaku*.

The challenge was communication. Dutch and Japanese are from different language families, with no vocabulary in common and dissimilar syntax and morphology. There had been attempts to bridge the gap before. The Shogun Yoshimune authorized two Japanese scholars, Noro Genjo and Aoki Konyo, to study Dutch scientific and medical writing in 1740. Noro went on to publish *Oranda honso wage* (*Japanese Explanations of Dutch Botany*), but Aoki's contribution was more relevant: a small Dutch–Japanese dictionary, published in 1745. A more ambitious one was begun by Nishi Zenzaburo (1718–68), one of the hereditary interpreters, who learned Dutch in Dejima starting in 1722. By 1754 he had been promoted to chief interpreter, and he accompanied the Dutch on their trips to Edo several times. Zenzaburo worked on a Dutch–Japanese dictionary, with Pierre Martin's Dutch–French dictionary as his starting point, but he made little progress, getting only as far as the letter *B*. Shortly afterward, Maeno Ryotaku likewise started, and likewise left unfinished, a set of translations.

A large-scale bilingual dictionary was a necessity,[3] and one finally appeared before the end of the eighteenth century: the work known as the *Haruma-wage*, or sometimes the *Edo Haruma*. The dictionary itself is dull, difficult of access, and both untranslated and probably untranslatable in any useful sense—it is simply a list of Dutch words and their Japanese equivalents. Its existence, though, is one of the most illuminating bits of evidence about East-West interaction in the eighteenth century.

Haruma is the Japanese rendering of the French name Halma: in 1708, François Halma, a French book dealer living in Utrecht, had published a *Woordenboek der nederduitsche en fransche taalen* (*Dutch–French Dictionary*). A copy of the second edition, 1729, eventually made its way to Japan, where Inamura Sampaku, a physician's son, encountered it. While studying medicine in Nagasaki he was first introduced to Western medicine; while in Kyoto, he read Otsuki Gentaku's *Rangaku Kaitei* (*Introduction to Western Studies*, 1788), and he felt his eyes had been opened. Starting in 1792, he studied with Gentaku, who gave him a copy of Halma's dictionary. Sampaku explained his intention to create a definitive Dutch–Japanese dictionary to Gentaku, who advised him that someone else, Ishii Shosuke, was already at work on such a dictionary. Sampaku was delighted, and the two lexicographers began collaborating.

The *Haruma-wage* was the work of thirteen years. Unimpressive as a dictionary, it has been called "a crude dictionary or rather a wordbook . . . giving for each headword only a few Japanese equivalents represented by Chinese characters."[4] While there are a few phrasal verbs, there are no parts of speech, and a sprinkling of synonyms takes the place of serious definitions. What demands our attention, however, is not the quality of the lexicography, but the vocabulary considered worthy of inclusion. Not surprisingly, many words related to trade were included: *handel* 'trade', *handelaar* 'dealer', *vredehandel* 'peace trade', and so on. The word *god* received a bold, centered heading, followed by a series of words related to religion: *goddelijk* 'divine', *goddelijkheid* 'divinity', *godendom* 'godhead', and so on. Words such as *natie* 'nation' and *religie* 'religion' aimed at bridging the distance between Western and Eastern notions of statehood and spirituality.

TITLE: *Haruma-wage*, also known as *Edo haruma*

COMPILER: Inamura Sampaku (1758–1811), following François Halma

ORGANIZATION: Alphabetical by Dutch word, from *abboek* to *zy*

PUBLISHED: Edo, 1796

VOLUMES: 27

PAGES: 4,500

ENTRIES: 64,035

TOTAL WORDS: 630,000

SIZE: 10½" × 7" (27 × 18 cm)

AREA: 2,350 ft² (219 m²)

The *Haruma-wage*'s influence was limited, because just thirty copies were produced—the Japanese definitions had to be added by hand, and mass production was impossible. An abridged version, the *Yakken*, followed in 1810, available in a hundred copies; it was printed in movable type and featured about twenty-seven thousand headwords. A new project, also based on Halma, was prepared in Nagasaki by the chief of the Dutch enclave, H. Doeff and was completed in 1833. The so-called *Dufu Haruma* or *Nagasaki Haruma* was more influential than its Edo predecessor, and more useful because it featured sentences showing the words in context.[5] The book was finally published in 1855–58, and it was the last significant bilingual dictionary during the closed Sakoku era. In 1853 Commodore Matthew Perry's warships forced Japan to open to Western trade, and the Meiji Restoration of 1868 broke down the last of the barriers.

※

Haruma-wage linked two immense cultures, but the number of people who had any reason to care about this work at the time was tiny. A trivial number of Dutch traders were allowed into Japan, and a similarly trivial number of Japanese translators were permitted to interact with them. But another variety of imperial relation comes at the opposite end of the spectrum. From the middle of the eighteenth century to the middle of the twentieth, British traders and troops controlled the whole of South Asia (known as India before partition). Thousands of British civil servants came into direct contact with millions of Indians, and with the ripple effect, hundreds of millions of people on two continents were influenced by the Raj. And a dictionary played a major role in connecting the parties.

Henry Yule was born in East Lothian, Scotland, in 1820. When his father, an orientalist who knew Persian and Arabic and worked for the East India Company, was stationed in Bengal, Henry followed. He got a close-up view of Anglo-Indian culture: his father's boss, Sir David Ochterlony, had "gone native" to the extent of marrying thirteen Indian wives. Henry Yule entered the East India Company's Military College in 1837, and two years later he was appointed to the Bengal Engineers. Between 1840 and 1862 he worked in Indian railways and irrigation canals; at forty-two he retired with the rank of colonel and moved to Sicily. There he became interested in travel as a means of exploring other cultures. His publication of an English translation of Marco Polo's *Travels* earned him a gold medal from the Royal Geographical Society, and he "so completely identified himself with his favourite traveller" that he would sign articles he wrote "MARCUS PAULUS VENETUS or M.P.V."[6]

After his retirement he resolved to create a glossary of Anglo-Indian terms. In or around 1872, while working in the India Office Library in London, Yule met a thirty-two-year-old senior Indian civil servant named Arthur Coke Burnell. Burnell began his career as a student of Arabic and had become proficient in Sanskrit, Tamil, Tibetan, Coptic, Kawi, Javanese, Portuguese, Dutch, and Italian. It turned out that Burnell was also working on an Anglo-Indian dictionary, so, rather than produce competing works, the two decided to combine their energies.

They planned to cover "etymological, historical, and geographical" subjects, but they found it difficult to draw boundaries. Though their book, *Hobson-Jobson*, is in theory concerned only with the language, in reality it takes in many subjects related to the Raj. "Anglo-Indian" is a strange category: there is no such language as "Indian," so it is inherently multicultural. *Hobson-Jobson* was concerned with the English

TITLE: *Hobson-Jobson: A Glossary of Colloquial Anglo-Indian Words and Phrases, and of Kindred Terms, Etymological, Historical, Geographical and Discursive*
COMPILER: Henry Yule (1820–89) and Arthur Coke Burnell (1840–82)
ORGANIZATION: Alphabetical, *abada* to *zumbooruck*
PUBLISHED: London: J. Murray, 1886
PAGES: xlviii + 870
ENTRIES: 2,000
TOTAL WORDS: 750,000
SIZE: 9" × 6¼" (23 × 16 cm)
AREA: 361 ft² (33.8 m²)
PRICE: 36s.

language as spoken in what was then India. It includes words from Hindi, Tamil, and Urdu, Persian, Arabic, Malay, Marathi, Chinese, and even Portuguese.

The two worked together for a decade, Yule usually in England, Burnell in Madras. Burnell, victim of a constitution that did not respond well to the Indian climate, died of cholera and pneumonia in 1882, at the age of just forty-two, but Yule kept at it for another six years. A year before *Hobson-Jobson* appeared in 1886, a rival work, George Clifford Whitworth's *Anglo-Indian Dictionary*, came out. But *Hobson-Jobson* was more than twice the length of Whitworth's dictionary, and the range and depth of Yule's and Burnell's learning, combined with the quirkiness of their interests, left the competition far behind.

The strange title was Yule's idea. A friend who had published a book with the drab title *Three Essays* was disappointed with sales, and Yule wanted to avoid that fate. He thought of the Arabic phrase "Ya Hasan! Ya Hosain!," a mourning cry used in Shia Islam, which was variously anglicized as "Hosseen Gosseen," "Hossy Gossy," "Hossein Jossen," and "Jaksom Baksom." The version that caught on borrowed a pair of stock names, "Hobson" and "Jobson," used in the nineteenth century to stand in for unknown or concealed names, a paired version of "John Doe."[7]

The process by which foreign loanwords get twisted into new forms to suit the sound system of the receiving language has since come to be called "the law of Hobson-Jobson."

Many words in the dictionary have to do with colonial administration—only natural, given the nature of the Raj—including both words originally Indian (*peshwa*, "chief minister of the Mahratta power"; *dewaun*, "the head financial minister") and words originally English (*settlement*, "an estate or district is said to be *settled* when . . . the Government has agreed . . . for a fixed sum to be paid"; *civilian*, "covenanted European servants of the E[ast] I[ndia] Company"). Other words reveal social relations: *sahib* is "The title by which, all over India, European gentlemen, and it may be said Europeans generally, are addressed, and spoken of, when no disrespect is intended," and a *cooly* is "A hired labourer, or burden-carrier; especially, a labourer induced to emigrate from India, or from China, to labour in the plantations . . . sometimes under circumstances . . . which have brought the cooly's condition very near to slavery."

The list of words from Indian languages that made their way into standard English is long, and *Hobson-Jobson* reveals the pathway they took. Words for distinctively South Asian phenomena, such as *chutney*, *curry*, *guru*, *nirvana*, *pashmina*, *sari*, and *yoga*, are still associated in many minds with India. On the other hand, most English speakers have forgotten the Indian origins of words like *avatar*, *bungalow*, *cashmere*, *chintz*, *juggernaut*, *jungle*, *khaki*, *pariah*, *polo*, *pundit*, *typhoon*, and *veranda*. And to learn that words like *bangle*, *cummerbund*, *dinghy*, *dungarees*, *loot*, *shampoo*, *shawl*, *thug*, and *toddy* are all of Indian origin probably surprises everyone but etymologists. Conversely, English words have acquired new meanings in India. *Cheese*, for instance, came to mean "anything good, first-rate in quality, genuine, pleasant, or advantageous"; English *compass* developed into *kompáss* with a meaning expanded to take in all sorts of surveying instruments; and *ducks* was used as a "distinctive name for gentlemen belonging to the Bombay service."

The longer entries in *Hobson-Jobson* are often the most enlightening. The article on *boy* includes extensive comments on the situations in which the term was considered appropriate; *snake-stone* ("a substance, the application of which to the part where a snake-bite has taken effect, is supposed to draw out the poison") drew on mythology, history, and medicine; and the entry for *India* filled pages—"A book," the lexicographers say, "might be written on this name"—and should be included in any account of European attitudes toward South Asia. The entry for *home* is telling: "In Anglo-Indian and colonial speech this means England." The first quotation from 1837 makes it clear: "**Home** always means England; nobody calls India *home*—not even those who have been here thirty years or more, and are never likely to return to Europe." The article on *suttee*—"The rite of widow-burning; *i.e.* the burning of the living widow along with the corpse of her husband"—is one of the longest in the book; it combines a history of the practice with comparative anthropology, noting similar traditions in other faiths, and the quotations give a good account of how Europeans have understood it over the centuries.

An early review exulted that "'Hobson-Jobson' provides a practically inexhaustible supply of quaint and rare information, and the reader who grumbles at the heaviness of Oriental literature should find reason to moderate his complaint from a cursory inspection of its pages."[8] *Hobson-Jobson* is an impressively scholarly work; it is also, in the words of the poet Daljit Nagra, "a madly unruly and idiosyncratic work."[9] The etymologies are notoriously digressive, rambling into anthropological anecdotes and speculation. The book ends up being a social history despite itself.

The occasional condescending entries do make one wince—the definition of *naukar-chaukar*, "the servants," comes with this note: "one of those jingling double-barrelled phrases in which Orientals delight even more than Englishmen"—and sometimes the book engages in outright racism, using terms such as "barbarous display" and "ignorant natives" when discussing the Indians. But the more we examine the book, the more balanced, even enlightened, it becomes. Yule and Burnell took the trouble to get to know the languages and the cultures, and they believed they had much to learn about them. Every subsequent lexicographer of nonstandard English has been indebted to Yule and Burnell. James Murray (see chapter 18) read the book while it was still in proof, and the *Oxford English Dictionary* quotes *Hobson-Jobson* in nearly 150 entries, including citations for words such as *beri-beri, chit, nabob,* and *pundit,* and there are probably hundreds more for which the *OED* editors borrowed without citation. A second edition, edited, expanded, and indexed by William Crooke, was published in 1903 and had greater influence than the first.

Plenty of writers have valued *Hobson-Jobson*. Rudyard Kipling admiringly called it "neither glossary, vocabulary, dictionary or anything else that may be described in one word, but simply—*Hobson-Jobson*." For Anthony Burgess, it evoked the lost days of British India, and *India Ink* by Tom Stoppard—who spent part of his childhood in India—is riddled with allusions to the glossary. Amitav Ghosh praises *Hobson-Jobson* for revealing something about the way English was actually spoken in the nineteenth century: "I love dictionaries and have many, not just of English, but dictionaries of laskari and nautical language. If you read these dictionaries, it becomes perfectly clear that English people when they were living in India were certainly not speaking like Jane Austen or George Eliot. In fact, it is often said when these nabobs went back home to England, people couldn't understand them."[10] Salman Rushdie is also attentive to the influence of Indian speech patterns on the English when he calls *Hobson-Jobson* a "legendary dictionary" and views it as "eloquent testimony to the unparalleled intermingling that took place between English and the languages of India,"[11] though he complains that some offensive terms have been omitted from the modern abridgment.

※

Despite their priority and their importance, bilingual dictionaries get much less attention than the familiar monolingual ones. To many people, "dictionary" means works such as Johnson's, Webster's, and the Grimms'. Bilingual (and other multilingual) dictionaries, however, open up views on history that are hard to find elsewhere and that allow us to see something about interactions between peoples that is hard to see elsewhere. Whether it is the only point of contact between two cultures, as with the Dutch in Japan, or merely a "lexical snapshot of a truly strange and fascinating moment in world history,"[12] the bilingual dictionary is an indispensable reference genre.

A SMALL ARMY

Collaborative Endeavors

"THE TONE OF American encyclopedias," the famous cultural commentator Charles Van Doren complained in 1962, "is often fiercely inhuman. It appears to be the wish of some contributors to write about living institutions as if they were pickled frogs, outstretched upon a dissecting board."[1] For many modern books, this is precisely the point: "humanity" in an encyclopedia or a dictionary is a quirk, and a quirk is a failing. Most works strive to exclude personality. Even Wikipedia famously aspires to "objectivity"—a "neutral point of view" is the one inflexible rule governing that vast collaborative endeavor.

Individuality, though, has not always been a fault. Once upon a time, reference books had not compilers but authors. Samuel Johnson's uniquely powerful mind, for instance, is visible on every page of his *Dictionary*, and you can almost smell the revolutionary air blowing through the pages of the *Encyclopédie*. Pierre Bayle's *Dictionnaire historique et critique* could only have been written by that skeptical genius. Most early reference books, at least in Europe and America, were the work of a single person working more or less alone, with little more than clerical assistance. All the major English dictionaries through the middle of the nineteenth century, for instance, are known by the name of their author: Cawdrey, Bullokar, Phillips, Kersey, Johnson, Webster, Richardson . . . In books like these we get a hint of what the lexicologist John Considine calls "the lexicographer as hero."

These personal books gave us some amusing eccentricities. Johnson's swipes at some of his enemies—tax collectors (*excise*, "A hateful tax levied upon commodities, and adjudged not by the common judges of property, but wretches hired by those to whom excise is paid"), Lord Chesterfield (*patron*, "Commonly a wretch who supports with insolence, and is paid with flattery"), and the Scottish (*oats*, "A grain, which in England is generally given to horses, but in Scotland supports the people")—are so familiar that some people assume the whole *Dictionary* is nothing but put-downs. (The actual number of such disparaging entries is tiny.) The personal qualities make eponymous books not merely works of reference but also works of literature, worth reading long after all their research has been rendered obsolete.

But already in the seventeenth century, European dictionaries were identified not with individuals but with organizations: the Accademia della Crusca, the Académie Française. This was the age of the first big collaborative projects. By the end of the eighteenth century, the name of the lone genius was being traded for that of an impersonal committee. The *Encyclopædia Britannica*, almost entirely the work of William Smellie (except when he was plagiarizing others' work), omitted his name from the title page; it was by "A Society of Gentlemen," and there are mentions throughout to the "Editors and Compilers" as if there were more than one.[2] The *Deutsches Wörterbuch* by the Brothers Grimm, begun in 1838, and Peter Mark Roget's *Thesaurus*, published in 1852, may be the last great reference works to go by the names of authors rather than teams.

We now live in an age when dictionaries, encyclopedias, atlases, and so on are almost always the work of impersonal committees. The six-page masthead of the fifth edition of the *American Heritage Dictionary*, to consider one very fine modern example, advertises the contributions of a publisher, an executive editor, a supervising editor, a managing editor, a senior lexicographer, two senior editors, an editor, two associate editors, nine consulting editors, four proofreaders, two production supervisors, an editorial and production coordinator, three designers, three administrative coordinators, five editorial and production assistants, a prepress developer, thirty-four special contributors, forty-five previous consultants, and a usage panel made up of 178 experts still drawing breath and another 21 who did not live to see the work's publication. The total is well into the three digits, all working on one single-volume dictionary.

The *Oxford English Dictionary* is an even grander project, with a chief editor, a deputy chief editor, an editorial project director, an editorial director, a team of eighteen in charge of general revision, thirteen science editors, nine new-word editors, eleven etymologists, seventeen bibliographers, twenty-three library researchers, and so on. In addition to the current staff, the *OED* website lists everyone who has worked on the project since 1989, when *OED2* was completed: the list of current and former employees runs to 560 people, and that does not include the thousands upon thousands who have served as volunteer readers or answered the editors' queries. The *New International Encyclopedia* makes the case that collaboration is now the only choice: "No good general encyclopædia, at least, is now possible which does not include in its editorial staff a small army of men of science, historians, theologians, lawyers, and so on."[3]

The encyclopedic army has included some impressive recruits. The *Encyclopædia Britannica* has since the early days made a policy of recruiting experts—historians, scientists, politicians, philosophers—to write its entries. The entries have not always been signed, and many publishing house records have been destroyed, so we will never know who all the contributors were. But we can say for certain that editions of the nineteenth and twentieth centuries included articles by the likes of Isaac Asimov, J. B. Bury, Jimmy Carter, Bill Clinton, Marie Curie, Thomas De Quincey, Albert Einstein, Sigmund Freud, Edmund Gosse, the skateboarder Tony Hawk, William Hazlitt, Harry Houdini, Thomas Henry Huxley, Lee Iacocca, Pyotr Alekseevich Kropotkin, H. L. Mencken, Bertrand Russell, Ernest Rutherford, George Bernard Shaw, Algernon Charles Swinburne, John Addington Symonds, Leon Trotsky, Archbishop Desmond Tutu, and James Watt.

CHAPTER 15

KILLING TIME

Games and Sports

Edmond Hoyle	John Wisden
A Short Treatise on the	*Wisden Cricketers' Almanack*
Game of Whist	1864
1742	

N OT EVERY REFERENCE BOOK is strictly utilitarian—not every reference, in other words, tells us things we *need* to know. Many tell us what we simply *want* to know, and how we might amuse ourselves.

Games and sports go back at least as far as the archaeological record will take us—Senet was played in predynastic Egypt around 3000 B.C.E., Ur in first-millennium-B.C.E. Babylon, and Go in fourth-century-B.C.E. China—and the more complicated the game, the more necessary are written rules. Isidore described board games, dice games, and ball games in his *Etymologies*, but some games required more extensive treatment. Simple games like catch and tag require little strategy, but chess—sixty-four squares, thirty-two pieces falling into six classes, each with different rules for moving—cries out for codification. One estimate says there are about 100,000,000,000,000,000,000,000,000,000,000,000,000,000,000,000 possible positions in a chess game. An early aid to those zillions of games appeared in 1512, when the Portuguese pharmacist Pedro Damião of Odemira wrote *Questo libro e da imparare giocare a scachi et de li partiti* in Italian. The book was translated from Italian to French, and then from French to English in 1562, when it was called *The Pleasaunt and Wittie Playe of the Cheasts Renewed*, and the long subtitle to the English edition promises *Instructions Both to Learne It Easely, and to Play It Well*.

This four-ton slab of basalt is one of the oldest reference "books" known, the emperor Hammurabi's compendium of 282 laws from 1754 B.C.E., which helped consolidate the government of a great empire. *"Code de Hammurabi, roi de Babylone." Louvre Museum. Licensed under CC BY-SA 2.0 FR.*

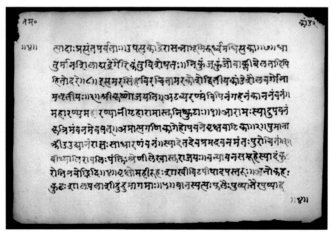

The *Amarakosha*—a third-century dictionary-cum-thesaurus of Sanskrit, seen here in an eighteenth-century manuscript—was one of the greatest intellectual achievements of ancient India, and influenced Peter Mark Roget a millennium and a half later. *Kislak Center for Special Collections, University of Pennsylvania Libraries.*

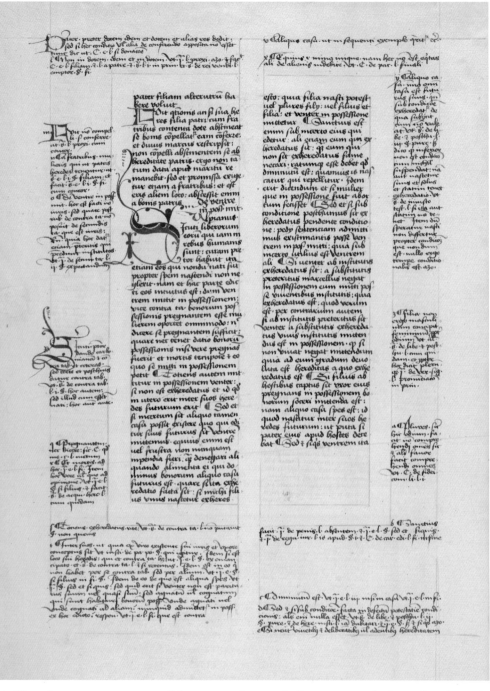

This fifteenth-century manuscript of the emperor Justinian's *Corpus juris civilis* shows that the sixth-century Roman legal code remained influential through Europe's Middle Ages. *Kislak Center for Special Collections, University of Pennsylvania Libraries.*

Claudius Ptolemy's *Geographike* described the entirety of the known world in the second century C.E., and informed European and Islamic cartography for hundreds of years. *"Claudius Ptolemaeus (Ptolemy). Woodcut by T. Stimmer, 1587" courtesy of Wellcome Images. Licensed under CC BY 4.0. "Tabulae geographicae" courtesy of the Beinecke Rare Book and Manuscript Library, Yale University.*

DOVERE tempore regis EDWARDI reddebat .xviii. libras. De quibus denariis habebat rex .E. duas partes. & comes Goduin' tercia. Contra hoc habebant canonici de sco marino medietate aliam...

[Facsimile of a page of the Domesday Book, containing the Kent (Chenth) entries beginning with Dover, written in abbreviated medieval Latin.]

William the Conqueror ordered a comprehensive accounting of the resources in his new country on Christmas 1085. The *Domesday Book* describes more than thirteen thousand places in England, and was not superseded until the nineteenth century. *Courtesy of Professor J. J. N. Palmer and George Slater. Licensed under CC BY-SA 3.0.*

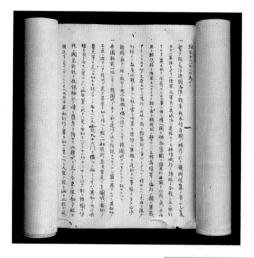

For centuries books took the form of scrolls, which were portable but ill-suited to quick reference. Few ancient scrolls survive intact, but this nineteenth-century Japanese example shows how readers searched for relevant passages. *Lawrence J. Schoenberg Collection of Manuscripts. Kislak Center for Special Collections, University of Pennsylvania Libraries.*

Saint Isidore of Seville's seventh-century encyclopedia, the *Etymologies*, is seen here in a thirteenth-century Spanish manuscript. The codex form made it much easier to search. It is fitting that Isidore has been proposed as the patron saint of the Internet. *Lawrence J. Schoenberg Collection of Manuscripts. Kislak Center for Special Collections, University of Pennsylvania Libraries.*

Avicenna's medical encyclopedia, the *Kitab al-Qanun fi al-tibb*, combined ancient Greek and medieval Islamic knowledge about pathologies and treatments. The book was written early in the eleventh century, but this copy was prepared at the very end of the fifteenth, a testament to Avicenna's long influence. *Lawrence J. Schoenberg Collection of Manuscripts. Kislak Center for Special Collections, University of Pennsylvania Libraries.*

In 1570 Abraham Ortelius of Antwerp published the *Theatrum orbis terrarum*, the first world atlas. It both reflected and made possible the age of Europe's colonial expansion into the New World. *"Ortelius Portrait" courtesy of the Rijksmuseum, Amsterdam. "Ortelius World Map Typvs Orbis Terrarvm, 1570" courtesy of the Library of Congress.*

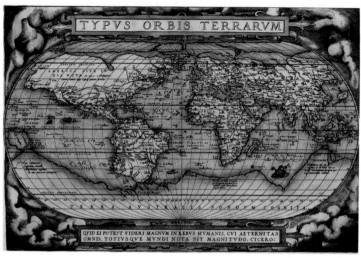

Scientific advances depend on ready access to vast amounts of information, and the numeric table served that purpose from antiquity until well into the computer age. This astronomical and astrological table was prepared in Naples in 1327. *Lawrence J. Schoenberg Collection of Manuscripts, Kislak Center for Special Collections, University of Pennsylvania Libraries.*

The German astronomer Johannes Kepler used his frontispiece to his *Rudolphine Tables* (1627) to pay tribute to two ancient and two modern predecessors: Hipparchus, Claudius Ptolemy, Nicolaus Copernicus, and Tycho Brahe. *Public domain.*

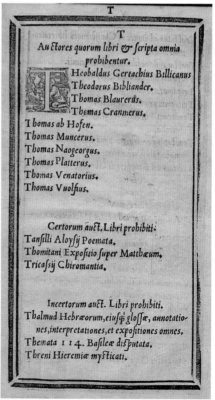

The Roman Catholic Church responded to the threats of the Reformation by compiling the *Index librorum prohibitorum* (1559), or index of forbidden books. The Protestant Thomas Cranmer's works and the "Talmud of the Jews" are among the proscribed heretical texts. *Courtesy of Bayerische Staatsbibliothek München.*

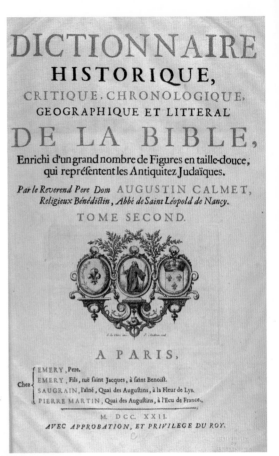

The *Dictionnaire historique* by the monastic scholar Antoine Augustin Calmet provided a comprehensive illustrated encyclopedia of the biblical world, aiding both the devout and the scholarly in understanding Scripture. *Kislak Center for Special Collections, University of Pennsylvania Libraries.*

Samuel Johnson—the son of a provincial bookseller, whose lack of money forced him to leave university after just a year—was an autodidact who compiled one of the greatest and most influential dictionaries in English. *Beinecke Rare Book and Manuscript Library, Yale University.*

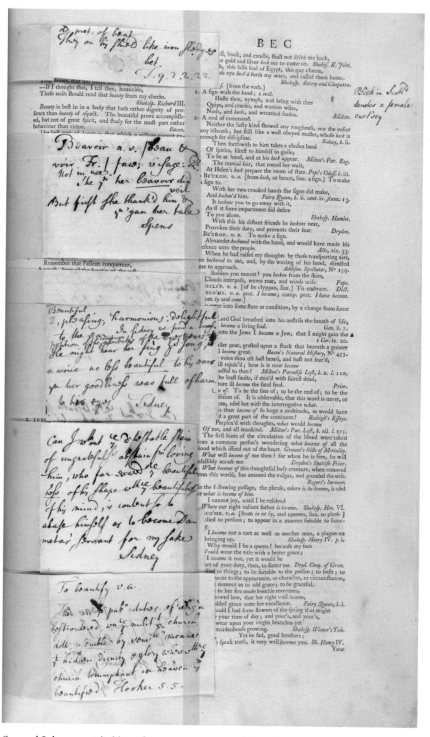

Samuel Johnson, aided by a few assistants, copied hundreds of thousands of passages from great English literature and used the slips as raw material for his *Dictionary of the English Language* (1755). *Beinecke Rare Book and Manuscript Library, Yale University.*

Two French polymaths, Jean le Rond d'Alembert (above) and Denis Diderot, assembled the team that produced one of the world's greatest, and most influential, reference books between 1751 and 1772. Some see the French Revolution as the *Encyclopédie*'s most important sequel. *"D'Alembert" from the author's collection. "Diderot" courtesy of the Rijksmuseum, Amsterdam.*

With the Deal.

7 to 6	— —	is 4 to 3
8 6	— —	2 1
6 6 is about	—	7 4

With the Deal.

8 7 is above	—	12 to 7
9 7 is about	—	12 8

8 to 9, upon the beft Computation made at Prefent, is about 3 and half in the Hundred, in Favour of 8 with the Deal; againft the Deal, the Odds is ftill, tho' fmall, in Favour of 8.

The *Laws* of the *Game at* WHIST.

1. If any Perfon plays out of his Turn, it is in the Option of the Adverfe Party to call the Card then played at any time in that Deal (in Cafe he does not make

make him revoke) or to call the Suit which he would have him play from; which done, it fhall then be in the Option of the Perfon called upon, either to name the Suit he choofes to have led, or to defire his Partner to lead as he pleafes; but in Cafe he names a Suit his Partner muft play it.

2. No Revoke to be claim'd till the Trick is turn'd and quitted, or the Party who revoked, or his Partner, have played again.

3. If a Revoke happens to be made the adverfe Party may add 3 to his Score, and the revoking Party, provided they are up, notwithftanding the Penalty, muft remain at 9; The Revoke takes place of any other Score of the Game.

4. If any Perfon calls at any Point of the Game, except 8, either of the adverfe Parties may call a new Deal; and they are at liberty to confult each other whether they will have a new Deal.

6. After the Trump-Card is feen no Body ought to remind his Partner to call.
6.

Edmond Hoyle started spelling out card-game strategies in 1742. Over the next few years he wrote reference books about games of all sorts, and before long the phrase "according to Hoyle" entered the English language. *Beinecke Rare Book and Manuscript Library, Yale University.*

For three centuries Dejima, a small artificial island connected to Nagasaki by a narrow footbridge, housed the only Europeans allowed to communicate with Japan. The Dutch–Japanese *Haruma-wage* (1796) was the intellectual equivalent of that footbridge, the only point of contact between Japan and the West. *Courtesy of the Rijksmuseum, Amsterdam.*

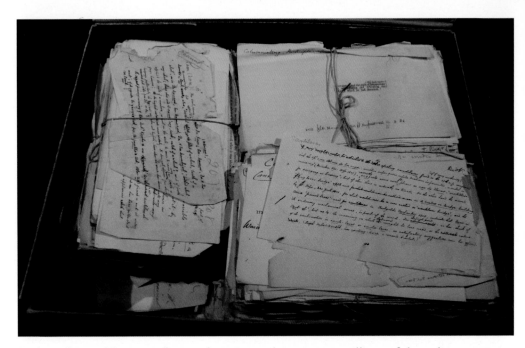

Both professional lexicographers and amateur volunteers sent millions of these slips containing dated quotations to Oxford, where James Murray used them to tell the history of every word in *A New English Dictionary* (1888–1933). The monumental work is known today as the *Oxford English Dictionary*. *Photo by Owen Massey McKnight. Licensed under CC BY-SA 2.0.*

Noah Webster, the American patriot who came to adulthood against the background of the War of Independence, used his *American Dictionary of the English Language* (1828) to create a national identity. His name is still synonymous with dictionaries in the United States. *Beinecke Rare Book and Manuscript Library, Yale University.*

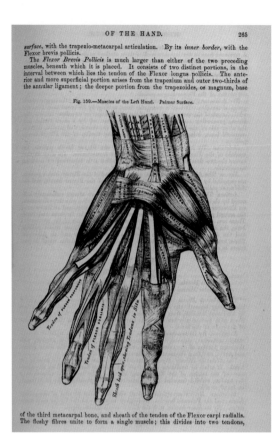

The world's most famous medical textbook, Henry Gray and Henry Carter's *Anatomy Descriptive and Surgical*, appeared in 1858 and has never gone out of print. The book now contains none of its original text or images, but the updated fortieth edition remains a staple of modern medical education. *Rare Book Collection, QM23 .G7 1859, Kislak Center for Special Collections, University of Pennsylvania Libraries*

Anthony Panizzi's radical politics forced him to flee Italy as a young man. After settling in London and finding employment at the British Museum, he initiated the catalog of the world's largest library. *Yale Center for British Art, Yale University.*

Convinced most encyclopedias showed an inexcusable bias against their religion, these five scholars compiled the authoritative seventeen-volume *Catholic Encyclopedia* between 1907 and 1914. *From the author's collection.*

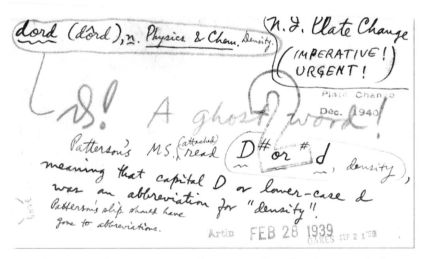

In *Webster's Second New International Dictionary* (1934), a lexicographer's note that either "D or d" was an acceptable abbreviation for "density" was accidentally turned into the non-word *dord*. On this slip a lexicographer realizes what happened and calls for an "URGENT!" deletion of the resulting "ghost word." *Used with permission of the publisher Merriam-Webster, Incorporated.*

No age took gaming more seriously than the eighteenth century. It was the great age of gaming, with card games, board games, and parlor games at the height of their popularity. Not coincidentally, the English idiom *to kill time* dates from exactly this period. And the king of the gaming table was Edmond Hoyle, who has held his position as the authoritative lawgiver for games since he wrote the first in a series of books on card games. He took it on himself to issue the rules, and nearly three centuries later, his name is a byword for authority.

Frustratingly little is known about him. He was probably born in 1671 or 1672, and he died in 1769. The best biographical source notes only that he "is said to have been a barrister by profession." In the early 1740s he lived in Queen Square, London—an upscale address—and he gave lessons on one of the most fashionable card games of the day, whist, similar to bridge. He "thought it would be doing no inconsiderable Service to many of my Countrymen," he wrote, "if I contributed a little to put them upon their Guard and preserve their Purses, while they are indulging themselves in what is elegantly called *Killing Time*."[1]

Hoyle began circulating handwritten copies of a short book on how to excel at the game, and eventually the private manual went public: he published his *Short Treatise on the Game of Whist* in 1742. Some sources say he received the astronomical sum of £1,000 for a published version. That is hard to believe—at the time, a working-class family could live on £30 a year—but he did sell copies for the outrageous price of a guinea, or twenty-one shillings, at a time when day laborers earned a shilling a day. Hoyle obviously had high-stakes players in mind when he priced his eighty-six-page pamphlet so extravagantly.

Most of what appeared in this first book was not really rules but suggestions or strategies. But one two-page section, "*The Laws of the Game at* WHIST," made fourteen rules explicit. A typical one: "I. If any Person plays out of his Turn, it is in the Option of the adverse Parties, either to call the Card then played at any Time in that Deal (in case he does not make him revoke) or the Person who is to lead, may demand his Partner to name the Suit, which he would have him play from." After spelling out the "laws," he offered "Some general Rules to be observed

TITLE: *A Short Treatise on the Game of Whist: Containing the Laws of the Game: And Also Some Rules, Whereby a Beginner May, with Due Attention to Them, Attain to the Playing It Well*

COMPILER: Edmond Hoyle (1672–1769)

ORGANIZATION: Chap. 1, general rules; chap. 2, particular rules; chap. 3–7, particular games; chap. 8, "A Case to demonstrate the Danger of forcing your Partner"; chap. 9, probabilities of various hands; chap. 10–12, directions for playing specific hands; chap. 13, cautions; chap. 14, playing sequences

PUBLISHED: London: printed by John Watts for the author, 1742

PAGES: viii + 86

TOTAL WORDS: 11,000

SIZE: 6½" × 3¾" (16.5 × 9.4 cm)

AREA: 15.3 ft² (1.4 m²)

WEIGHT: 7 oz. (196 g)

PRICE: 21s.

by Beginners," not actually the fundamental rules but tips for those who already knew the basics: "I. If you have Ace, King, and four small Trumps, with a good Suit," for instance, "you must play three Rounds of Trumps, or otherwise you may have your strong Suit Trumped." From there he worked his way up to discussions of strategy: chapter 5 spelled out "Particular Games to endeavour to deceive and distress your Adversaries, and to demonstrate your Game to your Partner."[2]

The book was a prompt success, and it encouraged him to tinker with the text. A second edition was called for within a few months, and while the first edition had omitted Hoyle's name, identifying its author simply as "a gentleman," this one bore "*By* EDMUND HOYLE, *Gent.*" on the title page. The following year, 1743, saw an amazing eight new editions, including a pirated one from Dublin. People clearly wanted Hoyle's wisdom without his extravagant price tag. Within a few years, pirated editions would outnumber the authorized London printings. Hoyle, aware that he could never compete with the pirated editions if he continued charging a premium, released his second for just two shillings a copy.

Hoyle soon began branching out into other games. After *A Short Treatise on the Game of Whist* in 1742 came *A Short Treatise on the Game of Back-Gammon* in 1743, and two works—*A Short Treatise on the Game of Quadrille* and *A Short Treatise on the Game of Piquet . . . To Which Are Added, Some Rules and Observations for Playing Well at Chess*—in 1744. These guides soon came together in one volume, as with *The Accurate Gamester's Companion: Containing Infallible Rules for Playing the Game of Whist . . . Also the Laws of the Game . . . to Which Are Added, the Games of Quadrille, Piquet, Chess and Back-gammon, . . . Likewise a Dictionary for Whist, and an Artificial Memory*, published in 1748, or *Mr. Hoyle's Games of Whist, Quadrille, Piquet, Chess, and Back-Gammon, Complete, in Which Are Contained, the Method of Playing and Betting, at Those Games . . . Including Also, the Laws of the Several Games*, published around 1755.

The early editions were not much interested in official rules. Hoyle's Piquet book, for instance, includes a section on chess that nowhere explains how the pieces move. But later editions gave more attention to the rudiments:

> The Chess-Board contains sixty-four Squares.
>
> The King and his Officers, being eight Pieces, are placed upon the first Line of the Board, the white Corner of it being towards your Right-hand.
>
> The white King must be upon the fourth black Square. The black King upon the fourth white Square: Opposite to each other.[3]

Hoyle aspired to teach players not merely the rules but the strategies behind them, and that meant teaching them some principles of probability and statistics. Both of these branches of mathematics were still in their infancy, and if even the professional mathematicians were largely ignorant of probabilities, laymen were completely in the dark. Hoyle therefore worked to introduce the amazing power of combinations:

First Quere, How many Chances are there upon six Dice?

Answer,	on 1	on 2	on 3	on 4	on 5	on 6	
Chances,	6	36	216	1296	7776	46656	[4]

The thought of probability turned his attention to less frivolous topics, like mortality. In a curious digression he prints a "Breslaw Table"—the name comes from such tables' early use in Breslau, now Wrocław, Poland—giving estimates of the proportion of people who can be expected to live to each age. Of every thousand infants born, 855 were expected to live into their second year, 680 to survive to the age of eight, 531 to be alive at thirty, and just 20 of the original thousand to live to age eighty-four.[5] Such a table served more than morbid curiosity: the new insurance industry was keen to know the likelihood of various disasters. "Suppose it was required to know the Odds of a Man of 25 Years of Age, dies within a Year?" Hoyle mused:

> Look in the Table and you will find in the Column against 25, that there is alive 567; in the following Year, *viz.* 26, there is only 560 living; therefore it is 560 to 7, that a Person of twenty-five Years of Age lives one Year. Or when reduced, 80 to 1.[6]

Or, more ghoulish still,

> If you would know how many Years a Man of forty has an equal Chance to live, look in the Table against 40, and you will find alive then 445; then look in the Table till you come to half that Number, *viz.* 222, which shews that is nearly an equal Wager that a Man of forty Years of Age, lives twenty-two Years.[7]

Hoyle's great achievement was to become not merely one gaming commentator among many, but the quasiofficial arbiter of how games are played. By collecting all the rules in one place, Hoyle turned an instruction book into a reference book. His was no longer a book to be read through before play began: instead, it was a book people turned to when they needed to settle arguments.

Keeping all the editions, expansions, abridgments, adaptations, and translations straight is a bibliographical nightmare, and not merely in England: Hoyle's work crossed the English Channel in 1763, when it was published in France as *Le Jeu de whist de M. Hoyle*. The proliferation of "Hoyles" caused problems—for Hoyle, of course, since he was not earning any money from the unauthorized copies, but also for his readers, since the whole point of having a book to settle disputes is to have a single, unimpeachable authority. Hoyle and his publishers began by putting notices on title pages to indicate the book was "Authoriz'd as revis'd and corrected under his [E. Hoyle's] own hand."[8] That formula proved insufficient, so beginning in 1743, he began warning them away from the competition: "The author has thought proper to inform the publick, that no copies of these books are genuine, but such as are signed by him."[9] (The books were far too popular for him to sign every copy; the publisher made do with a woodcut of his signature.)

Hoyle was impressively long-lived: he died in 1769, in his late nineties, beating the odds that appeared in his own tables. And though he published prolifically during his lifetime, his productivity only increased after his death. In 1775, for instance, Charles Jones published *Hoyle's Games Improved*, a work of 228 pages that went through multiple editions. In 1860 an *American Hoyle* appeared, and in 1887 *The Standard Hoyle, a Complete Guide upon All Games of Chance*. Some editions got smaller: *An Epitome of Hoyle, with Beaufort and Jones's Hoyle Improved; or, Practical Treatises* appeared around 1783, the word *epitome* in the title tipping off potential buyers that this was an abridgment. Even though it spelled out the rules and offered betting advice on thirteen separate games, from backgammon to tennis, it filled just 87 pages.

Hoyle quickly became a byword. He was famous enough to inspire an anonymous wag to publish *The Humours of Whist: A Dramatic Satire* in 1743, which took a few digs at Hoyle, such as insisting that "The genuine Books published by the Author, will be all signed with his Name."[10] Other literature of the day reveals Hoyle's place in high society. In *Tom Jones* (1748), Henry Fielding sketched a portrait of a young man about town who was scandalized to find four guests playing cards, and "my *Hoyle*, Sir,—my best *Hoyle*, which cost me a Guinea, lying open on the Table, with a Quantity of Porter spilt on one of the most material

Leaves of the whole Book."[11] In 1750, Samuel Johnson's *Rambler* series published a letter supposedly by the airheaded "daughter of a man of great fortune," who boasted, "Mr. Hoyle, when he had not given me above forty lessons, said I was one of his best scholars."[12]

By 1786, people were using the phrase "according to Hoyle" to mean "in accordance with the rules of games."[13] By the second decade of the nineteenth century, the expression had broadened its application further: it was now "in accordance with the rules," not only of card games, but of games of the heart. A novel from 1818, for instance, refers to a colonel who has "the stupidity to *boast* of non-payment" of his debts, "which is not thought exactly, according to Hoyle, in the *love* game."[14] Another novel describes the "ceremony" of kissing one's love letters, "which, in love affairs, is . . . according to *Hoyle*."[15] By the 1830s, a writer could explain that Hoyle's "name has become so familiar, as to be immortalised in the well-known proverb, 'According to Hoyle.' "[16] By the time the short story writer O. Henry used it in 1906—"The financial loss of a dollar sixty-five, all so far fulfilled according to Hoyle"—Hoyle had joined the very small number of reference-book writers whose personal names became synonymous with the authority embodied in their books: in the English-speaking world, only Johnson, Webster, and Roget enjoy a similar name recognition.

※

Though the Hoyle franchise eventually published guides to cricket ("The Ball must weigh not less than five Ounces and a Half, nor more than five Ounces and three Quarters"), tennis ("A Tennis Court is usually ninety-six or seven Feet long, by thirty-three or four in Breadth"), and so on,[17] most of Hoyle's attention was on the baize and the game board. But one book devoted entirely to an outdoor game became so successful that it became a brand name to rival Hoyle's.

Rheumatism forced John Wisden, a popular Victorian cricketer, to end his sporting career at the age of thirty-seven, and an impressive career it was. Wisden was born in Brighton in 1826 and, though he lacked the height that many players hoped for, he was an impressive underarm bowler. He went on to play not only for Sussex (82 matches, 578 wickets) but also for Kent and Middlesex. In one legendary match, he bowled all ten wickets in the second innings of the South v. North game on July 15, 1850. No one had ever done it before, and in the more than 165 years since, no one has done it again.

After his unexpected retirement in 1863, he founded John Wisden & Co. in a shop near Leicester Square, and from that location he ran a world empire of sports publishing, turning his attention to a publication that collected facts and figures about the sport he loved. He was not the first; *The Guide to Cricketers*, edited by a former associate of Wisden's, had been appearing annually since 1849. And Wisden's own first edition, published in 112 cramped pages, was undistinguished when it appeared in March 1864. Robert Winder, the historian of *Wisden*, has called the first edition little more than a "clump of scorecards."[18] Although the preface explained that "we have taken great pains to collect a certain amount of information," it was apparently cobbled together in a rush. It included only rules ("No umpires shall be allowed to bet") and scores, but no commentary: "We, of course, make no comments upon the matches, leaving the cricketer to form his own opinion with regard to the merits of the men, since a great many of our readers are at least equal, if not superior, to ourselves in arriving at a right judgement of the play."[19]

The first edition was not even limited to cricket. There are rules of other games—for instance, the rules of quoiting—and even miscellaneous reference information such as the dates of the English Civil War, the lengths of England's canals, and the dates of the Crusades was included. Gideon Haigh, the chronicler of Wisden's enterprises, describes this first edition as "a messy book, its scores surrounded with such factual bric-a-brac as winners of the Derby, Oaks at St Leger, a potted history of China, and the rules of pastimes like Knur and Spell," which "seemed destined for a short life."[20]

And yet, despite the unpromising beginning, its publication has been regarded as an epoch in the sporting world: "1864 should rank as the dawn of cricket," Haigh argues. "The publication of the first edition of *Wisden Cricketers' Almanack* was more than the minting of a distinguished imprint; it manifested the emergence of a record-keeping instinct in the game, now taken for granted, but intrinsic to its senses of continuity and context. The idea of records was a precondition for modern sport."[21]

TITLE: *The Cricketer's Almanack, for the Year 1864, Being*
  Bissextile or Leap Year, and the 28th of the Reign of Her
  Majesty Queen Victoria, Containing the Laws of Cricket,
  as Revised by the Marylebone Club . . . Together with the
  Dates of the University Rowing Matches, the Winners of
  the Derby, Oaks, and St. Leger; Rules of Bowls, Quoits,
  and Knur and Spell, and Other Interesting Information

COMPILER: John Wisden (1826–84)

PUBLISHED: London: W. H. Crockford, March 1864

PAGES: 112

SIZE: 6" × 3½" (15.2 × 9.3 cm)

AREA: 17 ft² (1.6 m²)

PRICE: 1s.

LATEST EDITION: *Wisden Cricketers' Almanack 2014*, 151st
  ed., by Lawrence Booth (London: Bloomsbury, 2014),
  1,584 pages

The first edition of the *Almanack* was followed by a second in the next year, and then a third—it became an institution, and a remarkably consistent one. As Winder notes, "We know next to nothing about the way the early volumes . . . were assembled."[22] As Wisden's role declined, the sportswriter W. H. Knight stepped in. The title went through a few permutations: *The Cricketer's Almanack* became *The Cricketers' Almanack* in 1869, and a year later *John Wisden's Cricketer's Almanack* to give the founder more prominence. Cancer took Wisden's life in 1884, but it did not affect the success of his publishing franchise. By that time the *Almanack* was edited by George West, the *Times* cricket correspondent. And the book kept growing, so that by 1892 it had reached 448 pages. Prospects for continued publication looked grim during the Great War, which threatened to put an end to the great Victorian sporting guide as it had put an end to so many Victorian institutions. But somehow the publishers kept it going, even though the tone of the book grew melancholy. Nearly two thousand cricketers were killed in combat, and the 1915 edition of *Wisden* featured forty-eight pages of obituaries.[23]

Once the war was over, the annual *Almanack* resumed its growth. It reached 727 pages in 1920; in 1924, it passed a thousand pages for the first time. Big changes came in 1938. The *Almanack* was acquired by a new publisher, J. Whitaker & Sons, who reorganized the book. Countries were now put in alphabetical order, and births and deaths were moved to the end of the book. Whitaker put money into improving the quality of the photographs. Most important, though, they added women's cricket to the venerable guide.

The Blitz in 1940 wiped out the company's archives, so that much of the early history of the *Almanack* is now lost, but the franchise continued to thrive, and more than a century and a half after the guide's premiere, its popularity is undimmed: it remains the world's longest-running and most widely read reference book on sports. "The Almanack, like cricket itself," the historian David Kynaston wrote, "represents something deep in the English psyche." For many it is a passion. "If I knew I was going to die today," the mathematician G. H. Hardy said, "I think I should still want to hear the cricket scores." Alec Waugh, the brother of Evelyn, dubbed it "the cricketer's bible" in the *London Mercury*, and the language used to describe it verges on the theological. Even Robert Runcie, then Archbishop of Canterbury, addressed the annual Wisden dinner in 1997 with a devotional metaphor: "All faiths need a sacred text. It's a big help if the faithful come to believe that it is well nigh infallible."[24]

Over the book's first 150 years, *Wisden* has taken up 133,000 pages, and they are interesting even to those who care nothing for cricket. John Fowles, Terence Rattigan, Sam Mendes, and King George VI all make cameo appearances, having played games that made it into the book. "Mr S. V. Beckett" appeared in 1925–26, and the notice of his death in 1989 described him as a left-hand opening batsman and left-arm medium-pace bowler and praised his thirty-five runs in four innings. Only in the last sentence does the obituary acknowledge, almost as an afterthought, that he was also "one of the important literary figures of the twentieth century." As befits a venerable reference book, *Wisden* has occasionally proven helpful in fields seemingly far from cricket. The British Library spent £27,500 for more than a hundred letters by the late playwright Harold Pinter. They all came from the years 1948 to 1960 but bore no more specific dates. A scholar, noticing references to cricket in nearly all of Pinter's letters, turned to Wisden to pin down when each was written. Where Pinter wrote of cricketer Doug Padgett, "Didn't he get a century yesterday, to bear out your words? . . . And what about Wilson being called back to continue his innings?," the librarians were able to turn to Wisden to discover that it had to be a reference to the Yorkshire–Warwickshire match of July 23, 1955.[25]

The *Wisden Cricketers' Almanack* is still published annually; it has never missed a year since 1864. Recent editions, published since 2008 by Bloomsbury, run around seventeen hundred pages a year and cover men's and women's cricket around the world. The game has changed a great deal since that first edition, and *Wisden* reflects those changes: the first South African was named Leading Cricketer of the Year in 2007, and the first Bangladeshi and Irish cricketers were in the top five in 2011. Claire Taylor was the first woman to make it into the top five in 2009. But it is still deeply conservative. The *Almanack*, with its iconic mustard-yellow jacket, has become an institution, and like so many institutions, it is slow to change. The few times the editors mustered up the courage to change direction—as when, in 1987, Graeme Wright decided to remove the old-fashioned laws of cricket from the guide—popular outcry forced them back in. The early volumes sell for thousands of pounds, because "A shelf-full of Wisdens," wrote sports historian Patrick Kidd, "is a sign of civilisation and a curious mind."[26]

⛬

It is only natural that the earliest reference books should be concerned with matters of life and death: promising an eye for an eye, prescribing remedies for diseases, keeping sailors from shipwreck on rocky coasts. But it is a testimony to the reference book's changing value in the culture that it was eventually adapted to purposes less utilitarian. The bibliography of game- and sport-related reference books is now long, and it includes many beloved titles. Some (like Hoyle's) teach particular skills to the players; others (like Wisden's) provide handy information for those on the sidelines; but they are all concerned with maximizing the pleasure that people take in their pastimes.

CHAPTER 15 ½
OUT OF PRINT

R EFERENCE BOOKS HAVE a natural life cycle: most have their day and are no more; the lucky few fill a niche and catch on. Time passes, and the work's shortcomings become clear—whether they were there from the beginning or imposed only by the passage of time. The publisher decides the world needs a revised version, and so appears the second edition. If all goes well, there may be a third, a fourth . . . A handful of fabulously successful reference works have histories that extend across centuries: *Wisden Cricketers' Almanack* has not missed an annual installment in more than a century and a half, Merriam-Webster's latest dictionaries are part of a direct lineage going back to 1828, and the *Dictionnaire de l'Académie française* will add its in-progress ninth edition to a series going all the way back to 1694. But most do not last nearly that long—they might get a second, even a third edition, and then they lapse into obscurity.

This much is natural. Every so often, though, there are episodes that seem to kill off entire genres, the bibliographical equivalent of a biological mass extinction. The Russian Revolution killed off a slew of dictionaries and encyclopedias from the czarist era. The invention of the pocket calculator put paid to the table of logarithms and sines. And we are now in the middle of one of the biggest mass extinctions ever. The name of the invasive species is the Internet.

Many once-proud reference franchises have fallen in the last few years. The *Brockhaus Enzyklopädie* traces its genealogy to Renatus Gotthelf Löbel and Christian Wilhelm Franke's *Conversations-Lexikon* (1796–1808), and it made it to a twenty-first edition in thirty volumes (2005–6). But after thriving for two centuries, Brockhaus could not figure out how to sell encyclopedias in the digital age. In 2009 they sold the intellectual property and fired the editorial staff. The legendary *Britannica* has been struggling mightily after several serious missteps since the mid-1990s. The company announced in 2012 that the 2010 version would be the last to appear in print—no surprise, now that printed books have fallen to less than one percent of the company's revenue.

Even for titles that have stayed healthy, print publication is unmistakably threatened. The *Oxford English Dictionary* is an institution, and it is unthinkable that it should shut down operation anytime soon—but the publishers are agnostic on whether there will be any further print editions.[1] The situation is the same at Merriam-Webster: a *Webster's Fourth* is in preparation, but no one can say whether it will have a physical existence.

This should not be an occasion for lamentation. Most of the effects of computerizing reference books are unambiguously good. Making them available in electronic form allows for searches that were unthinkable in the past. With the print *OED*, readers can search only by headword; with the online *OED*, they can look for all the words that entered English from Arabic between 1400 and 1500. (The answer is nine: *Alcoran, athanor, azoth, El Nath, gerfaunt, khan, Ramadan, resalgar,* and *sebesten.*) That would have been the work of years; it now takes seconds.

Online publication also makes possible much more frequent updates than were possible with books. Some of the most important reference books—the *Oxford English Dictionary*, the *Dictionary of National Biography*—average one, two, or maybe three editions a century, a pace determined by the world of print. With the references of the future, revisions could appear two or three times a year. It all depends on what we mean by "edition": the notion of numbered editions may be a relic of print culture that vanishes in the electronic age. The third edition of the *Oxford English Dictionary*, for instance, now in progress, may well be the last one to bear a number; later we may see only *OED*-of-the-afternoon-of-the-sixteenth-of-June-around-four-o'clock. The benefits of such currency for the users are obvious, though whether the editors and presses want the headaches of managing such perpetual flux, a Trotskyite permanent revolution, is an open question.

While online publication offers savings in materials, it also introduces new expenses and new challenges. Subscriptions and site licenses are the means publishers have devised to collect money for Internet-based resources, though pricing schemes are still being worked out. But those without institutional support may be shut out of the digital future: those without university IDs, even those with IDs from less affluent universities, may be left in the cold. In the old days, they could use expensive books in a library for free—distinguished professors from Ivy League universities and part-time lecturers at community colleges have always been on an equal footing in the New York Public Library, all drawing on the same resources. But when those resources are linked to student and faculty ID numbers, the computer age may make research impossible for the less fortunate. Some publishers have experimented with individual subscriptions and pay-per-view plans, but prices are almost always beyond the means of private researchers. The stratification of the academic haves and have-nots is already too pronounced, and the brave new research world may only make it worse.

When Britannica announced the end of their print edition, many declared they will miss the old hard copy. "I know I sound like a crotchety old grandfather on the porch reminiscing about the good old days of rumble seats," admits journalist A. J. Jacobs, who read the whole *Encyclopaedia Britannica*, "but I loved having pages you could actually turn, not click or swipe. I adored the literal weight of each volume (4 pounds), which somehow lent it metaphorical gravitas as well. I fell hard for the familiar smell of leatherette covers and the crinkling of the pages."[2] And some educators are concerned that the loss is more than sentimental: "The internet and its search boxes," a school librarian wrote, "do not encourage a sense of wonder. . . . We work to create inquiry-driven critical thinking in our students while we systematically remove the tools necessary to stimulate such thought."[3] "I love encyclopedias," a reference librarian wrote,

> and will miss the printed Encyclopaedia Britannica. . . . But we live in a complex world, too big for a few hundred people to cover completely, and too fast-moving for print volumes to keep up.[4]

But most of those who wipe away a tear of regret have to admit this is what progress looks like.

CHAPTER 16

MONUMENTS OF ERUDITION

The Great National Dictionaries

Noah Webster	Jacob and Wilhelm Grimm
An American Dictionary	*Deutsches Wörterbuch*
of the English Language	1852–1971
1828	

THE FRENCH ACADEMY's *Dictionnaire* and Johnson's *Dictionary* represent different approaches to the idea of a national language: one protected from foreign impurities, based on the "best" literary language, and enforced from on high; the other recognizing the impossibility of ever fixing the language, and concerned only with recording the language as accurately as possible. Dictionaries often reflect the cultures that produce them: since the rise of the modern nation-state in the seventeenth century, lexicographers have worked to reinforce, or even to build, a national consciousness.

Modern maps suggest that everyone in the area labeled SPAIN speaks Spanish; across the border to the west they speak Portuguese; across the border to the north they speak French. But maps can lie. Before the eighteenth century it was hard to tell how many languages were spoken in Spain or Portugal or France, and where the speakers of one left off and the next began. Dictionaries were partly responsible for consolidating national linguistic consciousness. The Della Cruscan *Vocabolario*, for instance, played a role not merely in recording but in creating the Italian language: it established a standard form of Italian, based on Tuscan, that would displace the dozens of local dialects spoken around the Italian peninsula. When Peter the Great wanted to consolidate a vast and growing Russia, he ordered his Academy of Sciences to regularize the Russian language with an academic dictionary. The six-volume dictionary published between 1789 and 1794 established vernacular Russian rather than Church Slavonic as the standard.[1] The Czech National Revival in part of the Austro-Hungarian Empire in the late eighteenth century led to the publication of a pile of reference books, of which Josef Dobrovský's grammar in 1809 and Josef Jungmann's *Ausfürliches und vollständiges deutsch–böhmisches synonymisch-phraseologisches Wörterbuch* of 1834–39—five volumes and 4,700 pages—were the most important.[2]

The connection between nation and dictionary may be clearest in Poland. By the end of the eighteenth century, the Commonwealth of Poland had come to an end and the country was partitioned among Russia, Austria, and Prussia, prompting Tadeusz Kościuszko to lead an uprising in 1794. It was defeated, but patriotic Poles held on to their sense of themselves as a nation. One passionate advocate for Poland's cultural identity was Samuel Bogumił Linde, part of the team that composed one of the first written national constitutions, Poland's so-called "Government Act" of 1788. Linde's constitution had a short life—the government it established was disbanded after just a year and a half—but his other contribution was more lasting: the *Słownik języka polskiego*, or *Dictionary of the Polish Language*, published in Warsaw in six volumes between 1807 and 1814. The first substantial dictionary of Polish, it defined sixty thousand words and provided a focus for linguistic, and therefore national, identity. The nineteenth-century French philosopher Constantin François de Chassebœuf, comte de Volney, knew what he was talking about when he said "Le premier livre d'une nation est le Dictionnaire de sa langue"—a nation's first book is a dictionary of its language.[3]

❦

Samuel Johnson had national ambitions in his *Dictionary*: "I have devoted this book, the labour of years, to the honour of my country, that we may no longer yield the palm of philology to the nations of the continent."[4] Johnson stood for England. Not all English speakers, though, were English, and not all the English-speaking nationalists shared Johnson's sense of the nation.

On the other side of the Atlantic one critic had serious complaints about the work everyone else seemed to admire. Noah Webster was born in West Hartford, Connecticut, in 1758, three years after Johnson's work was published. Webster, whose interest in the language was lifelong, found much to like about the *Dictionary*: Johnson's "great intellectual powers," his emphasis on morality, the definitions that let his abolitionist sympathies shine through (both Johnson and Webster despised American slavery). But Webster was an American patriot—at age nineteen he tried to fight in a battle in the American War of Independence in 1777 (though he arrived on the battlefield too late to be useful). Johnson, on the other hand, was notorious for his disparagement of the American rebels, whom he called "a race of convicts," adding that they "ought to be thankful for anything we allow them short of hanging." He was willing, he said, "to love all mankind, *except an American*."[5]

As the loyal American Webster became increasingly interested in the conjunction of language and nation, he came to scorn the English lexicographer whom he viewed not as a precursor but as an enemy. Before the Treaty of Paris officially ended the American Revolution, Webster wrote, "America must be as independent in *literature* as she is in *politics*, as famous for *arts* as for *arms*."[6] Johnson's *Dictionary*, he asserted, was "extremely imperfect and full of error," and "Not a single page of Johnson's *Dictionary* is correct."[7] He therefore decided to produce his own distinctively American dictionary, and he began by publishing a series of books on the English language in America— which he preferred to call "the American language"—in order to "promote the honour and prosperity of the confederated republics of America and cheerfully throws his mite into the common treasure of patriotic exertion."[8] His spellers, grammars, and readers, beginning with the *Grammatical Institute of the English Language* in 1783, were some of the bestselling books in America for more than a century, selling, by one estimate, a hundred million copies. He wrote essays and pamphlets advocating for spelling reform,[9] eager to widen the gap between British and American English: we owe to Webster most of the spellings marked "chiefly American" in modern dictionaries, in pairs like *colour/color*, *centre/center*, *programme/program*, and so on.

In 1806 he published *A Compendious Dictionary*. It was written, he said, "for my fellow citizens," and he had only scorn for those of his

TITLE: *An American Dictionary of the English Language: Intended to Exhibit, I. The Origin, Affinities and Primary Signification of English Words, as Far as They Have Been Ascertained; II. The Genuine Orthography and Pronunciation of Words, According to General Usage, or to Just Principles of Analogy; III. Accurate and Discriminating Definitions, with Numerous Authorities and Illustrations*

COMPILER: Noah Webster (1758–1843)

ORGANIZATION: Alphabetical, *abacist* to *zymome*

PUBLISHED: New York: S. Converse, 1828

VOLUMES: 2

PAGES: 1,920

ENTRIES: 70,000

TOTAL WORDS: 2.3 million

SIZE: 11" × 9" (28 × 23 cm)

AREA: 1,320 ft² (124 m²)

WEIGHT: 6 lb. (2.8kg)

PRICE: $20 (promptly lowered to $15)

LATEST EDITION: *Webster's Third New International Dictionary of the English Language, Unabridged* (1961)

countrymen "whose veneration for trans-atlantic authors leads them to hold American writers in unmerited contempt."[10] This was to be an American document through and through. But, though serviceable, it accomplished only a tiny fraction of what Webster hoped. Merely 408 small pages, with no etymologies or quotations, its definitions are skimpy, usually just a handful of synonyms:

Admit, v. to allow, suffer, grant, let in, receive
Different, a. unlike, distinct, contrary, various
Law, n. a rule, order, judicial process, justice
Moose, *n.* an American quadruped of the cervine genus very
    large

Take, v. took, pret. taken, pa. to receive, seize, trap, suppose, hire,
    please

Much of the work was not even original—many entries were lifted
whole from John Entick's *New Spelling Dictionary of the English
Language*, published in 1764.

Webster knew the limitations of his work, and he turned his attention to a much grander dictionary and worked on it for two decades. A
contemporary account showed him at work, using a custom-built

> large circular table . . . about two feet wide, built in the form of a
> hollow circle. Dictionaries and grammars of all obtainable
> languages were laid in successive order upon its surface. Webster
> would take the word under investigation, and standing at the right
> end of the lexicographer's table, look it up in the first dictionary
> which lay at that end. . . . He took each word through the twenty
> or thirty dictionaries, making notes of his discoveries, and passing
> around his table many times in the course of a day's labor.[11]

An American Dictionary of the English Language appeared in 1828,
when Webster was seventy. In two stout quartos, it was in most respects
the best dictionary of English on the market on either side of the
Atlantic. Not all the work was original: though Webster often disparaged Johnson he also leaned on him, adopting many of his definitions
verbatim and using others as the basis for his own. But lexicographers
today are almost universally agreed that while Webster took much from
Johnson, he also surpassed him in the clarity and precision of his definitions. Johnson was a very good definer, but Webster was a great one. He
announced that "the great and substantial merit" of a dictionary consists
of "the accuracy and comprehensiveness of its definitions," and he
delivered.

How far Webster came is clear in a comparison of an entry in the
Compendious Dictionary with the *American Dictionary*. This is how
Webster handled the word *language* in 1806:

Language, n. all human speech, a tongue, a style

Part of speech and three imprecise synonyms, nothing more. The entry for the same word in the dictionary of 1828 has grown exponentially, and with the length comes greater precision:

LAN´GUAGE, *noun* [Latin lingua, the tongue, and speech.]
1. Human speech; the expression of ideas by words or significant articulate sounds, for the communication of thoughts. *Language* consists in the oral utterance of sounds, which usage has made the representatives of ideas. When two or more persons customarily annex the same sounds to the same ideas, the expression of these sounds by one person communicates his ideas to another. This is the primary sense of *language* the use of which is to communicate the thoughts of one person to another through the organs of hearing. Articulate sounds are represented by letters, marks or characters which form words. Hence *language* consists also in
2. Words duly arranged in sentences, written, printed or engraved, and exhibited to the eye.
3. The speech or expression of ideas peculiar to a particular nation. Men had originally one and the same *language* but the tribes or families of men, since their dispersion, have distinct languages.
4. Style; manner of expression.
   Others for *language* all their care express.
5. The inarticulate sounds by which irrational animals express their feelings and wants. Each species of animals has peculiar sounds, which are uttered instinctively, and are understood by its own species, and its own species only.
6. Any manner of expressing thoughts. Thus we speak of the *language* of the eye, a *language* very expressive and intelligible.
7. A nation, as distinguished by their speech. Daniel 3:29.

What had been 9 words was now 240. Other pairings are even more extreme: the entry for *give* was 16 words in 1806, and 1,114 in 1828. In 1806 Webster covered *set*—noun and verb—in 43 words; in 1828 he took 2,490. The entry for *take* went from 13 words to 2,524. Joseph Friend calls his definitions "more accurate, more comprehensive, and not less carefully divided and ordered than any previously done in English,"[12] and to this day, professional lexicographers admire his definitions and strive to equal them.

Sales of the first edition were modest—about twenty-five hundred copies. Still Webster carried on, mortgaging his house to raise the money for a second edition. He entered into an acrimonious dispute with one of his former assistants, Joseph Worcester, who published his own *Comprehensive Pronouncing and Explanatory English Dictionary* in 1830, prompting accusations of plagiarism from Webster and a battle— the "dictionary wars"—that dragged on for decades. Webster's own second edition appeared in 1840, three years before he died at the age of eighty-four. His work had remarkable longevity, as the G. & C. Merriam Co. bought the intellectual property in Webster's *American Dictionary* and began marketing a series of revised and expanded editions: a New Revised edition in 1847, a Royal Quarto Edition in 1864, *Webster's International Dictionary* in 1890, *Webster's New International Dictionary* in 1909, a second edition in 1934, and *Webster's Third New International Dictionary* in 1961. The franchise remains the most prestigious in all American lexicography.

⁂

In one area, though, Webster is unambiguously inferior to his rivals, and that was etymology. Johnson's etymologies are sometimes inaccurate, but they were at least based on a reasonable method. Webster's were lousy because his theory of etymology was fundamentally unsound.[13]

Webster, writing in the early nineteenth century, was still looking backward, to seventeenth-century theories of the ways in which languages were related to one another. Early etymologists invented family trees for the world's languages that can be described only as wacky. The most superficial similarities between words were enough to suggest connections between languages. Webster bought into many of these theories and drew impossible connections between languages that had nothing in common. Webster had every reason to know better, because when he was a young man the biblical notion of the confusion of tongues at the Tower of Babel was dissolving from fact into myth. Sir William Jones, an English polymath, first made the argument that most of the languages of Europe and South Asia were related to one another. Everyone knew the Romance languages were descended from Latin. Other connections, though, were mysterious. Was English related to Greek? Did Latin and Swedish have anything in common, or Welsh and Russian? Did German or Portuguese share anything with Persian or Hindi? No one had a good answer before Jones lectured before the Asiatic Society in 1786 and compared Sanskrit to both Latin and Greek. He discovered similarities "so strong indeed, that no philologer could examine them all three, without believing them to have sprung from some common source, which, perhaps, no longer exists." He went even further: "There is a similar reason, though not quite so forcible, for supposing that both the *Gothick* and the *Celtick*, though blended with a very different idiom, had the same origin with *Sanscrit*; and the old *Persian* might be added to the same family, if this were the place for discussing any question concerning the antiquities of *Persia*."[14]

Jones laid the foundations for the study of what is now known as Indo-European, a language family that includes most of the languages of Europe and many of the Indian Subcontinent: English, Latin, French, Spanish, Italian, German, Dutch, Swedish, Norwegian, Greek, Russian, Polish, Czech, Persian, Hindi, Urdu, and dozens of others are all more or less distant cousins. Not all languages belong to this family: Swahili, for instance, has no known connections to English or Spanish or Greek, and no one has discovered any connections between Nahuatl and Dutch. But more than four hundred languages—some dead like Latin, some living like Polish; some major like French, some obscure like Chhattisgarhi—are all descended from the same original language, now known as Proto-Indo-European.

The most exciting etymological advances came from Germany, the center of international comparative and historical philology in the early nineteenth century. No nation-state with that name existed then; Germany was more an idea than a political reality. The Holy Roman Empire, centered mostly on the territory occupied by modern Germany, had been falling apart for generations, producing what became known as *Kleinstaaterei*, a proliferation of fragmented states. Historians cannot even agree on how many statelets there were: something on the order of three hundred, but no list has elicited consensus. German speakers wanted to know: What did it mean to be German? What defines a nation if it is not coterminous with a government? For many theorists in early nineteenth-century Germany, it was above all a culture, and the most important part of a culture was a shared language. Germans were not the people who lived in Germany, or even those who lived under German laws; they were the people who spoke German.

The Brothers Grimm, Jacob and Wilhelm, are best known today for their collection of folktales, including *Cinderella*, *Snow White*, and the *Frog Prince*. The Grimms' most important contribution to scholarship, though, was a dictionary, still the most authoritative dictionary of the German language nearly two centuries after it was begun. And though *Hansel and Gretel* may seem distant from innovations in comparative lexicography, both the dictionary and the folktales grow out of the same nationalist consciousness.

Jacob Ludwig Carl Grimm, born in 1785, was a child prodigy—he "could read books fluently," people said, "before others were beyond their alphabet"[15]—and his brother, Wilhelm Carl Grimm, born a year later, was nearly as brilliant. The family moved to Cassel in 1798; although the children started in the local school's lower levels, Jacob soon reached the top of his class, and Wilhelm was close behind. Jacob entered the University of Marburg in 1802, studying law on his father's advice, with Wilhelm once again in tow. Both found the lectures dull, but they came under the spell of a young lecturer named Friedrich Karl von Savigny. Wilhelm would later say that he owed all his achievements to Savigny.

When the royal library of Westphalia needed a librarian, Jacob's name was suggested. It was an easy enough job, requiring little effort, so Jacob took advantage of both his free time and the great library to begin his scholarly work in earnest. In 1811, both brothers issued their first learned publications: Jacob's *Über den alt-deutschen Meistergesang* (*On the Old German Mastersingers*) and Wilhelm's *Altdänische Heldenlieder, Balladen und Märchen* (*Old Danish Heroic Songs, Ballads, and Tales*). Together they published a collection of ancient German fragments, *Die zwei ältesten deutschen Gedichte des achten Jahrhunderts* (*The Two Oldest German Poems of the Eighth Century*). The German *alt* 'old' appears in all

TITLE: *Deutsches Wörterbuch*

COMPILER: Jacob Grimm (1785–1863) and Wilhelm
Grimm (1786–1859)

ORGANIZATION: Alphabetical, *a* to *Zypressenzweig*

PUBLISHED: 1852–1961; supplement 1971

VOLUMES: 32 + 1 vol. supplement

PAGES: 33,872 (34,824 including the supplement)

ENTRIES: 330,000

TOTAL WORDS: 42 million

SIZE: 10¾" × 6¾" (27.5 × 17 cm)

AREA: 17,000 ft² (1,600 m²), 17,400 ft² (1,630 m²) with the
supplement

WEIGHT: 185 lb. (84 kg)

---

three titles, and with reason: each was concerned with finding the ancient roots of German literary and cultural identity. The answer to the question of Germanness, they believed, was to be found in the deep past. The books were also concerned not with individual geniuses, but with an expression of *das Volk*—the people as a whole.

Das Volk was at the heart of the Grimms' most famous work. In 1812, the first three volumes of *Kinder- und Hausmärchen* (*Children's and Household Tales*) appeared. This foundational work in the study of folklore was one of the first great collections of popular stories. Having collected the tales, they moved on to the language of the folk. In 1819, Jacob published the first part of his four-volume *Deutsche Grammatik* (*German Grammar*), which has been described as "the first lengthy historical study of the Germanic languages" and which "laid the foundations of *Germanistik*, the study of Germanic philology."[16] Its publication marked an epoch, not merely for Jacob Grimm, not merely for German, but for the scientific study of language itself. As one contemporary remarked, "it for the first time demonstrated to the learned world what a language is. Its method was a complete revolution in the science of grammar,—the substitution of a natural and comparative process, in lieu of the former *a priori* rules."[17]

Eventually the brothers returned to Cassel, at which point Jacob Grimm wrote to Jules Michelet, spelling out the brothers' plan to write "a complete dictionary of the German language," one modeled not on the *Dictionnaire de l'Académie françoise*, with its prescriptivism and its invented quotations, but on the *Vocabolario* of the Accademia della Crusca, with its illustrative quotations drawn from the best writers. "Our object," wrote Jacob to another friend, "was first of all to open a complete archive of the language, as it actually exists and has existed during the time in question, let the practical use that shall be made of it be what it may."[18] The hard work began in 1838, and they likened their labors to splitting wood. They read hundreds of books, corresponded with Europe's leading philologists, and lined up volunteers to collect quotations. They particularly encouraged their contributors to pay attention to idioms and proverbs, and even invited them to report obscene words.[19]

Their work would bear the title *Deutsches Wörterbuch* (*German Dictionary*), and even that seemingly direct choice of title was a statement of nationalist consciousness. Most early reference books that listed words and meanings borrowed a name from the classical languages: Latin *glossarium, dictionarium*, or *vocabularius*, Greek *lexikon* or *thesaurus*. In late eighteenth-century Germany, though, a homegrown equivalent had begun to catch on: no longer a Latin *dictionarium* or a Greek *lexikon*, a German language reference book would be a *Wörterbuch* 'word book'. That is what Johann Christoph Adelung chose for his *Grammatisch-kritisches Wörterbuch der Hochdeutschen Mundart* (1774–86), the first great German dictionary, and what the Grimms chose for theirs decades later. It was a sign that German speakers were asserting their own identity, finding words rooted in the Germanic rather than the classical languages.

The most distinctive thing about the Grimms' *Wörterbuch* is the definitions—or, rather, the lack of them. Lexicographers like Johnson and Webster were determined to tease out all the subtle shades of meaning in every word. Not so the Grimms. Their plan was to give not proper definitions but simple translations of German words into Latin; when there was no Latin equivalent, as with modern scientific and technological developments, the Grimms used French or Dutch. Other lexicographers might spend pages explicating a word like *kaufen* 'buy', trying to pin down exactly which kinds of exchanges constituted a purchase. The Grimms simply gave the Latin words *mercari* and *emere*— no more. Jacob even ridiculed other lexicographers who wasted time on long definitions of words like *table* when they could simply give the Latin word for it.[20] (In practice, the Grimms' plan to define in Latin or French was not carried through, at least not systematically, and Latin became less and less common as the work went on. Most of the definitions are in German, though there are some Latin equivalents.)

A dictionary without definitions sounds like a very short work, but the *Wörterbuch* was anything but. It was based on extensive folkloric scholarship, but not fieldwork in the modern sense. The Grimms spent their time digging deep into linguistic history to trace the origins of every word in the German language, and they offered cognates in other Germanic and Indo-European languages in a vigorous workout of the methods of comparative historical linguistics. This attention to linguistic history and etymology was a Germanic tradition, appearing prominently in earlier works such as the Swedish *Glossarium suiogothicum* (1769). The Grimms turned to the quotations that showed the words in use in real German authors, ranging from Martin Luther and Hans Sachs in the early sixteenth century to Johann Wolfgang von Goethe in the early nineteenth. (Most of their attention went to the earlier writers, since they regarded the seventeenth and eighteenth centuries as periods of linguistic decay in Germany.)[21]

Their account of the verb *besetzen* 'occupy', to take an example, opened with an extensive etymological note, comparing German *besetzen* to Gothic *bisatjan*, Old High German *pisezan*, Modern Dutch *bezetten*, Anglo-Saxon *besettan*, English *beset*, Swabian *besätta*, and Danish *besätte*, and then offered an explanation: "land, stadt, burg, haus mit leuten besetzen, *occupare*," that is, "*besetzen* a country, city, castle, a house with people, *occupare*." The German illustrated of the kinds of objects the verb might take, but was not an explanation of what the verb means—the Latin verb *occupare* is as close as they came to a definition. Having got the origin and meaning out of the way, they turned their attention to the word's use in German literature, starting with a quotation from Martin Luther's translation of the Bible, then a trawl through medieval German poetry, a quotation from the sixteenth-century military writer

Leonhard Fronsperger, right up to their near-contemporaries, Goethe, Jean Paul, and Friedrich Schiller. The entry runs to nearly a thousand words.

Their dictionary shows on every page their fascination with the cultural hallmarks of Germanness, and they were determined that their book would be a "shrine"—in German, *Heiligtum*—"to language, to preserve its entire wealth, to hold access to it open for all."[22] Though it may have been open for all, it was hardly accessible to most; its erudition would have scared off all but the most learned readers, and its bulk would have put it beyond the means of most of the peasants they admired. Still, the *Wörterbuch* was to be a work of what was called *Germanistik*, a wide-ranging "German studies" that includes language, literature, history, culture, and folklore. The *Deutsches Wörterbuch* contributed to a sense of German national identity at a time when there was no nation to speak of, and even if the folk could make little sense of it, it made much of the folk.

The Grimms planned a dictionary of six or seven volumes, which would take perhaps ten years to complete. Of course they missed their target—by so much that both Grimms had been in their graves for nearly a century before their life's work was complete. The first install-ment appeared in 1852, when Jacob was sixty-seven and Wilhelm sixty-six, and the first complete volume was published two years later. Wilhelm worked on the *Wörterbuch* up to D but died in 1859, a victim of anthrax, before the second complete volume had appeared. His brother soldiered on until he died 1863, when he was working on the word *Frucht* 'fruit'. At that point the work was taken up by the Preußische Akademie der Wissenschaften (Prussian Academy of Sciences), and Göttingen became a center of German philology. The Grimms' successors had a comparable sense of the national mission of the book. Rudolf Hildebrand, who was instrumental in keeping the project going after the Grimms' death, gave a public lecture at the University of Leipzig in 1869, claiming that the dictionary served two purposes—"a scholarly one and a national one." For him the dictionary was a "treasure trove of German-language spirit," and he insisted that "language is [a] national treasure . . . in whose fate, flourishing, or disappearance the people [can] see its own fate as a people."[23]

After the division of Germany into East and West in 1945, work continued on both sides of the Iron Curtain, with centers in East Berlin and Göttingen. Cooperation was not always as smooth as it might have been. The Communist government of East Germany regarded lexicography as suspiciously *bürgerlich*—bourgeois—and the staff was sometimes reassigned to other tasks. Still the work continued, and the dictionary was completed on January 10, 1961—a century and a quarter after the work began. Much had happened in that time. The book was begun when there was no such country as Germany; the work lasted through the Franco-Prussian War and both World Wars, ending when Germany was not one nation-state but two. So even before the dictionary was complete, a team was put to work on bringing the older material up to date. In 1971 a supplement appeared, and the whole work, including the supplement, was now thirty-three volumes, a total of 34,824 pages.

❦

Webster and the Grimms were both engaged in lexicographical nation building, but they ended up taking very different approaches. Webster inspired a nation by dividing a linguistic community; the Grimms did so by uniting linguistic communities. For Webster, the problem was that the English-speaking world—what some have since called "the Anglosphere"—was too big and undifferentiated. The Brothers Grimm, on the other hand, lived in a world where no German nation-state existed, just many speakers of the German language spread out among many political organizations. For them, creating a German dictionary was a step toward creating a coherent German people.

COUNTING EDITIONS

ONE MEASURE OF the importance of a work of reference is the number of editions it goes through. The *Encyclopædia Britannica*, for example, is not just one work; there are actually fifteen different sets bearing that title, from *Encyclopædia Britannica; or, A Dictionary of Arts and Sciences, Compiled upon a New Plan*, published in three volumes from 1768 to 1771, through the *New Encyclopædia Britannica*, fifteenth edition, published in thirty-two volumes in 2010. Altogether, 274 volumes stretch over a quarter of a millennium, all part of this larger thing called the *Encyclopædia Britannica*. This does not include the hundreds of spinoffs: student editions, fact books, yearbooks, CD-ROM editions, and online versions. The Harvard University Libraries have 255 separate works with *Encyclopædia Britannica* in the title, the British Library has 386, and the Library of Congress 451.

Such is the story of all the great reference books. The *Grand Larousse gastronomique* is now in its sixth edition, the *Dictionnaire de l'Académie française* in its ninth, *Black's Law Dictionary* in its tenth, *Webster's Collegiate* in its eleventh, *Bartlett's Familiar Quotations* in its seventeenth, *Emily Post's Etiquette* in its eighteenth, the *Duden* German dictionaries in their twenty-fifth, and *Wisden Cricketers' Almanack* in its 152nd. For a reference work to be superseded is a badge of honor, meaning that the work did its job. The only works that never change are the dead ones.

But numbers like ninth, eleventh, and twenty-fifth can be misleading. Some works go through so many versions, so poorly coordinated and labeled, that it can be difficult to count them. Even a task that should be simple—tallying the number of editions of Johnson's *Dictionary*—can induce headaches. Samuel Johnson's *Dictionary of the English Language* is famous for its appearance in 1755, but pirated editions, abridgments (both authorized and unauthorized), miniature versions, international issues, unlabeled reprints, and so on, were often advertised with meaningless edition numbers. According to the best count so far, there have been at least 52 separate editions of the full *Dictionary*, 13 adaptations of it, 141 abridgments, and 315 miniature versions. Thus at least 521 different books can in some sense be called "Johnson's *Dictionary*," and that does not count the modern facsimiles and electronic editions. And previously unrecognized editions still turn up from time to time. Because every one of these involved a separate setting of type, no two editions are exactly the same, though no one has yet had the energy to go through all of them to figure out which edition borrowed from which, or where they differ from one another.

Nineteenth- and twentieth-century publishing depended on a new technology, the stereotype or electrotype plate, that allowed publishers to reprint a book without resetting the whole thing in type. Mini-editions could be issued, each slightly different from those that came before, but only modest changes were possible in each, and nothing that altered the pagination. In this system, new edition numbers were reserved for major top-to-bottom revisions. There are many printings of *Webster's Third New International Dictionary*, for instance, with the later ones correcting the errors of the early ones, and sometimes new entries squeezed in when space could be found. The *World Book Encyclopedia* actually had a practice of issuing stickers and telling subscribers to paste them over the old pages to bring information up to date.[1]

The confusion is only becoming worse. In the electronic age, "editions" become close to meaningless. Software sometimes bears an edition number (Windows 8.1), or uses the year of its release as part of a trademark (Office 2010). But it feels meaningless to assign an edition number to, say, Wikipedia. Many guides to citation recommend giving the date of access, but even a date may not be enough. A Wikipedia entry may say one thing at 11:07 in the morning, and something very different at 11:08, and then be tweaked a dozen more times before noon.

CHAPTER 17

GRECIAN GLORY, ROMAN GRANDEUR

Victorian Eyes on the Ancient World

Henry George Liddell and	August Pauly and
Robert Scott	Georg Wissowa
A Greek–English Lexicon	*Real-Encyclopädie der classischen*
1843	*Altertumswissenschaft*
	1893–1980

ICTIONARIES OF THE ancient languages are among the earliest reference books we know—though the languages were not ancient when the first dictionaries were compiled. Even the ancient Greeks needed help with ancient Greek. By the late fourth century B.C.E., Greeks were already having trouble with Homer's language from four centuries earlier. Scholars compiled dictionaries and grammars, most notably at the great Library of Alexandria and the Mouseion—the home of the Muses, the origin of our word *museum*.[1]

Bizarre stories circulate about Philetas of Cos, a late fourth-century-B.C.E. lexicographer. "He was remarkable," wrote Sir John Sandys, "for the delicacy of his frame; it is even stated that he was compelled to wear leaden soles to prevent his being blown away by the wind."[2] His *Ataktoi glossai* (*Miscellaneous Glosses*) collected difficult words from Homer and other early writers and earned Philetas both a statue in his native town of Cos—a rare honor for a lexicographer—and a ribbing in the works of the comic playwright Strato.

Latin posed the same problems as Greek.[3] Even in the Middle Ages, when scholars and clerics were still speaking Latin, the language had evolved to the point that many words in ancient literature were no longer understood. Despite rearguard efforts to keep Latin alive, by the seventeenth century only a tiny population spoke any Latin, and the written language was kept on scholarly life support. Greek was in even worse shape, at least in the West. For as long as Greece was part of the Byzantine, and then the Ottoman, Empire, the West had little contact with Greek as a living language; few Greek texts were in libraries, and no Greek grammars or dictionaries.

In 1478 Giovanni Crastoni published the first printed Greek–Latin dictionary, opening the works of Aristotle and Plato to scholars across Europe. The most important Greek lexicon of the age of print, though, was the *Thesaurus linguae graecae* that Henri Estienne—in Latin, Henricus Stephanus—published in four volumes in 1572. Estienne came from a learned family: his father, Robert, a distinguished Parisian printer, was the first to divide the Christian Bible into verses in his Greek New Testament in 1551. When Robert died in 1559, Henri took over the family printing business, specializing in classical texts, especially in Greek. He devoted himself to a project his father had begun, a dictionary of the ancient Greek language, translating the still-little-known Greek into the international language of scholarship, Latin.

Estienne needed a title for his wordbook. He could have chosen *dictionarius* or *lexicon*, but he instead followed his lexicographer father, who had settled on a less familiar Greek word: *thesaurus* 'treasure-house'. The *Thesaurus linguae graecae* (*Treasure-House of the Greek Language*) frustrated Estienne endlessly. One of his assistants, Joannes Scapula, stole the page proofs and released a plagiarized *Lexicon græco-latinum* in 1579, forcing Estienne to compete in the marketplace with his own work sold at a discount.[4] Still, the *Thesaurus* is a model of lexicography: its coverage is close to comprehensive, given the knowledge of the day; it lays out multiple senses of words clearly; and it includes plentiful illustrative quotations from a wide range of Greek authors.

As the decades passed, though, more ancient texts were discovered and more meanings were revealed. Estienne was reprinted over and over, often with additions and corrections, but after two hundred years, it was time for someone to redo the job from scratch. The new project came from a German scholar named Johann Gottlob Theaenus Schneider, who published his *Kritisches griechisch–deutsches Hand-wörterbuch* (*A Concise Critical Greek–German Lexicon*) in 1797–98. Though Schneider's work is little used today, it deserves credit as the

first Greek lexicon that was more than a repackaged *Thesaurus*. Unlike
Estienne, who translated Greek into Latin, Schneider translated it into
German, since the most advanced linguistic and classical scholarship in
the world was then written in that language.

Another German classicist, Franz Ludwig Carl Friedrich Passow,
was appointed in 1807 to a professorship in Greek thanks to a letter from
his friend Johann Wolfgang von Goethe, then putting the finishing
touches on the first part of *Faust*. One of his students was the philosopher Arthur Schopenhauer, who boarded in Passow's house. In 1812
Passow published *Zweck, Anlage, und Ergänzung griechischer Wörterbücher*
(*The Purpose, Planning, and Completion of Greek Dictionaries*), in which
he insisted lexicographers should strive to show the origin of every word,
as well as every shift in the form or the meaning of that word over the
centuries, supported with chronologically arranged quotations showing
the word in use in actual literature. Earlier lexicographers had included
quotations, but their arrangement was not systematic, and they did not
appear with dates. Passow strove to be comprehensive in laying out his
historical evidence. "Every word," he wrote, "should be made to tell
its own story,"[5] which became a mantra for historically minded philologists in the nineteenth century.

Passow put his principles into action. He used Schneider's
Handwörterbuch as the basis of his own, producing the *Handwörterbuch
der griechischen Sprache* (*A Concise Dictionary of the Greek Language*, 2
vols., 1819–24). It sports quotations from the whole range of classical
Greek literature, and with "semantic bridges," Passow showed how one
basic sense ramified over the centuries into many other senses. This
major contribution to what the Germans call *Gräzistik*, or ancient
Greek philology, sold well—three editions and more than ten thousand
copies by 1827. Those first few editions bore Schneider's name prominently, but following a tradition in lexicography, the original compiler's
name eventually faded from view. By the fourth edition of 1831, it was no
longer *Johann Gottlob Schneiders Handwörterbuch der griechischen Sprache*,
but *Handwörterbuch der griechischen Sprache von Franz Passow*.

Passow would in turn get his comeuppance. He is remembered only
because someone incorporated his work into an even greater lexicon—
the greatest Greek lexicon of them all.

If Henry George Liddell is known at all to the larger world, it is not for his achievement in classical lexicography but for his daughter. Alice Liddell is still one of the most famous girls in the world, even if virtually nobody knows her last name. As a little girl she entranced a young mathematician and photographer, Charles Lutwidge Dodgson, who wrote several books about the imagined adventures of a girl named Alice under his pen name, Lewis Carroll.

But Henry Liddell deserves to be known in his own right. He was born in 1811 in County Durham to a clerical family with roots in the ancient nobility. An unpublished memoir describes his introduction to classical studies: "On my sixth birthday I was promised a great honour and reward. My father took me up into his study and inducted me into the mysteries of the Eton Latin Grammar. I remember the day, the place, and the fact as clearly as if it were yesterday." That the future classicist was a great reader, particularly fond of *Robinson Crusoe*, *The Swiss Family Robinson*, and the children's stories of Maria Edgeworth, is fitting. But despite his love of learning, his time at school was insufferable. "I do not think that any sorrow of youth or manhood," he recalled, "equalled in intensity and duration the blank and hopeless misery which followed the wrench of transference from a happy home to a school such as that to which received us in the summer of 1819." He spent seven dismal years at Bishopton Grove, remembering about it nothing but "the sense of desolation, the utter despair, the wish that I could die on the spot." He was no happier at the famous seventeenth-century Charterhouse School in Surrey: one letter to his father was dated from "Beastly Charterhouse."[6] He did, however, become friendly with the student who sat next to him, William Makepeace Thackeray.

After thirteen unhappy years, Liddell left for Oxford in 1829. "Never," he wrote, "did pilgrim departing from an inhospitable mansion shake the dust from off his feet with more hearty satisfaction than I did on quitting the noble foundation" of Charterhouse.[7] His mood picked up when he arrived at Christ Church, Oxford, where he received nearly perfect marks. His first-class honors in classics and mathematics led to his appointment as a tutor at Christ Church in 1836, and he became an

TITLE: *A Greek–English Lexicon, Based on the German Work of Francis Passow*

COMPILER: Henry George Liddell (1811–98) and Robert Scott (1811–87)

ORGANIZATION: Alphabetical, α and Ἀάατος to Ὠώδης

PUBLISHED: Oxford: Oxford University Press, 1843

PAGES: xviii + 1584

ENTRIES: 104,000

TOTAL WORDS: 2.3 million

SIZE: 10" × 6¼" (25 × 16 cm)

AREA: 685 ft² (64 m²)

WEIGHT: 5 lb. (2.27 kg)

PRICE: £2 4s.

LATEST EDITION: *A Greek–English Lexicon*, 9th ed., rev. and augmented by Henry Stuart Jones with Roderick McKenzie (Oxford: Clarendon Press, 1996)

Anglican priest two years later. He held a series of increasingly distinguished titles in the college, in the university, and in the church, rising to be domestic chaplain to Prince Albert himself—the husband of Queen Victoria. ("It is only an *Honorary* appointment," he wrote to his sister, "i.e. there is no pay. Still it is an honour.... My name is not unknown or unnoticed in high quarters.")[8]

At Christ Church, Liddell met some soon-to-be-big names—William Ewart Gladstone, a future prime minister, was a fellow undergraduate; later, John Ruskin would be among his students, calling him "the only man in Oxford among the masters of my day who knew anything of art." The most momentous of his contacts, however, was a fellow student, Robert Scott. Liddell and Scott were both born in 1811, and both came from clerical families. Both were also impressive academics, for within months of his arrival at Oxford, Scott was awarded a series of scholarships, and like his colleague he took first-class honors. A distinguished Latin essay won him both a prize and the opportunity to become a fellow of Balliol College, Oxford, in 1835, the year in which he, too, was ordained a priest. Like his fellow lexicographer, Scott held a series of academic and ecclesiastical posts. Despite the similarities, though, Liddell and Scott were not an obvious pair. They were political opposites, with Liddell supporting the Liberals and Scott the Tories. Still they managed to find a modus vivendi, and they began their collaboration in the early 1830s—what Christopher Stray calls "an exemplary case of lexicographical amity."[9] What led them to begin their lexicon is unclear. It may have been a publisher's project: Talboys of Oxford may have reached out to them.[10] Others think another tutor at Oxford urged them to work on the book.

"This is what we proposed to ourselves," they wrote, "viz. to carry on what Passow had begun." Passow's fourth edition was the best Greek lexicon on the market, so it made sense that they would base their own work on it. The first plan was simply to translate Passow's German into English, answering the need for a serious Greek–English dictionary, as the few attempts in English were weak. But they discovered that they needed to go beyond mere translation, and they resolved to out-Passow Passow, making their work an avowedly historical lexicon: "Our Plan has been that marked out and begun by Passow, viz. *to make each Article a History of the usage of the word referred to.*" It was a much larger task than they had expected when they agreed to the project, and finding the time for the work was difficult. Through a decade's labor, Liddell and Scott "had only spare hours to bestow."[11] Every evening at seven o'clock, Scott would walk from Balliol, along the Cornmarket and St. Aldate's, to Christ Church, where the two of them would work together.

Their *Greek–English Lexicon* finally appeared in 1843. Its definitions are sound, and the book gives full expositions of all the subtle shades of meaning. The dictionary is especially strong in providing cross-references from irregular forms to the proper entries. Most important, everything is based on actual literature: Liddell and Scott often provided full quotations from actual Greek literature, from the eleventh century B.C.E. into the Hellenistic period. The erudition can be intimidating:

Τρίπους, ποδος, ὁ, ἡ, -πουν, τό, (τρι-, πούς) *three-footed, three-legged* or *with three feet*: and so—I. *measuring three feet*, τρ. τὸ ευρος, Hdt. 3, 60.—II. *going on three feet*, proverb. of an old man who leans on a staff, τρίποδας ὁδοὺς στείχει, Aesch. Ag. 80; cf. τριτοβάμων, and see the Sphinx's riddle in Argum. Soph. O. T.: hence—2. usu. as subst., τρίπους, ὁ, *a tripod, a three-footed brass kettle*, Il. 18, 344, sq., Od. 8, 434, etc.; τρίπους ἐμπυριβήτης, Il. 23, 702; so, τρ. ἀμφίπυρος, Soph. Aj. 1405:—besides these we hear of τρ. ἄπυροι, vessels *untouched by fire*, which seem to have been of fine workmanship, used only for ornament, Il. 9, 122, 264, cf. 18, 373, sq., Paus. 4, 32, 1. In Hom., tripods are often given as prizes, Il. 11, 700; 23, 264, 485, etc.; also as gifts of honour, Il. 8, 290, Od. 13, 13. In aftertimes, tripods of fine workmanship, bearing inscriptions, were placed as votive gifts in the temples, esp. in that of Apollo at Dephi; these were then called τρ. ἀναθηματικοί, Δελφικοί, and were sometimes of precious metals, even gold, Hdt. 8, 82, Ar. Plut. 9, Thuc. 1, 132, Paus. 10, 13, 9, cf. Dict. Antiqq.:—hence, a street of Athens adorned with these gifts was called οἱ Τρίποδες, Paus. 1, 20, 1.—III. *any thing with three legs*, generally, *a three-legged table*, etc., Xen. An. 7, 3, 21:—esp. *the stool of the Delphic priestess*, Eur. Ion 91, Or. 163, etc.; proverb, ὡς ἐκ τρίποδος λέγειν, i. e. authoritatively, Ath. 37 fin.

The information is densely packed. Liddell and Scott dwell on the ways literal meanings shade into figurative ones, and they even stray from purely linguistic information to provide insights into Greek folkways and material culture. Citations to parallels in other works abound. The eras that get the most attention from scholars and students get the most thorough treatment: the detail is greater for classical Attic than later Hellenistic or biblical Greek. This sometimes unbalances the *Lexicon*, since the most-quoted authors are not necessarily most typical of the language, but it does show Liddell and Scott's devotion to pedagogy.

The reviews were strong. As one reviewer noted, "The merits of this work ... will drive every other Greek dictionary out of circulation, wherever the English language is spoken, and will continue to be used for years, perhaps for generations to come."[12] In that he was correct. One splenetic reviewer, J. R. Fishlake, tried his best to complain about Liddell and Scott, but even he had trouble finding things to object to:

"having examined this Lexicon word by word through many, very many pages, we have not discovered in it more defects of this kind than might fairly have been expected, in proportion to its size, and considering it to be a first edition; and those which we have seen are not generally of a glaring character, nor of any very material consequence." He was obliged, almost against his will, to declare, "it constitutes already a sterling addition to the library; and reflects indisputably very high honour on its authors."[13]

Success was immediate, and only grew. The first edition appeared in a print run of three thousand copies, but by the time of the sixth edition, 1869, the presses turned out fifteen thousand copies. Over the years it continued to be improved. Liddell revised the seventh (1883) and eighth (1897) editions himself, and the ninth edition, the first to be undertaken after Liddell's death, was a major revision, carried out by Sir Henry Stuart Jones and Roderick McKenzie. Jones's contribution was important enough that modern editions are known as "Liddell-Scott-Jones," or "LSJ."

But before Jones's name was added to the masthead, one other name was dropped. In the first edition, the editors acknowledged their debt to their most important German predecessor: "our Work is said to be 'based on the German Work of FRANCIS PASSOW.' We cannot too fully express our obligations to this excellent book, without which ours never would have been attempted."[14] The second and third editions continued to praise their great predecessor. But their graciousness did not last: the fourth edition of 1855 dropped Passow's name from the title page.

⁂

Liddell and Scott drew a sharp line between the lexical and the encyclopedic, and they stayed firmly on the lexical side. Others, though, sought to illuminate the ancient world in more wide-ranging works.

William Smith, an Englishman, knew that "scarcely a single subject included under the general name of Greek and Roman Antiquities . . . has not received elucidation from the writings of the modern scholars of Germany."[15] He therefore planned to collect the latest in German antiquarian knowledge, scattered through many learned volumes, and to bring it together in a one-volume compendium suited to the needs of students. It would come with citations to the best modern scholarship that would allow the more diligent students to follow the leads. His *Dictionary of Greek and Roman Antiquities* appeared in 1842.

The most extensive treatment the classical world has ever received, though, followed not long after. Like Liddell and Scott's *Lexicon*, it began as a revised version of something that already existed. August Friedrich Pauly started publishing his German encyclopedia of the classical world in 1837, and though Pauly died young, his work was completed and supplemented by Wilhelm Siegmund Teuffel and Christian Waltz as the *Realencyclopädie der classischen Altertumswissenschaft in alphabetischer Ordnung* (*Encyclopedia of Classical Knowledge in Alphabetical Order*, 6 vols. in 9 parts) in 1852.[16] But Pauly's work was superseded by a French *Dictionnaire des antiquités grecques et romaines* (1873–1919), and it would hardly be remembered today but for a successor, Georg Wissowa, who was not even born when Pauly died. Wissowa was the main force behind a revised version of Pauly, known today as Pauly-Wissowa.

The revised version fills an entire bookcase and then some. Though it was begun at the end of the nineteenth century, it is still essential for anyone interested in ancient Greece or Rome. The German word *Altertumswissenschaft* gives some idea of the book's scope: it means "knowledge of ancient times," and anything at all related to antiquity— history, literature, drama, clothing, food, philosophy, numismatics, military tactics, language, architecture—was included. It was cultural studies applied to the glory that was Greece and the grandeur that was Rome. The learning manages to be both dense and wide-ranging, as in this entry on *Draco*:

7)Δράκων, *Serpens, Anguis,* large constellation in the northern hemisphere, see S t e r n b i l d e r. The mythological D. was regarded as the dragon who guarded the apples of Hesperides and, after Heracles killed him, was placed in the sky by Hera or Zeus. According to Pherecydes (see frg. 33), the Earth gave the golden apples to Zeus and Hera at their wedding, and Hera planted them in the garden of the gods, near Atlas. But since the Hesperides always picked the apples, Hera placed the dragon to guard the garden (Eratosth. Catast. 3. Hyg. astr. II 3. Schol. Arat. 45. Schol.

TITLE: *Paulys Realencyclopädie der classischen Altertumswissenschaft: Unter Mitwirkung zahlreicher Fachgenossen: Hrsg. von Georg Wissowa*

COMPILER: August Pauly (1796–1845), Wilhelm Siegmund Teuffel (1820–78), and Georg Otto August Wissowa (1859–1931)

ORGANIZATION: Alphabetical, *Aal* to *Zythos*

PUBLISHED: Stuttgart: J. B. Metzler, then Druckenmüller, 1893–1980

VOLUMES: 83 + 15 vols. supplement

PAGES: 68,000

ENTRIES: 15,334

TOTAL WORDS: 55 million

SIZE: 10" × 7½" (25 × 19 cm)

TOTAL AREA: 35,000 sq. ft. (3,230 m²)

WEIGHT: 202 lb.; 285 lb. with supplements (91.8 kg; 130 kg with supplements)

LATEST EDITION: *Der neue Pauly: Enzyklopädie der Antike: Altertum*, ed. Hubert Cancik and Helmuth Schneider (Stuttgart: J. B. Metzler, 1996–2003), 16 vols. in 19

Germ. BP 60, 7ff. G 116, 21. S 117, 1ff., s. H e s p e r i d e n). The dragon is in conjunction with the nearby constellation of Heracles (ὁ Ἐνγόνασιν), who, placed by Zeus among the stars, places his foot on the D.'s head (Eratosth. 4. Hyg. astr. II 6. Schol. Arat. 74. Schol. Germ. BP 61, 3ff. G 118, 18ff. S 118, 2ff.; on the relationship between Eratosth. 3 and 4 see O l i v i e r i I catasterismi di Eratostene, S.-A. in Stud. ital. di filol. class. V 1ff.). There were a number of other interpretations. Either the D. was the Python's dragon (ὡς δὲ ὁ πολὺς λόγος, ὁ ὑπὸ Ἀπόλλωνος ἀναιρεθεὶς Πύθων), or the dragon killed by Cadmus (Schol. Arat. 45), or a dragon that Athena, in a fight with the giant Mimas, threw into the sky, where he still slithers (Hyg. astr. II 3. Schol. Germ. BP 60, 15ff.). According to a Cretan myth, Zeus, to escape the persecutions of his father Kronos, changed himself into a snake and his attendants into she-bears. When he later took charge, he immortalized this event in the stars (Schol. Arat. 46). Finally, it could be the snake that Dionysus led as a sign of the shield and placed in the sky as a token of the virginity of Chalcomede (Nonn. Dionys. XXV 402ff. XXXIII 370ff.).

The major characters behind Pauly-Wissowa were great scholars, but neither lived an especially interesting life. Pauly was a classical philologist, educated at the University of Tübingen, then and now one of the most prestigious universities in Germany. He spent most of his career teaching Greek and Latin literature at the Gymnasium in Stuttgart and died in 1845 just shy of his forty-ninth birthday. Georg Wissowa was born in 1859 in Wrocław, in what is now Poland, and attended the local university. He landed a job as a classical philologist at the University of Marburg, where he specialized in Roman religion. He was known in his time for revising another reference book, Theodor Mommsen's *Handbuch der römischen Alterthümer* (*Manual of Roman Antiquities*).

The original idea for a revised Pauly came from a scholar named Otto Crusius, but Crusius quickly changed his mind and relinquished the task to Wissowa, who declared his intention to produce a wholly new work, not merely a light revision. The plan was for a work in ten volumes in as many years. The story should be familiar by now: it wound up in ninety-eight volumes in nearly as many years. Wissowa, who lived to be seventy-one, died as the encyclopedia had reached *M*, and after his death the editorship passed to a series of philologists: Wilhelm Kroll, Karl Mittelhaus, Konrat Ziegler, Hans Gärtner. Inevitably a work published over several decades will be inconsistent, and that is true of Pauly-Wissowa. New scholarly discoveries make their appearance, and shifting scholarly interests and fashions give the volumes slightly different characters. Some scholars have noted hints of Nazi ideology in the volumes from the 1930s and '40s, followed by a shift away from those principles after the Second World War came to an end. The project was finally completed in 1980.

The reviews, which began appearing shortly after the first volume was published in 1894, were not so much glowing as awestruck. Many were amazed at the breadth of the coverage. As one early reviewer pointed out, "it includes all the names of persons of any historical importance whatsoever"—so, for instance, we get more than a hundred people named *Alexandros* and 127 named *Annius*.[17] But it had depth as well as breadth, and the real strength of Pauly-Wissowa shows up in the long entries—extended essays, some dozens of pages long, signed by the contributors, with extensive references to the scholarly literature. The article for *princeps* occupied thirteen columns of small type; *Praxiteles* filled twenty-three; *praetor* twenty-seven; *prähistorische Kulturen* ninety-eight. *Praefectus* took up ninety columns in the main alphabetical sequence, with another eighty-eight in the supplement at the end of the volume.

The encyclopedia's greatest virtue was the quality of the scholarship. The specialized knowledge in every one of the subjects it covered— military history, literature, philology, archaeology, monumental inscriptions, even the history of agriculture—was greater than what had appeared in any comparable reference work before.[18] Modern encyclopedias are collaborative endeavors, and editors work to line up contributors in various areas of expertise. Getting the best person for every article is difficult, and editors often have to settle for someone who is merely good enough. Wissowa, though, somehow managed to get the best people in the field, or, more accurately, fields. He initially signed up 119 experts, mostly German university professors, but as the work stretched out over multiple generations, more signed on, and the roster became more international. Eventually 1,096 contributors pitched in. The result is the first port of call for anyone working on the Greek or Roman world.

⁂

Both works discussed in this chapter have had significant afterlives. The first edition of Liddell and Scott appeared in 1843; today, in its ninth edition (1925–40), it remains the authoritative work in the field. Its three versions—the abridged edition, the intermediate edition without citations, and the unabridged edition—are known affectionately as the "Little Liddell," the "Middle Liddell," and the "Great Scott."

But much has happened over the decades: new texts and unknown words have turned up in manuscripts and inscriptions, and new research has revealed word origins unsuspected by earlier generations. A new definitive take on Greek is needed, and it is coming in the form of the *Diccionario Griego–Español* (*DGE*) being developed at the Instituto de Lenguas y Culturas del Mediterráneo y Oriente Próximo at Madrid's Centro de Ciencias Humanas y Sociales. When complete, the *DGE* will be three times the length of Liddell and Scott, with an even broader scope, taking in some of the earliest Greek writings from Mycenae as well as the Christian Church Fathers. It will also be more open to encyclopedic information by including personal names and place names. Volume 1 appeared in 1980, covering the alphabet from *a* to *alla*, and volume 7 (*ekpelleuo–exauos*) arrived in 2009.

Pauly-Wissowa, too, has been both abridged and revisited. Between 1964 and 1975 a *Kleine Pauly* (small *Pauly*) appeared in five volumes, mostly an abridgment of the *Real-Encyklopädie* but with updates to some of the older entries. But the more significant work is the *Neue Pauly* (new *Pauly*), eighteen volumes published between 1996 and 2003, with twelve supplementary volumes between 2004 and 2012. While this work was inspired by Pauly-Wissowa and written in the same tradition, the scholarship was original and reflected the latest thinking in the study of antiquity. The new version appeared in two independent alphabetical sections, one covering "Antiquity" and the other the "Classical Tradition." An English version, *Brill's New Pauly*, was published in twenty-eight volumes between 2002 and 2014.

CHAPTER 17 ½
LOST PROJECTS
What Might Have Been

ANY ANCIENT BOOKS have disappeared. Seven plays each by Aeschylus and Sophocles have survived, and eighteen or nineteen by Euripides. But Aeschylus is believed to have written between seventy and ninety plays; Sophocles wrote more than a hundred, and Euripides had ninety-five to his credit. The others are lost, presumably forever. The same fate has befallen many early reference books. Verrius Flaccus wrote *On the Meaning of Words* early in the first century C.E.; only a later summary survives. Cato the Censor's encyclopedia, compiled around 158 B.C.E., is gone leaving hardly a trace, as is Marcus Terentius Varro's *Disciplines*. Only the medical parts of A. Cornelius Celsus's encyclopedia survive. The first known Chinese encyclopedia, *Huang Ian*, written around the year 220 C.E., has vanished.

The survival rate is better in the medieval world, though many reference books celebrated in their time have never been seen today. The *Hortus deliciarum* (*Garden of Delights*) was composed in the twelfth century by Herrad of Landsberg, the abbess of Hohenburg. The original manuscript was beautifully illustrated in color, and the book survived intact for seven centuries. But when the Prussians besieged Strasbourg in August 1870 during the Franco-Prussian War, fire destroyed both the city's Museum of Fine Arts and its Municipal Library, where the *Hortus* had been kept. We know of its contents only from earlier lithographic reproductions, but the glorious colors of the original are lost.[1] Fire also did in what would have been a magnificent Czech lexicon. Jan Ámos Komenský, or Comenius, an important Moravian humanist and educator, began work on his *Linguae Bohemicae thesaurus* in 1612, while he was still a student, and spent forty years on it.

But it was burned to ashes during the Habsburg occupation of the town of Leszno during the Swedish-Polish War in 1656.

Water has been equally damaging. Louis de Jaucourt worked for almost twenty years on a six-volume folio medical dictionary. In 1750, nearing the finish line, he was negotiating with a Dutch publisher to bring the book out. He had the manuscript carefully packed in a box and sent on a ship from Rouen to Amsterdam—but the ship sank to the bottom of the sea somewhere off the Dutch coast, taking the only copy of his work with it. Recognizing that it was too late to start again from scratch, he turned to the editors of *L'Encyclopédie* and offered his services there.[2]

Probably the most painful loss the world of reference books has ever suffered is the *Yonglè dàdian*, also called the *Yongle Encyclopedia*. This king-sized work was ordered by the Emperor Cheng Zu and carried out at the Wen Yuan Pavilion in the imperial library. When the encyclopedia was completed in 1407 it occupied 22,937 scrolls in 11,095 books. In the sixteenth century, prudence dictated that a copy be made, so in 1567 a team set to work transcribing it—by which time something like 10 percent of the original work had gone missing. That original has now disappeared entirely, and no one knows what happened to it. Even the backup copy has suffered serious indignities. In the nineteenth century, the English and French visited China as part of their imperial projects and thought it reasonable to take pieces of the encyclopedia home as souvenirs. A fire wiped out eight hundred volumes. By 1875, less than half of the original work survived; by 1894, just 7 percent; and today, less than 4 percent.[3]

But every so often we get lucky, and a long-lost work turns up. James Boswell, famous as Samuel Johnson's biographer, worked in the 1760s on a Scottish dictionary. "The Scottish language is being lost every day," he lamented in his diary, "and in a short time will become quite unintelligible. . . . To me, who have the true patriotic soul of an old Scotsman, that would seem a pity. It is for that reason that I have undertaken to make a dictionary of our tongue."[4] But no such dictionary had ever been published, and even the discovery of tens of thousands of pages of Boswell's manuscripts in the 1920s produced nothing lexicographical. Critics assumed Boswell never made much progress on his dictionary, or, if he did, it had been destroyed, but it was hiding in plain sight all along, on the shelves of one of the world's great libraries. Some unknown owner in the late eighteenth or nineteenth century bound the unpublished manuscript with John Jamieson's *Etymological Dictionary of the Scottish Language*—a published Scottish dictionary sharing a binding with an unpublished Scottish dictionary—and when Oxford University's Bodleian Library bought the volume, they cataloged it only under Jamieson's name, convinced the manuscript was his. Boswell's work sat undetected until in 2010 lexicographer Susan Rennie, pursuing research on Jamieson in Oxford, discovered the handwritten material and began to suspect it was not Jamieson's. After consulting Boswell experts, she was able to confirm that the long-neglected manuscript was the work begun in the 1760s.

CHAPTER 18

WORDS TELLING THEIR OWN STORIES

The Historical Dictionaries

Matthias de Vries	Sir James A. H. Murray
Woordenboek der	*The Oxford English*
Nederlandsche taal	*Dictionary*
1882–1998	1884–1928

THE GRIMMS SHOWED the lexicographical world what a dictionary could be: a monumental work of scholarship, surveying the whole of a language's literary inheritance and providing a historical account of its development. But the *Deutsches Wörterbuch*, though 34,000 pages and the work of a century and a half, is neither the largest nor the slowest of the great dictionaries.

⯑

The *Woordenboek der Nederlandsche taal*, the historical dictionary of the Dutch language, is called the longest dictionary in the world. The *Deutsches Wörterbuch* was its most important inspiration, but whereas the Grimms were seeking to establish a national identity, Dutch lexicographers were self-consciously dealing with an international language. Dutch is spoken in both the Netherlands and the Flemish parts of Belgium, two countries that had once been part of a United Kingdom of the Netherlands. With the Belgian Revolution of the 1830s, though, what had been the Southern Netherlands became a new nation-state, Belgium. The *Woordenboek* is often identified with an "integrationist" movement, an attempt to create an international version of the language. Both nations provided financial support for the project.

People had been lamenting the lack of a reliable Dutch dictionary since the early eighteenth century, and the moaning grew louder in the

TITLE: *Woordenboek der Nederlandsche taal*
COMPILER: Matthias de Vries (1820–92)
ORGANIZATION: Alphabetical, *a* to *zythum*
PUBLISHED: 's-Gravenhage: Martinus Nijhoff & Sdu,
  1882–1998
VOLUMES: 40 + 3 vols. supplement
PAGES: 45,805; 49,255 including supplements
ENTRIES: 375,000
TOTAL WORDS: 36.6 million; 39.4 million including
  supplements
SIZE: 10¼" × 6½" (26 × 16.5 cm)
AREA: 21,000 ft² (1,963 m²); 22,600 ft² (2,113 m²) including
  supplements
WEIGHT: 110 lb. (50.2 kg); 119 lb. (54 kg) including
  supplements

nineteenth.[1] The plan to publish a dictionary arose at the first Nederlandsch Congres, an annual gathering of Dutch-speaking linguists that alternated its meetings between the Netherlands and Belgium. The meeting that began on August 26, 1849, was hosted by the University of Ghent in Belgium, where Gerth van Wijk of the Netherlands urged a dictionary "for our common tongue." It would eventually become the *Woordenboek der Nederlandsche taal*, or *WNT*. After a year's preparation, the 1850 congress—this time in Amsterdam—made it official: Matthias de Vries was to be the editor.

As a young man, de Vries was fascinated by all things Dutch, especially the literature of the Middle Ages. He had studied classics at Leiden University, earning a Ph.D. in 1843, and became a private tutor in classical studies at Leiden. In 1846 he took another position, as a teacher at the city's grammar school, but he was determined to bring the study of Dutch to the level of scientific inquiry that had been achieved in the classical languages. In 1849 he published *De Nederlandsche taalkunde, beschouwd in hare vroegere geschiedenis, tegenwoordigen toestand en eischen voor de toekomst* (Dutch philology: past, present, and future), and was appointed professor of Dutch language and literature at Groningen University, but a few years later he returned to Leiden, where he remained for nearly forty years, until his retirement in 1891.

One of de Vries's contemporaries wrote that "Language is the soul of the nation, it is the very nation itself," and de Vries was so impressed with that formulation that he made it the motto for the entire dictionary.[2] He valued the historical study of a living language, for in a living language he could discern the true spirit of a nation. But there was something special about Dutch. De Vries believed that the Romance languages were now "benumbed" in the people's minds, but that the Germanic languages were still vigorous, still vital. De Vries's most important predecessor as both lexicographer and Leiden-based philologist, Matthijs Siegenbeek, believed that the point of studying the Dutch language was to achieve eloquence. Not so de Vries, who thought it was to achieve a scientific understanding of the language, including the old, the hackneyed, the awkward, "just as to the botanist the most insignificant weed is as important as the most splendid flower."[3] By paying attention to the language in all its registers, he hoped to extract the laws that guided its development—and that could be achieved only through a solid grounding in linguistics. In this de Vries was channeling the spirit of August Schleicher, a German linguist who had made similar calls for a scientific approach to language.

The practical work on the *WNT* began in 1852, with the publication of de Vries's *Ontwerp van een Nederlandsch woordenboek* (Proposal for a Dutch dictionary). De Vries was originally planning a dictionary only of contemporary—which is to say nineteenth-century—Dutch, with some background going back to the early seventeenth century. He was eventually persuaded to cover the whole of the modern form of the language, and to that end he built up a database that eventually reached 1.7 million quotations.

In 1863, de Vries teamed up with Lamert Allard te Winkel, another philologist eleven years his senior. Te Winkel lived only another five years, so he had a short tenure with the *WNT*, but the work he did was fundamental. He developed a new systematic approach to spelling. Most of the European languages had achieved a high degree of standardization in their orthography by the mid-nineteenth century, but Dutch was still chaotic. The system worked out, still known as the *de Vries–te Winkel spelling*, became official—mandated by law—in both countries.

The fruits of their efforts appeared in 1864, when the first part, covering *A–Aanhaling*, came out. But it was not an entire volume, just a fascicle. Another eighteen years passed before the first full volume appeared, *A–Ajuin*, in 1882. Already the character of the dictionary was visible. Each entry provided information on the part of speech and, for nouns, the gender and the plural forms; historical information, with minimal speculation on etymological questions; definitions, given in Dutch; and quotations drawn from Dutch literature. Unlike the Grimms, with whom he traded ideas, de Vries decided to forgo Latin definitions in favor of the vernacular. There was information on pronunciation only in difficult or ambiguous cases, but no dates of quotations appeared in the text proper, though a long bibliography provided them.[4] De Vries also included usage notes, and he was not shy about offering value judgments: from time to time he declared his own opinion was better than widespread usage, even the usage of the best authors. Nonstandard dialect was systematically excluded. He laid out policies, not always strictly followed, for including or excluding foreign borrowings; borrowings from French that he considered insufficiently Dutch often did not make the cut.

De Vries retired in 1891 at age seventy, having reached only the word *gitzwart* 'pitch-black'. The project was taken over by the Instituut voor Nederlandse Lexicologie, under the aegis of the Dutch Language Union, and over the next hundred years a series of editors worked on it. One of the most important was Jacoba van Lessen, who joined the editorial staff in 1929 and was promoted to chief editor in 1946, a position she held until her death in 1951, making her one of the very few women at the helm of a major reference project.

The *Woordenboek* has a prominent place among the other great historical dictionaries of that era, the *Deutsches Wörterbuch*, the *Oxford English Dictionary*, and Émile Littré's *Dictionnaire de la langue française*; of the three, it is the largest, but also the least consistent in carrying out its policies.[5] Over the course of the dictionary, for instance, the period it covered changed several times: the starting date for quotations was originally 1637 (the publication of the *Statenbijbel*, the most important Bible translation), then it got pushed back to 1580, then even further to 1500; the ending date was always the present, but the present kept extending, and when it reached 1971, it was suddenly pushed back to 1921. The nature of the source material also changed over time. De Vries imagined a dictionary of literary usage, but the dictionary was eventually opened to nonliterary sources: legal writing, diaries, letters, and so on. Even foreign and dialect words that are widely used in Dutch-speaking countries made their way in. In the 1940s and '50s a supplement appeared, bringing the early part of the dictionary into line with the new editorial policies.

At long last, 134 years after the first volume appeared and 146 years after the dictionary was proposed, the team presented the fortieth volume, *Zuid–Zythum*, to Albert II of Belgium and Queen Beatrix of the Netherlands on June 16, 1998. Three supplementary volumes, bringing the early parts of the dictionary up to date through 1976 and bringing the page count up to 49,255, appeared in 2001. It was the work of five generations.

❧

The story of the *Oxford English Dictionary* begins in 1857. Johnson's was still the reigning English dictionary, and it had appeared in dozens of editions. Webster was also taken seriously, especially in the United States, and was in some ways superior to Johnson—his definitions are often more precise, and of course he was able to include words from the seventy-five years that came between Johnson's *Dictionary* and his own. Another major English dictionary had appeared in 1835–37, written by Charles Richardson, a protégé of the eccentric philologist John Horne Tooke. Richardson adopted Horne Tooke's strange notion that every word has one and only one meaning, which can be determined by looking at the etymology. He therefore wrote a dictionary without definitions. With the space he saved, he expanded the etymologies, the subject closest to his heart. That most of those etymologies were pure bunk did little for the quality of the dictionary.

By 1857, Johnson's *Dictionary* was too old, Webster's too weak in his
etymologies, and Richardson's too eccentric to serve the growing
English-speaking world. Worst of all, none of them was designed on a
scientific plan. The Germans had shown what was possible when scientific method was brought to bear on a language. So in Richard Chenevix
Trench's lecture that year before the Philological Society, later published
as *On Some Deficiencies in Our English Dictionaries*, he demanded a
proper historical dictionary of English, from the earliest days to the
present. At its heart should be quotations from English literature.
Johnson, of course, had included quotations, and Webster followed, but
neither of them was concerned with finding the first and (in the case of
obsolete words) last occurrences, or of showing how senses developed
over time. Remembering Passow's edict that "Every word should be
made to tell its own story," Trench argued that "the study of language is
. . . the most potent means of all for planting in us the true past of our
country; and of this it is proposed in great part to deprive us by those
who would make our Dictionaries the representations merely of what
the language now is, and not also of what it has been."[6]

The Philological Society released a *Proposal for the Publication of a
New English Dictionary* in 1859, and in it the debt to Passow was explicit.
Passow's mantra about words telling their stories was again invoked and
expanded upon:

> In the treatment of individual words the historical principle will
> be uniformly adopted;—that is to say, we shall endeavour to show
> more clearly and fully than has hitherto been done, or even
> attempted, the development of the sense or various senses of each
> word from its etymology and from each other, so as to bring into
> clear light the common thread which unites all together.[7]

Macmillan was to be the publisher, but they had little idea of what
they were signing on to. They imagined a moderate-sized dictionary,
perhaps four quarto volumes, and were prepared to devote ten years to
the project. Little did they know the length would be exceeded by a
factor of four and the time by a factor of seven. The lexicographers
needed a quarter century simply to get to the letter *A*. The snail's pace

eventually led Macmillan to back out and to hand the project over to Oxford University Press, which had more experience dealing with over-extended scholars.

The work—titled simply *A New English Dictionary*—was plagued by a series of problems in the early days. The first editor, Herbert Coleridge, was the grandson of the poet and a literary boy wonder. Unfortunately, he was never given the chance to show what he was capable of, because he died almost as soon as he took the reins, having just turned thirty years old. The next in line was Frederick Furnivall, a distinguished lawyer and the secretary of the Philological Society. While he loved establishing clubs and societies of every description, he could not bring himself to do any real lexicographical work, and what little he did in those early days was sloppy.

The next editor, though, was a winner: a forty-two-year-old Scot named James Murray. (Later he would pick up a knighthood and a pair of middle initials, becoming Sir James A. H. Murray, but the initials do not seem to stand for anything.) While still a young child, Murray taught himself to read several languages, and he kept up the passion the rest of his life. As he boasted, "I at one time or another could read in a sort of way 25 or more languages."[8] Murray and his team decided to produce a historical dictionary, covering the English language from the year 1150, traditionally recognized as a boundary between Old and Middle English, to the present. Words that had died out during the Old English period would be excluded, but anything that survived past 1150 would go in. None of the other historical dictionaries presumed to cover so many centuries.[9] The Grimms dealt with a canon of about three centuries, and de Vries was initially interested in the Dutch language over just two centuries, though the scope was widened to four. But the *OED* was dealing with a continuous literary tradition more than a thousand years long.

The dictionary was prepared according to a much-expanded version of Johnson's method. Everything had to be based in actual written sources, so the first step was to read widely in English. Words would be included and defined based solely on how they had been used in writing by others; the compilers would resist the urge to single out "good" or "bad" words, and on principle they refused to make up or tinker with

TITLE: *A New English Dictionary on Historical Principles;*
Founded Mainly on the Materials Collected by the
Philological Society

COMPILER: Sir James A. H. Murray (1837–1915)

ORGANIZATION: Alphabetical, *a* to *zyxt*

PUBLISHED: Oxford: Oxford University Press, 1 Feb.
1884–19 April 1928; supplement, 1933

VOLUMES: 12 + 1 vol. supplement (1933); 4 further
supplements (1972–86)

PAGES: 15,487; 21,217 including supplements

ENTRIES: 252,200, defining 414,800 word forms

TOTAL WORDS: 38 million; 52 million including
supplements

SIZE: 13" × 10¼" (33 × 26 cm)

AREA: 14,200 ft² (1,328 m²); 19,500 ft² (1,820 m²) including
supplements

WEIGHT: 145 lb. (66 kg); 198 lb. (90 kg) including
supplements

PRICE: £52 10s. to £57 15s., depending on binding

LATEST EDITION: 2nd ed., 1989, in 20 vols. and 21,730
pages, running to 59 million words; 3rd ed., in progress,
online

quotations. All of those things were characteristic of Johnson's *Dictionary*, but the *OED* editors were determined to be as close to comprehensive as possible. And this involved reading exceedingly widely—a reasonable approximation of everything in the English language.

No single human being could hope to read all this, of course, so Murray organized a small team of professional lexicographers, who in turn energized a vast team of volunteer readers, and they were able to do an impressive approximation of the task. The readers were encouraged to read everything they could get their hands on, with occasional specific requests and advice coming from the editors; it would hardly make sense, after all, to have everyone reading *Hamlet*. As they read, they were told, they should keep an eye out for interesting words, and not merely obscure ones; the dictionary needed instances of the usage of ordinary words such as *tree* and *walk* and *little*. Whenever the readers saw something worthy of notice, they were told to write the word in the upper left corner of a slip of paper, to transcribe the whole quotation below it, to provide a precise citation, and to send the slip to Murray's office in Oxford. This office, a prefab building, was fondly known as the Scriptorium, an echo of and tribute to the monastic scriptoria that Cassiodorus had developed nearly a millennium and a half before.

Over the course of five decades the list of volunteers grew to more than a thousand people, and they submitted around 5 million slips. These, combined with the more focused reading project carried out by the in-house lexicographers, formed the raw material from which the dictionary was compiled. Once they had sorted the millions of quotation slips into pigeonholes, first by headword and then by year of publication, the lexicographers worked through the alphabet, pulling all the slips for a given word. By reading through the accumulated evidence they determined how many different senses a word had. Murray's approach to defining owes much to Johnson and Webster, both of whom believed in long and precise definitions, with many meanings broken out into numbered senses. Definers can be "lumpers," who try to cover the whole range of meaning in a small number of broad definitions, or "splitters," who propose a separate definition for every slightly different meaning. Richardson was the ultimate lumper, insisting every word had just one meaning, which he believed would be obvious from context. Murray, on the other hand, was a card-carrying splitter, preferring a large number of distinct definitions.

Murray believed that a proper historical dictionary should tell the story of every word, and every story should start at the beginning. He took seriously Trench's recommendation: "the *first* authority for a word's use in the language which occurs should be adduced; . . . the moment of its entrance into it, . . . the register of its birth, should be thus noted."[10] (Trench was thinking of both Passow's principle and John Jamieson's *Etymological Dictionary of the Scottish Language*, which in 1808 was the first to offer coverage of the birth of every word.) And so Murray resolved to track down the first written occurrence of every word in the English language, along with at least one citation for every sense for each century, and, in the case of obsolete words, the last known citation.

How to recognize, in the Victorian era, the first occurrence of a word was a challenge. Trench was a keen reader, and he was among the first to state a principle that has guided lexicographers every since: "But if it be thus desirable to note in every case, so far as this is possible, the first appearance of a word, then all those tokens which will sometimes cleave to words for awhile, and indicate their recent birth, ought also to be diligently noted. None are more important in this aspect than what one may fitly call 'marks of imperfect naturalization.'"[11] In other words, readers were asked to look for signs that a word was still novel to the audience. When someone read in one of Lord Chesterfield's letters of 1768 that "I feel what the French call a general *mal-aise*, and what we call in Ireland an *unwellness*," the phrase "what the French call" suggested that the English did not: it is the first known occurrence of *malaise*. Likewise, when a reader of W. Abney's *Treatise of Photography* (1878) came across the sentence "The next lens . . . is what is known as a 'wide angle' doublet," the telltale phrase "what is known as" suggested that the term was still unfamiliar to readers, and so it appeared as the first occurrence of *wide angle*.

All these pieces came together to form the dictionary. For 252,000 entries, covering 414,800 words and word forms, Murray and his team provided the headword, along with all its attested spellings and when they were current; pronunciation; an etymology; a series of numbered definitions; and under each definition, quotations to illustrate the word in use. (Whereas the Grimms gave leisurely passages from the great German writers, Murray trimmed his quotations carefully, leaving enough to get the sense of a sentence but no more.)[12] Altogether there are 1,861,200 quotations, covering 4,500 works by 2,700 authors.

The information in each entry includes a pronunciation, then a list of accepted spellings used over the centuries:

Forms: 3–4, 7 **elemens** (*pl.*), 4 **ela-**, **elemente**, 5 **elymente**, 6 **elyment, elemente**, 4– **element**.

Space is at a premium, so single digits indicate centuries ("3–4," for example, means "current in the thirteenth and fourteenth centuries"). For some words, the list of spellings can go on for many lines. Then comes a discussion of the word's origin. Curt, even single-word etymologies are usually adequate, but when necessary, Murray provided long and detailed descriptions of a word's derivation:

[a. OF. *element*, ad. L. *elementum*, a word of which the etymology and primary meaning are uncertain, but which was employed as transl. of Gr. στοιχειον in the various senses:—a component unit of a series; a constituent part of a complex whole (hence the 'four elements'); a member of the planetary system; a letter of the alphabet; a fundamental principle of a science.]

Definitions, sometimes running to dozens of numbered senses, are laid out in a hierarchical outline, with meanings grouped into families. Daggers indicate obsolete definitions:

I. A component part of a complex whole.
* of material things.
1. One of the simple substances of which all material bodies are compounded.
†a. In ancient and mediæval philosophy these were believed to be: Earth, water, air, and fire. See examples in 9. *Obs.* exc. *Hist.*
†b. In pre-scientific chemistry the supposed 'elements' were variously enumerated, the usual number being about five or six. (See quots.). . .
c. In modern chemistry applied to those substances (of which more than seventy are now known) which have hitherto resisted analysis, and which are provisionally supposed to be simple bodies. . . .
2. In wider sense: One of the relatively simple substances of which a complex substance is composed; in *pl.* the 'raw material' of which a thing is made. . . .
3. The bread and wine used in the Sacrament of the Eucharist. Chiefly *pl.*

Under each definition appears a series of quotations, in chronological order:

1813 SIR H. DAVY *Agric. Chem.* i. (1814) 8 Bodies..not capable of being decompounded are considered..as elements. **1830** M. DONOVAN *Dom. Econ.* I. III Sugar is composed of three elements, carbon, hydrogen, and oxygen. **1841** EMERSON *Ess. Hist. Wks.* (Bohn) I. 17 Fifty or sixty chemical elements. **1854** BUSHNAN in *Circ. Sc.* (*c*1865) II. 6/1 The proximate elements are formed by the union of several ultimate elements. **1881** WILLIAMSON in *Nature* No. 618. 414 The foundation of..chemistry was laid by the discovery of chemical elements.

The *New English Dictionary on Historical Principles*—such was the original title—took far longer than the early planners expected. Murray died in 1915, having completed *Q*; his assistants carried on to the end of the alphabet. The tenth volume, *wise–zyxt*, appeared on April 19, 1928, and it was followed in 1933 by complete republication with the contents rejiggered into twelve volumes, with a thirteenth supplemental volume that brought some of the early material up to date and corrected some errors. The title was also changed in the reissue: now that Oxford University Press was firmly in charge, it was officially the *Oxford English Dictionary*.

A series of supplements appeared in the 1970s and '80s, bringing the Victorian material up to date; in 1989, the supplements were merged with the main body of the dictionary into one long sequence to produce the second edition, or *OED2*. A third edition is now under way, but this time it will be a top-to-bottom rewrite: most of the work in *OED2* dates back to the late nineteenth or early twentieth century. Updates continue apace, made easier now that the whole is maintained online. As I write, the *OED* contains 2,674 words first used in the 1970s (*benchmarking, carjacking, factoid, mail bomb, retro*), 1,580 from the 1980s (*biodiversity, bitch-slap, gaydar, power-walk, studmuffin*), 632 from the 1990s (*bootylicious, cybercafe, dotcom, smackdown, spammer*), and 64 from the 2000s (*bromance, crowdsource, podcast, selfie, waterboarding*). As time passes, recent decades will be more fully represented.

The accomplishment of these historical dictionaries—begun in the era of the quill pen, completed in the era of the typewriter—is astonishing. The searches made possible by computers and huge textual corpora have revolutionized historical lexicography; we can now turn up the evidence required for a dictionary entry with little effort. But de Vries, Murray, and their successors did it all with only sharp eyes and patient attention. Any modern lexicographer who has closely examined the quality of this work, conceived and largely carried out in the nineteenth century, has to admire their achievement in making every word tell its own story.

CHAPTER 18 ½
OVERLONG AND OVERDUE

W
HEN CHARLES DICKENS's young hero David Copperfield arrives at a new school he meets the elderly schoolmaster, Dr. Strong, a true scholar, "always engaged in looking out for Greek roots" for his classical dictionary. But while Strong had convinced himself "he had been advancing with it wonderfully," his progress was not all it might be. One of David's classmates with "a turn for mathematics" looked at how long he had been working, how much he had completed, and how much he had yet to do, and delivered the estimate, "It might be done in one thousand six hundred and forty-nine years, counting from the Doctor's last, or sixty-second, birthday."[1] Dr. Strong's progress is all too typical of actual reference books. Every major reference project ends up overlong, overdue, and over budget.

The editorial apology for missed deadlines is an essential part of every dictionary or encyclopedia preface. Thomas Blount apologized for his *Glossographia* (1656), which "has taken me up the vacancy of above Twenty years";[2] Abraham Rees's *Cyclopædia* (1802–20) also trickled out over two decades, prompting him to write, even more embarrassed, "Some apology may, perhaps, be thought necessary for the extension of this work beyond the limits first proposed."[3] But twenty years is nothing in the world of reference publishing. The Académie Française started its *Dictionnaire* in 1635 and spent fifty-nine years on it—during which time two rival dictionaries were begun and finished. The same story is written today. DICTIONARY REACHES FINAL DEFINITION AFTER CENTURY reads a BBC headline of August 31, 2014, reporting the completion of *The Dictionary of Medieval Latin from British Sources*, launched in 1913 and completed, with an entry for *zythum*, 101 years later.[4]

Extra time almost always means extra space. The French *Encyclopédie* was planned for ten volumes, eight of text and two of illustrations. Had it appeared in that format, it still would have been longer than any of its competitors in France or England.[5] But it ended up 250 percent over its projected size, with seventeen volumes of text and eleven of illustrations. Charles Joseph Panckoucke declared confidently that his *Encyclopédie méthodique*, planned for twenty-one volumes, would be finished in five years, but, as one historian notes, "he was already wondering if his estimate of the number of volumes was entirely accurate."[6] He was right to wonder. The encyclopedia began appearing in November 1782, but it was not completed until 1832, when it occupied more than two hundred volumes, exceeding his estimates of both time and length by a factor of ten.

Some projects chug along at a reasonable pace for a while, only to hit a snag. The *Videnskabernes Selskabs Ordbog*, the great Danish dictionary sponsored by the Academy of Sciences, began appearing in 1781, with the first full volume coming out in 1793. Volumes appeared every few years until 1853, when the dictionary had reached *U*. The final volume, though, *V–Z*, did not appear until 1905, fifty-two years after the prior volume. Altogether it took 112 years to get from volume 1 to volume 8.

The early plan for what became the *Oxford English Dictionary* called for a book about the size of Webster's *American Dictionary*, to be completed in ten years. Five years into the project, half the projected time for the whole dictionary, the lexicographers had reached the word *ant*, and they had not published a page. The publishers (Macmillan—Oxford University Press had not yet come on board) were concerned about the length. They thought 2,000 pages about right, and drew a firm line at 4,000. The Philological Society came back with a counteroffer of 5,000 pages, thinking it would probably end up closer to 6,000. Macmillan, eager to compromise, settled on 4,800 pages.[7] But both the page count and the calendar kept increasing. Ten years turned into seventy-five, and 2,000 pages into 15,487.

Because of these delays—often stretching over several generations— reference books sometimes change their character over the decades.

Some compilers make the same estimate that David Copperfield's classmate did and realize that, at their current scale, their projects will take lifetimes, and they resolve to pick up the pace. Volume 1 of the first *Encyclopædia Britannica*, for example, covered *Aa* through *Bzo*. Had William Smellie continued to allot pages at the same rate throughout the project, the result might have been ten or a dozen volumes. But plans changed: he rushed through the rest of the alphabet in just two volumes. The early seventeenth-century Spanish dictionary by Sebastián de Covarrubias is similarly unbalanced: the entries for A, B, and C are much longer than those for the rest of the alphabet. Covarrubias, who was sixty when he began his project, feared he might not live to see its completion.

Usually, though, later volumes take a more leisurely approach to publication. In 1732, Johann Heinrich Zedler thought his *Grosses voll-ständiges Universal-Lexicon* would occupy twelve volumes; by the time he reached the middle of the alphabet he had already published eighteen. Instead of picking up the pace, he slowed down even further: the second half of the alphabet took not eighteen volumes but an additional forty-six—"with the letter *U* alone occupying six volumes and the letter *S* occupying nine."[8] The would-be-twelve-volume encyclopedia eventually filled sixty-four. (Even that looks puny next to Johann Georg Krünitz's *Oekonomische Encyclopädie oder allgemeines System der Staats- Stadt- Haus- und Landwirthschaft*, 1773–1858, in an overwhelming 242 volumes and 170,000 pages.) And over the century and a half it took to appear, the Grimms changed policy on quotations in their *Wörterbuch*, partly because there was much more German literature to quote. The amount of detail also increased in the later volumes: to pick three related adjectives, *blau* 'blue' appeared in 1860 and took up two columns; *rot* 'red' in 1893 occupied thirteen; *grün* 'green' in 1935 filled twenty-six.[9]

The Assyrian Dictionary, based at the University of Chicago, is an all-too-typical case of how reference publishing progresses. The project was mapped out in 1921: a six-volume dictionary of three thousand pages. But after the Second World War, when the team had worked for a quarter century with no volumes to show for it, the publishers began applying pressure. The staff was ordered to begin publishing in 1947 and to finish no later than 1957. Those deadlines began slipping almost immediately. The first volume appeared in 1956, and by then it was clear that six volumes would not be enough—they would need twenty.

In 1972, more than half a century into the ten-year project, the team promised to finish by 1980; by 1977, when volume 14 appeared, the completion date was pushed back to 1984. In 1991, the project's seventieth anniversary, the annual reports began talking about imminent completion and thinking about what the Oriental Institute would do next: "While the completion of the Chicago Assyrian Dictionary is the immediate goal . . . we have also started formulating plans for the future use of the data." Still the work dragged on. In 1995 the editorial board was reorganized, and a three-year grant in 1997 made clear that the project would go into the next millennium. At some point the press informed the Library of Congress that the project would be finished by 2006—the date that appears in the catalog—but even that deadline was missed.

A single volume tells the story. The editors started on *P* in 1994, thinking it the work of about a year. At first they seemed more or less on track: "Final editing of the P Volume occupied Professors Reiner and Roth," the annual report for 1995–96 declared, "and they have finished editing most of the volume. The edited articles are prepared for final checking." In June of the next year, they had "finished editing the last of the draft articles for the P." But "During the 1997/98 academic year, the staff of the CAD continued to devote most of our energy to the P and R volumes." The next year's report opens with essentially the same sentence: "During the 1998/99 academic year, the staff of the Chicago Assyrian Dictionary Project devoted most of our energy to the P volume." Only in the 1999–2000 annual report were they able "to report that . . . we sent the P volume of the *Chicago Assyrian Dictionary* (CAD) to press." By 2000–1 the book was in galleys. They were still reading those galleys in 2001–2, and in 2002–3 it was finally "being typeset." Only in July 2005 did the volume appear. The product of eleven years' intensive labor, *P* took longer than the original editors projected for the entire dictionary.[10] The entire project was completed in 2011, twenty-six volumes and ninety years in the making.

Things are no swifter in the high-tech twenty-first century.

The third edition of the *Oxford English Dictionary* was begun in the mid-1990s, with plans to finish by 2010. But by 2010, the editors had completed less than a third of the alphabet, and current estimates place the final publication date sometime around 2034—though the smart money says that when 2034 rolls around, the editorial team will still be valiantly working its way through the alphabet.

CHAPTER 19

AN ALMS-BASKET OF WORDS

The Reference Book as Salvation

John Bartlett	E. Cobham Brewer
A Collection of	*Dictionary of*
Familiar Quotations	*Phrase & Fable*
1855	1870

HIGH-MINDED VICTORIANS TOOK reference books seriously as a way of improving the lot of the less fortunate. Nineteenth-century compilers wanted their works to be useful in as many ways as possible.

One handy guide that would be owned by virtually every reader in Victorian England was *Bradshaw's Railway Time Tables and Assistant to Railway Travelling* (1839), the earliest (and most long-lasting) guide to moving around Great Britain on the newly invented railroads. George Bradshaw—born in Lancashire, England, in 1801—arrived in the world at nearly the same time as the locomotive, which was invented in 1804, and for more than a century, his name was synonymous with the technology that revolutionized travel.

Another technology was behind another ubiquitous reference book, the phone book.[1] The first one, *The Telephone Directory*, appeared in New Haven, Connecticut, in 1878. In his *Dictionary*, Samuel Johnson had noted that the word *Bible* came from Greek *biblion* 'book', adding that "The sacred volume in which are contained the revelations of God" was "called, by way of excellence, *The Book*." One hundred thirty years later, in a story in the December 1885 issue of *Cassell's Family Magazine*, a character mused, "In a minute Charlie was in my boudoir, and was ringing to the Central Exchange. I looked in the book; the fire number was something—I forget what." "The book" had taken

on a whole new meaning as the telephone directory became central
to people's lives.

₰

Aristotle advised students in his *Rhetorica* to take good notes on their
reading and to arrange them under topical headings, rubrics such as "on
goodness."[2] Latin readers, too, were told to look for *sententiae*—that
is, maxims, aphorisms, or memorable statements. These "sentences"
were bits of wisdom that could be carried around and trotted out
when appropriate. Good readers were advised to collect important
quotations for themselves. Blank books gave readers the chance to
copy their favorite passages. At their worst, these so-called common-
place books were little more than clichés mindlessly strung together,
reflecting no actual reading or wisdom, just the ability to parrot
moralistic bromides. Shakespeare's Polonius, for instance, is a walking
commonplace book: "Neither a borrower nor a lender be . . ." But these
compendia were an essential part of a Renaissance education, and at
their best, they encouraged readers to read with newfound attention.
For a keeper of a commonplace book, reading and writing were linked
activities.

Commonplace books were originally do-it-yourself exercises, but
eventually people began publishing collections of commonplaces. At
the end of the fifteenth century and into the sixteenth, for instance,
Desiderius Erasmus began publishing his quotations in a work known
as the *Adagia* (*Adages*, 1500), which went through dozens of editions,
growing larger with each new publication. Throughout the sixteenth
century, these collections were bestsellers all over Europe. John
Merbecke's *Booke of Notes and Common Places, with Their Expositions,
Collected and Gathered out of the Workes of Diuers Singular Writers, and
Brought Alphabetically into Order* (1581) helped Protestant readers find
their way around religious writings. English readers were especially
fond of Italian compilations. Giovanni Andrea Grifoni published *A
Comfortable Ayde for Scholers, Full of Variety of Sentences* in the sixteenth
century, and David Rowland provided an English version in 1568;
Francesco Sansovino's *Quintesence of Wit: Being a Corrant Comfort of
Conceites, Maximies, and Poleticke Deuises* came out in English in 1590.

Sansovino collected his wit and wisdom from a range of classical authors, including Aristotle, Julius Caesar, Cicero, Plato, Plutarch, Sallust, Suetonius, Thucydides, and Xenophon. Sansovino's 803 snippets appear in no particular order, but a topical index at the end directs readers to the entries on subjects such as "Affirmations," "Agents," "Old Age," "Ambition," "Art of warre," and so on. His "sentences," though, appear without citations—not even authors' names. The result is a collection of wisdom, authorized by a list of great names, belonging not to individual writers but to the culture as a whole.

Later came the single-author quotation collection. One successful example is *Beauties of Shakespear*, a two-volume work that appeared in London in 1752. Its compiler was William Dodd, then a deacon in the Church of England but eventually a prominent priest. Dodd spent some time serving as tutor to the Earl of Chesterfield, the would-be patron of Johnson's *Dictionary*, and he would write a *Commentary on the Bible* in the late 1760s. At the beginning of his career as a writer, though, he was interested in a different kind of scriptural exegesis—that of England's greatest writer. Shakespeare's supremacy was not yet taken for granted in 1752; he was still making the long transition from very good old-fashioned playwright to literary demigod. An entire reference book dedicated to an English writer would still have struck most people as a questionable enterprise. But Dodd insisted that Shakespeare was uniquely deserving of a collection of quotations, and he was proud to serve up "such a collection of *Beauties*, as perhaps is no where to be met with, and, I may safely affirm, cannot be parallell'd from the productions of any other single author, ancient or modern. There is scarcely a topic, common with other writers, on which he has not excelled them all; there are many, nobly peculiar to himself, where he shines unrivall'd." Many of Shakespeare's greatest lines are reproduced in Dodd's *Beauties*. The famous "To be or not to be" soliloquy appears, for instance, under the heading "Life and Death weigh'd"; under "The different sorts of Melancholy" is this passage from *As You Like It*: "I have neither the scholar's melancholy, which is emulation; nor the musician's, which is fantastical; nor the courtier's, which is proud; nor the soldier's, which is ambitious; nor the lawyer's, which is politic; nor the lady's, which is nice; nor the lover's, which is all these."[3]

Dodd hoped his *Beauties* would not merely entertain his readers but would edify them as well—from Shakespeare, readers would learn valuable lessons of morality. But he should have paid more attention to a passage he included under "A Father's Advice to his Son, going to travel," in which Polonius adviseed Laertes against being a borrower or a lender. In 1777, Dodd found himself in debt, and he forged Lord Chesterfield's name on a bond worth £4,200—this at a time when a middle-class family could live comfortably on less than £100 a year. When the forgery was discovered, he was sentenced to death by hanging. Samuel Johnson pleaded for mercy, and more than twenty thousand people joined in signing a petition begging the crown to commute the sentence. It was in vain. Dodd was hanged at Tyburn in 1777, after prompting one of Johnson's more memorable quotations: "Depend upon it, Sir," he said, "when a man knows he is to be hanged in a fortnight, it concentrates his mind wonderfully."[4]

The most influential of the published commonplace books came out of nineteenth-century Cambridge, Massachusetts. John Bartlett, of a distinguished New England family, was an early reader—"he was able to read a Bible verse to his mother at the age of three; by nine he had read the entire Bible aloud"—and he must have been an excellent recorder of commonplaces.[5] At the age of sixteen he started working at the Harvard University bookstore, and he eventually bought the shop. He became a fixture in Harvard Square, known for his willingness to chat with customers, and especially for his ability to find apt quotations. "Ask John Bartlett" became proverbial among Harvard students. Eventually the constant questions about quotations gave him the idea of publishing his own little collection of bons mots, a descendant of the Erasmian *Adagia*. With the aid of a Harvard student, Henry W. Haynes, he pieced together his favorite tags from American, English, and world literature. "The object of this work," Bartlett explained in his preface, "is to show, to some extent, the obligation our language owes to various authors for numerous phrases and familiar quotations which have become 'household words.'"[6]

Bartlett claimed he took all his quotations from their original sources rather than depending on reprints of reprints of reprints. If that is so, his reading was extensive and hit most of the high points recognized by

TITLE: *A Collection of Familiar Quotations, with Complete Indices of Authors and Subjects*

COMPILER: John Bartlett (1820–1905)

ORGANIZATION: First the Bible, then Shakespeare, then English-language poets in chronological order, then foreign authors, then prose writers

PUBLISHED: Cambridge, Massachusetts, 1855

PAGES: vii + 295

ENTRIES: 1,600

TOTAL WORDS: 38,000

SIZE: 6¾" × 4" (17 × 10 cm)

AREA: 54½ ft² (5.1 m²)

WEIGHT: 13 oz. (367 g)

PRICE: 75¢

LATEST EDITION: 17th ed. (2003)

nineteenth-century America. The book opens with "Holy Scriptures," arranged by book of the Bible: "It is not good that the man should be alone" (Gen. 2:18); "For dust thou art, and unto dust shalt thou return" (Gen. 3:19); "Am I my brother's keeper?" (Gen. 4:9); and so on. All the most memorable passages were included: "He kept him as the apple of his eye" (Deut. 22:10); "A man after his own heart" (1 Sam. 13:14); "How are the mighty fallen" (2 Sam. 1:25); "A still, small voice" (1 Kings 19:12); "Pride goeth before destruction, and a haughty spirit before a fall" (Prov. 16:18); "Set thine house in order" (Isaiah 38:1); "Man shall not live by bread alone" (Matt. 4:4); "Ye are the salt of the earth" (Matt. 5:13); "Neither cast ye your pearls before swine" (Matt. 7:6); "For many are called, but few are chosen" (Matt. 22:14); "Physician, heal thyself" (Luke 4:23); "He that is not with me is against me" (Luke 11:23); "In my Father's house are many mansions" (John 14:2); "I am made all things to all men" (1 Cor. 9:22); "For now we see through a glass, darkly" (1 Cor. 13:12); "I have fought the good fight" (2 Tim. 4:7).

Bartlett was especially drawn to the more legalistic parts of the Bible, and he had a particular fascination with judgment: "Whoso sheddeth man's blood, by man shall his blood be shed" (Gen. 9:6); "Eye for eye, tooth for tooth, hand for hand, foot for foot" (Deut. 19:21); "Out of thine own mouth will I judge thee" (Luke 19:22); "Whatsoever a man soweth, that shall he also reap" (Gal. 6:7). Right after the Bible came the *Book of Common Prayer*—together, the Scriptures and the prayer book got twenty-five pages.

Then Bartlett presented the author who, for English speakers, came closest to holy writ: Shakespeare received sixty pages to himself, more than twice as much as the Bible. Of course, these passages are removed from plays and dropped into a collection of quotations; speeches are reproduced without speech prefixes—in other words, it is impossible to tell who said what. The result is that Shakespeare seems to be speaking, not his characters. The Bard authorizes whatever appears under his name, even if he intended it to be understood ironically.

A procession of literary worthies followed, starting with the English and American poets lined up in chronological order. Many of them are predictable—John Milton, for instance, got ten pages—but, as a reminder that the literary canon evolves, John Donne, today one of the most respected poets, earned just two quotations, a total of five lines, and none of his now-famous ones: no "Death be not proud" or "No man is an island." George Herbert received similar treatment, and John Keats got only four lines. Bartlett was generous, though, with American authors, including William Cullen Bryant, Henry Wadsworth Longfellow, and Oliver Wendell Holmes. Foreign writers (Thomas à Kempis, Rabelais, Cervantes) and prose writers (Bacon, Hobbes, Benjamin Franklin) closed out the quotations, making a total of 169 featured authors. A topical index rounded out the volume to aid those who remember keywords: "Abundance, every one that hath"; "Accidents by flood and field"; "Accoutred as I was"; "Aching void"; "Action, suit the, to the word"; "Actions of the just"; "[Actions] like almanacs"; "Acts, little nameless."

Bartlett went on to have an interesting post-*Quotations* life. In 1862, when the U.S. Civil War was heating up, he sold his bookshop and took a position as a paymaster in the Navy. He returned to Boston the following year and went to work for Little, Brown and Co., one of the leading publishers in the city. By this time they were interested in Bartlett's book, which he had self-published through three earlier editions. He did well at Little, Brown, working his way up to senior partner in 1878. After his retirement in 1894, he produced a concordance to the works of Shakespeare. By the time he died in 1905, his *Familiar Quotations* was in its ninth edition, having sold more than three hundred thousand copies, and new editions continue to appear—along with countless imitators.

Bartlett has had some high-profile supporters. "It is a good thing for an uneducated man to read books of quotations," advised Winston Churchill. "Bartlett's *Familiar Quotations* is an admirable work, and I studied it intently. The quotations, when engraved upon the memory, give you good thoughts. They also make you anxious to read the authors and look for more."[7] Browsing Bartlett's, in its dozens of editions since 1855, remains one of the best ways to get insight into our culture's collective psychology. As James Gleick put it in a review of a recent edition, "Dorothy Parker and Robert Benchley have become ancient sages; to capture the words now on our lips and pens, the new edition has felt obliged to canonize less venerable authors like the Doors ('Come on, baby, light my fire'), Sesame Street ('Me want cookie!') and Monty Python's Flying Circus ('This parrot is no more. It has ceased to be. It's expired and gone to meet its maker. This is a late parrot. It's a stiff. Bereft of life, it rests in peace. If you hadn't nailed it to the perch, it would be pushing up the daisies. It's rung down the curtain and joined the choir invisible. This is an ex-parrot')."[8]

The nineteenth-century concern with practicality gave reference books an almost missionary purpose. Eminent Victorians hoped to offer their social inferiors a path to betterment by becoming learned, giving the proletarians the information once available only to gentlemen.

One of the nineteenth century's most enduring and beloved reference books is one of its quirkiest, born out of "the need to make the fruits of nineteenth century scholarship accessible to an ever widening range of readers."[9] The Reverend Ebenezer Cobham Brewer had nobly paternalistic intentions, perfectly in keeping with his upbringing: to provide the working classes with access to high culture. Those who had been denied a good education might still turn to his guide to proverbs, idioms, folklore, history, and mythology. If idioms and mythology seem an odd combination, it is characteristic of the book as a whole; all of Brewer's diverse and eccentric interests and hobbyhorses are expressed in it.

Brewer, born into a large family, was privately educated by his schoolmaster father in Norfolk. In 1832 he entered Trinity Hall, Cambridge, where he won prizes for Latin, English, and mathematics. But he ended up studying none of these, and instead took first-class honors in civil law. Meanwhile he was ordained a deacon in 1834 and a priest in 1838. Still, he neither practiced law nor held a position in the church. Instead, he taught in his father's school and wrote widely—books on education, translations, a *Poetical Chronicle*, and a bestselling *Guide to the Scientific Knowledge of Things Familiar*—making good use of an excellent reference library in his chambers. For six years in the 1850s he relocated to Paris, where he traveled in fashionable and aristocratic circles. After marrying he returned to England, settling first in Bloomsbury, then in Paddington, and finally in Sussex.

There he worked on his most famous book. His nephew recalled his study: "The walls of this room were papered with a plain white paper, upon which he used to write in pencil stray memoranda and the names of any particularly interesting visitors and the dates on which they came to see him. These names included that of the Duchess of Portland, then one of the most beautiful women in the country. She insisted on going upstairs to my grandfather's own room and carried on a long conversation with him, sitting on his bed, a highly informal proceeding in those days, which particularly pleased the old gentleman!" Brewer was a devoted note taker, recollecting the old commonplace habit that Bartlett made use of. But Brewer carried it further, sorting his notes into categories. His nephew again described his workspace: "In the middle of the room . . . there was a long wooden box arrangement. The front was open and divided into pigeon-holes, lettered from A to Z, in which were the slips of paper on which were written the notes and references he made and continued to make daily."[10]

TITLE: *Dictionary of Phrase and Fable: Giving the*
   Derivation, Source, or Origin of Common Phrases,
   Allusions, and Words That Have a Tale to Tell
COMPILER: Ebenezer Cobham Brewer (1810–97)
ORGANIZATION: Alphabetical by keyword, *A* to *Zulfagar*
PUBLISHED: London: Cassell & Co., 1870
PAGES: viii + 979
ENTRIES: 20,000
TOTAL WORDS: 750,000
SIZE: 7¾" × 5¼" (19.7 × 13.3 cm)
AREA: 275 ft² (25.6 m²)
PRICE: 10s. 6d.
LATEST EDITION: 19th ed. (2012)

Describing the *Dictionary of Phrase and Fable* is notoriously challenging, and Brewer himself admitted "it will be difficult to furnish an answer in a sentence." He introduced it by saying, "We call it a 'Dictionary of Phrase and Fable,' a title wide enough, no doubt, to satisfy a very lofty ambition, yet not sufficiently wide to describe the miscellaneous contents of this 'alms-basket of words,'" but that was not a description. Coming closer to an answer, he claimed, "It draws in curious or novel etymologies, pseudonyms and popular titles, local traditions and literary blunders, biographical and historical trifles too insignificant to find a place in books of higher pretension, but not too worthless to be worth knowing."[11]

Whatever it was, it had some antecedents: William Hone's *Every-Day Book* (1825–26) and John Timbs's *Things Not Generally Known* (1856) both collected miscellanea that might be some approximation of useful. Brewer's book contains elements of an encyclopedia, with many entries covering real-world subjects, especially mythology. It also is dictionary-like in its attention to word origins: etymology "forms a staple of the book, which professes to give 'the derivation, source, or origin of words that have a tale to tell.'"[12] And it is also partly a dictionary of proverbs.

Once Brewer settled on the kind of book he wanted to write, he sought a publisher. He turned to an editor he knew well, but, in Brewer's own words, "it was his opinion that the book would have no sale as it would be wholly impossible to exhaust the subject." It is hard to blame the editor. At length Cassell hesitantly agreed to take the book, though they were "doubtful whether the book would pay the expense of printing."[13] Cassell had to exert some influence on Brewer. The manuscript he submitted was far too long to publish; the editors demanded he cut it severely, down to one third of the length he wanted. Charged with tossing out two of every three curious facts he had collected, he was still left with about twenty thousand entries.

Brewer excluded most Greek and Latin fables because they were too well known, focusing instead on "Scandinavian and other mythology, bogie-land and fairy-land, ghouls and gnomes, and a legion of character-words, such as *Bumbledom* and *Podsnappery*, *Lilliputian* and *Utopian*."[14] Biblical allusions feature regularly: "Mammon. The god of this world. The word in Syriac means riches." *Sowing wild oats* (alphabetized under *oats*) was explained as "He has left off his gay habits and is become steady." The entries often underscored the origin of familiar phrases: *A1*, for instance, "means first-rate—the very best. In Lloyd's Register of British and Foreign Shipping, the character of the ship's hull is designated by *letters*, and that of the anchors, cables, and stores by figures. A 1 means hull first-rate, and also anchors, cables, and stores; A 2, hull first-rate, but furniture second-rate." Always concerned about utility, Brewer provided guides to pronunciation, indicating accented syllables to save the inexperienced from embarrassment: "Bar´becue (3 syl.). A West Indian dish, consisting of a hog roasted whole, stuffed with spice, and basted with Madeira wine. Any animal roasted whole is so called."

The glory of the book is its marvelous heterogeneity—it packed with information of every sort. Why do we call the time after marriage a honeymoon? "So called from the practice of the ancient Teutons of drinking honey-wine (*hydromel*) for thirty-days after marriage. Attila, the Hun, indulged so freely in hydromel at his wedding-feast that he died." If you come across "O.H.M.S.," turn to Brewer and discover it means "On Her Majesty's Service." The derivation of the phrase "drinking out of the skulls of your enemy" makes sense of a gruesome-sounding practice: actually, "This promise of our Scandinavian forefathers is not unfrequently misunderstood. Skull means a cup or dish; hence a person who washes up cups and dishes is called a scullery-maid." Brewer enjoyed "reduplicated words": "Chit-chat, click-clack, clitter-clatter, dilly-dally, ding-dong, drip-drop, eye-peep, fal-lal, fiddle-faddle, flip-flop," and so on, through "higgledy-piggledy," "namby-pamby," "pell-mell," "roly-poly," "tip-top," and "wishy-washy." Regarding dwarfs, he wrote:

The most remarkable are:

Phile'tas, a poet (contemporary with Hippoc'ratës), so small "that he wore leaden shoes to prevent being blown away by the wind." (Died B.C. 280.)

Niceph'orus Calistus tells us of an Egyptian dwarf not bigger than a partridge.

Aris'tratos, the poet, was so small that Athenæ'os says *no one could see him.*

Sir Geoffrey Hudson, born at Oakham, in Rutlandshire, at the age of thirty was only eighteen inches in height. (1619–1678.)

Owen Farrel, the Irish dwarf, born at Ca'van, hideously ugly, but of enormous muscular strength. Height, three feet nine inches. (Died 1742.)

The reviews were gratifying. The *Daily Telegraph* declared that it "fills a decided gap in our instructive literature." The *Standard* declared it "intrinsically good" and called it "a most valuable accession to every library." The *Manchester Examiner* found it "well calculated to afford much pleasant and profitable employment." Like the good Victorians they were, they often put the emphasis on utility: the *Daily Telegraph* called it "really a most useful volume"; the *Daily News* said it was "extremely useful and judiciously compiled"; the *Sheffield Independent* praised its "vast amount of useful information."

Brewer planned his *Dictionary* as the first part of a trilogy, and he wrote two follow-ups at ten-year intervals: the *Reader's Handbook* in 1880 and the *Historic Note-Book* in 1890. Both did well enough, but neither entered the pantheon of classic reference books. The *Dictionary*, though, did exceptionally well. After a number of so-called editions that were really no more than reprints, Brewer released a revised edition in 1894, in which he got to restore some of the material he had left on the cutting-room floor—this time the book was a third longer than the first edition. By this year, sales of the *Dictionary* had passed a hundred thousand copies, and soon editions began being advertised as "110th Thousand," "129th Thousand," and so on, like the classic "Billions Served" signs at McDonald's.

The high-minded purpose of these high-Victorian works comes through on every page. Bartlett and Brewer saw their works in nobly educative terms: they were bringing enlightenment to the masses. These books testify to the increasing prominence of an aspiring middle class— literate in a way their grandparents may not have been, able to buy at least a few improving books, but lacking the refinement and educational privilege of the to-the-manner-born aristocracy. Both Bartlett and Brewer were devout Christians, but they carried out their missionary endeavors with a Bible in one hand and a reference book in the other.

READING THE DICTIONARY

I HAVE DEFINED A reference book as one nobody reads from start to finish. The thought of *reading* a dictionary or encyclopedia strikes many as the height of absurdity, an emblem of futility. Business writer George S. Day, a professor at the Wharton School of Business, offers advice on "Converting Information into Strategic Knowledge," and he begins by warning executives that "Simply packing the shared knowledge base with undigested information is about as useful as reading an encyclopedia cover to cover."[1] *Are You a Geek?* asks Tim Collins, offering *10³ Ways to Find Out*. One of the signs: "You've read a dictionary cover to cover for pleasure." (Worse still: "It was an Elvish or Klingon dictionary.")[2] And yet some people, not all of them geeks, *have* read dictionaries and encyclopedias from cover to cover—or, since many of these works are in multiple volumes, from cover to cover to cover to cover to cover to cover . . .

Some people have to read them. When Robert Burchfield was commissioned to supplement the *Oxford English Dictionary*, he began by reading the whole thing through—all thirteen volumes, all 15,490 pages, all 1,827,306 quotations, all 178 miles of type. It is more text than many people will read in a lifetime, but the only way Burchfield could prepare himself to be editor.

Others read dictionaries and encyclopedias when they have time on their hands. George Eliot's idealistic young doctor Tertius Lydgate, for instance, was such a passionate reader in his youth that he would go through "any sort of book that he could lay his hands on: if it were Rasselas or Gulliver, so much the better, but Bailey's Dictionary would do," and when bored "he took down a dusty row of volumes with gray-paper backs and dingy labels—the volumes of an old Cyclopaedia."[3]

And Bertolt Brecht, in his *Threepenny Novel*, wrote of the ridiculous George Fewkoombey, who amuses himself with a tattered volume of the *Encyclopaedia Britannica* he found in a lavatory.

Others have even more time—time that has been forced upon them. When Nicolas Fréret, an eighteenth-century French scholar, was confined in the Bastille, he "was permitted only to have Bayle for his companion"—Pierre Bayle's *Dictionnaire historique et critique*.[4] Two centuries later, while Malcolm X sat in prison, he, too, read a dictionary. Frustrated by his limited vocabulary—"Every book I picked up had sentences that contained anywhere from one to nearly all the words that might as well have been in Chinese"—he resolved to do something about it. "I saw that the best thing I could do was get hold of a dictionary." After two days of "riffling uncertainly through the dictionary's pages," he

> began copying. In my slow, painstaking, ragged handwriting, I copied into my tablet everything printed on that first page, down to the punctuation marks.
>
> I believe it took me a day. Then, aloud, I read back, to myself, everything I'd written on the tablet. Over and over, aloud, to myself, I read my own handwriting.[5]

The next day he moved on to the next page, and before he knew it he had reached the end of the letter *A* and the end of his notebook. Rather than stopping, he found another tablet and kept going. "That was the way," he wrote, "I started copying what eventually became the entire dictionary."

And some read dictionaries for the intellectual challenge. Historian William Robertson, a friend of Samuel Johnson, was a fan of his largest book; Johnson was "pleased . . . to be told by Dr. Robertson, that he had read his Dictionary twice over."[6] When the young Robert Browning "was definitely to adopt literature as his profession," wrote a nineteenth-century biographer, "he qualified himself for it by reading and digesting the whole of Johnson's Dictionary."[7] Later he told James Murray that he planned to do the same with the *Oxford English Dictionary*—but Browning died not long after *A* was published.

Many great writers have been great readers of reference books. Walt Whitman was "an avid reader of dictionaries, which he realized were the compost heap of all English-language literature, the place where all the elements of literature, broken down, were preserved. . . . The nation's unwritten poems lay dormant in that massive heap of words."[8] Leo Tolstoy loved encyclopedias, and his diary included a resolution in February 1851: "To rise at 9; to occupy myself with the Encyclopædia of Law"—Constantine Alexeyevich Nevolin's *Encyclopædia of Jurisprudence*, which he read every morning from eight until noon and again from six until nightfall. His letters and diaries are full of dictionaries, encyclopedias, and Greek lexicons. The Beat poet Lawrence Ferlinghetti "went through *Webster's Unabridged Dictionary*, cover to cover, with particular attention to etymologies."[9] No reader of Jorge Luis Borges, creator of the fantastic "Chinese encyclopedia" called *Celestial Empire of Benevolent Knowledge*, will be surprised by his reminiscence of reading *Britannica* and "the German encyclopedias of Brockhaus or of Meyer" when he was a child,[10] and Vladimir Nabokov kept a dictionary on his bedside table, passing insomniac nights by turning its pages.[11] Aldous Huxley was another *Britannica* reader; he took a complete twelfth edition with him on holiday. Bertrand Russell recalled, "It was the only book that ever influenced Huxley. You could always tell by his conversation which volume he'd been reading. One day it would be Alps, Andes and Apennines, and the next it would be the Himalayas and the Hippocratic Oath.'"[12] Even young Bill Gates read the 1960 edition of *The World Book Encyclopedia* nearly all the way through,[13] and Wikipedia cofounder Jimmy Wales fondly remembers reading his parents' copy of *World Book*.[14]

A few readers have simply been curious to the point of masochism; others have read for the sake of reading. The *Encyclopaedia Britannica* office routinely received letters along the lines of "Dear Sir, You will be interested to know that I have just finished reading every word in all the 24 volumes of the *Britannica*. I believe I am the first person who has ever done this."[15] Making clear the magnitude of that task, A. J. Jacobs read the complete *Britannica* in a single year, and he reported on the experience in his book *The Know-It-All*. When the parcel arrived, Jacobs was overwhelmed by the magnitude of my quest. I'm looking at 33,000 pages, 65,000 articles, 9,500 contributors, 24,000 images. I'm looking at thirty-two volumes, each one weighing in at a solid four pounds, each packed with those giant tissue-thin pages. The total: 44 million words.[16]

To put 44 million words in perspective, *War and Peace* is only around 560,000 words, Shakespeare's collected works weigh in at 900,000 words, and you could read from Genesis to Revelation fifty-three times in a row in the time it would take you to read *Britannica*. As Jacobs immersed himself in the text, "the mind-blowing diversity of everything" made the biggest impression.[17] "It's the perfect book for someone like me," he wrote, "who grew up with Peter Gabriel videos, who has the attention span of a gnat on methamphetamines. Each essay is a bite-sized nugget. Bored with Abilene, Texas? Here comes abolitionism. Tired of that? Not to worry, the Abominable Snowman's lurking right around the corner."[18]

Writer Ammon Shea performed a similar experiment with the *Oxford English Dictionary*, pointing out, "If you were to sit down and force yourself to read the whole thing over the course of several months, three things would likely happen: you would learn a great number of new words, your eyesight would suffer considerably, and your mind would most definitely slip a notch."[19] He offered his book-length account of his efforts, *Reading the OED*, as "the thinking person's CliffsNotes to the greatest dictionary in the world," but he had to admit it is also "an account of the pain, headache, and loss of sanity that comes from spending months and months searching through this mammoth and formidable dictionary—and pulling together all of its most beautiful and remarkable words."

CHAPTER 20

MODERN MATERIA MEDICA

Staying Healthy

Henry Gray and Henry Vandyke Carter *Anatomy Descriptive and Surgical* 1858	*Diagnostic and Statistical Manual of Mental Disorders* 1952

M EDICAL INFORMATION WAS first written down because its volume had grown beyond the bounds of the individual healer. As the centuries passed, the volume of accumulated medical knowledge only increased. The scientific revolution brought empiricism to health, and clinical trials let practitioners figure out whether a treatment was more or less likely to lead to a cure. Meanwhile the rise of scientific journals and the systematic collection of data made medical knowledge both more accurate and more specialized. Reference books had to work hard to keep up.

Comparing two major works on health separated in time by one long lifetime highlights the differences between Victorian confidence and modern anxiety over what constitutes health. These two works—one focusing on physical, one on mental health—trace the evolution of ideas about the relationship of the mind to body and explore the kinds of authority with which specialists made claims about both.

❦

Few Victorian textbooks have inspired prime-time soap operas, but one legendary guide to human anatomy has become so famous over the centuries that its name is now proverbial.

One of the longest-lasting medical references in history had as its declared mission "to furnish the Student and Practitioner with an accurate view of the Anatomy of the Human Body, and more especially the application of this science to Practical Surgery."[1] Surgery was undergoing exciting changes in the 1850s. Anatomical education in England improved by leaps and bounds when the Anatomy Act of 1832 made it possible to get cadavers for dissection as part of a medical education without having to depend on grave robbers. And the availability of anesthesia—both ether and chloroform had been approved for use in the 1840s—was allowing surgical interventions that would once have been impossible.

Henry Gray—"diligent and hard-working, focused, clever, ambitious"—was born in 1827 and was eager to be recognized as a great surgeon at St. George's Hospital in London.[2] Beyond that, we know next to nothing about him; he left virtually no traces of his private life. We do not even know where he attended school, only that he was a London surgeon and that the most famous of all anatomy textbooks bears his name. *Gray's Anatomy* is not entirely Gray's; he provided the text, but the woodcuts—among the most useful features of the book, and the most distinctive—were provided by a colleague, another surgeon, named Henry Vandyke Carter. We know much more about Carter, who kept a detailed diary in tiny handwriting from the time he was fourteen. Carter came from a less privileged background; he could not easily afford a university education, so he trained first as an apothecary and used his income from that, combined with money he earned as an illustrator, to advance his education. He was devastated when he failed his surgical exam the first time, but a year later he passed with honors.

We know from Carter's writings that the two men met in 1850, when both were working at St. George's Hospital. Having discovered that Carter was an accomplished illustrator, Gray sought his assistance on an essay he was writing, eventually published in book form as *The Structure and Use of the Spleen* (1853). Carter was glad of the payment, but he was wounded when he saw the published book: Gray had neglected to credit his contribution. "See Gray's Book on Spleen takes no notice of my assistance," he noted in his diary, "tho' had voluntarily promised." Despite his Victorian stoicism, his fragmentary comment, "rather feel it," leaves no doubt that the omission rankled.[3] It was only the first of a series of struggles between the two for prominence.

TITLE: *Anatomy Descriptive and Surgical, by Henry Gray, F.R.S. Lecturer on Anatomy at Saint George's Hospital: The Drawings by H. V. Carter, M.D. Late Demonstrator of Anatomy at St. George's Hospital: The Dissections Jointly by the Author and Dr. Carter*

COMPILER: Henry Gray (1827–61) and Henry Vandyke Carter (1831–97)

ORGANIZATION: By bodily system: osteology, articulations, muscles and fasciae, arteries, veins, lymphatics, nerves, sense organs, viscera, respiration, urinary organs, male then female generative organs, inguinal and femoral hernia, perineum and ischio-rectal region

PUBLISHED: London: John W. Parker and Son, 1858

PAGES: xxii + 754

SIZE: 9½" × 6" (24.5 × 15.5 cm)

AREA: 315 ft^2 (29.5 m^2)

WEIGHT: 3 lb. 8 oz. (1.6 kg)

PRICE: 22s.

LATEST EDITION: *Gray's Anatomy: The Anatomical Basis of Clinical Practice, Expert Consult*, 40th ed., edited by Susan Standring (Churchill Livingstone, 2009), 1,576 pages

Gray aspired to write a truly comprehensive one-volume guide to human anatomy, superseding all the other books on the market. In November 1855, Carter made a note of a conversation: "Little to record. Gray made proposal to assist by drawings in bringing out a Manual for students: a good idea but did not come to any plan . . . too exacting, for would not be simple artist."[4] Carter was slow to agree to the project. Though he had already qualified as a surgeon and apothecary, he was still completing his MD degree. He was also probably still smarting from his treatment on the earlier book. Gray's offer of £10 a month for fifteen months, though, seems to have tipped the balance in Carter's mind, and he began in January 1856. Once they decided to work together, they moved quickly—from planning to publication in less than three years. They worked together on dissections, Gray taking notes while Carter made sketches. Dissections were no simple matter in the 1850s. They had to be done in winter, because cadavers would decay too quickly in the summer, but daylight being shorter then, they began work as soon as the sun rose high enough. Still they worked systematically through the body, preparing materials for the definitive work on human anatomy.

Gray was the motive force for the project, and he secured a publisher. He had already published his essay on the spleen with John Parker, so Parker was the obvious choice to publish the *Anatomy*. But, having done that work, Gray abruptly walked out in the middle of the project when he accepted an invitation to serve as personal physician to the Duke of Sutherland on his private yacht. He got a leave of absence from his hospital duties, providing the remainder of his contributions to the book by mail and leaving Carter to handle the details of production.[5]

The work is structured systematically: under the broad head "Osteology" comes a series of introductory articles—"General Properties of Bone," "Chemical Composition of Bone," "Structure of Bone," and so on—followed by sections on the major classes: the spine, the skull, the thorax, the pelvis. Within each of those classes are more specific entries: "The Spine" opens with "General Characters of the Vertebræ" and "Characters of the Cervical Vertebræ," followed by "Atlas," "Axis," "Vertebra Prominens," and on through the bones of the spine. Sometimes an entry is even more specific: under the broad head "The Lymphatics" is an entry on "Cerebrum"; under "Cerebrum" comes "Boundaries of, and Parts forming the Lateral Ventricles"; under that comes "Thalami Optici." As befits a clinical book, the tone is always clinical: the sections on "Male Generative Organs" and "Female Organs of Generation" have no time for moralizing on the one hand or tittering on the other. The language is never vulgar; Latin takes the place of the vernacular when the subject gets too explicit. But neither is there any shying away from delicate matters: "The SCROTUM is a cutaneous pouch, which contains the testes and part of the spermatic cords. It is divided into two lateral halves, by a median line, or raphe. . . ."[6]

The book features detailed drawings—hand-colored in some editions—of the sex organs, the sort of thing that distressed nineteenth-century moralists. Carter's illustrations, made directly onto the woodblocks that would be used to print the images, are exemplary, providing just the right balance of naturalistic detail and schematic clarity. Carter introduced an innovation to anatomical illustration by putting his labels directly on the parts they identify, rather than relying on a clumsy system with numbers and arrows. The drawings are beautifully engraved, presumably by someone on the publisher's staff. But the illustrations provoked last-minute panic when someone discovered that the woodblocks were almost an inch too large to fit on the paper size they had chosen.[7] Recreating the images was out of the question, as was moving to a larger page size. Fixing the problem involved frantic scrambling to rearrange the pages and reduce the captions whenever possible; if no other option remained, they would have to trim the woodblocks themselves.

A more delicate problem arose after the book was in proof. On the first proof of the title page, both contributors' names appeared in the same size of type, though Carter's appeared well below Gray's; already the hierarchy of the contributors was being asserted. Gray, however, was not content. In marking the proof he crossed out Carter's name and qualifications and added a notation for the typesetter: "Type size of the name below," that is, smaller than his own. Where Carter's new job title, a prestigious professorship, appeared, Gray crossed it out, adding explicit instructions—"To be omitted"—and his authorizing initials, "H.G." The message was clear: this was to be H.G.'s *Anatomy*, not H.G.'s and H.V.C.'s *Anatomy*.[8] To add injury to insult, Gray never paid Carter any of the royalties he had earned.

The book appeared in summer 1858, in time to be adopted in medical schools for the upcoming academic year. Gray and Carter were stung by one early bad review—"low and unscientific in tone . . . inconsistent with the professions of honesty which we find in the preface. . . . A more unphilosophical amalgam of anatomic details and crude surgery we never met with"—but most of the other notices were strong, and sales were good. The review in the *British Medical Journal* is typical, calling *Anatomy Descriptive and Surgical* "far superior to all other treatises," and "a book which must take its place as *the* manual of Anatomy Descriptive and Surgical." A review from 1869 listed *Anatomy* among the essential books for medical students.[9]

The book brought together the best information on anatomy and physiology the age had to offer, and it quickly became the standard book in the field. The medical knowledge did Gray himself little good; he died at age thirty-four of "confluent smallpox" in June 1861. Carter's post-*Anatomy* career was more fortunate. He took a position as principal of Grant Medical College in Bombay, India, where he did groundbreaking work on the nature of leprosy. But the book remains one of the classics in the field and has never gone out of print. When the thirteenth edition appeared in 1892, an advertisement declared that "*Gray's Anatomy* has been the standard work used by students of medicine and practitioners in all English-speaking races." The ad quotes the *Cleveland Medical Gazette*—"Teachers of anatomy are almost unanimous in recommending 'Gray' as the standard work"—and the *University Medical Magazine*—"the recognized text-book for the great majority of English-speaking students of medicine . . . the most perfect work of its kind extant." *Gray's Anatomy* is now in its fortieth edition, the work of eighty-five (properly credited) experts. Though none of Gray's text or Carter's illustrations remain, for generations of medical students, getting their copy has been a professional rite of passage.

❦

The *Diagnostic and Statistical Manual*, better known as the *DSM*, is not much to look at—small, paperbound, nine inches high by six inches wide, and just 142 pages long. It does not even seem particularly controversial on first reading. It advances no theological heresies, no maxims for political revolutionaries, no threats to the established order. It simply tallies the recognized psychological disorders and assigns to each a number: childhood schizophrenic reaction is 000–x28, sleepwalking is 000–x74, and "psychophysiologic endocrine reaction" is 008–580. And yet how much power lies in that classification!

Classifying illnesses has a long history. François Boissier de Sauvages de Lacroix, a friend of Carl Linnaeus, compiled a *Nosologia methodica* in 1763, applying the Linnaean taxonomy of plants to diseases. Sauvages

> **TITLE:** *Diagnostic & Statistical Manual, Mental Disorders*
> **COMPILER:** The Committee on Nomenclature and
>   Statistics of the American Psychiatric Association:
>   George N. Raines, Moses M. Frolich, Ernest S.
>   Goddard, Baldwin L. Keyes, Mabel Ross, Robert S.
>   Schwab, and Harvey J. Tompkins
> **PUBLISHED:** Washington, D.C.: American Psychiatric
>   Association Mental Hospital Service, 1952
> **PAGES:** xii + 130
> **ENTRIES:** 106 disorders
> **TOTAL WORDS:** 25,000
> **SIZE:** 6" × 9" (15.2 × 22.9 cm)
> **AREA:** 53 ft² (5 m²)
> **WEIGHT:** 10 oz. (300 g)
> **LATEST EDITION:** *Diagnostic and Statistical Manual of
>   Mental Disorders: DSM-5* (Washington, D.C.:
>   American Psychiatric Association, 18 May 2013),
>   xliv + 947 pages

identified ten classes, including insanity as number eight. The various classes were all divided into genera and species, for a total of twenty-four hundred diseases.[10] The *International List of Causes of Death* (1893), prepared by the International Statistical Institute, took recent medical thinking into account. As the nineteenth century turned into the twentieth, medicine became increasingly bureaucratic. Two forces pushed it toward statistics and classifications. The first was modern war, as more and more lethal weapons piled bodies higher and higher. Medical statistics in wartime translated into the ability to count, and perhaps thereby to reduce, various causes of mortality on the battlefield. The other was the insurance industry: the country doctor gave way to the bean counter, and the black bag was traded for red tape. Some of the world's earliest health insurance statutes were introduced in Germany in 1883, the United Kingdom in 1911, and France in 1945; universal or near-universal health care plans followed in the Soviet Union in 1937, New Zealand in 1939–41, Canada in 1946, and the United Kingdom in 1948. In the United States, Blue Cross and the Ross-Loos Medical Group were both founded in 1929—the beginning of the reign of the big health insurance companies. All demanded extensive paperwork.

Classifying mental disorders, though, proved more challenging than classifying physical disorders. It is comparatively easy to agree on what is ailing those suffering from the large majority of physical problems; though physicians are still unable to cure many conditions, they usually agree that this bone is broken, that sore is infected, or this organ is inflamed. Disorders of the mind are infinitely more complicated. Are there different kinds of mental, emotional, psychic, or spiritual unsoundness? If so, what are the categories, and how can we tell which sufferers have which diseases?

Classifying mental disorders is also exceedingly consequential. Expert witnesses in criminal trials often have to base their claims in the collective wisdom of the psychiatric profession, and that collective wisdom is contained in the reference books authorized by the professional societies. In most criminal prosecutions, our legal system demands a *mens rea*, an intention to do wrong. A psychiatric diagnosis that a defendant is incapable of distinguishing right from wrong may be enough to save him from imprisonment, even execution. The right diagnosis can keep a killer from the electric chair; the wrong one, conversely, can keep an otherwise qualified diplomat from government service, or an otherwise qualified soldier from serving in the military. A code in a reference book might be responsible for locking someone in an asylum.

What constitutes a mental disorder, and who gets to say? Are soldiers who refuse to rush into battle victims of shell shock?—of battle fatigue?—of PTSD?—or are they, as some have called them, merely cowards hiding behind a diagnosis? The boundaries of insanity are ill-defined, and they are easily influenced by the worldview of those drawing the lines. In 1851, Samuel Cartwright, a physician based in Louisiana who wrote *Diseases and Peculiarities of the Negro Race*, developed a pair of mental diagnoses that he said were characteristic of black slaves. The first, "dysaesthesia aethiopica," accounted for their laziness; the second, called "drapetomania," was an unaccountable desire on the part of slaves to escape from servitude. With the right treatment, Cartwright maintained, "this troublesome practice that many Negroes have of running away can be almost entirely prevented."[11] He thus demonstrated that all manner of preconception or prejudice can be elevated to the level of quasiscientific diagnosis.

In the 1840s, the U.S. Census recognized just one variety of mental illness, identified as "idiocy" or "insanity." The American Psychiatric Association devoted part of its founding year, 1844, to classifying patients in asylums, and began enumerating varieties of insanity.[12] By 1880, the list of maladies recognized by the census had grown from one to seven: mania, melancholia, monomania, paresis, dementia, dipsomania, and epilepsy.[13] The *Statistical Manual for the Use of Institutions for the Insane* (1918), the first attempt of the National Committee for Mental Hygiene to classify psychological disorders, included twenty-two diagnoses.

The number continued to rise over the first half of the twentieth century, culminating in 1952 in the American Psychiatric Association's *Diagnostic and Statistical Manual, Mental Disorders*, universally known as the *DSM*. It laid out a taxonomy of 106 mental disorders as understood in the early 1950s—that is, an essentially Freudian understanding of the world— backed up with epidemiological data. The word *reaction* appeared often in its pages, reflecting the understanding that most mental disorders were responses to stresses in the outside world—repressed trauma, unresolved tensions with family members, inadequately absolved guilt. When conditions in the *International Statistical Classification of Diseases*, concerned with somatic illnesses, had a connection to psychiatry, the *DSM* shared the appropriate code: nail biting is 324.3, cancerophobia is 313, weight loss is 788.4, and moral deficiency is 320.5. Much of the book is tabular:

PERSONALITY DISORDERS

−X DISORDERS OF PSYCHOGENIC ORIGIN OR WITHOUT CLEARLY DEFINED TANGIBLE CAUSE OR STRUCTURAL CHANGE

000–x40	Personality pattern disturbance	*(320.7)**
000–x41	Inadequate personality	*(320.3)*

000–x42   Schizoid personality   *(320.0)*
000–x43   Cyclothymic personality   *(320.2)*
000–x44   Paranoid personality   *(320.1)*

The first edition of the *DSM* reveals much about the state of psychiatry at midcentury, but the interesting story appeared in its subsequent revisions. Fourteen years after the *DSM* came *DSM-II*. It was a little shorter than its predecessor—136 pages rather than 145—but included more conditions. Children's behavioral disorders were recognized for the first time, including "hyperkinetic reaction," akin to what would later be called attention deficit hyperactivity disorder. More telling, the word *reaction* got much less use in *DSM-II*, and an essay appended to the manual justified the exclusion: the editors did not want the book to reflect any particular school of thought, and "reaction" was too tightly bound to Freudian psychoanalysis.

DSM-II was a critical dud, and within a few years of publication, the discontent translated into plans for a third edition. In the meantime, several developments had prompted a change in thinking about mental pathologies. In 1972 a large comparative study of diagnosed cases of schizophrenia in both London and New York City revealed the incidence was twice as high in New York as in London—forcing psychiatrists to think hard about the need for precise diagnostic criteria. More important, medications were showing promise in controlling what had been conceived of as strictly mental disorders: mania and depression seemed to be responding to pharmaceuticals.

The result was a walloping increase in the number of conditions identified—and in the size of the *DSM*. The original edition had identified 106 conditions, the second 182. By 1980, *DSM-III* was 494 pages long and included 265 diagnoses, arranged in a new classification system. In the first two versions, psychopathologies were regarded as manifestations of underlying subconscious states. This makes diagnosis difficult, since one behavior might be an expression of dozens of underlying conditions. Starting in the 1980s, the editors strove for a classification system that would be agnostic on questions of etiology. Instead they proposed a taxonomy based strictly on symptoms—on objective expressions in the real world. The buzzwords were now "objectivity" and "truth," and the manual was billed as a victory for science. Not everyone, though, regards *DSM-III* as a step forward. For some it was a victory not for science but for the pharmaceutical industry: the supposedly objective system of classification, dependent on no particular theory, paved the way for the medicalization, and therefore monetization, of many behaviors that had never before counted as pathologies.

Subsequent versions continued moving in the same direction. No sooner had *DSM-III* appeared than there were plans for *DSM-IIIR* ("revised") in 1987. Seven years after that came a *DSM-IV*, and six years later a *DSM-IV TR* ("text revision"). By the time of the fourth edition, the book had grown to 886 pages, backed up by four volumes of sources, and the number of diagnoses now stood at 279. The ever-finer distinctions among diagnoses partly reflected the best scientific thinking, but they also represented the influence of insurance companies that demanded billing codes.

With each change, the sorts of behavior considered "normal" or "pathological" were readjusted, often with real-world consequences. Michael First, a Columbia University professor of psychiatry who worked on *DSM-IV*, described the stakes: "Anything you put in that book, any little change you make, has huge implications not only for psychiatry but for pharmaceutical marketing, research, for the legal system, for who's considered to be normal or not, for who's considered disabled." There were dangers: "the more disorders you put in," First continued, "the more people get labels, and the higher the risk that some get inappropriate treatment."[14] Many think psychiatry has gone overboard with "disorders" such as binge eating and gambling, while excluding Internet addiction and sex addiction.[15] And as some putative mental illnesses are added, other long-familiar conditions simply disappear through fiat. Hysteria, a common diagnosis for millennia, was defined out of existence in the revision of 1980.

Probably the most controversial change in the history of the *DSM* was the editors' decision that one condition was no longer to be considered a disorder. The original *DSM* included, as number 000–x63, "Sexual deviation," with the instruction to "specify the type of the pathologic behavior, such as homosexuality, transvestism, pedophilia, fetishism and sexual sadism (including rape, sexual assault, mutilation)."[16] This classification reflected the general, if not universal, consensus of the profession in the 1950s: psychoanalysis saw homosexuality as a pathological "inversion." But times change, as do moral judgments about behavior. After Alfred Kinsey's groundbreaking *Sexual Behavior in the Human Male* (1948) reported that 37 percent of otherwise "normal" men had at some time engaged in this "pathology," though, it became more difficult to consider the behavior—increasingly thought of as an identity —as a "disorder." The meeting of the American Psychiatric Association (APA) in 1970, just months after the so-called Stonewall riots, was marked by controversy: protesters were out in numbers; they blocked the entrance to the conference and destroyed a booth that sold equipment for "aversion therapy" to "cure" homosexuality. The APA responded, as bureaucracies are wont to do, by forming a committee, this one headed by Robert Spitzer. The committee's report came to four conclusions:

(1) Expert opinion was divided over whether homosexuality was pathological;

(2) Many homosexuals seemed satisfied with their own sexual orientation;

(3) But there are also many homosexuals who want to change their orientation;

(4) It is possible to change the sexual orientation of some proportion of homosexuals.

Convinced that these findings were inconsistent with other pathologies, they ended by unanimously recommending that homosexuality be removed from the list of mental illnesses. In 1973, just four years after Stonewall, the professional consensus had changed: the sixth printing of *DSM-II* removed homosexuality from the list of diseases. Millions of "sick" people were instantly pronounced healthy.

Revision of the manual continues, and controversies about the classification system continue to grow. *DSM-5* appeared in May 2013, the work of fifteen years by thirteen subcommittees, each working on its own subspecialty. The page count reached 947, and again the number of ailments—potentially treatable, and therefore potentially profitable—rose: the count now tops three hundred, although changes to the classification

system make it impossible to come up with a precise number. New diagnoses include hoarding disorder, restless leg syndrome, and social communication disorder. Meanwhile, Asperger's syndrome has dissolved into a
more general "autism spectrum disorder," leaving millions of families
wondering what that will mean for the treatment of their children.

Some find the whole enterprise pointless. "Has there ever been a task
more futile," asked writer L. J. Davis about the *DSM*, "than the attempt
to encompass, in the work of a single lifetime, let alone in a single work,
the whole of human experience? . . . Not even Shakespeare could
manage it." The reductio ad absurdum leads inevitably to the conclusion
that "human life is a form of mental illness." Davis's cynical interpretation is that the *DSM* is a "catalogue," and "The merchandise
consists of the psychiatric disorders described therein, the customers are
the therapists, and this may be the only catalogue in the world that
actually makes its customers money: each disorder, no matter how
trivial, is accompanied by a billing code, enabling the therapist to fill out
the relevant insurance form and receive an agreed upon reward."[17]

⚕

Gray's Anatomy and the *DSM* seem to be worlds apart. One is concerned
with the body, the other with the mind; one tells a story of Victorian
positivism, the other of postmodern insecurity about the limits of our
knowledge. Both, though, reveal the power exercised by the classifying
function of the reference book. Gray and the nearly forgotten Carter
got to determine how generations of physicians approached the human
body, and their decisions have shaped the thinking of medical profes-
sionals for a century and a half. The *DSM*, too, has been shaping
thinking, but it has been easier to see the work that went into shaping
it, and thus easier to see how contingent many of its judgments are.
Both books offer an opportunity to think about how much depends on
the decisions made by the writers of our handbooks.

INCOMPLETE AND ABANDONED PROJECTS

I N THE BACK alleys of intellectual history are scattered the abandoned wrecks of would-be dictionaries and encyclopedias. When publishing projects stretch out over decades, money runs out, editors die, publishers go out of business, manuscripts burn, wars intervene. The remarkable thing isn't that some works peter out before they're finished; more amazing is that any of these works ever make it to completion.

Some books never make it past the gleam-in-the-author's-eye stage. Read literary biography and you'll find no end of people who considered writing a dictionary or encyclopedia. Many poets thought about trying their hand at lexicography—only natural for people who devote their lives to language—but few have finished. Alexander Pope and Walt Whitman both dreamed of being lexicographers, but only a few notes survive of their planned dictionaries.[1] Oliver Goldsmith—novelist, poet, playwright, historian, and journalist—"for some time . . . entertained the project of publishing a 'Universal Dictionary of Arts and Sciences'" featuring contributions from friends including Samuel Johnson and Sir Joshua Reynolds—but, despite the progress he made on the proposals, he died before publishing any of it. One scholar discovered evidence of fifty-four English dictionaries that were conceived but abandoned between just 1755 and 1828.[2]

Others got a little further. Oxford's Bodleian Library holds tantalizing evidence of a dictionary from around 1570, which, had it been completed, would have been the first monolingual English dictionary, coming decades before Cawdrey's.[3] Franz Fügner began a *Lexicon Livianum* but called it quits after the letter *B* because he could not raise enough money.[4] In 1793, the Portuguese Academy published the first volume of the *Diccionario da lingoa portugueza*. This promised to put the

Portuguese language on the same academic foundation as French, Italian, and Spanish, but it was abandoned after *A*. The Portuguese would have to wait until 2001 for a serious academic dictionary. Elsewhere on the Iberian peninsula, Rufino José Cuervo worked on a *Diccionario de construcción y régimen de la lengua castellana*, more comprehensive than any other Spanish dictionary—the preposition *a* alone fills twenty-seven pages. But the project died after 2,270 pages took Cuervo only as far as the letter *D*.[5] A French *Dictionnaire historique* released volume 1 (*a–actualité*) in 1865 and started on volume 2 in 1878; at that rate they would have finished in 2,990 years. Perhaps it is just as well that they gave up in 1894, having completed only *A*.[6]

Some efforts got pretty far along before something caused them to fall apart. The seventeenth-century French encyclopedist Jean Magnon worked on *La Science universelle*, an encyclopedia in verse—around ten thousand lines, roughly the length of *Paradise Lost*—but he never finished it. Perhaps we need not agonize over the loss; one nineteenth-century source calls him "Jean Magnon, poëte français très-médiocre," a description unlikely to need translation.[7] Vincenzo Coronelli, a Venetian monk and cartographer at the beginning of the eighteenth century, planned a *Biblioteca universale sacro-profana, antico-moderna* in forty or forty-five folio volumes. Had it been completed, it would have been among the first major encyclopedias arranged entirely in alphabetical order—but funds dried up when Coronelli's manuscript had reached *M*. Just the first seven volumes—covering *A*, *B*, and part of *C*—appeared in print between 1701 and 1706; the remainder has never been published.

One of the grandest of the abandoned wrecks is the *Allgemeine Encyclopädie der Wissenschaften und Künste*, or *Universal Encyclopedia of the Sciences and the Arts*. It was begun in 1818 and would have been one of the greatest encyclopedic projects of all time. It took most of the century: in 1889, seventy-one years after publication began, volume 167 appeared. And yet this was still less than half of its projected size. The team that devoted seven decades to the project managed to finish only the entries for *A* through *Ligatur*, and then *O* through *Phyxios*—the rest of the alphabet was untouched.[8]

A few dictionaries were actually finished, or nearly so, but never saw the light of day. Fernando del Rosal completed his *Origen y etymologia de todos los vocablos originales de la lengua Castellana* in 1601. But it was never printed, and the handwritten copy remains in the archives of Madrid's Biblioteca Nacional. Matthias Moth did virtually all the work on an imposing Danish dictionary between 1680 and 1717, producing more than sixty folio volumes in manuscript, but could not push it across the finish line; the work has never been published.[9] Ilyn Fedorovich Kopievskii compiled a more or less complete *Nomenclator in lingua latina, germanica et russica*—a trilingual dictionary of Latin, German, and Russian—in 1700, but he left it unpublished at the time of his death.

Shake-ups in the publishing economy, coming from both the rise of electronic publication and the collapse of library budgets, have caused some projects to sputter to a halt. Literary scholars depend on the *Cambridge Bibliography of English Literature* or *CBEL*, which first appeared between 1940 and 1957, followed by a *New* edition—known as the *NCBEL*—between 1969 and 1977. At the end of the twentieth century a third edition was planned: thousands of contributors were lined up and thousands of contracts signed. (I was tapped for *Boswell, James* and *Johnson, Samuel*.) The volumes were worked on independently, and volume 4, covering the nineteenth century, appeared in 1999, to mostly good reviews. But between the issuing of the contracts and the delivery of the finished typescripts, the bottom fell out of print reference publishing. Cambridge University Press realized it could not sell enough hard-copy volumes, and it saw no way to recover its costs on an online version. All the contributors were released from their contracts, the project was scrapped, and volume 4 remains orphaned in the world's libraries, doomed never to sit between volumes 3 and 5.

Politics can also kill a reference work. The *Brockhaus-Efron entsik-lopedicheskii Slovar* came out in Russia between 1890 and 1907, after which a revised *Novyi entsiklopedicheskii Slovar* was planned. That project got under way in 1912, but this revolutionary decade was not a good time for reference publishing, especially for an old-fashioned reflection of the czarist world. Five years after the first volume appeared, the encyclopedia had reached twenty-nine volumes and the letter *O*. But the October Revolution of 1917 meant the end of the *Novyi entsiklopedicheskii.*[10]

A few abandoned projects are especially tantalizing because they might have been works of genius. Samuel Taylor Coleridge, one of the towering intellects of the early nineteenth century, provided the introductory treatise to what was going to be a trailblazing *Encyclopædia Metropolitana* in 1817, but it was just another of the utopian dreams that Coleridge entertained over the course of his career, and he withdrew.[11] Just as lamentable is the loss of W. E. B. Du Bois's proposed *Encyclopædia Africana*, a "comprehensive compendium of 'scientific' knowledge about the history, cultures, and social institutions of people of African descent: of Africans in the Old World, African Americans in the New World, and persons of African descent who had risen to prominence in Europe, the Middle East, and Asia." The project occupied Du Bois's mind for nearly half a century.[12] He wrote to dozens of experts, hoping to establish a pair of editorial boards—"One Hundred Negro Americans, African and West Indian Scholars," along with a second panel of white advisers—though "the real work," he told a friend, "I want done by Negroes."[13] Nearly everyone he asked said yes, and progress was expected to be rapid. Printed stationery promised the first volume in 1913, "the Jubilee of Emancipation in America and the Tercentenary of the Landing of the Negro," with four more volumes coming out over the next four years. But the funding never materialized. Du Bois tried again during the Great Depression, but progress was even harder then.[14] A one-volume project on this plan—*Africana: The Encyclopedia of the African and African American Experience*, edited by Kwame Anthony Appiah and Henry Louis Gates—finally appeared in 1999, but for all its value, it's hard not to lament the lost *Africana* by a father of African studies.

CHAPTER 21

THE FOUNDATION STONE

Library Catalogs

Anthony Panizzi	The National Union Catalog
General Catalogue of	*Pre-1956 Imprints*
Printed Books	1968–81
1881–1900	

W HEN A LIBRARY holds just a few dozen books, life is simple. Need a book? The librarian can locate it for you off the top of his or her head. But books have a habit of piling up, and when those piles become too big, someone is charged with coming up with a useful list of what is where. And so was born the library catalog.

The royal library of Ashurbanipal in seventh-century-B.C.E. Assyria had some sort of catalog, though we know nothing of its form. Better evidence survives from the Library of Alexandria, founded in the late fourth or early third century B.C.E. The library had a vigorous acquisitions policy. When ships arrived in Alexandria, all their books would be seized and copied. When they were ready to depart, they were given the copies instead of the originals, which stayed at the library. Techniques like this turned the Library of Alexandria into what was, by ancient standards, a prodigiously large collection, far too large for any librarian to know by heart.[1] And so in the late third century Callimachus wrote the *Pinakes* (*Tables* or *Tablets*), the most thorough list of books in the ancient world. Callimachus divided literature into categories, including philosophy, oratory, history, law, medicine, lyric poetry, tragic poetry, and miscellaneous, and within each category he listed the authors' names in alphabetical order—a rare classical example of alphabetical order in a reference book. The list occupied 120 "books," or scrolls.[2]

Only bits survive today, but those fragments provide a guide to other Greek literature that is now lost, presumably forever.

Callimachus had Greek and Roman successors, but after the collapse of the Western Roman Empire, few impressive libraries existed in Europe. A medieval European library with five hundred books would have been exceptional. The oldest intact library in the Western world is a small room in Cesena, Italy, near Rimini, a building dating from the middle of the fifteenth century—as traditionally dated, the end of the Middle Ages and beginning of the Renaissance. There the original collection of books remains in situ: a grand total of fifty-eight volumes.[3] Most European libraries, like this one, numbered their books in the tens or hundreds of titles. The great libraries of China and the Islamic world, on the other hand, numbered theirs in the tens or hundreds of thousands, and that is where the interesting works on library cataloging are found in this period. Abu Tahir Tayfur, a ninth-century bookseller from Baghdad, followed Callimachus in giving short biographies and alphabetical lists of works of major authors. In 987, Ibn al-Nadim cataloged as many Arabic-language books as he could identify, and the resulting book, the *Fihrist*, is the most thorough collection of medieval Arabic knowledge known today.[4] And the Chinese scholar Zheng Qiao (1103–62) wrote *Jiao zhou luo* (*Theory of Library Science and Bibliography*), which gave a rationale guiding the purchase of new acquisitions.[5]

❧

The number of books and readers in the West was far lower than in the Arabic and Chinese worlds, and so the number of libraries remained lower. Early in the sixteenth century, though, movable type caused libraries to develop at an unprecedented rate. Now even the most capacious memory could not hope to recall the location of every book. And as the great libraries grew, and opened their collections not merely to the nobles who owned them but to the scholars who visited them, the need for catalogs became even greater.

Most of the impressive libraries in early modern Europe were royal collections, or the personal collections of wealthy aristocrats, and they were cataloged only sporadically. Oxford University's Bodleian Library was first cataloged in 1605, with a four-part index covering the arts, theology, law, and medicine, with a separate index of authors.[6] When Edward Harley—the son of the bibliophile Robert Harley, First Earl of Oxford and Earl Mortimer—died in 1741, his father's collection of more than 7,000 manuscripts, 50,000 rare books, and 350,000 pamphlets was purchased by the British government, and one of the young scholars hired to produce a catalog was Samuel Johnson, who spent several years in his early thirties describing the collection.

One of the world's greatest feats of cataloging came in the late nineteenth century, when Britain's national library was a division of the British Museum in London. The person who made it possible was an Italian revolutionary who became the most English of establishment Englishmen. Antonio Panizzi, born in Reggio Emilia, resented Austrian rule over Italy and involved himself in revolutionary causes. According to his biographer, the political struggles were "to determine radically the course of his whole life and to influence his conduct, even into old age."[7] Several friends were arrested for their radical politics, and eventually the inevitable happened: a warrant for Panizzi's arrest was issued. Rather than defend himself he decided to flee. After saying goodbye to his family and close friends in 1822, he slipped across the border, using a small boat he had hidden among the reeds, and made his way through Europe with virtually no resources and no support. After arriving in England he taught himself English, gained the friendship of some powerful Whig politicians, and in 1831 landed a job at the British Museum Library, the largest in England. As he worked through the ranks at the library, he was given the task of cataloging the collection of nearly a quarter million printed books.

There had been earlier attempts. The two-volume *Librorum impressorum qui in Museo Britannico, adservantur catalogus* (*Catalog of the Printed Books Kept in the British Museum*, 1787) was followed by a seven-volume version (1813–19). Neither was very good. Plans for a more comprehensive edition resulted in the *Catalogue of Printed Books in the British Museum*—but only the first volume, covering *A*, saw the light of day, in 1841, before the project was abandoned.

It was Panizzi's job to make a proper catalog. He first set his staff to work identifying exactly what they had—a more difficult task than it seems. For one reader, anything called *King Lear* on the title page is good enough. For another, only the edition that says *M. William*

TITLE: *Catalogue of Printed Books in the Library of the British Museum*

COMPILER: Anthony Panizzi (1797–1879)

ORGANIZATION: Alphabetical by author

PUBLISHED: London: W. Clowes & Sons, 1881–1900; supplement, 1901–5

VOLUMES: 393 parts in 95 volumes + 44 parts in 13 vols. supplement

PAGES: 59,000

TOTAL WORDS: 45 million

SIZE: 13¾" × 10¼" (35 × 26 cm)

AREA: 57,800 ft² (5,370 m²)

PRICE: £76 10s. for subscribers; free to public libraries in the UK

LATEST EDITION: The last printed version was *The British Library General Catalogue of Printed Books to 1975* (360 vols., London, 1979–87) with supplements (6 vols., London, 1987–88); the current catalog is now online at catalogue.bl.uk

Shakspeare: His True Chronicle Historie of the Life and Death of King Lear and His Three Daughters. With the Vnfortunate Life of Edgar, Sonne and Heire to the Earle of Gloster, and His Sullen and Assumed Humor of Tom of Bedlam, published by Nathaniel Butter in 1608, will do. And only a serious specialist, well versed in early modern bibliography, will know that this is not the same book as the one that says on the title page that it was published by Nathaniel Butter in 1608 but was actually published by William Jaggard in 1619. Panizzi's impatient superiors thought a printed catalog could be completed in just a few years, and they fretted when Panizzi spoke of "years of unremitting and heavy labour." But he insisted the work had to be done right.[8]

Panizzi's real contribution was a system for organizing the records in the catalog. Most works were to be listed alphabetically by author; when that was impossible, they were to appear alphabetically under predictable headings. To this end he compiled a set of ninety-one rules, issued in 1841. Even many librarians disparaged them. But as another librarian admitted in 1869, "The ninety-one rules, ... so foolishly ridiculed for their number, have probably been increased to twice as many by the subsequent experience of that vast establishment."[9]

We assume that alphabetical order is easy, but real-world examples quickly become difficult. What to do with names in foreign alphabets? Where to alphabetize a book "By a Lady" or "By Publicus"? Should *Tom Sawyer* go under "Twain, Mark" or "Clemens, Samuel Langhorne"? "Sand, George" or "Dupin, Amantine-Lucile-Aurore"? What about authors using the names of real authors as their pseudonyms? What about nobles: alphabetize under "Wilmot, John, 2nd Earl of Rochester" or "Rochester, John Wilmot, 2nd Earl of"? What about a book published by the Kaiserliche Akademie der Wissenschaften in Wien? *Euclid, Book V: Proved Algebraically So Far as It Relates to Commensurable Magnitudes* was published by Charles L. Dodgson, M.A., and *Alice's Adventures in Wonderland* by Lewis Carroll, even though they are the same person.

A few rules give a taste of Panizzi's system:

I. Titles to be written on slips, uniform in size . . . .
Titles to be arranged alphabetically, according to the English
     alphabet only (whatever be the order of the alphabet in which
     a foreign name might have to be entered in its original
     language) under the surname of the author, whenever it
     appears printed in the title, or in any other part of the book. If
     the name be supplied in MS. the work must nevertheless be
     considered anonymous or pseudonymous . . . .
V. Works of Jewish Rabbis, as well as works of Oriental writers
     in general, to be entered under their first name . . . .
XI. Works of authors who change their name or add to it a
     second, after having begun to publish under the first, to be
     entered under the first name, noticing any alteration which
     may have subsequently taken place.[10]

The brilliance of Panizzi's system lies in the way it provided consistent ways of dealing with all the complications that inevitably arise once you begin cataloging real books. Alphabetize by author: easy enough. But what about a book published, by, say, "W.S."? Rule XXII: "Works published under initials, to be entered under the last of them; and should the librarian be able to fill up the blanks left, or complete the words which such initials are intended to represent, this is to be done in the body of the title, and all the supplied parts to be included between brackets."[11] Rule XVIII governed long titles: "The title of the book next to be written, and that expressed in as few words and those only of the author, as may be necessary to exhibit to the reader all that the author meant to convey in the titular description of his work; the original orthography to be preserved."[12] Rule LIV—"No work ever to be entered twice at full length. Whenever requisite, cross-references to be introduced"[13]—was especially prescient; it ensured that when changes were necessary, they would be made in just one place, not all over the catalog.

The wars between Panizzi and the trustees of the Museum dragged on, and they sometimes got ugly and personal. As the decades passed, though, Panizzi won most of his battles, and his efforts made his library one of the greatest in the world. He worked first to pass, then to enforce a new Copyright Act, ensuring that the British Museum would be a legal deposit library. Panizzi also drew up the initial plans for the legendary round Reading Room, which opened in 1857 and hosted generations of scholars— those in the know could identify the desks used by Karl Marx, Oscar Wilde, Virginia Woolf, and Mahatma Gandhi. (Since the British Library moved into its own quarters in 1997, the Reading Room has mostly been used for exhibitions, though discussions are ongoing about how best to use the space.) For this work he received a long series of honors, culminating in a knighthood in 1869. No longer Antonio Panizzi, he was now Sir Anthony, and seemingly worlds away from the radical firebrand who slipped out of his native Italy.

Panizzi died in 1879 and did not live to see the completion of his catalog, but its compilation was governed to the end by the rules he had written. The first printed version of the catalog came out between 1881 and 1900. The *General Catalogue of Printed Books*, known by the shorthand GK—the job that the trustees thought would be a simple clerical task, completed in a few years—ended up occupying 393 volumes, with another 44 in the *Supplement* added between 1900 and 1905.[14] GK2, bringing the original up to date, covered only the early parts of the alphabet, but GK3 covered holdings through 1955, and *The British Library General Catalogue of Printed Books to 1975* in 360 volumes, published between 1979 and 1987, with six supplements in the late 1980s, brought it up to date. GK now abides in the ether with 57 million items, far more than even Panizzi could have imagined: the library had just a quarter million volumes when he started, and more than half a million when he died.

GK has been called "a research tool of undisputed importance for historians of European civilisation from the invention of printing to the present day,"[15] and every major catalog since has been indebted to Panizzi. "Panizzi's '91 Rules,'" wrote K.G.B. Bakewell, "marked the beginning of the modern era of cataloguing."[16]

⁂

Even the best library catalogs from Callimachus to Panizzi and beyond share one major drawback: they are *library* catalogs, not *libraries'* catalogs. What if someone needs a book but does not know who owns a copy? Once, the searcher would have had to check library after library. The thirteenth century, though, sees the birth of a new reference genre, the "union catalog," which brings together the holdings of several libraries. The abbey of Savigny in Normandy, for instance, compiled a catalog not only of the library in Savigny, but of those in four nearby Benedictine abbeys.[17] English Franciscan monks likewise assembled the *Registrum Angliae de libris doctorum et auctorum veterum*, a list of works by roughly a hundred authors, with notes on which English and Scottish monastic libraries owned them.[18]

The union catalog took a great leap forward early in the fifteenth century, when a monk—usually identified as Boston Buriensis, or John Boston of Bury—put together a *Catalogus scriptorum ecclesiae* covering 195 libraries in English monasteries. He listed 674 authors, and he used the books of the Bible as an organizing principle—under each book came a list of the authors who had written about it, as well as a list of English libraries where the curious could find the books.[19] These manuscript catalogs were necessarily of limited use because they were not widely available. In print, though, they became accessible to a large audience, and the first great printed union catalog came in 1545, when

TITLE: *The National Union Catalog, Pre-1956 Imprints: A Cumulative Author List Representing Library of Congress Printed Cards and Titles Reported by Other American Libraries*

ORGANIZATION: Alphabetical by author, *A* to *Zzays, Jgo Wan*

PUBLISHED: London: Mansell, 1968–81

VOLUMES: 685 + 69 vols. supplement

PAGES: 528,000

ENTRIES: 11.6 million

TOTAL WORDS: 580 million

SIZE: 13¾" × 10¼" (35 × 26 cm)

AREA: 510,000 ft² or 11.8 acres (48,000 m² or 4.8 hectares)

WEIGHT: 2.7 tons (2,450 kg)

PRICE: $15.18 for the first volume; prices rose over time

Conrad Gesner devoted years to his *Bibliotheca universalis* in 1545, covering around ten thousand books by some three thousand authors.[20]

The greatest of the union catalogs, though, is a twentieth-century American production—a work so immense that it was recognized as a national strategic asset during the Second World War and involved an airlift operation whose logistics had some of the complexity of the war itself.

The first inklings of an American union catalog came from Charles Coffin Jewett, the librarian of the Smithsonian, who in 1850 proposed the distribution of stereotype plates of printed library catalogs. Nothing came of such a complex plan, but soon a practical development in the way local catalogs were maintained eased some of that complexity. Libraries have to deal with growing collections: new books are constantly coming in, and they need to find space both on the shelf and in the catalog. Librarians would routinely leave blanks between the entries in their handwritten catalogs, allowing for new entries. But maintaining alphabetical order in a bound manuscript is a losing battle, because it is never possible to know where the additions will be. The solution to the growing collection was surprisingly elegant: catalogs were prepared not in bound volumes but on cards, which could be arranged in purpose-built drawers. Harvard was using 2" × 5" cards in the 1860s, though eventually 3" × 5" became standard in the United States and the United Kingdom.[21]

Once catalog entries were on cards that could be removed from their drawers, the American Library Association proposed finding means to share the cards. In June 1898, the Library of Congress offered copies of their own cards for newly cataloged books, available by subscription. This made life infinitely easier for small public libraries, which could now rely on the experts in D.C. to catalog their new acquisitions. But this one-way traffic, with the Library of Congress providing cards for other libraries, did not do anything to report on other libraries' holdings.

The Library of Congress therefore proposed a scheme in 1901 to share cards from the major American research libraries, including the New York and Boston Public Libraries, the Harvard University Libraries, and others. The first step would be combining cards into one alphabetical sequence, an effort begun in 1909. They expected to collect about six hundred thousand cards. Two things became clear as soon as they started comparing collections systematically: how many books existed and how few any one library had. By 1926, they had assembled 1.96 million cards, and their work was barely a quarter of the way to completion. Even the biggest libraries had just a tiny fraction of the books that were in circulation. Spot-checking revealed that the Library of Congress—by far the largest library in America—owned just 7 percent of the titles in the new combined list. Of the others, only another 7 percent were owned by more than one library. The nation's collections were both vast and vastly different. This discovery served only to make the need for a central catalog clearer.

In 1926, John D. Rockefeller, Jr., gave a gift of $250,000 over five years—enough to employ thirty-one staffers to work on what was nicknamed Project B. The team identified 8.3 million copies of a total of 6.8 million works to add to the catalog. In the 1930s, as Rockefeller's grant ran out, the Works Progress Administration stepped in, producing regional union catalogs that would feed into the central project. Evidence continued to mount as to how many books in these regional libraries were not in the master list.

Although it was very much a work in progress, by the late 1930s the union catalog was being recognized as a genuinely useful resource—and it got a new use as the United States entered the Second World War. Knowledge was power, especially in the development of weapons, and the government began making requests to the Library of Congress, asking especially for books on scientific and technical subjects. Once again people were surprised by just how incomplete even the most comprehensive list of books in the country was: about a third of the books the government requested could not be located even on the library's master list.

By the early 1940s, this master catalog had become so cyclopean, and so valuable, that it was moved out of Washington to protect it during wartime. The catalog had become a strategic military asset, and government action had to be taken to guard it from enemy action. The Library of Congress decided to issue a printed version, even though the work was far from complete, in order to make their labors available to the rest of the country. About 1.9 million cards were reproduced in *A Catalog of Books Represented by Library of Congress Printed Cards Issued to July 21, 1942*, an interim publication of a mere 167 volumes, followed by a 42-volume supplement. Dozens of libraries subscribed to the printed set, checking their own holdings against the master list and making a note whenever their holdings included something not in the central catalog. Within a year, another eighty thousand books were added to the master list.

The war ended; the work continued. Halsey William Wilson published *A Proposed Plan for Printing Library of Congress Cards in Cumulative Book Form* in 1946, and in 1948 the effort received the official name of National Union Catalog. A formal proposal for printing a carefully collated set came in 1953, and the agreement was reached in June 1964. The National Union Catalog Publication Project (NUCPP) was officially established in February 1967. The first decision was to draw a line: only books from before 1956 would be included. This would ensure that all the volumes would have the same coverage. The printed catalog would contain every card in the Library of Congress catalog, and the cards would be annotated with all the locations where a book might be found. If a major American library owned a book that was not in the Library of Congress, that library's card would appear in the book, again with location information. The plan called for sixty printed volumes a year over the course of ten years, for a total of 610 volumes, each of around 700 pages. Photographic reproduction would capture a few dozen index cards on each page.

The challenges were nearly overwhelming. The Library of Congress, having canvassed the country's other major research libraries, was sitting on more than 20 million cards, with no standardization of size, format, or the kinds of information they contained. Some were detailed records with precise transcriptions of the title pages, publication information, and even bibliographic collation formulas; others were single-line records that merely acknowledged the existence of a title. Some slips had to be cut to fit in the drawers built for them; others were too small and had to be mounted on cards. Duplicates had to be weeded out. When a book existed in the records of more than one library, they had to select the most reliable record. But it was not always clear when there were duplicates. Did two similar, but not perfectly identical, records point to the existence of two editions?—or was one merely a "ghost," the result of sloppy cataloging in the first place?

Between twenty-five and thirty project editors each worked through fourteen hundred cards a week. When they had done the necessary sorting, the cards were hastily microfilmed to provide a backup in case a shipment was lost, and then they were flown in batches, with almost military efficiency, to a London publisher, Mansell, for printing. Mansell won the contract because they had developed a technique by which blank space was removed from photographed copies, thereby avoiding wasted space. Even with the compactness offered by Mansell, the catalog is still huge. Volume 445, for instance, takes five hundred pages to get from *Patronato Central* to *Pavlovskii Leibgvard II*; the Smiths start in volume 550 and end in volume 552. But the team continued the five-volumes-a-month pace without missing a deadline until the project was completed, with volume 685 in June 1979.

The *National Union Catalog* has been called "the bibliographical wonder of the world." From conception to completion, it took eighty years and $34 million. One reviewer, holding the first volume, could offer little more than stunned silence: "A reviewer is normally expected to say something about the value of the title being reviewed. ... This catalog is so tremendous, with such a great potential, and appears to be so well done so far that it is felt better to delay such a review for maybe ten years or so. Maybe then one can do justice to it."[22] But when the reviewers could find words, they were glowing. One review of the first five volumes opened with "Has ever a bibliographical enterprise been so eagerly awaited, by so many, for so long?" The same reviewer called it "by far the largest constellation in the Gutenberg galaxy."[23]

⁂

These days the cataloging action is online. Even before the printed set of the *National Union Catalog* was finished, computers were appearing, with the Ohio College Library Center (OCLC) introducing the first electronic library catalog in August 1971. The Library of Congress considered getting into the computer catalog business itself but decided to support OCLC instead; its mission expanded from Ohio to the United States, and then to the whole world, and in the process the initials were repurposed as the Online Computer Library Center. Today their catalog, WorldCat, contains records from 72,000 libraries in 113 countries, with 2,223,658,162 items in the catalog, including books, archives, magazines, maps, CDs, DVDs, and databases.[24] And yet the cataloging project is far from complete. Many libraries are even now only partially cataloged, and of those that have been cataloged, not all their holdings have made it into the electronic catalogs—about a quarter of the books in the *National Union Catalog* are not (yet) in WorldCat.[25] Old books regularly turn up whose existence no one was aware of. As one of Harvard's librarians put it as long ago as 1869, "The cataloguer should not expect to be satisfied with his work."[26]

"Good cataloging," writes John Overholt, the curator of the Donald and Mary Hyde Collection at Harvard, "is the foundation stone of librarianship. If you have an item and can't find it, you don't really have it." When administrators propose cutting cataloging staff, Overholt cautions, "Saving money on cataloging only externalizes the costs in public services staff labor, duplicate purchases, and patron frustration."[27] The same sentiment was put more poetically a century and a half earlier: "A library is not worth anything without a catalogue," said Thomas Carlyle; "it is a Polyphemus without any eye in his head."[28]

CHAPTER 21 ½

INDEX LEARNING

S GOOGLE MAKING us stupid?

That was Nicholas Carr's question in 2008. "Over the past few years," he worried, "I've had an uncomfortable sense that someone, or something, has been tinkering with my brain, remapping the neural circuitry, reprogramming the memory." In the Google age, the danger is that "we will sacrifice something important not only in our selves but in our culture."[1] The logic is that ease of access is incompatible with profound contemplation—as information access gets easier, we'll take it increasingly for granted, and then knowledge itself will become superficial. Because I can know any fact I want to know in seconds without even getting off the sofa—Mount Kilimanjaro is 19,341 feet (5,895 m) high; the B side of Elvis Presley's "Heartbreak Hotel" was "I Was the One"; cricket was first played in India in 1721—I need not take the time to stock my brain with knowledge, and without deep knowledge, I can never aspire to wisdom.

This anxiety about ready access to information has a long history. Centuries before people worried about Google and Wikipedia, they worried about reference books and other scholarly apparatus. The first alphabetical indexes date to the fourteenth century,[2] and the paraphernalia of learning, which had long been the preserve of classical scholars, began showing up in the modern languages in the seventeenth century. In eighteenth-century Britain, some readers felt particularly threatened by the rise of indexes, glossaries, and concordances, all of which let the merest impostor appear as learned as the greatest sage. Alexander Pope dismissed this kind of knowledge as mere "Index-learning":

How Prologues into Prefaces decay,
And these to Notes are fritter'd quite away:
How Index-learning turns no student pale,
Yet holds the eel of science by the tail.[3]

Someone who depends on indexes is getting erudition on the cheap. In his bizarre satire on "modern" learning, *A Tale of a Tub*, Pope's friend Jonathan Swift took aim at all literary aids to comprehension, including marginalia, footnotes, dictionaries, and indexes—especially indexes. He blames those superficial scholars who hope "to get a thorough Insight into the *Index*, by which the whole Book is governed and turned, like *Fishes* by the *Tail*." The satirical *Grub Street Journal* complained in 1735 that "One of the principal causes of the decay of Learning is . . . the over great care that has been taken to preserve it. . . . The multitude of *Abridgements*, of *New Methods*, of *Indexes*, of *Dictionaries*, have damped that lively ardour which made scholars; and they have thought to know, that without any study, which they were assured might be learned with but moderate pains."[4] And the novelist Samuel Richardson wrote to a friend in 1750 complaining about "this age of dictionary and index learning, in which our study is to get knowledge without study."[5] The index, that is to say, amounts to cheating. "An index," literary historian Paul Tankard writes, "as an (albeit institutionalized) short cut, is always subversive; it suggests the possibility of avoiding the author's prose, of undermining the linearity of the text, of re-writing it. An index treats all prose as (mere) rhetoric."[6]

Actually, the fear is even older than the index—it is as old as writing itself. We see exactly the same anxiety in one of Plato's dialogues composed around 370 B.C.E. Socrates lectures Phaedrus about "a famous old god, whose name was Theuth," an inventor, whose greatest creation was writing. Theuth offered to share the gift of letters with the Egyptian people: "This, said Theuth, will make the Egyptians wiser and give them better memories; it is a specific both for the memory and for the wit." The Egyptian king, though, is unconvinced. Writing sounds like a gift, he says, but it will simply "create forgetfulness in the learners' souls, because they will not use their memories; they will trust to the external written characters and not remember of themselves." The result will be a race of dilettantes: "they will be hearers of many things and will have learned nothing; they will appear to be omniscient and will generally know nothing; they will be tiresome company, having the show of wisdom without the reality."[7] Two and a half millennia later, and we continue to fret about the inevitable decline.

CHAPTER 22

THE GOOD LIFE

The Arts and High Society

Sir George Grove	Emily Post
A Dictionary of Music	*Etiquette in Society*
and Musicians	1922
1879–99	

M ANY REFERENCE BOOKS are grimly utilitarian, concerned only with what we *need* to know: legal codes to settle the penalty for adultery, logarithm tables to aid artillery batteries, dictionaries to settle Saxon etymologies. But reference books can also tell us things we *want* to know. They can be just as useful in helping us find *le mot juste* for a poem, guiding us through the world's great museums, or advising us on which wine is worth a week's salary. Reference books, that is to say, can help us live the good life.

❀

George Grove was born in Clapham, just south of London, in 1820. Though far from rich, he managed to get a decent education, and at the age of sixteen he was apprenticed to a Scottish civil engineer. Soon he began working on the Birmingham–London railway. His passion, though, was music. His earliest musical memories were of hearing his mother play parts of Handel's *Messiah* on the piano. As a boy he was a regular at the Clapham parish church—partly, no doubt, for the doctrine, but largely to hear the music there, since the organist was especially fond of Johann Sebastian "Bawk."[1] When he worked in London, he heard as many concerts as he could, and he spent hours at the British Museum copying out long-neglected scores.

When he finished his apprenticeship he qualified as a graduate of the

Institution of Civil Engineering and traveled first to Glasgow, then to Jamaica and Bermuda, working as an engineer on building projects. Jamaica was under direct British rule in the heyday of the Empire, and Grove played his part in the imperial project. As his biographer tells the story—in an attempt to make him sound humane—"It is characteristic of Grove's considerateness that he was most anxious to get his white men away from the spot on the earliest possibility before the setting in of the unhealthy season."[2] Grove was a product of his age, when a white European life was worth more than a brown or black life.

Back in England, Grove worked on the new railway station at Chester, but he also made a point of hearing as much music as possible at the cathedral. When he heard the organist there playing a Bach fugue, he knew he had found a kindred spirit, and the two became fast friends. Together they started a singing club. Eventually Grove came into contact with some of the highest-profile civil engineers working in Britain, including Isambard Kingdom Brunel. On their urging—he facetiously says "they forced me"[3]—he became secretary of the Society of Arts in London at a time of great cultural excitement, since London was preparing for the Great Exhibition of 1851. Grove was responsible for much of the planning, and after the Exhibition, he became secretary in charge of the Crystal Palace, the gigantic glass structure that had been built for the event. He spent the rest of his life hosting concerts—first with a wind band, then with a full orchestra—at the Crystal Palace. He routinely chose the program and wrote program notes for the concerts, signing them simply "G."

Grove had many notable friends—Alfred, Lord Tennyson, Henry Morton Stanley, Benjamin Jowett, Clara Schumann, Arthur Sullivan ("a constant visitor at his house")[4]—and he hosted a wide range of programs, including the great Germans and Austrians of the Classical period, the French Romantics, and up-and-coming British composers. Bach—no longer "Bawk"—was a particular passion. Bach's reputation among the general public was not high in the mid-nineteenth century; he was regarded as learned but difficult. But for Grove, writing in the *Spectator* for a music-loving audience, Bach was marked not by learning but by "feeling, tender passionate sentiment, a burning genius, and a prodigious flow and march of ideas."[5] Grove also championed Franz Schubert, then little known in Britain. Sullivan and Grove traveled to Vienna to track down Schubert manuscripts and discovered music thought lost, which was first played at one of Grove's Crystal Palace concerts.

His writing talent made him a natural to become assistant editor of the *Bible Dictionary* being prepared by William Smith. He threw himself into the task, quickly providing a list of two hundred topics he might write on that started with just the letters *A* and *B*. He even paid two visits to the Holy Land to do research for the project, and as he worked on his contributions, often sat up until sunrise. He ultimately contributed around eleven hundred pages to the dictionary. He became the editor of *Macmillan's Magazine*, one of Victorian England's most popular periodicals, and did the job for fifteen years, securing contributions from the likes of Bret Harte, Christina Rossetti, Robert Louis Stevenson, W. H. Lecky, Thomas Henry Huxley, George Eliot, George Meredith, Matthew Arnold, Walter Pater, Margaret Oliphant, William Morris, and even the Russian novelist Ivan Turgenev.[6]

As Grove later recalled, "One dictionary led to another."[7] In 1874, the Macmillan publishing house approached him with an idea for a new dictionary of music, and he resigned his secretaryship of the Crystal Palace to devote himself to the project. In January 1874, Macmillan published a prospectus for a two-volume *Dictionary of Music and Musicians*. The publishers noted that interest in music had grown by leaps and bounds over the previous twenty-five years—the years, by no coincidence, during which Grove had been proselytizing in London—and that people were now curious about an art they had long neglected. But where to get answers? "There is no book in English," they wrote,

> from which an intelligent inquirer can learn, in small compass, and in language which he can understand, what is meant by a Symphony or Sonata, a Fugue, a Stretto, a Coda, or any other of the technical terms . . . or from which he can gain a readable and succinct account of the various branches of the art, or of the use and progress of the pianoforte and other instruments, or the main facts and characteristics of the lives of eminent musicians.[8]

TITLE: *A Dictionary of Music and Musicians (A.D. 1450–1889) by Eminent Writers, English and Foreign: With Illustrations and Woodcuts*

COMPILER: Sir George Grove (1820–1900)

ORGANIZATION: Alphabetical, *A* to *Zwischenspiel*; last volume devoted to the index

PUBLISHED: London: Macmillan, 1879–99

VOLUMES: 5

PAGES: XXXV + 3,312

TOTAL WORDS: 3.5 million

SIZE: $9\frac{1}{2}$" × 6" (24 × 15.5 cm)

AREA: 1,325 ft² (125 m²)

PRICE: £5 5s.

LATEST EDITION: *The New Grove Dictionary of Music and Musicians*, ed. Stanley Sadie, 29 vols. (New York : Grove's Dictionaries; London: Macmillan, 2001); *Grove Music Online*, 8th ed.

Grove was able to draw on his network of musical acquaintances to assemble an unimpeachable roster of contributors, as well as authorities whose names appear nowhere in the dictionary but who answered Grove's queries by mail or in person. He established a few principles: to minimize technical language; to make the musical examples available to readers, rather than locked away in libraries; and to cover European music broadly, with particular attention to English musicians. He began his coverage in 1450, "the most remote date to which the rise of modern music can be carried back." Anything earlier he dismissed as "mere archæology."[9] In this he was a creature of his age: early music was not yet in vogue.

Even as he worked on the music dictionary, he could not resist taking on side projects. "I have no temptation to be idle," Sir Walter Scott once wrote, "but the greatest temptation when one thing is wanted of me [is to] go and do something else"—Grove understood that urge deep in his bones.[10] He wrote a geography primer, as well as monographs on Beethoven, Mendelssohn, and Schubert. He also worked to raise money for the Palestine Exploration Fund, hoping to develop scholarly knowledge about the Holy Land.

Oddly, the highly productive writer found writing wearing. "My botherations often won't let me work,"[11] he complained. He had much to complain about. He suffered the death of several friends and, at the end of 1886, the death of his daughter; he had a deeply unhappy marriage. At times he let hyperbole get the best of him in complaining about his lot:

> How cruel life is! I declare to you I lead the life of a slave. From the moment I wake up till the moment I close my eyes it is one fight to do what it is impossible to get through. Hard work is a delight, but when it comes to giving up everything that you care for, and being always in anxiety, always in difficulty, never to have a quiet or a good time undisturbed by the thought of masses of duty left undone, then really life is not worth having.[12]

But, despite his grousing, the work was thorough. The entry for *appoggiatura*, for instance, goes on for four pages, with examples from Mozart's *Sonata in A Minor* and *Fantasia in C Minor*, Bach's *Passionmusik*, *Adelaide*, and *Suites Françaises*, Beethoven's *Andante in F*, Haydn's *Sonata in Eb*, and so on. Grove wrote his Schubert article "at least four times over, each time quite differently. Each time I think now I have got it, and then the next morning I find that it won't do." It finally appeared in 1882, and has been praised as "perhaps his most remarkable contribution to the Dictionary."[13]

What was going to be two volumes turned into four, appearing in 1878, 1880, 1883, and 1889. Among musicologists in the English-speaking world, "Grove" is now as familiar as "Webster" or "Roget": the name has come to stand for the book. After his work appeared, Grove was rewarded with a knighthood. Grove—by then Sir George—suffered a stroke early in 1899, and he continued to decline until his death at the end of May 1900. His book, though, remained a fixture in every musician's library for decades, until its place was taken in 1980 by an even larger *New Grove Dictionary of Music and Musicians*, not four volumes but twenty, with 22,500 articles. The edition of 2001 hit twenty-nine volumes, the first to be available online.

Grove informed the more learned members of the cultured world about what they might hear in the world's great concert halls, but Emily Post was more concerned about how to behave when they got there.

Born Emily Price to a socialite family in either 1872 or 1873 (the records are unclear), she was educated at home, then spent some time at Miss Graham's finishing school in New York. "For years I was made to carry a sandbag on my head," she recalled. "With this I had to curtsy to my governess, who pretended to be my hostess; and then in turn I, playing hostess to her, would smile and bow, and dance and walk across a polished floor without swinging my arms or resting a hand on my hip. And of course I sat bolt upright on a backless chair."[14]

The debutante life seemed to pay off with a marriage to a wealthy banker, Edwin Main Post, in 1892, but all was not well. Edwin, no dutiful husband, had a string of affairs. At the turn of the century any divorce was scandal, but *Post v. Post* was more scandalous than most. The scandal sheet *Town Topics* found out about Edwin's affairs and tried to blackmail him to avoid the details appearing in the paper. He refused, and both Posts had to suffer the embarrassment of being tabloid fodder against the background of police stings. Once on her own, Emily Post was forced to make a living with her pen. Still she had no thought of writing the kind of book that made her famous.

That changed after a series of letters. "For several days in succession," she recalled, "the same message was brought to me that Mr. D. of an important publishing house wanted to speak to me about an encyclopedia." She wanted nothing to do with the importunate salesman. "As I already had five encyclopedias," she wrote, "I sent word that another was one thing in the world I did not need. Mr. D.'s reply at last made it plain: 'We do not want you to buy an encyclopedia, we want you to write one.'"[15]

That got her attention. "Mr. D." was Richard Duffy of Funk & Wagnalls, and she agreed to meet him over tea and discuss what he had in mind, though she was "unable to imagine what kind of encyclopedia it might be." When the answer came, though—an encyclopedia of etiquette—"all the lovely balloons of vague fantasy collapsed." Etiquette, she thought, "meant a lot of false and pretentious fuss over trifles. I

TITLE: *Etiquette in Society, in Business, in Politics and at Home: By Emily Post (Mrs. Price Post)*

COMPILER: Emily Post (1872–1960)

ORGANIZATION: Topical

PUBLISHED: New York and London: Funk & Wagnalls, 1922

PAGES: ix + 627

TOTAL WORDS: 200,000

SIZE: 9½" × 6" (24 × 15 cm)

AREA: 253 ft² (23.5 m²)

PRICE: $4

LATEST EDITION: *Emily Post's Etiquette: Manners for a New World*, 18th ed. (New York: William Morrow, 2011)

refused even to talk about it, and thought the matter closed." Duffy kept at her, though, and at one point sent her a stack of books about etiquette mostly to show her how bad they were. That tactic worked. "*I will* write the book for you," she told Duffy, "and at once! It will be only a little primer—just a few of the essential principles of taste. I'll begin it tomorrow morning."[16] After eighteen months of work, the "little primer" grew to a typescript of 692 pages.

In 1922, Post's audience was largely made up of the newly rich, as those who climb the social ladder are often eager for information on what is expected of them in their new station. Nowhere was class insecurity greater than in the United States. After the First World War, America found itself a world power, richer than all the others. Many of Europe's cultural treasures were being snapped up by Americans: European dukes and viscounts with impeccable pedigrees found themselves in dire need of cash, and wealthy Americans were looking for cultural cachet. It therefore made perfect sense that there would be an American market for a book on etiquette. Richard Duffy of Funk & Wagnalls explained at the time that "We Americans are members of the nation which, materially, is the richest, most prosperous and most promising in the world." And yet, while "America . . . has her ancient manners to remember and respect," there were difficulties with "the rapid assimilation of new peoples into her economic and social organism." The book was necessary: "The perfection of manners by intensive cultivation of good taste, some believe, would be the greatest aid possible to the moralists who are alarmed over the decadence of the younger generation."[17]

Early in 1922 Funk & Wagnalls published *Etiquette in Society, in Business, in Politics and at Home: Illustrated with Private Photographs and Facsimiles of Social Forms*. Post opened with a meditation on the nature of "best society"—"an ambiguous term," she warned; "it may mean much or nothing." For her it was not based on inherited rank or wealth, though she rarely ventured too far down the socioeconomic ladder. She included a heading "Money Not Essential to Social Position," and she worked to put the less well-off at their ease—"The fact that you live in a house with two servants, or in an apartment with only one, need not imply that your house lacks charm or even distinction"—but she did not consider the possibility that some houses had only one servant, and many apartments had none at all. Post said that "A very well-bred man intensely dislikes the mention of money, and never speaks of it (out of business hours) if he can avoid it,"[18] though it was much easier not to mention money if one had a lot of it. Not caring about money can be expensive.

Some of the advice seems worlds away from twenty-first-century life:

> The younger person is always presented to the older or more distinguished, but a gentleman is always presented to a lady, even though he is an old gentleman of great distinction and the lady a mere slip of a girl.
>
> No lady is ever, except to the President of the United States, a cardinal, or a reigning sovereign, presented to a man.[19]

Alongside the positive advice came the negative. "Do *not* say: 'Mr. Jones, shake hands with Mr. Smith,' or 'Mrs. Jones, I want to make you acquainted with Mrs. Smith.' *Never* say: 'make you acquainted with' and do not, in introducing one person to another, call one of them 'my friend.'"

And if that is not bad enough: "Under no circumstances whatsoever say 'Mr. Smith meet Mrs. Jones,' or 'Mrs. Jones meet Mr. Smith.' Either wording is equally preposterous."[20]

Being preposterous was bad, but being vulgar was worse. The lurking bogeyman throughout the book is vulgarity. We may expect the proletariat to be vulgar: "A 'show-girl' may be lovely to look at," Post acknowledged, but the moment she opened her mouth and said something like "My Gawd!" her "vulgar slang" immediately convicted her as insufferably low. But even those traveling in the best circles could find themselves among the vulgar. "Acceptances or regrets," for instance, "are always written. An engraved form to be filled in is vulgar." Elaborate designs on tablecloths "inevitably produce a vulgar effect." A man wearing diamonds? "Nothing is more vulgar than a display of 'ice' on a man's shirt front, or on his fingers." Flowers in the hearse at a funeral were not just vulgar but "very vulgar." A hat too fancy for the occasion was so vulgar that one might as well have been running naked through the jungle: "Vulgar clothes . . . are always too elaborate. . . . The woman of uncultivated taste has no more sense of moderation than the Queen of the Cannibals." Post archly considered it "unnecessary to add that none but vulgarians would employ a butler (or any other house servant) who wears a mustache!"[21]

Conversation was also governed by Post's rules. How should one speak to the valet ("pronounced val-et not vallay")? "In a dignified house, a servant is never spoken to as Jim, Maisie, or Katie, but always as James or Margaret or Katherine, and a butler is called by his last name." Sometimes the rules were complicated, but that is why a book like *Etiquette in Society* was essential: "A gentleman on the street never shakes hands with a lady without first removing his right glove. But at the opera, or at a ball, or if he is usher at a wedding, he keeps his glove on." "On very informal occasions, it is the present fashion to greet an intimate friend with 'Hello!' . . . This seemingly vulgar salutation is made acceptable by the tone in which it is said. To shout 'Hul*low!*' is vulgar, but 'Hello, Mary' or 'How 'do, John,' each spoken in an ordinary tone of voice, sound much the same."[22]

A great historical distance separates our world from Post's, but at the core of all her rules, even those most alien to us, was the imperative to put people at their ease. For Post, manners were part of ethics. She summed up this principle well in the golden rule of etiquette:

> Consideration for the rights and feelings of others is not merely a rule for behavior in public but the very foundation upon which social life is built.
>
> Rule of etiquette the first—which hundreds of others merely paraphrase or explain or elaborate—is:
>
> Never do anything that is unpleasant to others.[23]

"Post's guiding precept," wrote one commentator, "was that good manners began with consideration for the feelings of others and included good form in speech, knowledge of proper social amenities, and charm of manner. She believed that there was a right or best way to do almost everything and that that was the way that pleased the greatest number of people and offended the fewest."[24]

Post's *Etiquette*—she called it her "little blue book," a charming phrase for a work of 627 pages—was a great success. Sales were slow at first but picked up as 1922 passed. Through the autumn of that year she found herself nearly at the top of the *Publishers Weekly* chart, bouncing around between fifth and second place. Finally, in March 1923, she claimed the number one spot. *Etiquette* was America's bestselling nonfiction book in 1923, and it remained in the top ten throughout 1924—and on the list for more than a decade. Post became a superstar. She was besieged by requests for endorsements: makers of glassware, silver, linens, even ginger ale ("a refreshing drink to serve at parties!") were eager to get Post to promote their wares.

The popularity of *Etiquette* unleashed a large number of questions—in one year alone, she received twenty-six thousand queries—and she did what she could to answer them. Most came from women, but Post estimated that around one letter in ten came from a man—mostly young men. When she realized her answers might be of interest to more than the original writers, she published them in a column syndicated in more than 150 newspapers across the United States. In answering all these unexpected queries, she began developing material for a new edition. Five years after the first edition, a second appeared in 1927, now with a subtitle: *The Blue Book of Social Usage*. Further editions followed in 1931 and 1934, while she was hosting a radio program on etiquette. In 1946 she opened the Emily Post Institute "to study problems of gracious living."

The reference books that promote the good life are a comparatively neglected genre. They deserve more attention. Books such as Joshua Poole's dictionary for poets, *The English Parnassus; or, A Helpe to English Poesie* (1657), with its list of rhymes and its "excellent choice and variety of apposite *Epithets*,"[25] and Nicolas Slonimsky's *Thesaurus of Scales and Melodic Patterns* (1947), a radical synthesis of music theory that inspired classical musicians as well as John Coltrane and Frank Zappa, played a role in shaping artistic sensibilities. Ludwig von Köchel's *Chronologisch-thematisches Verzeichnis sämtlicher Tonwerke Wolfgang Amadé Mozarts* (1862) is still the authoritative catalogue of all of Mozart's compositions, and the source of the *K* that appears before the numbers of all his works. And the great works on food and drink, from Prosper Montagné's *Larousse gastronomique* (1938) through Jancis Robinson's *Oxford Companion to Wine* (1994), are more examples of the reference genre being deployed to make life a little sweeter. These and the works of Grove and Post are instances of a thriving genre that has too often been neglected by those who study reference books.

SOME UNLIKELY REFERENCE BOOKS

BIBLIOPHILE ILAN STAVANS reports on his own explorations in the card catalog: "Browse the catalogue web page of the Library of Congress and allow yourself to be flabbergasted."[1]
I have in fact browsed that catalog, along with the catalogs of the world's other great libraries, and can confirm Stavans's report. The following are some of the less likely published works of reference. All are real books, and all required someone's interest in the subject, an author's willingness to devote months or years to the project, and a publisher's calculation that a substantial number of people or libraries would be willing to buy the book:

American Rabbit Breeders Association. *Standard of Perfection for Rabbits, Cavies, Mice, Rats, Skin and Fur Bearing Animals.* Cleveland: American Rabbit Breeders Association, 1920.

Baltimore Bottle Book: Being an Annotated List of 170 Years of the Collector Bottles of Baltimore City and Baltimore County, 1820–1990. 2nd ed. Baltimore: Baltimore Antique Bottle Club, 2002.

Baron, Frank R. *Commercial Fish Decoys: Identification & Value Guide: Collectible Decoys and Implements Used in the Sport of Ice Spear Fishing.* Paducah, KY: Collector Books, 2002.

Behang encyclopedie. Rijen: Behangselpapier Industrie N.V., 1970. After more than forty years, still the definitive Dutch-language encyclopedia of wallpaper.

Brams, Koen. *Encyclopedie van fictieve kunstenaars: van 1605 tot heden.* Amsterdam: Nijgh & Van Ditmar, 2000. Available in translation into both German (*Erfundene Kunst: Eine Enzyklopädie fiktiver*

Künstler von 1605 bis heute) and English (*The Encyclopedia of Fictional Artists*).

Bricquet, Charles-Moïse. *Papiers et filigranes des archives de Genes 1154 à 1700*. Geneve: H. Georg, 1888. The authoritative guide to watermarks on Genevese paper.

Browne, Phillis. *The Dictionary of Dainty Breakfasts*. London: Cassell, 1899. Breakfast food from *anchovies* to *whiting* in 131 pages.

Bull, Donald. *A Price Guide to Beer Advertising Openers and Corkscrews*. Trumbull, CT: D. Bull, 1981.

Cassin, Barbara. *Dictionary of Untranslatables: A Philosophical Lexicon*. Princeton: Princeton University Press, 2014. A glossary of philosophical terms that cannot be translated. The whole book is, of course, a translation of *Vocabulaire européen des philosophies: Dictionnaire des intraduisibles*.

Charny, Israel W. *Encyclopedia of Genocide*, 2 vols. Santa Barbara: ABC-CLIO, 1999.

Dan'shina, Mariia Stepanovna. *Protozoogeneticheskii slovar'*. Kishinev: Shtiintsa, 1990. The best protozoogenetical dictionary in the Moldovan language.

Davidson, Gustav. *A Dictionary of Angels, Including the Fallen Angels*. New York: Free Press, 1967.

De Morgan, Augustus. *Encyclopedia of Eccentrics*. La Salle, IL: Open Court, 1974. Originally published in 1915 as *A Budget of Paradoxes*.

Erardi, Glenn, and Pauline C. Peck. *Mustache Cups: Timeless Victorian Treasures: With Price Guide*. Atglen, PA: Schiffer, 1999.

Frasier, David K. *Show Business Homicides: An Encyclopedia, 1908–2009*. Jefferson, NC: McFarland, 2011. The sequel to Frasier's *Suicide in the Entertainment Industry: An Encyclopedia of 840 Twentieth Century Cases* (2002).

Galoyan, Sergey A. Harut'yunyan, and T. Khach'atryan, eds. *Gogheri ashkharhe: Teghekatu*. Erevan: "Areresum" Ani, 1997. "World of Thieves," with a guide to criminals' tattoos and a Russian–Armenian dictionary of terms associated with thieves.

High, Will B. [pseud.]. *Weed-o-pe-dia: A Totally Dank A–Z Reefer Reference*. Avon, MA: Adams Media, 2010. "Offers information and illustrations stoners should know, including: why the subtle flavour of bubbleberry makes it a rich pothead's drug of choice; how to properly make a bong out of a coconut for maximum highness . . ."

Hischak, Thomas S. *Disney Voice Actors: A Biographical Dictionary.* Jefferson, NC: McFarland, 2011. A 282-page guide to the nine hundred actors who provided voices for the Disney animated films from *Steamboat Willie* to *Tangled.*

Lindenberger, Jan. *Collectible Ashtrays: Information and Price Guide.* Atglen, PA: Schiffer, 1999. With more than 460 color photos.

Manguel, Alberto, and Gianni Guadalupi. *The Dictionary of Imaginary Places.* New York: Macmillan, 1980.

Mas, Carles Constantino, and Josep L. Siquier Virgós. *Petita guia dels bolets de les Balears.* Mallorca: Govern Balear, Conselleria d'Agricultura i Pesca, 1985. A Catalan-language guide to the edible wild mushrooms of the Balearic Islands.

Muroi, Hiroshi. *Takerui goi.* 1968. A 290-page Japanese dictionary of bamboo.

Newton, Michael. *Bad Girls Do It! An Encyclopedia of Female Murderers.* Port Townsend, WA: Loompanics Unlimited, 1993. Nearly all the reviews feature the word "macabre."

Newton, Michael, and Judy Ann Newton. *The Ku Klux Klan: An Encyclopedia.* New York: Garland, 1991. *Library Journal* says "This highly specialized book will be of interest only to the most ardent students of the Ku Klux Klan."

Oliphant, Samuel Grant. *Queer Questions and Ready Replies: A Collection of Four Hundred Questions in History, Geography, Biography, Mythology, Philosophy, Natural History, Science, Philology, Etc., Etc., with Their Answers.* Boston: New England Publishing Co., 1886. "Considerable time and pains have been given to the selection of the matter herein contained, and to the verification of the same."

Oppenheimer, Harold L. *Cowboy Arithmetic: Cattle as an Investment.* Danville, IL: The Interstate, 1961.

Østrem, Gunnar. *Atlas over breer i Nord-Skandinavia.* Oslo: Norges vassdrags- og elektrisitetsvesen, 1973. A Norwegian atlas of the glaciers of northern Scandinavia.

Parker, James N., and Philip M. Parker. *Rectal Bleeding: A Medical Dictionary, Bibliography, and Annotated Research Guide to Internet References*. San Diego: ICON Health Publications, 2004.

Pessemesse, Pierre. *Lou voucabulàri de la massounarié*. Berre l'Etang: CIEL d'Oc, 2014. A comprehensive Provençal-language guide to the vocabulary of masonry.

Phillips, Sir Richard. *A Million of Facts, Connected with the Studies, Pursuits, and Interests of Mankind: Serving as a Common-place Book of Useful Reference on All Subjects of Research and Curiosity*. New York, 1839.

Rand Corporation. *A Million Random Digits with 100,000 Normal Deviates*. Glencoe, IL: Free Press, 1955. Exactly what the title promises: "10097 32533 76520 13586 34673 54876 80959 09117," and so on, for 625 pages. "One distinguishing feature of the digit table," the introduction explains, "is its size."

Redfern, Nicholas. *The Zombie Book: The Encyclopedia of the Living Dead*. Canton, MI: Visible Ink Press, 2014. "A fascinating, informative collection that anyone interested in the history of zombies will want to read. It's funny, scary, and sometimes shocking"—*Library Journal*.

Sagastizabal, Joxean. *Zorotariko euskal hiztegia*. Irun: Alberdania, 1996. A dictionary of Basque humor.

Serafini, Luigi. *Codex Seraphinianus*, 2 vols. Milan: F. M. Ricci, 1981. An Italian architect produced this large and elaborately illustrated encyclopedia in a language no one else can decode.

Sifakis, Carl. *Encyclopedia of Assassinations*. New York: Facts on File, 2001.

Smith, John C. *The Doorstop Book: The Encyclopedia of Doorstop Collecting*. Atglen, PA: Schiffer, 2006.

Stern, Jane, and Michael Stern. *The Encyclopedia of Bad Taste*. New York: HarperCollins, 1990.

Stimpson, George W. *A Book about a Thousand Things*. New York: Harper, 1946.

Stone, Geo. *Suicide and Attempted Suicide: Methods and Consequences*. New York: Carroll & Graf, 1999. "This is essentially a guide on how to commit suicide"—*Kirkus Reviews*.

Taormino, Tristan. *The Big Book of Sex Toys: From Vibrators and Dildos to Swings and Slings*. Beverly, MA: Quiver, 2009.

Tole, Vasil S. *Sprovë për një fjalës të muzikës popullore homofonike të Shqipërisë se Veriut*. Tiranë: Akademia e Shkencave e Shqiperisë, 2010. The most recent biographical dictionary of Albanian folk musicians.

Van Boxsel, Matthijs. *De Encyclopedie van de Domheid*. Shanghai: Shanghai Literature and Art Publishing House, 1999. A Dutch and Chinese *Encyclopedia of Stupidity*.

Vermeersch, Arthur, *De castitate et de vitiis contrariis: tractatus doctrinalis et moralis* (*On Chastity and Its Opposing Vices: A Moral and Doctrinal Treatise*). Rome: Università Gregoriana, 1919.

Yannes, James A. *Collectible Spoons of the 3rd Reich: With Extensive Historical Exposition*. Victoria, BC: Trafford, 2009. By the author of the more wide-ranging *Encyclopedia of Third Reich Tableware*.

Zeynal oglu Dünyamaliyev, Mämmädäli. *Fitosanitariya terminlärinin izahli lügäti*. Baki: Nurlan, 2008. An Azerbaijani glossary of the vocabulary of plant quarantine.

CHAPTER 23

PRESUMED PURITY

Science in a Scientific Age

Merck's Index	CRC Handbook of Chemistry
1889	and Physics
	1913

B Y THE MIDDLE of the nineteenth century, the modern scientific establishment was in place. Knowledge about the natural world came not from tradition, not from authority, but from empirical research no longer carried out by gentleman amateurs in potting sheds, but by white-coated specialists in academies or universities, with laboratories fitted with expensive equipment paid for by grants. The amateurs were crowded out by the professional scientists (the English word *scientist* was coined in 1834), and the volume of research exploded. The rapidly generated knowledge required reference works to be updated constantly.

☙

Pity the nineteenth-century physician or pharmacist, who had to keep pace with an overwhelming amount of new scientific and medical knowledge. Medical people had always been learned, but before modernity they could hope to keep up with all the relevant publications. By the nineteenth century, though, new scientific research was coming in a torrent. This is the world in which one of the most successful of all scientific reference books, the *Merck Index*, came into being.

Merck & Co. has deep roots. In 1668, Friedrich Jacob Merck bought a small shop in Darmstadt, Germany, known as the Engel-Apotheke, or Angel's Pharmacy, and made it his own. Merck's nephew took it over on his death, and the business passed from generation to generation. In the

TITLE: *Merck's Index of Fine Chemicals and Drugs for the Materia Medica and the Arts: Comprising a Summary of Whatever Chemical Products Are To-day Adjudged as Being Useful in Either Medicine or Technology, with Average Values and Synonyms Affixed; a Guide for the Physician, Apothecary, Chemist, and Dealer*

ORGANIZATION: Alphabetical by chemical, *Absinthin* to *Zymase*

PUBLISHED: 1889

PAGES: 170

ENTRIES: 6,500

TOTAL WORDS: 50,000

SIZE: 10" × 7" (25 × 18 cm)

AREA: 82 ft² (7.65 m²)

PRICE: $1

LATEST EDITION: *The Merck Index: An Encyclopedia of Chemicals, Drugs, and Biologicals*, 15th ed., 2013.

---

late eighteenth century, it was run by Johann Heinrich Merck, a close friend and collaborator of Johann Wolfgang von Goethe. (Goethe later claimed he drew the character of Mephistopheles from Merck, who committed suicide in 1791.) In 1816, Heinrich Emanuel Merck—a descendant of the original Friedrich Jacob, and the sixth of that surname to run the company—took over the store. Heinrich had studied pharmacy in Berlin and Vienna, and he had ambitious ideas about the family business.

The company was turning its attention from compounding drugs for its own purposes to manufacturing them for the rest of the profession. In 1827 they opened a manufacturing plant in Darmstadt, and by 1850, several dozen employees worked there. By this time the long-established business had ties with some of the most important scientific interests in Germany and throughout Europe—Emanuel Merck, for instance, supplied Sigmund Freud with his cocaine.[1]

Merck had its eye on the American market, and they began selling in the United States under the E. Merck trademark in the nineteenth century—eventually they would incorporate there as Merck & Co. To advertise their offerings, in 1889 they released *Merck's Index of Fine Chemicals and Drugs for the Materia Medica and the Arts*. Unlike so many of the reference works considered here, this one was not compiled with the improvement of humanity in mind: it began its life simply as a company's catalog of "the full line of my products, numbering to-day upwards of 5,000 medicinal, analytical, and technical Chemicals."[2]

Whoever wrote the copy for the *Index* (it is signed "E. Merck," but there is no reason to assume Emanuel wrote it himself) was a serious marketer. The tone is signaled with breathless exclamation points: "The most vital interests of your patients, gentlemen physicians!—and of your customers, gentlemen of the pharmaceutical profession!—depend, as you are well aware, on the reality of the Presumed Purity, of the Prescribed Strength, and of the Correct Condition of the materials employed in filling prescriptions." The *Index* looked backward to its long history—a grand-looking patent, in Gothic letters, from the Landgrave of Hesse to George Frederick Merck in 1668 was followed by a list of "a few of the HONORABLE AWARDS extended to the firm of E. MERCK" over the years, including a gold medal from the Pharmaceutical Society of Paris in 1830 "For the Relief of Mankind"[3]—but it also looked forward to the future. The company promised rapid delivery, taking advantage of a new American office and American factories rather than depending on steamships.

Buy only the real thing, Merck exhorted: "I would earnestly entreat my friends, throughout both professions, to insist rigidly that Merck's Chemicals be furnished to them, by dealers, in the *original* packages."[4] At the bottom of every page appeared

☞ When ordering, specify: "MERCK'S"!

The *American Monthly Microscopical Journal* found this approach distasteful: "This indicates an advertising purpose in the volume, and seems to us an unnecessary blemish."[5] But the author reminds readers not to let the apparent hucksterism turn them off: "One remark may be needed by my professional friends, as to the Price-notes placed opposite the names of most substances in the following List. *Those Price-notes are* **not** *intended to give this work the character of a commercial or business Price-list.*"[6]

The chemicals appear in alphabetical order, though *Merck's Index* wrestled with the problem of inconsistent nomenclature. It used the system adopted by the Chemical Society in England but also included many older, common names, with cross-references: "But, **whichever** the 'odd names' thus received may be,—the substance in question is *invariably listed under a proper chemical name* **also**, and is, as a rule, *detailed* and *priced* **there!**"[7] There was also a strange mix of metric and imperial units, and a list of abbreviations in the back explained that "gm" refers to "gramme[s] (=15.42328—or, about 15½—grains)," and "cm" means "centimetre[s] (=0.3937—or, about 4/10—of an inch)."

Turning the pages of the *Index* provides an education in the cutting edge of the chemical sciences a century and a quarter ago. Various acids occupy the first eight pages; pure caffeine could be had for $8 per ounce; $1.75 would buy fifteen grams of pure gold. Aspirin was not offered; the name was still a trademark owned by Bayer. But "acid, salicylic" was available for anywhere from 75¢ to $3.00 a pound, depending on process.

While all of these things appear in chemical catalogs today, other offerings remind us that this was a different era, including essential spirits of prunes and "Blood, bullock's, (Sanguis Tauri [Bovis]), dry, powdered." Most surprising to modern eyes is the list of narcotics available to anyone who wanted them. What are now known as controlled substances were not controlled then. In the United States, the Pure Food and Drug Act of 1906 started to require labeling information about ten "addictive" or "dangerous" substances, including alcohol and opium. The first edition of *Merck's Index* includes cannabinon (a resin made from cannabis flowers); later editions include other forms of cannabis. Fully eighteen varieties of cocaine could be had for the asking, along with eleven forms of codeine, thirty-two forms of morphine, and one that mixed codeine and morphine together. Laudanum—opium dissolved in alcohol, a favorite treatment for pretty much any malady— cost $1.50 a pound. The International Opium Convention did not convene until 1912; before that, opium could be had legally without so much as a doctor's prescription, and an advertisement in the back offered METCALF'S COCA WINE FROM FRESH COCA LEAVES. Even more nervous-making are all the poisons offered for sale. A pound of hemlock would set one back four bits. Curare could be had for 25¢ per 15 grams, arsenic trioxide ("arsenious acid") for a dollar a pound, strychnine for two dollars per eighth-ounce vial, and pure potassium cyanide for four dollars a pound. For two dollars an ounce, one could get "Ouabain . . . an aqueous extract from whose root and bark forms the arrow-poison of the East-African Comalis," which could be used as a "heart-poison." (Pharmaceutical companies still sell many of these "addictive" and "dangerous" compounds, but the regulatory paperwork required is daunting.)

The first *Merck's Index* is in reality a 170-page advertisement, but it was useful in its way; it collected all the chemicals and medicines any physician or pharmacist might need. It impressed early reviewers with the range of medicines on offer, as well as the background information it compiled. "This work is essentially a price list," wrote one review, "covering the whole range of drugs and compounds used in medicine, and it will be of value to the large body of physicians who have to dispense their own medicines, and to many others who like to know the cost of the drugs which they use or order. Incidentally it contains a great deal of useful knowledge about the drugs employed."[8] Over time its commercial purpose shifted: as the *Index* grew in subsequent editions, the organizing principle was not "chemicals offered for sale by Merck" but chemicals, period.

The Merck Index spawned a related *Merck's Manual* in 1899, properly *Merck's Manual of the Materia Medica: Together with a Summary of Therapeutic Indications and a Classification of Medicaments: A Ready-Reference Pocket Book for the Practicing Physician*. It opened by justifying the need for another manual: "Memory is treacherous. . . . When the best remedy is wanted, . . . it is difficult, and sometimes impossible, to recall the whole array of available remedies so as to pick out the best." And so the *Manual*—part 1 covering "a descriptive survey, in one alphabetic series, of the entire Materia Medica," part 2 "a summary of Therapeutic Indications for the employment of remedies, arranged according to the Pathologic Conditions to be combated," and part 3 "a

Classification of Medicaments in accordance with their Physiologic Actions"—was there to offer a comprehensive list of the medicines on offer.[9] It remains in use today as the *Merck Manual of Diagnosis and Therapy*, among the bestselling medical books in history.

Merck & Co. has had its ups and downs. In 1917, the U.S. government seized all the American assets of the German-based Merck—a chemical company operated by the enemy during a time of war—and turned it into an independent American company. A century later, the wounds have still not healed: in March 2010, the German company Merck KGaA sued Facebook for allowing the American Merck & Co. to claim the name "Merck" on the social networking site. But today the American Merck is one of the largest pharmaceutical companies in the world—with its merger with Shering-Plough in 2009, it became the second largest.

The *Index* and the *Manual* are still thriving, though they are mostly used online today. A review of the fourteenth edition in 2007 began, "Over time, certain reference books achieve such an outstanding reputation that any review of a new edition is almost unnecessary. Such is true of *The Merck Index*."[10] The entries, called "monographs," in the current *Merck Index* are more systematic than in the early editions, and include a CAS registry number, by which the Chemical Abstracts Service assigns a unique number to every known chemical substance; all the names, synonyms, and trade names that might appear in the chemical literature; a chemical formula and structural formula; the molecular weight of the substance; physical properties such as density and melting and boiling points; the therapeutic category; citations to the scientific literature; and so on. Especially important is advice on the potential hazards of each chemical listed. The companion, the *Merck Manual of Diagnosis and Therapy*, is in its nineteenth edition, at an overwhelming thirty-five hundred pages, and now represents the collected knowledge of three hundred contributors. A *Merck Manual of Medical Information, Home Edition*, is aimed at lay folk, available both in print and online.

⚜

A slim 116-page pamphlet issued by the Chemical Rubber Company, known in the trade as *The Rubber Handbook*, hardly sounds like a promising work of scholarship, especially since its intention did not go beyond selling rubber and related chemicals. But it mutated into *The CRC Handbook of Chemistry and Physics*, a work essential to everyone working in the laboratory sciences for the better part of the last century.

A Handbook of Chemistry and Physics: A Ready-Reference Pocket Book of Chemical and Physical Data appeared in 1913. This was not even a list of products offered for sale, like *Merck's Index*; it was instead primarily a means of keeping the name of the Chemical Rubber Company in front of practicing scientists, much in the same way that companies give out pens and calendars bearing their names and logos. It is a list of miscellaneous information that a lab scientist might need to keep at hand. The work was "carefully selected by W[illiam] R[eed] Veazey, Ph.D., Chemistry Department, Case School of Applied Science," supported by "more than a thousand members of high standing in the Chemical and Physical profession."[11]

The contents are impressively heterogeneous. The *Handbook* opened with a table of "International Atomic Weights," according to the latest cutting-edge standards of 1911: all eighty-one elements then known were listed with their chemical symbols and atomic weights to two decimal places. (Astatine, francium, hafnium, promethium, protactinium, rhenium, technetium, and all the transruanic elements were not discovered until after the first *Handbook* was published, and what is now known as nobium was then columbium.) Then, without transition, came a page of a dozen "Antidotes of Poisons": "*Hydrocyanic Acid.—* Hydrogen peroxide internal, and artificial respiration, breathing ammonia or chlorine from chlorinated lime, ferrous sulphate followed by potassium carbonate, emetics, warmth."[12] Then appeared, with just as little warning, "Vapor Tension of Water in Millimeters of Mercury $-2°$ to $+36°C$." Scattered throughout the guide were lists of fusible alloys, comparisons of wire gauges, density of water at temperatures from $0°$ to $36°$ in tenth-degree intervals, with figures given to six decimal places, and other miscellanea. More than two and a half pages were devoted to "One Hundred Completed Chemical Equations," such as "$3Hg(NO_3)_2 + 6FeSO_4 = 2Fe(NO_3)_3 + 2Fe_2(SO_4)_3 + 3Hg$."

The sheer range of material is striking, and the *Handbook* was frank about its randomness: one section was headed simply MISCELLANEOUS

TITLE: *Handbook of Chemistry and Physics: A Ready-Reference Pocket-Book of Chemical and Physical Data: Compiled from the Most Recent Authoritative Sources and Published by the Chemical Rubber Company, Cleveland, Ohio*

COMPILER: William R. Veazey (1883–1958)

ORGANIZATION: Miscellaneous

PUBLISHED: 1913

PAGES: 116

TOTAL WORDS: 40,000

SIZE: 6¾" × 4¼" (17 × 11 cm)

AREA: 23 ft² (2.16 m²)

PRICE: $2

LATEST EDITION: 95th ed., 2014

DATA AND FORMULAE. Some of it was clearly written for novices, some for experts. The section on FUNDAMENTAL CHEMICAL THEORIES, for instance, with entries such as *"The Atomic Theory.*—All elementary forms of matter are composed of very small unit quantities called atoms," contained information obvious to anyone working in the field, but students still needed the reminder. Likewise the guide to the metric system—by 1913 the standard throughout Europe, but still novel to American scientists, so the *Handbook* included tables converting feet, gallons, and troy ounces to meters, liters, and grams. Professional chemists, on the other hand, benefited more from a section, one of the longest in the book, headed GRAVIMETRIC FACTORS AND THEIR LOGARITHMS.

A list of PHYSICAL CONSTANTS OF INORGANIC COMPOUNDS— solubility, molecular weight, specific gravity, melting and boiling points for 651 compounds from acetic acid to zinc sulphide blende—was just the sort of information a chemist would want to have nearby. The *Handbook* also offered some unexpected information: it ventured into nutritional science, as with "Functions and Uses of Food in the Body" ("*Protein.*—Builds and repairs tissue") and a table of the amount of protein, fat, carbohydrates, ash, water, and calories in a few dozen foods: "Candy stick . . . Herring, smoked . . . Lard . . . Parsnip." Formulas for converting temperatures among the Fahrenheit, Celsius, and Réaumur scales were useful then. Likewise the table of BASICITY OF ACIDS WITH VARIOUS INDICATORS—the modern notion of pH had been developed as recently as 1909 and would not be common among scientists for another decade. Toward the end is a section on TEXT BOOKS, MANUALS AND REFERENCE BOOKS, providing standard citations such as Lodge's *Elementary Mechanics* and Bottone's *Electrical Instrument Making*.

"We shall feel amply rewarded for our effort and expense," wrote W. R. Veazey in 1913, "if this volume proves to be of use and convenience to the profession."[13] They have indeed been amply rewarded. The Nobel laureate Linus Pauling summed up the importance of the *Handbook*: "People who have interviewed me have commented on the extensive knowledge that I have about the properties of substances. I attribute this knowledge in part to the fact that I possessed the Rubber Handbook." Sixty years after the first edition appeared, the Chemical Rubber Company stopped making chemicals and rubber, but they continued issuing the manual, which had become more important than their entire manufacturing business. A review of the seventy-fifth edition (1994) calls the *CRC Handbook* "a classic must for scientists in all areas,"[14] and CRC Press, now part of Taylor & Francis, continues to issue new editions of the *CRC Handbook*, which is now in its ninetieth edition. The *CRC Standard Mathematical Tables and Formulae* went through a major change in 1991, when most of the functions available on pocket calculators were nixed to make room for more useful material.

The *Handbook* is no longer a book but a franchise, with a tremendous suite of related books: the *CRC Handbook of Laboratory Safety*, the *CRC Handbook of Tables for Probability and Statistics*, the *CRC Handbook of Environmental Control*, the *CRC Handbook of Radiation Measurement and Protection*, the *CRC Handbook of Antibiotic Compounds*, the *CRC Handbook of Animal Models for the Rheumatic Diseases*, the *CRC Handbook of Imunoblotting of Proteins*, the *CRC Handbook of Lubrication*, the *CRC Handbook of Avian Body Masses* . . . the list goes on and on. But even these dozens of tables available from CRC are just a small selection of the information modern scientists need to keep at hand.

The range of tables available to the scientist at the end of the twentieth century was gigantic: a 214-page reference book called *Handbooks and Tables in Science and Technology* is needed just to list the other reference books.[15]

※

The science historian Lynn Thorndike's claim—"Encyclopedias are perhaps the most important monuments of the history of science and of civilization"[16]—may sound like hyperbole. Surely legendary works of scholarship like Newton's *Principia Mathematica*, Darwin's *Origin of Species*, and Einstein's famous papers of 1905 are the real monuments of science. But it takes nothing away from the towering geniuses of science to remember that the day-to-day operations in the laboratory and in the classroom owe much to the practical works that have sat on every lab bench for generations. Otto Lueger's *Lexikon der gesamten Technik* (1894) was updated through the twentieth century, and we continue generating gigantic reference works such as the *Human Genome Project* (2003), the effort to identify and catalog the billions of base pairs that make up human DNA. Works like the *Merck Index* and the *CRC Handbook* rarely get their due in the history of scientific endeavor; they are taken for granted, treated as part of the background of scientific discovery rather than part of the story itself. That assumption should change.

CHAPTER 23 ½

AT NO EXTRA COST!

The Business of Reference Books

"INFORMATION," ACCORDING TO the slogan, "wants to be free." But compiling that information is work, and the people who do it expect to be paid, though very few have gotten rich in the process. It has always been difficult to break even. Johnson's *Dictionary* was published by booksellers working together in an ad-hoc consortium, a "conger," that allowed all of them to minimize risk. They paid Johnson £1,575— maybe around £200,000 or $300,000 today—and they covered the costs of printing and distribution. They planned to break even if they sold a thousand sets for £4 10s., but that was several months' wages for a day laborer. Sales were disappointing. After a few months the booksellers tried to sell the *Dictionary* in pieces: 165 parts, one a week, at sixpence each (which came out to the same £4 10s. as the original). The results were no better. The *Dictionary* had received strong notices, and those in the know recognized it as a major work—but it seemed to be a commercial flop.

At that point the idea for an abridged edition came up. Johnson took his hefty *Dictionary* and tightened up the definitions, trimmed the etymologies, and stripped out the 115,000 quotations—the very feature that made it such a lexicographical milestone. The result was two much smaller volumes, octavos instead of folios, called *A Dictionary of the English Language ... Abstracted from the Folio Edition*. Finally the publishers had something that made money. Over Johnson's lifetime, the folio *Dictionary* sold about five thousand copies, compared to thirty-five thousand of the abridged editions.[1] To history, "Johnson's *Dictionary*" is the monumental work of 1755, but to the large majority of its actual users, "Johnson's *Dictionary*" did not have a single quotation. When Becky Sharp threw a copy of Johnson's "dixonary" out the carriage window in William Makepeace Thackeray's *Vanity Fair*, it was no doubt the little one.

The pattern has been much followed over the centuries. The big unabridged dictionaries take years of work and almost never earn back their expenses. This is true even of monuments like the *Oxford English Dictionary*—its editor's biographer wrote, "Looked at from a business angle the Dictionary was clearly a failure."[2] Publishers would go broke if they had to depend on sales of flagship products. Oxford University Press and Merriam-Webster make their money where Johnson's publishers did: selling abridged versions of their flagship dictionaries to a large audience.[3]

Encyclopedias are, if anything, an even harder sell. In the 1770s Charles-Joseph Panckoucke confidently began compiling his own *Encyclopédie méthodique* as an answer to the *Encyclopédie*, and a back-of-the-envelope calculation suggested he would break even with between fifteen thousand and twenty thousand advance subscriptions. When he was ready to start writing, he tallied up his subscribers and found a grand total of just one hundred sixty-two.[4] Clearly, more aggressive salesmanship was required. "The industry believes encyclopedias are sold and not bought," said the editor of the American Library Association's *Reference Books Bulletin*. "You must have representation from a salesman."[5]

And so salesmen were called in. Through most of the twentieth century, as many as 90 percent of American encyclopedias were sold door to door.[6] Salesmen (and, on occasion, saleswomen) knocked on the doors in suburban neighborhoods and extolled the virtues of their wares—a compendium of knowledge that would enlighten, entertain, and even impress the neighbors by making the room look classy. The ritual was scripted, starting with the "opener," or initial sales pitch, with reference to local satisfied customers; moving to the "spread," which involved opening sample volumes and pamphlets around the room; and ending with the "close," which was supposed to end with a check in the salesman's pocket.[7] Children were the real target. What about Tommy's book report in Mrs. Davis's class? Where else will he be able to find the population of Guatemala or the chemical formula of formaldehyde? The pitch might continue that the fifteen-volume *Britannica Junior* might be sufficient, but to excel in school, the deluxe reference package was better choice: the twenty-four-volume encyclopedia, the *Britannica World Atlas*, the *World Language Dictionary*, and the *Book of the Year*, updated—at no extra cost!—every year for a decade![8]

The best salesmen got very good at it. They were selling not books but a lifestyle, a future, a promise of social mobility. Having *Britannica* on the shelves proved the family was cultivated, literate, and curious, even if, a month or two after the set was delivered, odd volumes were serving as a baby's booster seat or propping up uneven table legs. One *Britannica* salesman, J. S. Dalton, became legendary in company lore. He once ran his car off the road and barely escaped while it was hanging over a cliff. Two other motorists stopped, pulled him to safety, and saved his life. In the time it took for help to arrive, Dalton managed to sell one of them a complete set of encyclopedias.[9]

The sales pitch could be assertive—encyclopedias were sold by high-pressure hucksters, not always remarkable for their honesty and integrity. *Britannica* paid no salaries, leaving the sales force to live entirely on commissions.[10] All sorts of improper means were used to get the foot in the door, and all sorts of promises made that the salesman had no expectation of keeping. The best—or worst?—of the sales force could teach a thing or two to *The Music Man*'s Harold Hill: Yessir, order now and get the dee-luxe one-hundred-percent gen-yoo-wine faux leatherette binding.

Sellers found all sorts of ways to mislead potential buyers, like pretending to be taking surveys or distributing raffle tickets.[11] Even when the pitches weren't outright lies, the pressure could be unseemly. Not buying an encyclopedia? Well, ma'am, if you're the type of mother who isn't concerned for her child's future, I suppose there's nothing I can do to change that . . . The spirit of the era is caught in an all-too-accurate Monty Python sketch, in which a man seeks to enter a woman's apartment by pretending to be a thief:

SALESMAN: Burglar, madam.
WOMAN: What do you want?
SALESMAN: I want to come in and steal a few things, madam.
WOMAN: Are you an encyclopaedia salesman?

SALESMAN: No madam, I'm a burglar, I burgle people.

WOMAN: I think you're an encyclopaedia salesman.

SALESMAN: Oh, I'm not. Open the door, let me in, please.

WOMAN: If I let you in you'll sell me encyclopaedias.

SALESMAN: I won't, madam! I just want to come in and ransack the flat. Honestly.

The moment she opens the door, he begins: "Mind you, I don't know whether you've really considered the advantages of owning a really fine set of modern encyclopaedias ..." In the United States it got bad enough that in 1972, the Federal Trade Commission lodged a complaint against several encyclopedia publishers for deceptive practices. A 1978 ruling determined that they were indeed breaking the law. A series of rulings led to a new regime: sales representatives had to declare immediately that they were selling encyclopedias.[12] But the age of door-to-door sales was nearly at an end. *Britannica* watched its market fall apart with the arrival of online resources. In the 1970s they had more than two thousand door-to-door sales people selling $2,000 sets of encyclopedias across the country. *World Book*, even more assertive, had forty-five thousand door-to-door representatives by the late 1980s.[13] But by 1996—the year when the last one thousand door-to-door salespeople were laid off—*Britannica*'s sales had fallen by 60 percent.[14]

Britannica was not ready for the electronic age, and they stumbled badly—but then so have many publishers. Print sales of multivolume reference books are all but dead, and the industry is still struggling to figure out how to make money online. Some dictionaries and encyclopedias are prepared by national academies or other organizations that can write off the loss as a public service. Many reference publishers have given up on marketing to individuals and count on university libraries for all their sales. Others charge monthly or annual fees, though competing with free services like Wikipedia and Dictionary.com is not easy. Others still provide free access and depend on advertising revenue. Even the free services sometimes have to beg for spare change, as when Wikipedia goes on public-television-inspired fundraising drives. Which plan will win? It is the biggest unanswered question in the reference world today.

CHAPTER 24

FULL AND AUTHORITATIVE INFORMATION

Doctrine for the Modern World

The Catholic Encyclopedia	Bol'shaia sovetskaia
1907–14	entsiklopediia
	1926–47

ANY REFERENCE BOOKS end up with an authority they never sought for themselves. We consider "the dictionary" the authoritative word on language, and we feel something must be true if it's in an encyclopedia. Few lexicographers or encyclopedists want that authority, but it is often thrust on them nonetheless. A few reference books, though, demand to be treated with deference and claim to lay down the law.

∞

The early twentieth century was a rough time for doctrine, and traditional belief systems were increasingly challenged. The process began in the European Enlightenment and picked up steam over the revolutionary era of the early nineteenth century. Nietzsche, Darwin, Marx, and Freud demolished old certainties. By the end of the nineteenth century, one conventional piety after another had been challenged, discredited, or simply ignored.

The Catholic Encyclopedia was compiled to meet a need: orthodoxy was under attack. At the beginning of the twentieth century, prominent Roman Catholics were concerned that other encyclopedias were not merely indifferent to this attack, but actually aiding the forces of evil with their own anti-Catholic bias. Diderot and d'Alembert's *Encyclopédie* had enraged many, and the Catholic Church was high on the list of aggrieved parties. It responded by putting the *Encyclopédie* on the *Index*

TITLE: *The Catholic Encyclopedia: An International Work of Reference on the Constitution, Doctrine, Discipline, and History of the Catholic Church*

COMPILER: Charles George Herbermann (1840–1916), Edward A. Pace (1861–1938), Condé Benoist Pallen (1858–1929), Thomas Joseph Shahan (1857–1932), and John J. Wynne (1859–1948)

ORGANIZATION: Alphabetical, *Aachen* to *Zwirner*

PUBLISHED: New York: Robert Appleton Company, March 1907–April 1914

VOLUMES: 17

PAGES: 13,600

ENTRIES: 9,700

TOTAL WORDS: 19 million

SIZE: 10½" × 7½" (26.5 × 19 cm)

AREA: 7,300 ft² (685 m²)

WEIGHT: 112 lb. (51 kg)

PRICE: $90 for buckram binding, $120 for ¾ morocco, $225 for full morocco

LATEST EDITION: *The New Catholic Encyclopedia*, 2nd ed. (New York: Thomson, Gale, 2003), 15 vols., with 4 vols. of supplements

---

expurgatorius in 1759 and nearly excommunicating Diderot. And while the great encyclopedia from the other side of the Channel was less radical in its freethinking tendencies, Catholics pointed out that the *Encyclopædia Britannica* treated only Protestantism with respect, while "Roman Catholicism receives more censure than Judaism."[1]

"The need of a Catholic Encyclopedia in English," the editors of *The Catholic Encyclopedia* wrote, "was manifest for many years before it was decided to publish one. Editors of various general Encyclopedias had attempted to make them satisfactory from a Catholic point of view, but without success."[2] A London-based Catholic magazine, *The Month*, published a brutal review of the new *Britannica* in 1911, lashing out at its "anti-Catholic animus." The reviewer worried that articles "on purely Catholic topics" were too often assigned to writers who were not Catholic; as a result, the entries on "Church History" were nothing but "a series of articles thoroughly Protestant and necessarily incorrect." *The Catholic Encyclopedia* was conceived, written, and marketed as a response to this sort of "unscholarly bigotry."[3] The introduction promised "full and authoritative information on the entire cycle of Catholic interests, action and doctrine,"[4] and that is what the team of editors and contributors delivered.

For the encyclopedia to be Catholic meant that it must exclude "facts and information which have no relation to the Church." Catholics may need to know the length of the Nile and the atomic weight of sodium as much as anyone else, but these subjects did not make the cut because "there is no specifically Catholic science," and "mathematics, physiology and other branches of human knowledge are neither Catholic, Jewish, nor Protestant." Nor does the *Encyclopedia* include entries on prominent people who happen to be Catholic. Instead it is about Catholic saints, martyrs, doctrine, and liturgy. There is another respect, though, in which *The Catholic Encyclopedia* lived up to its name: it presumed to give authoritative answers to questions of faith. As the preface explained, "Designed to present its readers with the full body of Catholic teaching, the ENCYCLOPEDIA contains ... precise statements of what the Church has defined."[5] Coverage of questions on which the Church itself had no definitive answers was balanced, but once a verdict was handed down from the Vatican, the matter was considered settled.

The planners resolved to embark on their encyclopedia at a meeting on December 8, 1904. They found models in a few comparable works, including the recent *Jewish Encyclopedia* (12 vols., 1901–6). On January 11, 1905, five editors—all Catholic educators with editorial experience— came together: Latin professor and CUNY librarian Charles G. Hebermann, Catholic University philosophy professor Edward A. Pace, *Catholic World* editor Condé B. Pallen, Catholic University professor of church history the Rt. Rev. Thomas J. Shahan, and *Messenger* editor John J. Wynne. The German-born Hebermann took the helm. The team gathered on Sixteenth Street in New York City, the offices of *The Messenger*, and over the next few years met a total of a hundred thirty-four times to plan the encyclopedia and monitor its progress.

They signed a contract on February 25, 1905, and issued a specimen of their planned encyclopedia containing the text of the preface and a few sample entries and illustrations.[6] Printing was to be overseen by the Robert Appleton Company—even though there was no such company at the time. The publisher was incorporated in February 1905 specifically to print *The Catholic Encyclopedia*, and that was the only job it handled.

This project, unlike so many, moved at a brisk clip. The first volume, *Aachen–Assize*, appeared in March 1907, just two years after work began, and the final volumes of the main text, covering *Simony–Tournely* and *Tournon–Zwirner*, followed five years after that, right on time. A master index was added in 1914. It took less than a decade to get from the initial meeting to the last volume, a pace that puts many other reference editors to shame. As is only fitting for a work on Roman Catholic doctrine, *The Catholic Encyclopedia* received a thumbs-up from the Church: Remy Lafort issued the *nihil obstat*, permitting it to be printed, and Archbishop John Murphy Farley issued the imprimatur.

The *Encyclopedia* makes no pretense to treating most subjects even-handedly: this was an avowedly Catholic book. Look up a term like *sola scriptura*, the Protestant notion that reading the Bible unaided is enough for salvation, and the *Catholic Encyclopedia* will explain that "The belief in the Bible as the sole source of faith is unhistorical, illogical, fatal to the virtue of faith, and destructive of unity." Look up *Reformation* in *Britannica* (1911) and you will read that it was "the religious and political revolution of the 16th century, of which the immediate result was the partial disruption of the Western Catholic Church and the establishment of various national and territorial churches." For the *Catholic Encyclopedia*, though, it was "the religious movement which ... while ostensibly aiming at an internal renewal of the Church, really led to a great revolt against it, and an abandonment of the principal Christian beliefs." To be fair, *Britannica* was not always a model of impartiality. In *Britannica*, the entry for *confession* starts with an overview of the place of confession in Judaism, then says that "In the Gospels confession is scarcely mentioned." A history of bitter controversy among early Christians follows, riddled with contradictions and scandals and petty rivalries. *Britannica* gives a condescending account of the origins of the Catholic sacrament, noting that "the constant repetition of confession and reconciliation, together with the fact that the most tender consciences would be the most anxious for the assurance of forgiveness, led to the practice being considered a normal part of the Christian life." Contemporary Catholic practice is brushed off, suggesting that even the priests do not take the idea too seriously: "As confession is now administered in the Roman Church, the disciplinary penance is often little more than nominal, the recitation of a psalm or the like." Thus it is not hard to see where the charge of "anti-Catholic bias" came from.

In *The Catholic Encyclopedia*, the reader is told that "Penance is a sacrament of the New Law instituted by Christ in which forgiveness of sins committed after baptism is granted through the priest's absolution to those who with true sorrow confess their sins and promise to satisfy for the same." In discussing the Inquisition, *Britannica* invokes the terms "reign of terror," "burning at the stake," "terrible measures of repression," "massacre," and "persecution"; the *Catholic Encyclopedia* explains that "Christian Europe was so endangered by heresy . . . that the Inquisition seemed to be a political necessity" and says that the many deaths were merely "the occasional executions of heretics [that] must be ascribed partly to the arbitrary action of individual rulers, . . . and in no wise to ecclesiastical law or the ecclesiastical authorities."

Not all the entries are so parti pris, and most of the encyclopedia is learned and balanced. On subjects that did not prompt Protestant-Catholic quarrels—entries such as *Kabbala* and *oratorio* and *dome* and *Septuagint*—*The Catholic Encyclopedia* is a superb source for everyone. Many biographical entries—on popes, bishops, priests, even minor abbots and scholars—and historical entries are models of clarity and sometimes without rival even today, more than a century after they were written. Of course, on questions of Catholic doctrine and tradition— *faith, rule of*; *Purgatory*; *natural law*; *extreme unction*—there is no better place to turn for official policy. Even entries on subjects with which we might expect the Church to be uncomfortable—*evolution, Galileo, Copernicus*—are often balanced and frank.

Most Catholics were happy with the encyclopedia, but some critics emerged. The United States was not friendly to Roman Catholics in the 1910s. Only about 16 percent of Americans were Catholic in an overwhelmingly Protestant United States, and many of them were immigrants from what many considered "undesirable" countries—Ireland and Italy above all. In the 1920s, the recently refounded Ku Klux Klan had Roman Catholics high on their list of enemies. A legal struggle therefore ensued over whether the U.S. Constitution's separation of church and state permitted public libraries to spend money on *The Catholic Encyclopedia*. Virtually no one had complained about public money buying works that reflected a Protestant worldview, but nativist bigotry viewed Roman Catholicism as a particular threat. The *Encyclopedia* triumphed in the lawsuits, and it remains a triumph as a monumental work of scholarship.

⁂

Not all doctrine is grounded in religious belief. Noah Webster's dictionaries and spellers, for instance, were all about a different kind of doctrine, one grounded in American nationalism. Legal compilations such as the *Code Napoléon* (1804) were both reference sources and definitive statements, in this case of the emperor's conception of the law. In 1839–40, Pierre Leroux and Jean Reynaud served up their own variety of doctrinal document in their three-volume *Encyclopédie nouvelle*, a party-line socialist account of the contemporary world.

One of the most engaging of the doctrinal reference books, though, came out of a nation-state that did not even exist when Webster, Napoleon, Leroux, and Reynaud were writing. On July 17, 1918, Czar Nicholas II, Emperor and Autocrat of All the Russias, was executed. Not long afterward, in December 1922, the Russian Empire collapsed and the Union of Soviet Socialist Republics took its place. A new nation had come into being.

Reference books abounded in czarist Russia. The *Dictionary of the Russian Academy* appeared in six parts in St. Petersburg from 1789 to 1794, with editions through the nineteenth century. Although German and French encyclopedias were popular in Russia, local versions could also be had. Late czarist Russia divided the encyclopedic field with two works bearing the same title: *Entsiklopedicheskii Slovar*, or "encyclopedic dictionary." One, based on the German *Konversations-Lexikon* published by Brockhaus, came to be known as the *Brockhaus-Efron*; the other took the name of the two brothers who published it, *Granat*.

After the Russian Revolution, the works of the previous regime became deeply suspect. They reflected an old-fashioned conception of the world and had to be replaced. Since reference books often help to create a coherent national and cultural identity, the new USSR demanded a new set of reference works to cement its identity. More than that: the Russian Revolution was not only a political revolution but an intellectual one as well, operating on the premise that society ran on different principles than the world had assumed. New models of economics, history, linguistics, religion, even evolutionary biology were introduced. Dialectical materialism was the order of the day, and Marxism-Leninism was the lens through which the entire world was to be seen: the editors of the Soviet encyclopedias said as much in their prefaces.

Through the Soviet period, the *Bol'shaia sovetskaia entsiklopediia* (*Great Soviet Encyclopedia*) was the most important work of general

TITLE: Большая советская знциклопедия *(Bol'shaia sovetskaia entsiklopediia)*

ORGANIZATION: Alphabetical

PUBLISHED: Moskva: Sovetskaia entsiklopediia, 1926–47

VOLUMES: 65

PAGES: 28,000

ENTRIES: 65,000

TOTAL WORDS: 17 million

SIZE: 10" × 6¾" (25.5 × 17 cm)

AREA: 13,000 ft² (1,210 m²)

WEIGHT: 55lb. 7 oz. (25.2 kg)

LATEST EDITION: 3rd ed. of the *Great Soviet Encyclopedia*, 30 vols., 1969–78; the *Great Russian Encyclopedia*, 30 vols. (2004–9)

reference. The publication history is notoriously complicated. The first edition was begun in 1926, with four volumes appearing that year. The volumes came out serially, but not in alphabetical order. By the time it was finished, its sixty-five volumes, 65,000 articles, 12,000 illustrations, and 1,000 maps covered a tremendous range of subjects, virtually all of them seen through a Marxist-Leninist lens. The fifteen-page entry for *encyclopedia*, for example, features a prominent tribute to Diderot and d'Alembert, who are credited with sparking the French Revolution— explicitly identified as a precursor to the Russian Revolution.[7]

The *Entsiklopediia* was forward looking. It was a new era, and the sooner the past was forgotten, the better. All of Russian history from the beginning to 1917 got three pages of text; the entry on the Russian Soviet Federated Republic got a hundred twenty. Recent accomplishments, such as the Moscow Canal, were celebrated in rapturous terms; czarist accomplishments were often passed over in silence. Coverage of scientific accomplishments is one of the weaknesses, but the biographies and historical entries are strong. Considerable attention is devoted to the major figures in Soviet history. The entry on *Leninism* took up more than eighty pages, and *Stalin* got forty to himself. Lenin and Stalin were themselves credited with contributing to the forty-page entry on *Marxism*.

But the nature of the coverage shifted over the time it took to produce the book. As one reviewer wrote, the encyclopedia "took more than twenty years to complete, a long time by any encyclopedic standard, but an even longer and more eventful period when viewed through the prism of Soviet history."[8] The period between the first volume and the last, 1926 through 1947, was one of almost unimaginable turmoil in the Soviet Union. In 1926, Leon Trotsky was expelled from the Politburo, and eventually from the Communist Party; Nikolai Bukharin would follow in 1929. Stalin began his five-year plans in 1928. The Moscow Trials of sixteen dissidents took place in 1936. Stalin's constitution went into effect in 1936, and the Great Purge of 1937 rooted out anti-Soviet elements. Lithuania, Latvia, and Estonia were incorporated into the Soviet Union; Poland, Romania, Hungary, and Czechoslovakia were invaded.

Writers of reference books are charged with representing the world around them, and if that world is changing in unpredictable ways, their work will represent it. Early volumes of the *Entsiklopediia* were published in the 1920s, and they are filled with Bolshevik energy. As Stalin's brand of leadership sank in, though, many of the early figures who were celebrated enthusiastically fell from favor. In 1931, the editorial board looked back on their work to date and came to the conclusion that some of the articles—no one specified which or how many—were not appropriately orthodox in their commitment to Marxism-Leninism. The publication plan was shaken up. And as political attitudes shifted, the subsequent volumes of the encyclopedia had to be rejiggered to reflect the new orthodoxy. Bukharin, for instance, at the heart of the October Revolution in 1917, was still in good standing in the 1920s, but when he stood up to Stalin and opposed his consolidation of power, he fell from grace. Though his name was at the top of the list of editors in the volumes published in 1930, he found himself demoted in the volumes published in 1932. In 1937, Bukharin disappeared from the masthead entirely. It was a grim harbinger of his fate: in 1938, he was arrested and executed. Later he would suffer the posthumous indignity of not even appearing in the entry on the October Revolution, published in 1939.[9]

Not every shift in coverage can be explained by an individual's getting on Stalin's bad side. The entries for Great Britain and Germany were written early, and these two nations received more or less sympathetic treatment. But Italy, Japan, China, and France, all appearing later in the Russian alphabet, paid the price for their poor standing with the Soviet Union in the years leading to the Second World War. The entry for the United States was relatively positive, because by 1945, when the relevant volume appeared, the Americans and the Soviets were working together to defeat the Axis powers.[10]

As soon as the first edition was complete, the editorial team turned its attention to a second edition. Rapid progress was part of the national ideology, as was achieving ideological purity. The Council of Ministers therefore issued a decree:

> The second edition of the Great Soviet Encyclopedia should elucidate broadly the world-historical victories of Socialism in our country, which have been attained in the USSR in the provinces of economics, science, culture, and art. ... With exhaustive

completeness it must show the superiority of Socialist culture over the culture of the capitalist world. Operating on Marxist-Leninist theory, the encyclopedia should give a party criticism of contemporary reactionary bourgeois tendencies in various provinces of science and technics.[11]

The first edition reached the end of the alphabet in 1947; the second edition began appearing in 1949. It was concerned less with extending the first edition than with replacing it.

The second edition explicitly took sides in the cold war. The Soviet Council of Ministers instructed the editorial board "to show with exhaustive completeness the superiority of socialist culture over the culture of the capitalist world. Based on Marxist-Leninist theory, the *Encyclopedia* should give the party's criticism of reactionary bourgeois tendencies in various fields of science and technique."[12] But Soviet history did not stop making life confusing for the encyclopedists. Stalin died in 1953, and Nikita Khrushchev's rethinking of Stalin's rule required the editors to be fast on their feet. We can trace the decline in the adulation directed at Stalin in the volumes published after 1953. The once-beloved leader had the misfortune to have a name beginning with *S*, which put his own entry late in the encyclopedia. By the time his volume appeared, his reputation was already in tatters. At the same time, many of the figures who were "disappeared" in the Stalinist purges of the 1930s and excluded from the first edition of the *Entsiklopediia* reappeared in the second.

The second edition, which drew on the work of a mind-blowing 15,820 contributors, was complete in fifty-one volumes by 1958. The scientific coverage is better than before; the entries are both more extensive and more accurate, showing less of the concern with dialectical materialist doctrine. It also deserves credit for sticking to its publication schedule, and it is a more attractive and more usable book than its predecessor. The third edition, ordered by the Central Committee in 1967, is smaller— thirty volumes instead of fifty-one—a condensation achieved partly by shortening the entries and partly by printing them in smaller type. Still it featured 100,000 articles, 36,000 illustrations, and 1,650 maps, prepared by more than ten thousand scientists, headed by Aleksandr Prokhorov, winner of the Lenin Prize and the Nobel Prize in physics. It appeared between 1970 and 1978, with an index of names appearing in a separate volume in 1981. By this time the Soviet Union was looking abroad, and it authorized translations into the major European languages: Italian, Greek, Spanish, and English. The English publisher was eager to distance itself from the doctrine that prompted the encyclopedia in the first place: they were presenting a document of cultural interest without endorsing the Marxist-Leninist ideology that created it:

> This English edition of the Great Soviet Encyclopedia is a faithful translation of the Soviet national encyclopedia, unannotated and as true as possible to the content and meaning intended by the editors of the original edition in Russian. The publisher and editors of this work do not embrace the ideology or endorse the views expressed by the Soviet Editors and authors of the Encyclopedia, nor do they believe it is meaningful or valuable to its users in English for them to comment on the material. Rather, the purpose of this translation is to convey the scope and point of view of the Great Soviet Encyclopedia and to bring to scholars and others with a serious professional interest in Soviet affairs a primary source through which they can gain a richer knowledge and understanding of the contemporary Soviet Union.[13]

Most of the Western reviews of the *Great Soviet Encyclopedia* were just as much a part of the Cold War mentality as the *Encyclopedia* itself. "Objectivity" became the favorite word of hostile critics, who contrasted putatively "objective" Western publications with the "doctrinaire" or "ideological" work of the Soviets. A reviewer points to the "half-comical and half-macabre megalomania" of the book.[14] And yet Western encyclopedias have no shortage of doctrine and propaganda; their entries on *democracy* and *Smith, Adam* can be every bit as propagandistic as Fascist and Communist publications. And when the English third edition of the *Great Soviet Encyclopedia* appeared in 1991, shortly after the fall of the Berlin Wall, some American reviews were positively gloating. "What's more out of date than a leisure suit, denser than the caveats to an insurance policy and a whole lot bigger than a breadbox?" asked the *St. Petersburg Times*—Florida, not Leningrad. "Try a multivolume set of the Great Soviet Encyclopedia, a master compendium of the world's most outmoded, misleading and downright untrue knowledge."[15]

⚭

Other twentieth-century ideologies were enshrined in encyclopedia form. The *Enciclopedia Italiana di scienze, lettere ed arti* (36 vols., 1925–37) was determined to support the Fascist state, and the entry *fascismo* was signed by Benito Mussolini himself (though it was probably ghost-written by philosopher Giovanni Gentile, editor of the series).[16] Nazi Germany had no exact equivalent. *Der Große Brockhaus* (20 vols., 1928–37) rejected Nazi influence, but *Meyers Lexikon* (8 vols., 1936–42) shows contemporary concern with race. And the *Zhongguo Da Baike Quanshu* (*China Great Encyclopedia*) began appearing in 1978.

It is well to remember, though, that some Western encyclopedias are every bit as ideological, even as they vigorously deride ideology. After an education at Cornell and Yale and a career as a literary critic and theorist, E. D. Hirsch, Jr., achieved prominence as the director of a college writing program. He became increasingly concerned that his students lacked the background needed to be good readers and writers of important literature. Quoting Samuel Johnson's invocation of "the common reader," Hirsch noted that in the eighteenth century "there did exist a commonality of literate people who shared much the same grammar school education, who had ready many of the same ancient and modern authors, who continued to read many of the same periodicals, . . . and who could be counted on to have a certain range of shared knowledge and attitudes." He rejected the increasing politicization of literary studies and called for a "Back-to-the-Classics" approach to teaching writing: "back to content, shared knowledge, cultural literacy."[17] The concern culminated in the bestselling *Dictionary of Cultural Literacy* (1988), an attempt to delineate essential shared knowledge in an age of increasing relativism and intellectual fragmentation. But adherence to a canon of classics is itself an ideological position, and in the *Dictionary of Cultural Literacy*'s most vehement denunciations of doctrine, it reveals its true genealogy among other doctrinal encyclopedias.

CHAPTER 24 ½

UNPERSONS

Damnatio Memoriae

ISTORY, IT IS said, is written by the winners. More important, history is often *rewritten* by the winners—or, even more, *unwritten*. Nowhere is that seen more clearly than in encyclopedias and biographical dictionaries.

The Roman practice of *damnatio memoriae*—Latin for "condemnation of memory," though the term was not used by the ancients—is the removal of every trace of an enemy of the state from history. When the Roman Senate pronounced an *abolitio nominis* on someone, an "abolition of the name," the abolition was literal. Statues were knocked over, mosaics pried up, inscriptions chiseled out, and coins bearing the hated image removed from circulation.[1] Even the person's family name was removed from circulation. He became what George Orwell in *1984* called an "unperson."

Though the term is Latin, the practice was not limited to Rome. The Hebrew Bible records threats of punishment: "his name shall be covered with darkness," says Ecclesiastes 6:4. And Christians could remove people from history by excommunicating them.[2] The most notorious modern examples of *damnatio memoriae*, though, came from the Soviet Union.

Readers of volume 5 of the second edition of the *Great Soviet Encyclopedia* in 1950 might have been interested to read of the career of Lavrentii Pavlovich Beria, the state security chief under Stalin. There they would have learned about his childhood in Georgia, his rise through the ranks of the Georgian State Political Directorate, his appointment as secretary of the Communist Party for the entire Transcaucasus, and his eventual promotion to the Central Committee of the Communist Party in 1934. They would have read about how he became one of Stalin's favorites, and how he reached the post of commissar general of state security. All of this was captured, in suitably patriotic detail, in the encyclopedia.

In the early 1950s, though, Beria underwent a rapid downfall, as Stalin had begun to suspect his loyalty. Stalin's death offered Beria only a temporary reprieve, because after a coup by Nikita Khrushchev and a few others, Beria was arrested, tried for "criminal activities against the Party and the State" in a trial where he was not permitted to defend himself, and found guilty of terrorism and treason. He was executed in December 1953.

The Party found itself in an embarrassing position: the official state encyclopedia now included a laudatory entry on a traitor. In 1954, therefore, subscribers to the encyclopedia received—at no extra charge!—a new set of pages 21 through 24. They were instructed to cut out the original pages "with a small knife or razor blade" and to paste the new ones in their place. The new pages included extended coverage of the Bering Sea, as well as of Vitus Bering, the Danish explorer whose name it bears. Readers got expanded information on Friedrich Wilhelm von Bergholz, an eighteenth-century courtier and diarist, and on philosopher George Berkeley's subjective idealism. All this new information, though, left no room for an entry on Lavrentii Pavlovich Beria, who disappeared completely. Beria would not appear in any official history or memoir for the next thirty years.[3]

Beria is the most famous, but far from the only, instance of *damnatio memoriae* in the *Great Soviet Encyclopedia*. Leon Trotsky's entry came and went in the book as his reputation among party officials rose and fell. Nikolai Bukharin, Grigory Zinoviev, and Lev Kamenev, eliminated from positions of power by Stalin, were eliminated from the encyclopedia by loyal editors. Even literary figures and scientists found their entries rewritten or eliminated from subsequent printings if party doctrine became less tolerant of their work.

While Soviet revisionism was extreme, as Charles W. Hedrick wrote, "all societies, including modern Western liberal democracies, have necessarily been selective about what they remember and what they forget. Even contemporary American businesses may treat embarrassing executives in a manner reminiscent of the *damnatio memoriae*."[4]

Disgraced CEOs and indicted insider traders have suffered the indignity of watching their oil portraits come off the wall in boardrooms and halls of distinguished alumni. A twenty-first-century twist is provided by the services that seek to remove unflattering information about their clients from the major databases and search engines. A recent European Union law asserts the "right to be forgotten," empowering the living to decide which facts about them should be forgotten.

CHAPTER 25

NOTHING SPECIAL

Books for Browsers

Norris and Ross McWhirter	Ben Schott
The Guinness Book of Records	*Schott's Original Miscellany*
1955	2002

R EFERENCE WORKS EVOLVED to serve practical needs. Essential information, having grown too copious and unwieldy to be retained in memory, had to be laid out in documentary form for quick access. But eventually the books pervaded the culture, and the reference form was used for other purposes, begetting full-length reference books containing information no one will ever need to refer to. These books are meant entirely for browsers, with no pretense to being "useful" at all. They are instead reference-book-shaped compendia of trivia—the word got its modern sense of "Trivialities, trifles, things of little consequence" as recently as 1902—and they have become a publishing phenomenon.

As with every reference genre, books of trivia have deep roots. Jeremiah Whitaker Newman's *Lounger's Common-Place Book* (1792–93) is typical of late eighteenth-century miscellanies: the subtitle promises an *Alphabetical Arrangement of Miscellaneous Anecdotes: A Biographic, Political, Literary, and Satirical Compilation, in Prose and Verse*, and that is what the book delivers. Some four pages are devoted to Robert Adair, then the same to Anabaptists, to Tomaso Aniello, John Arbuthnot, Polly Baker, and so on—a gathering of people with nothing in common. Volume 2 starts over at the beginning of the alphabet, this time trading biographical for topical entries: "Benefit of Clergy," "Black Hole" (of Calcutta), "Burton-upon-Trent." Whitaker confessed his scholarship was sometimes shoddy. "From the nature of this production," he wrote, "authors have been occasionally referred to generally by memory; sometimes I have imagined myself quoting, when in fact I was not, and sometimes I have quoted without being conscious of it." For readers who discovered his quotations "have not been exactly and literally correct," he "claim[ed] the reader's indulgence for an omission, which I hope he believes did not originate from a mean design of plucking feathers from the nightingale, to deck a parrot, whose merit at best is to repeat by rote."[1] But the quotations hardly have to be correct. No one will ever turn to the *Lounger's Common-Place Book* as part of a scholarly investigation into Burton-upon-Trent. It was meant only for curious browsers.

⁂

The golden plover or the grouse?—They *needed to know.*

Sir Hugh Beaver, a "classical, colonially inspired child of the British empire"[2] who managed the Guinness brewery, was convinced the plover was the fastest game bird. His companions maintained just as adamantly that it was the grouse. The debate arose during a shooting party in County Wexford, Ireland, in 1951. The party returned to their host's house and browsed his books, hoping to find the answer, but without success. With enough hours of research in encyclopedias and bird guides they might eventually have come up with an answer, but no single source told the story. Sir Hugh thought that a convenient collection of facts of that sort might prove useful in settling bets like this. And so was born one of the bestselling books in the world.

The Guinness brewery had no connection with the publishing world, but they decided to enter the business because a book to settle drunken wagers might be a way to promote their beer in Britain's 84,400 pubs. Christopher Chataway, a Guinness executive, suggested the project, and he proposed the people to edit it. Norris and Ross McWhirter were born in 1925, the athletic and congenitally curious identical twin sons of a newspaper editor. After attending Trinity College, Oxford, they served in the Royal Navy during the Second World War. When the war ended, they headed to London and found work as journalists, setting up a fact-checking business called McWhirter Twins Ltd.

The brothers were strangely fact-obsessed. Their father, who managed three national newspapers, brought an astounding 150 newspapers home

TITLE: *The Guinness Book of Records*

COMPILER: Norris McWhirter (1925–2004) and Alan Ross McWhirter (1925–75)

ORGANIZATION: Twelve sections: Universe, Natural World, Animal Kingdom, Human Being, Human World, Scientific World, World's Structures, Mechanical World, Business World, Accidents and Disasters, Human Achievements, and Sport

PUBLISHED: London: Guinness Superlatives Ltd., September 1955

PAGES: vi + 198; sixteen plates

ENTRIES: 4,000

SIZE: 10" × 7½" (25 × 19 cm)

AREA: 104 ft² (9.7 m²)

PRICE: 5s. (available to Guinness employees for 2s. 6d.)

LATEST EDITION: *Guinness World Records 2015*

every week. The twins were enraptured, and they made a point of reading the papers and setting aside clippings. "As boys, the pair had charted the deepest lakes, the longest tunnels and the tallest buildings. As adults, they had started an agency to supply sports trivia to British newspapers."[3] Norris was one of the founding members of the Association of Track and Field Statisticians, an organization that continues to keep track of facts and figures related to field sports. The Guinness executives met the brothers and quizzed them: the widest river that has ever frozen, the longest time for pole squatting, the longest filibuster in the U.S. Senate. Norris found their questions "fairly simple." When Sir Hugh mentioned his frustration in trying to find someone to translate documents from English to Turkish, Norris

interposed that I could not see why Turkish should be a particular problem since the language had only one irregular verb. Sir Hugh stopped dead and said "Which is the irregular verb?" I replied

"imek, to be." "Do you speak Turkish?" he asked, so I admitted
I didn't. "Then how on earth do you know that?" he queried.
"Because records of all kinds interest me and I had learnt that fact
in trying to discover which language had the fewest irregular verbs."
. . . Sir Hugh seemed to decide that he had discovered people with
the right kind of quirkish mind for producing the book.[4]

Doing the research for the project was no small task: they had only
sixteen weeks to meet Guinness's production schedule. They put in
ninety-hour weeks "extracting '-ests' (i.e., highests, oldests, richests,
heaviests, fastests, etc.) from 'ists' (dendrochonologists, helminthologists,
paleontologists, and vulcanologists, etc.)."[5] Letters by the thousand left
their office at 107 Fleet Street, London, and went to experts in more than
a hundred countries: museum curators, librarians, professors, government
officials. (The first edition thanks the British Speleological Association,
the United States Coast Guard, and the Embassy of Japan.)[6] The brothers'
biggest frustration was exaggerated reports: one of their sources claimed
to have clocked a fly traveling 820 mph (1,320 kph), faster than the speed
of sound. Their fact-checking prowess proved handy.

The Guinness Book of Records, featuring a foreword by Rupert Guinness,
Earl of Iveagh, was bound on Saturday, August 27, 1955, and offered for
sale in early October. That first edition informed readers that Walt Disney
had won more Oscars than anyone else, that the champion rat-killing dog
was named Jacko, that Mount Everest is 29,160 feet high, and the fastest
time to run a mile was John Landy's 3:57.9. The print run was tremendous,
fifty thousand copies, but not as a result of large orders. W. H. Smith,
Britain's biggest bookseller, ordered a total of six copies. "It was a marketing
give away," said Beaver; "it wasn't supposed to be a money maker." At first
they gave them away, accompanying shipments to pubs with this letter:

Dear Sir,
                    "Guinness Book of Records"

Where is the biggest pub in Great Britain? Who was Britain's
fattest man? Which team has played in most F.A. Cup Finals?
Where is the rainiest spot in the United States?

These and hundreds of similar questions, are discussed in the inns and pubs of Britain every day. We have designed "The Guinness Book of Records" to provide authoritative answers to as many questions of this kind as we could think of, and we hope that it will prove useful to landlords. It must, of course, be produced at just the right moment, that is, after the contestants have derived all the enjoyment and thirst possible from the argument but before they proceed to the "lie direct."

Please accept this copy with our compliments. It has been given a special waterproof, and beer-proof, binding so that it may stand up to handling in a busy bar.[7]

It turned out, though, that people were willing to pay cash money for this giveaway product. On publication even W. H. Smith upped its order from six to a hundred, and just a few hours later to a thousand, and then by week's end to ten thousand. The *Guinness Book* became a surprise bestseller for Christmas; four printings were issued by January. An American edition followed in 1956, and revised editions were released every year. In retrospect the success makes sense: it was a golden age of trivia in Britain and America, with pub trivia contests and television quiz shows proving some of the most entertaining ways to pass the time.[8] As soon as Guinness realized they had a hit on their hands, the price went up: the price of the five-shilling first edition went to nine shillings and sixpence for the second, as the page count jumped from 198 to 272. Over time, the book's annual editions proved an astonishing success, setting its own record: the bestselling book in copyright in history, with more than 120 million copies in circulation. Only the Bible, the Qur'an, and Mao's *Little Red Book* have sold more.[9]

Early editions gave much attention to natural phenomena—the longest rivers, brightest stars, fastest land animals, and so on. They were facts about the world, not things on which people could compete:

The world record for any breed of sheep is 5,500 guineas   Sheep
(£5,375) for a Kent ram at Fielding, New Zealand, in
January 1951.

The British auction record is £2,500 by B. Wilson for
a Scottish Blackface ram lamb owned by J. M. Wilson
at Lanark in October, 1954.

The world's record price for a pig is $10,200 (£3,643)   Pigs
paid in 1953 for a Hampshire boar "Great Western"
for a farm at Byron, U.S.A.

The British record is 3,300 guineas (£3,465) paid for
the Landrace gilt "Bluegate Ally 33rd" at Keating on
2nd March, 1955.

There were, however, exceptions; the first edition featured a man
who ate twenty-four raw eggs in fourteen minutes. But these stunts
have grown in popularity over time, and the later editions' fondness for
outré personal achievements has generated controversy. Critics refer to
the "Guinness effect": "when a measurement is created, persons come
forth to be measured by it."[10] This was a concern from early on.
Norris McWhirter worried about stunts from the beginning, and he
insisted that all records must be in "universally competitive, peculiar,
or unique" areas. Over time, though, his resolve weakened, and
"gradually he began to include such records as eating a bicycle ground
into metal filings and the longest time spent in a bathtub with live
rattlesnakes."[11]

Some personal records are harmless enough—the largest collection of
Charlie's Angels memorabilia (5,569 items, owned by Jack Condon), the
largest wine flute (56.25 liters, produced by Agrofirm Zolotaia Balka of
Ukraine), most hopscotch games completed in twenty-four hours (434,
by Ashrita Furman, who also holds the records for long-distance pogo
stick jumping, the most glasses balanced on the chin, and the fastest time
to pogo-stick up the CN Tower). Others, though, celebrate behavior that
probably should not be encouraged. When Christie Glissmeyer set a
world record by taking her kayak down a twenty-five-meter waterfall in
May 2009, she seemed only to be inviting someone else to take a kayak
down a twenty-six-meter waterfall. Sage Werbock, who performs under
the stage name "the Great Nippulini," lifted 31.9 kg on chains attached
by piercings to his nipples; it is only a matter of time before someone
goes for an even 32. Beginning in December 2008, Thailand's Kanchana

Ketkaew lived for thirty-three days in a small glass box with 5,320 scorpions. We can keep checking the *Guinness Book* for news of someone who spends thirty-four days in a box with 5,321 scorpions.

As a result, *Guinness* has stopped accepting some records—those in "life-threatening categories"—for fear that ambitious adventurers will be prepared to risk their lives for the immortality that comes with an entry in *Guinness*.[12] On the advice of physicians, and perhaps advice of counsel, *Guinness* no longer accepts records related to headstands, sleep deprivation, or hunger strikes; gone are the records for smoking the largest number of cigarettes or chugging the greatest amount of alcohol. Even when records are not rejected for being dangerous, though, many are omitted because there is no end to what ingenious aspirants can make up. About sixty-five thousand claims come to the *Guinness* offices every year, but only about one in seven is even considered. As a journalist explains the book's policy for inclusion,

> Many are too specific. Most People Crammed into a '63 Chevy? Sorry, but Guinness accepts car-cramming records only for "iconic" cars such as the Volkswagen Beetle. Oldest Pit Bull? Guinness does not categorize pet records by breed. "People often try to claim a record by complicating it," says Guinness' Keeper of the Records, Stewart "The Oracle" Newport: "They'll say they have the record for Longest Standing on the Corner of Such and Such a Street While Playing a Banjo."[13]

And which was the fastest game bird, the golden plover or the grouse? Neither, it turns out. The wood pigeon holds the record.

❦

The *Guinness Book* contains information no one particularly needs to know, but it is nonetheless a genuine compendium of superlative information. You may not need to know the cost of the world's most expensive hamburger, but if you want to know it, you know you can turn to the latest *Guinness* for the answer ($5,000 at Juicys Outlaw Grill).

❦

A few reference books go even further than Guinness in the direction of gloriously unconnected trivia, and the perfect example of this genre may be *Schott's Original Miscellany*, described on the title page as "Conceived, written, and designed by BEN SCHOTT." As the author's website advertises, the book is an "indispensable collection of essential trivia, uncommon knowledge and vital irrelevancies." However irrelevant, it has kept browsers happy for more than a decade; as the review in *Newsweek* put it, "Part encyclopedia, part anthology, part lexicon, the book is a collection of inconsequential tidbits that you never knew, never thought to ask, but will love knowing." The *Sunday Telegraph* was similar: "This bizarre little book manages to be both totally useless and nearly indispensable."

Schott's Original Miscellany is the reason the word *quirky* was invented. It opens with a meditation on its own form:

> An encyclopaedia? A dictionary? An almanac? An anthology? A lexicon? A treasury? A commonplace? An amphigouri? A vade-mecum?
>
> Well . . . yes. *Scott's Original Miscellany* is all of these and, of course, none.

Its declared purpose is "to gather the flotsam and jetsam of the conversational tide," and while it "makes very few claims to be exhaustive, authoritative, or even practical," it does "claim to be essential."[14]

TITLE: *Schott's Original Miscellany*
COMPILER: Ben Schott (1974–)
ORGANIZATION: God only knows
PUBLISHED: London: Bloomsbury, 2002
PAGES: 159
TOTAL WORDS: 37,837
SIZE: 8¾" × 4½" (186 × 115 mm)
AREA: 36.6 ft² (3.4 m²)
WEIGHT: 8 oz. (230 g)
PRICE: £9.99
LATEST EDITION: A series of *Miscellanies* and *Almanacs*

Ben Schott—not yet thirty when the *Miscellany* appeared—was a photographer with a politics degree from Gonville and Caius College, Cambridge. He has done a good job cultivating an air of mystery, so there are vague rumors about his collection of cufflinks and his 1967 Mercedes. He used to send handmade Christmas cards to friends that took the form of little booklets of trivia. The cards suggested the book, which Schott not only wrote but designed and typeset. The small print and eccentric layout, reminiscent of Victorian self-help books, are among the most distinctive features of the book, at once beautiful and frenzied. The manic miscellaneity evokes Victorian hodgepodges like *Beeton's Dictionary of Universal Information* (1870–73).

It is tempting to say that the *Miscellany* includes facts like the weight classes of sumo wrestlers, the names of people on the cover of *Sgt Pepper's Lonely Hearts Club Band* (Carl Jung, Bob Dylan, Marlene Dietrich, Karl Marx), the months on the French revolutionary calendar, and who supplies bagpipes to the Queen—but what facts are "like" these? The first few pages do, however, give a taste of the rest. The main text opens with "Golf Stroke Nomenclature," then moves without transition to a discussion of the Hat Tax, followed immediately by a set of "Characteristics of Living Things" (movement, respiration, sensitivity . . .), and then abruptly segues into "Shoelace Length"—and so on. The curious reader comes across the Victorian rules for mourning, with the proviso that widows were expected to mourn their husbands two to three years, while widowers could get on just three months after their wives' deaths. They are not the only deaths to be featured: see also "Curious Deaths of Some Burmese Kings," including Anawratha, "gored by a buffalo during a military campaign," and Tabinshweti, "beheaded by his chamberlains while searching for a fictitious white elephant."

Schott is drawn to anything that can be numbered: Isaac Asimov's three laws of robotics, the thirty *Carry On* films, the Three Wise Men, the five regular Platonic solids, the three-to-fifteen-point range of the Glasgow Coma Scale. Astronomical numbers are even better: the odds of a royal flush in poker are 649,739 to 1. Any set that is (a) limited and (b) unexpected has appeal, such as a complete list of Bond Girls or all the recognized sizes of icebergs and eggs. He revels in obscure words, as in his list of phobias including pteronophobia (tickling with feathers), xenoglossophobia (foreign languages), scorodophobia (garlic), as well as in his tour through various techniques of divination, including gelo-scopy (the interpretation of laughter), bletonism (analyzing currents of water), and sciomancy (shadows or ghosts).

Part of the book's charm is its *incompleteness*. A comprehensive list of patron saints would be too useful, so instead we get a defiantly arbitrary selection: wine growers claim St. Joseph; gravediggers, St. Anthony; bricklayers, St. Stephen; syphilitics, St. George. Other entries get their allure from being categories that no one ever thought of as categories before, such as the list of "Notable Belgians," or things proverbs say you can't do (have it both ways, have your cake and eat it, get blood out of a stone). Instructions are always fun: Schott will teach you how to wrap a sari, calculate bra sizes, and convert shoe sizes (a British 9 is an American 10½ or a European 42.5). Historical trivia is always welcome, like the first-class dinner menu for the *Titanic* on April 14, 1912, and lengths and opening dates of the lines on the London Underground.

The book came out on November 4, 2002, and initially got little publicity. When the early reviewers got their copies, though, it was love at first sight. Stuart Jeffries's *Guardian* review was one of the first to celebrate the "publishing sensation of the year," and two days later Robert McCrum published a review under the title "God Bless You, Mr Schott, for Your Pointless yet Perfect Miscellany," calling the book "without doubt the oddest, nay maddest, and possibly merriest, title you will come across in a long day's march through the shimmering desert of contemporary publishing. . . . strangely unputdownable . . . Schott is a snapper-up of unconsidered trifles, a mad magpie at large in the wide world of facts and words . . . the work of a jackdaw mind."[15] These reviews and others like them made it the hit of the Christmas book buying season, and over the next four weeks the book sold more than two hundred thousand copies.

Schott continues to cultivate a mysterious public image. He was voted one of *GQ*'s Men of the Year in 2003, but he turned down the honor, as he turned down an invitation to a party with Elton John. After the *Original Miscellany*, he turned his attention to matters culinary, with *Schott's Food & Drink Miscellany*. "The London 'miscellanist' returns," wrote *Publishers Weekly*, "bestowing upon hungry readers every random thing they've ever wondered about the culinary arts and then some. . . . Servants' wages, rates of digestion, blessings for wine and bread, dining times for monks, cognac nomenclature, Laotian cooking measures, ways to ask for the bill in 22 languages, microbial count in raw meat, Latin names for herbs—Schott addresses all these subjects and more, hopping between completely useless (though always fascinating) information and eminently practical tidbits."[16]

❦

Reviewing *Schott* for the *Christian Science Monitor*, Mark Luce linked the two works of this chapter: "The last time I experienced such a response to a compendium of useless information was in fifth grade, when a 1980 edition of 'The Guinness Book of World Records' landed in my grubby mitts."[17] *Guinness* and *Schott* are part of a genre that includes Michael Powell's *Back in the Day: 101 Things Everyone Used to Know How to Do*, *Mental Floss Presents Condensed Knowledge: A Deliciously Irreverent Guide to Feeling Smart Again*, and *Slate* magazine's *Explainer*. The Library of Congress has assigned some of these the brilliantly nonspecific subject heading "Handbooks, vade-mecums, etc."

Their shared success is noteworthy. "More intriguing than any mere fact in Schott's," JoAnn Gutin observed on its first appearance, "is the philosophical question raised by its popularity. In A.D. 2003, when anyone with a high-speed Internet connection can get the basics of any subject within 10 seconds, does the world need collections like this?" Her conclusion: "From an informational standpoint, probably not."[18] Perhaps the ready availability of so much information, when any idle curiosity can be settled with only a few seconds' labor, makes books about nothing special—that is to say, things we would never search for—all the more desirable. They remind us that reports of the death of hard-copy reference books, even in the age of Google and Wikipedia, are considerably exaggerated.

THE WORLD'S INFORMATION

The Encyclopedic Dream

I N NOVEMBER 1619, the young René Descartes had a series of dreams.[1] In the first, a powerful whirlwind blew past his college, knocking him down. In the second, he saw and heard an explosion coming from the small stove in his room. In the third, he saw on his desk a familiar collection of Latin poetry, the *Corpus poetarum*, next to a huge dictionary. Descartes used the word *dictionnaire*, but it seems he had something more like an encyclopedia in mind—the word *encyclopédie* was not common when he wrote. On waking, Descartes interpreted the dictionary in his dream as representing "toutes les Sciences ramassées ensemble," "all knowledge gathered together." This was part of the turning point in the life of the young philosopher. He concluded, "I thought I could do no better than . . . devote all my life to cultivating my reason and advancing as far as I could in the knowledge of the truth."[2]

We have dreamed about that dictionary for millennia, though we might call it an encyclopedia, a miscellany, even a database: at that level the distinctions between genres break down. The notion of collecting all the world's knowledge in one place has been a goal—for some, an obsession—for as long as there has been writing. All fifty of the primary works considered here, as well as the thousands that were not included, are in some sense failures, even if many of them are glorious failures. Every dictionary, every encyclopedia, every atlas leaves questions unanswered. As the historian of encyclopedias Richard Yeo puts it, "Encyclopaedic dreams have almost always outrun achievements."[3]

The encyclopedic dream echoes throughout history. In the seventh century B.C.E., Ashurbanipal, king of Assyria, assembled a library—"the first documented attempt to collect all knowledge systematically."[4] A more famous attempt came a few centuries later, in the Library of

Alexandria. In the modern era, in 1895, a Belgian professor of law named Paul Otlet and a legislator named Henri La Fontaine founded an Institut International de Bibliographie, later named the Mundaneum, which accumulated 16 million index cards in an attempt to catalog the world's knowledge according to their new system, the Universal Decimal Classification. Eventually, more ambitious souls aspired to collect the world's information not in a library but in a single book, albeit a large one, thinking their work would render all previous books unnecessary.[5]

The Chinese have a long tradition of encyclopedias that aspire to be comprehensive. One of the most impressive is the *Four Great Books of Song*, by Li Fang and others in tenth- or eleventh-century China. The text runs to 14 million words, making it one of the largest works ever written to that point. Even that looks scrawny, though, compared to one of its successors, the *Yonglè dàdian*, or "Great Canon or Vast Documents of the Yongle Era," sometimes known as the *Yongle Encyclopedia*. This work, put together between 1403 and 1408 by a large team—five chief directors supervised twenty subdirectors, who oversaw 2,169 scholars—once ran to 11,095 volumes and about 370 million words. It was compiled in the hope of collecting "everything that had ever been written on Confucian religion, history, philosophy, arts, and sciences,"[6] and it incorporated into itself the full text of between seven and eight thousand classical Chinese works. The book was too long to be printed, and the consequences were grim: most of it has been lost. But another Chinese encyclopedia from 1725 to 1726, the *Qinding Gujin tushu jicheng* (*Complete Collection of Writings from Earliest to Current Times*), was printed in more than three quarters of a million pages and 100 million words, making it one of the longest works ever printed.[7]

The dream was every bit as alive in the West. Medieval philosophers and theologians aspired to write a *summa*, a single work that would encapsulate everything known, at least everything worth knowing. Thomas Aquinas's *Summa theologica* (1265–74) is the most famous of the summae, but splendidly immodest titles like Radulfus Ardens's *Speculum universale* (*Universal Mirror*) and Rabanus Maurus Magnentius' *De rerum naturis*, sometimes known as *De universo* (*On the Universe*), show the kind of thing they had in mind. Most of these works were meant to be read through—though with Aquinas's *Summa theologica* running to more than 2 million words, how many people have actually done so is open to question—but Nicholas de Byard's *Summa de abstinentia* (late thirteenth century) and Bartolomeo of San Concordio's *Summa de casibus coscientiae* (1338) were presented in alphabetical order, aligning them with reference books.

In the modern era the presumption grew. Ephraim Chambers, for instance, boasted in 1727 that his *Cyclopaedia* would "answer all the Purposes of a Library,"[8] and Victorian booksellers turned out keys to all mythologies with admirable regularity. What is not to love about a work called *Enquire Within upon Everything* (1856)? H. G. Wells, Britain's leading man of letters a century ago, waxed messianic when he wrote about a "world encyclopaedia" that would solve all our species' problems. This "new social organ" would be "the means whereby we can solve the problem of that jig-saw puzzle and bring all the scattered and ineffective mental wealth of our world into something like a common understanding."[9] One of Wells's early commentators saw the connection of his project with the ancient and medieval summae: "The impossible dream of intellectual order is at least a dream of respectable antiquity, and it is being dreamed still by thousands if not millions of people. It sees the human mind as ultimately concerned with all that is knowable in the universe."[10]

The encyclopedic dream got a technological inflection in the middle of the twentieth century when Vannevar Bush proposed a device he called a "memex," which would not only assemble the world's knowledge but make it more easily accessible than ever before. He imagined microphotographic technology installed in a workstation the size of a large desk, with links between microfilm frames that would allow users to zip easily around the world's knowledge—a clear precursor of the hypertext technology that makes the World Wide Web possible. "The *Encyclopedia Britannica* could be reduced to the volume of a matchbox," Bush wrote as the Second World War came to an end:

> A library of a million volumes could be compressed into one end of a desk. If the human race has produced since the invention of movable type a total record, in the form of magazines, newspapers, books, tracts, advertising blurbs, correspondence, having a volume

corresponding to a billion books, the whole affair, assembled and compressed, could be lugged off in a moving van.

The technology was not yet developed in 1945, when Bush published *As We May Think*, but by the early 1990s, networked personal computers had taken the place of microfilm, photocells, and servomotors.[11]

Comprehensive reference books show up in fiction, too. Gustave Flaubert's Bouvard and Pécuchet (1881) try to read everything ever written on every branch of human knowledge and to summarize the results. Isaac Asimov's "Foundation" (1942) features an *Encyclopedia Galactica*, and Douglas Adams's *Hitchhiker's Guide to the Galaxy* (1979) gives us the greatest of them all:

> In many of the more relaxed civilizations on the Outer Eastern Rim of the Galaxy, the *Hitchhiker's Guide* has already supplanted the great *Encyclopaedia Galactica* as the standard repository of all knowledge and wisdom, for though it has many omissions and contains much that is apocryphal, or at least wildly inaccurate, it scores over the older, more pedestrian work in two important respects.
>
> First, it is slightly cheaper; and secondly it has the words DON'T PANIC inscribed in large friendly letters on its cover.[12]

Today we tend to have our encyclopedic dreams on the Internet. Google's corporate mission is "to organize the world's information and make it universally accessible and useful." Wikipedia "Imagine[s] a world in which every single person is given free access to the sum of all human knowledge."[13] And while some reference books have left their mark on the language, Google is unique in having become a verb. Within just thirteen months of its public unveiling in September 1998, it became possible *to Google*. We turn to Google for information on just about anything. Never before in history has a single reference held such monopolistic power over information.

Wikipedia, the student's savior and the teacher's bane, is the product of a confluence of several technologies. In 1994, early in the age of the World Wide Web, the programmer Ward Cunningham developed a series of programs to allow people to work together on a database using only their web browsers. Since it was a quick and easy way to edit text, he remembered the name of a bus at the Honolulu International Airport, the "Wiki Wiki Shuttle," itself named for the Hawaiian word for "quick." At first the community of participants was limited to the computer-savvy, but eventually it became accessible even to amateurs. And when, in 2000, Wiki ran into a project called Nupedia—a fairly conventional encyclopedia, a for-profit venture with a managing editor, expert contributors, and a seven-step approval process for entries—a new approach to reference publishing came into being.[14]

Wikipedia was launched into the world with very few rules, the most famous of which was summed up as IAR—"ignore all rules." "If rules make you nervous and depressed," one early version read, "and not desirous of participating in the Wiki, then ignore them and go about your business."[15] But they added three central policies that have guided Wikipedia ever since: NPOV, or "neutral point of view"; V, or "verifiability"; and NOR, or "no original research." No one knew what to expect in a dictionary written by unpaid volunteers with no editorial supervision, but within just one year, twenty thousand articles had been written, and the volume of the encyclopedia and the number of queries were straining their computing power. By March 2003, more than a hundred thousand articles had been drafted, roughly the number in many of the major commercial encyclopedias. But soon they would leave the commercial encyclopedias far behind. On March 1, 2006, the one millionth entry was contributed: an article on Jordanhill, a Scottish railway station. As historian Stacy Schiff points out, the history of that article is typical of the way Wikipedia entries mutate: "Its author, Ewan MacDonald, posted a single sentence about the station at 11 P.M., local time; over the next twenty-four hours, the entry was edited more than four hundred times, by dozens of people."[16]

These two resources have displaced so many others that they constitute an epoch in reference publishing: future ages will divide their histories of publishing into before and after. Nicholson Baker, a man who knows the joys of obsessive research, has already started the division. "Let me tell you," he says, "I remember the old days, the antegoogluvian era. It was O.K.—it wasn't horrible by any means. There were cordless

TITLE: Wikipedia: The Free Encylopedia

COMPILER: Jimmy Wales (1966–) and Larry Sanger
(1968–)

PUBLISHED: January 15, 2001

VOLUMES: 0

PAGES: 0

ENTRIES: 4,681,440 in English, written and revised by
23,584,715 volunteers; 1.8 million in Dutch, 1.7 million in
German, 1.6 million in French, 1.6 million in Swedish,
1.3 million in Waray-Waray, 1.2 million in Chinese, 1.2
million in Russian, 1.2 million in Visayan, 1.1 million in
Spanish, 1.1 million in Polish, 1.1 million in Vietnamese,
938,000 in Japanese, 848,000 in Portuguese, 785,000 in
Chinese, 535,000 in Ukrainian, 441,000 in Catalan,
428,000 in Persian, 400,000 in Norwegian, 359,000 in
Finish, 350,000 in Indonesian, 336,000 in Arabic,
308,000 in Czech, 294,000 in Korean, 274,000 in
Serbo-Croatian, 271,000 in Malay, 270,000 in
Hungarian, 254,000 in Romanian, 254,000 in Serbian,
237,000 in Turkish, 222,000 in Minangkabau, 210,000
in Kazakh, 205,000 in Esperanto, 204,000 in Basque,
196,000 in Slovak, 192,000 in Danish, 169,000 in
Bulgarian, 168,000 in Lithuanian, 166,000 in Hebrew,
149,000 in Croatian, 143,000 in Slovene, 128,000 in
Estonian, 108,000 in Simple English, 101,000 in Greek,
105,000 in Hindi, 91,000 in Thai, and 3.7 million more
in 193 other languages, for a total of 33.4 million

TOTAL WORDS: 2.714 billion in English, 18 billion total

SIZE: none

AREA: none

WEIGHT: none

PRICE: free

LATEST EDITION: Every edition is the latest edition

telephones, and people wore comfortable sweaters. . . . But the haul was haphazard, and it came in slow."[17] And the site that is often the first hit on Google is just as enthralling to Baker's jackdaw consciousness:

> Wikipedia is just an incredible thing. It's fact-encirclingly huge, and it's idiosyncratic, careful, messy, funny, shocking, and full of simmering controversies—and it's free, and it's fast. In a few seconds you can look up, for instance, "Diogenes of Sinope," or "turnip," or "Crazy Eddie," or "'Bagoas," or "quadratic formula," or "Bristol Beaufighter," or "squeegee," or "Sanford B. Dole," and you'll have knowledge you didn't have before. It's like some vast aerial city with people walking briskly to and fro on catwalks, carrying picnic baskets full of nutritious snacks.[18]

There is much to love about Google, Wikipedia, and other online reference sources. Encyclopedias and unabridged dictionaries are hard to tote around; computers can be small, and phones fit in a pocket. Reference books need constant updating, which pushes old editions into landfills; online sources can be revised several times a day without any additional cost or waste. Information is now more timely than it has ever been: by the time the news announces the death of a prominent person, the relevant Wikipedia page has been updated.

And yet Google and Wikipedia have serious limitations. Wikipedia, for instance, shows a strong presentist bias: the first George to serve as president of the United States, Washington, has a Wikipedia entry of roughly 19,000 words; the most recent President George, this time W. Bush, gets 27,000. Wikipedia also famously favors the fashionable. The English-language entry for Zoroaster—the prophet who developed the world's first monotheistic religion—gets fewer than 8,000 words, and the religion he founded another 9,000; combined, the two entries are the length of Lady Gaga's entry. Thomas Aquinas weighs in at just over 37,000 words on his life and major works; Michael Jackson warrants five times the space. The notorious and infamous do well: the account of O. J. Simpson's life and criminal trials occupies nearly 21,000 words, more than the entries for Florence Nightingale and Mother Teresa combined. Popular culture tends to fare much better than high culture. Perhaps we should expect the pages on the *Legend of Zelda* video games to get more space in Wikipedia than Shakespeare's *Hamlet*, but those pages, at more than 160,000 words, are more than four times the length of *Hamlet* itself.

Anxiety about reliability may be the greatest problem with these online resources. Google serves up "hits" without regard for the authority of the source; Wikipedia is assembled by uncredentialed volunteers. As a result, some teachers forbid reference to them. Middlebury College's history department, for instance, voted to ban citations of websites in student papers.[19] That is almost certainly an overreaction, not least because some online resources are every bit as thoroughly vetted as print resources, and some are just scanned versions of authoritative print encyclopedias. Even Wikipedia, for all its lapses, is valuable. Physicist Freeman Dyson captures the paradox well: "Among my friends and acquaintances, everybody distrusts Wikipedia and everybody uses it."[20] I confess that, even though I adore dusty dictionaries and surround myself with them, I wrote hardly a page of this book without turning to Google, Wikipedia, or both. But these free online sources need to get more reliable, and, just as important, users need to become more sophisticated in evaluating the sources they use.

The bigger danger, to my mind, is that Wikipedia, despite being noncommercial, still poses many of the dangers of a traditional monopoly, and we run the risk of living in an information monoculture. We are in a strange position in the second decade of the third millennium. More information is more readily available to more people than at any time in human history—not merely an incremental increase on previous ages, but an exponential explosion. A rural twelve-year-old with a $250 laptop and a slow Internet connection now has access to more information than the wealthiest scholars and librarians at the richest universities just a generation ago, and anyone with a smartphone owns orders of magnitude more information than fit in the Library of Alexandria. But the new world order remains nervous-making. The information at our fingertips is more diverse than ever before, but in some ways it is more limited. Google has become the first—and, for many people, only—stop for seeking information on everything.

This is the paradox of research in the "postgoogluvian era." We are now nearer to the encyclopedic dream than any society has ever been. From one source—not a library, not a set of books, but a computer connected to most of the other computers around the world—we come closer than ever before to having all the world's information at our fingertips. I hope my survey of attempts to collect the world's information from the third millennium B.C.E. through today serves as a reminder of the sheer variety of information sources out there and helps to keep us attentive to the need for multiple sources of information, multiple ways of organizing the world, multiple points of view. I hope, too, that the lesson about the impossibility of ever achieving the encyclopedic dream induces a healthy skepticism about the sources we do have.

abecedarium Used in the Old English period to refer to the alphabet, taking its name from *A, B, C, D*. It was later used to refer to dictionaries, glossaries, and primers.

almanac A mystery: it shows up in the thirteenth century, and it seems to come from the Arabic *al-manakh*—except that no one has found *manakh* in Arabic. Chaucer was the first English writer to mention this kind of book, which provided information on the calendar and positions of the stars and planets. Later almanacs have included information on holy days, weather, tide tables, and planting dates.

annals Latin *annus* 'year' provides the root; annals are histories organized year by year.

atlas In Greek mythology, Atlas was a Titan who bore the weight of the heavens on his shoulders. Gerardus Mercator included a depiction of Atlas on his collection of maps, and since then the word has been applied to cartographical compilations that cover a wide area.

bibliography Greek βιβλίον (*biblion*) 'book' and γράφειν (*graphein*) 'to write'. A relative newcomer to English, showing up with its meanings "the study of books" and "a list of books" only in 1814.

book Most Germanic languages have a form like *book*; they may be derived from *beech*, perhaps because early books were made from the bark or wood of beech trees. Like Latin *liber* (source of French *livre*, Spanish *libro*, and Italian *libro*) and Greek βιβλίον (*biblion*), English *book* has been applied to various forms of text packaging, from scrolls to codices to e-readers. Its meanings are slippery: it can refer to a section of a longer work (as in an epic poem), or one volume in a multivolume set, or the whole title in however many volumes; it can mean both a single copy and a full edition. See also *codex*.

catalog(ue) Greek κατά (*kata*) 'down' and λέγειν (*legein*) 'pick, choose' combined to form κατάλογος (*katalogos*) 'register, list', which made its way into Latin as *catalogus*, then into French as *catalogue*. When it appeared in English in 1460 it meant any list; since the 1660s it has implied "systematic or methodical arrangement, alphabetical or other order." The French phrase *catalogue raisonné* is sometimes used in English for a systematic list of all the works of an artist.

chronology Χρόνος (*chronos*) is Greek for "time"; λογία (*logia*) has many meanings, but "discourse" is one. *Chronology* has long meant the understanding of the passage of time, but since the seventeenth century, at least in English, it has also meant a timeline, a list of events arranged in chronological order.

codex Latin *caudex* means tree trunk, or a tablet made from its wood. Eventually the word came to mean a book formed by hinged leaves joined along a spine, as opposed to a scroll. The word *codex* is also the source of the word *code*, in the sense of both "legal code" and "cipher."

companion See *vade mecum*.

concordance From Latin *concors* 'concord, agreement'. Originally a collection of parallel passages "in concord" with one another. The *OED*'s definition of the modern sense is elegant: "An alphabetical arrangement of the principal words contained in a book, with citations of the passages in which they occur."

corpus The Latin word for "body" has expanded to mean "A body or complete collection of writings or the like; the whole body of literature on any subject" (*OED*). In the 1950s, another sense arose: "The body of written or spoken material upon which a linguistic analysis is based" (*OED*). *Corpus linguistics* refers to studies based on a defined collection of texts, like the 350-million-word *Russian National Corpus*, the 650-million-word *Bank of English*, the 2.5-billion-word *Oxford English Corpus*, or the 4-billion-word *Deutsches Referenzkorpus*.

database Latin *data* 'things given' started being used in English in the seventeenth century. *Base*, from Latin *basis* 'lowest point', started being used in English for architectural foundations in the fourteenth century. The two words were first combined in Harvard's *Quarterly Journal of Economics* in 1955, which called for a "data-base . . . for this kind of stabilization policy." Soon it was understood to signify structured information stored in a computer.

definition Latin *finis* means end or boundary; *definire* is to terminate something—to mark its boundaries. That was one meaning of *define* when it was used by Chaucer in 1384, but he also used it to mean "To state exactly what (a thing) is; to set forth or explain the essential nature of." The noun *definition* followed quickly. Lexicographers and philosophers of language argue over whether they provide true *definitions* or merely *explanations*.

dictionary Latin *dico* means "I say"; speech is *dictio*; spoken things are *dictiones*. In 1225, an English monk, Joannes de Garlandia, coined the Latin word *dictionarius* to refer to a collection of words. The Romance languages inherited the term, as in French *dictionnaire*, Italian *dizionario*, and Spanish *diccionario*. They provide information about words—generally the grammatical classes to which a word belongs, its origin or etymology, and one or more definitions. Dictionaries can be *monolingual, bilingual,* or *polyglot*; they can be *general* or *specialized*; they can be *synchronic* (looking at the language at one moment) or *diachronic* (looking at language change over time). Other terms for what we call a *dictionary* have included *abecedarium, alphabetum* or *alphabet, alvearium* or *alveary, biblioteca, declaration, descriptio, expositor, glossarium* or *glossary, hortus, lexicon, liber floridus, manipulus, medulla, promptuarium, promptorium, repertorium, summa, tabula, terminarius, thesaurus* or *thrésor* or *treasury, vocabularius* or *vocabulary, vulgaria,* or *wordbook*. The word *dictionary* is also sometimes used for more encyclopedic collections, as with a *biographical dictionary*.

directory The classical Latin *dirigere* means "to direct"; in the Middle Ages, something that helps to direct—to give directions—became known as a *directorium*. James Harrison made it an English word in 1543 when he promised his book would include "An alphabetycall dyrectorye or Table." The word has been applied to many varieties of reference books, especially guides to authorized prayers in the seventeenth century and "lists of the inhabitants of any locality, with their addresses and occupations" in the eighteenth. Telephone numbers were added to directories early in the twentieth century.

enchiridion The Greek χείρ (*kheir* or *chir*) means "hand"—the same root appears in *chiropractor* (one who works with his hands) and even in *surgeon*, which was once spelled *chirurgeon*. An *enchiridion* is therefore something small that goes in the hand—a handbook. In 1541, Miles Coverdale suggested that in compiling the first five books of the Bible, Moses made "an enchiridion and sum of all the acts of his time."

encyclopedia From Greek ἐγκύκλιος παιδεία (*enkuklios paideia*). The -*cyc*- root is from Greek κύκλος (*kyklos*) 'circle', and the -*ped*- or -*paed*- root is from παιδεία (*paideia*), ultimately from παῖς (*pais*) 'child', which means education or child rearing; the same root appears in *pediatrician* and *pedagogy*. The late Latin word *encyclopaedia* was long assumed to mean "the circle of learning" or "the circle of the sciences," but it actually meant something like "rounded education." Not until 1644 did the English use it to refer to a kind of book.

entry French *entrer* comes from Latin *intrare* 'go into'. The noun *entry* 'that by which any place is entered' appears in 1297, and 'the action of coming or going in' in 1330. A few decades later clerks could *enter* names and numbers into records, and the things so registered have been called *entries* since 1556.

etymology In Hellenistic Greek, ἔτυμον (*etymon*) is the "true" or literal sense of a word. It got picked up in postclassical Latin, where it meant "word" more generally. *Etymology*, which started being used as an English word a little before 1400, is the study of word origins.

folio From Latin *folium* 'leaf', referring to the leaves of a book. A folio is the largest format of codex book, with sheets folded just once before being bound. A typical folio book is 15–20" (38–50 cm) tall, though a so-called "elephant folio" can be as tall as 50" (127 cm). Other formats are smaller: a *quarto*, with the sheets folded twice, is typically about 12" (30 cm) tall, and an *octavo*, with the sheets folded three times, about 9" (23 cm) tall.

gazetteer A *gazetta* was a small coin used in early modern Venice. The Italian word made its way into French and then English. Because, some speculate, Venetian newspapers typically cost one *gazetta*, it came to mean a news sheet, and a *gazetteer* was a news reporter. In 1692, Laurence Echard used the word in the title of *The Gazetteer's, or, Newsman's Interpreter: Being a Geographical Index*, and the term stuck for geographical dictionaries.

glossary Greek γλῶσσα (*glossa*) means "tongue" or "language." Originally a *gloze*, *glose*, or *gloss* was a word written in the margins or between the lines of a manuscript to explain the text. These marginal or interlinear explanations in the Bible or in legal texts were *glosses*; when they were all collected together, to give a list of words and passages that needed explanation, they became a *glossary*.

ghost word A word that appears in a dictionary accidentally, without having any existence in the larger world. See chapter 10½.

handbook The English was inspired by Latin *liber manualis* (the origin of our word *manual*) and Greek *enchiridion*. *Handbook* first showed up in English around the year 1000, when the monk Byrhtferð of Ramsey wrote of his "enchiridion (þæt ys manualis on Lyden and handboc on Englisc)"—"that is, *manual* in Latin and *handbook* in English." Around 1538 the author of the *Encheridyon of a Spyrytuall Lyfe* explained the name: "It is called encheridion, in englysh, an hand booke, not only bycause it is small and portatyue [portable], but bycause it is (for the fruyte and vtylite [utility] therin) worthy and necessary to be had in in euery mans hande." Related words appear in many Germanic languages: Dutch *handboek*, German *Handbuch*, Old Icelandic *handbók*.

headword An obvious etymology from a pair of English words for the word that serves as a heading in a reference book—the word being defined in a dictionary, the entry being discussed in an encyclopedia. Headwords are often typographically distinctive (capitals, boldface, indented, large type) to facilitate skimming. Sometimes known as a *lemma* (plural *lemmas* or *lemmata*), from Greek λῆμμα 'something taken'. Headwords are often reduced to their most basic form: *approvingly* appears under *approve*. The process of reducing words to this form is called *lemmatization*.

herbal Latin *herba* 'grass, green crops' became French *erbe* became Middle English *erbe* around 1290, a plant without a woody stem. In medieval Latin a book about plants was a *liber herbalis*, which led to the practice of referring to an English book about plants—especially the medical uses of plants—as a *herbal* in 1516.

index Latin *index* 'forefinger' comes from *dic-* 'to point out'—compare *indicate*. English picked up the forefinger meaning at the end of the fourteenth century; it came to mean any sort of pointer, literal or metaphorical, at the end of the sixteenth century. One of those "pointers" was the list of names or subjects that "pointed" to the places they appeared in a book. Early modern books often had more than one index: an *index nominum* for names, an *index locorum* for places, and an *index rerum* for subjects.

information A complicated word with a complicated history—as James Gleick notes, the revised *OED* entry for the word "now runs 9,400 words, the length of a novella. It is a sort of masterpiece—an adventure in cultural history." The Latin root *forma* 'shape, appearance' led to *informare* 'to give form to, to shape'. An act of giving shape is Latin *informatio*, which could also mean "teaching"—the word's first English meaning, starting in the late fourteenth century. From there it came to encompass knowledge or news more generally. Mathematicians came up with formal definitions starting in the early twentieth century, and they discovered surprising connections between information and entropy.

latent words Latin *latens* 'lurking, hiding' gives us *latent*. Some lexicographers use the term *latent words* to refer to those for which there are no records of their ever having existed, especially derived forms. *Restaurantlike, pentagonality, liturgicalness,* and *uncruciform* are perfectly plausible English words—they are not *ghost words*, which are the result of accident—but they may never have been used in the real world. Some dictionaries, eager to run up their word count for advertising purposes, list many such words.

lexicographer A postclassical Greek word, from λεξικόν (see below) and γράφειν (*graphein*) 'to write'. Since 1658, *lexicographer* has been the English word for a writer of dictionaries. Samuel Johnson's famous definition may be the final word on the subject: "a writer of dictionaries; a harmless drudge, that busies himself in tracing the original, and detailing the signification of words."

lexicon We can trace it all the way back to Greek λέγειν (*legein*) 'to speak'; from that root came the noun λέξις (*lexis*) 'word, phrase' and the adjective λεξικός (*lexikos*) 'related to words'. A βιβλίον λεξικόν (*biblion lexikon*) was a wordbook. Today *lexicon* is often used interchangeably with *dictionary*, although in German-speaking countries it is often used for encyclopedic works.

manual See *handbook*.

mountweazel An invented entry in a reference book, giving information on something that does not exist. See chapter 10½.

pharmacopoeia Greek φάρμακον (*pharmakon*) has a disconcerting range of meanings, running from "medicine" to "poison"; ποιεῖν (*poiein*) means "to make." The art of compounding drugs became *pharmacopée* in French in 1571, and by 1618 a book listing approved drugs and how to make them was known as a *pharmacopoeia* or *pharmacopeia*.

reference The verb *refer* comes from Middle French *referer* or *referir* 'put in connection', which in turn comes from Latin *re* 'back' + *ferre* 'bear, carry'. The verb showed up in English in the late fourteenth century and got its meaning of "consult" in 1574. The noun *reference* was used in English from the end of the sixteenth century, and the compound *reference book* from 1771.

table One of the oldest words in English. Latin *tabula*, its source, had a range of meanings, including a piece of furniture with legs supporting a flat surface and a tablet on which laws were written. It already meant "a systematic arrangement of numbers, words, symbols, etc., in a definite and compact form" in the Old English period, around the year 1000.

thesaurus Greek θησαυρός (*thesauros*) is a treasury or a storehouse—it is the root of *treasure*. It appears in the titles of a number of word-books: Thomas Cooper's Latin–English dictionary of 1565 was titled *Thesaurus linguæ romanæ et britannicæ* and Henri Estienne published his *Thesaurus linguae graecae* in 1572. It took on new life, and a new meaning, when Peter Mark Roget used it to refer to his thematically organized dictionary in 1852.

union catalog Latin *unus* 'one' produced *unio* 'oneness, unity.' A *union catalog(ue)* brings together the holdings of many libraries into one sequence.

vade mecum The Latin is simple enough: "come with me." An easily carried book that promises to guide its reader through complexities.

vocabulary Latin *vocare* 'to call or name' gives *vocabulum* 'something called or named', and a collection of these *vocables* is a *vocabulary*. Today it often means a list of words a beginner is striving to learn, or the total number of words an individual knows, but it is also used as a synonym for *dictionary* or *lexicon*.

volume Latin *volumen* comes from *volvere* 'to roll'; it recalls the days when books were scrolls. Today *volume* usually refers to a codex. Because there is a practical limit to how many leaves can be bound together, long reference books often fill multiple volumes. A near synonym, and the word used in the Romance languages, *tome*, is from τόμος (*tomos*) 'section of a book', itself derived from τέμνειν (*temnein*) 'to cut'.

wordbook The Germanic roots *word* and *book* are both very ancient, but it took until 1598 for John Florio to combine them as *word-book*. In English, says the *OED*, "The term is sometimes used specifically to avoid the implication of completeness or elaboration of treatment characteristic of a dictionary or lexicon." Dutch *woordboek* and German *Wörterbuch*, though, have no such connotations.

ACKNOWLEDGMENTS

To DO THIS properly, I'd have to thank pretty much everyone I've spoken to in the last half dozen years, since there's hardly a soul who has escaped my requests for suggestions. But I'll single out a few for particular thanks: Lauren Avirom, David Azzolina, Celia Barnes, Lisa Berglund, Kevin Berland, Brycchan Carey, Paul Charosh, Elizabeth Denlinger, Jonathan Ellis, Mimi Ezust, Janet Ing Freeman, Cynthia Gibson, Anthony Grafton, Tom Guilbert, Steve Gustafson, Rachel Hadas, Kristine Haugen, Joe Holub, Simon Hornblower, Jacqueline Hylkema, Dale Ireland, Jan Lewis, Tabitha McIntosh, James J. O'Donnell, Ann Peters, John Pollack, Jessica Richard, Rebecca Shapiro, Ammon Shea, Jesse Sheidlower, Peter Sokolowski, Peter Stallybrass, Kory Stamper, Tim Stewart-Winter, John Stone, Christopher Stray, Dan Traister, Sarah Werner, Phil Yeagle, and Ben Zimmer.

My research assistant, Rachel Niemczyk, has been indispensable, helping me collect and organize close to a million words of notes.

As always, it has been a pleasure to work with George Gibson at Bloomsbury, for whom I hope the chapter "Overlong and Overdue" has served to put my own missed deadlines in some kind of perspective.

BIBLIOGRAPHY

Abbott, John P., and Allan G. Scherlen. "National Union Catalog: Asset or Albatross?" *Proceedings of the Charleston Library Conference*, 2012. www.loc.gov/coll/nucmc/oclcsearch.html.

Académie Française. *Le Dictionnaire de l'Académie françoise: Dedié au Roy*. 2 vols. Paris, 1694.

Adams, Douglas. *The Hitchhiker's Guide to the Galaxy*. London: Pan, 1979.

Adams, Michael. "The Dictionary Society of North America: A History of the Early Years (Part I)." *Dictionaries: Journal of the Dictionary Society of North America* 35 (2014): 1–35.

Alford, Henry. "Not a Word." *New Yorker*, August 29, 2005.

Alston, Robin, and M. J. Jannetta. *Bibliography, Machine-Readable Cataloguing and the ESTC*. London: British Library, 1978.

Anderson, Benedict. *Imagined Communities: Reflections on the Origin and Spread of Nationalism*. Rev. ed. London: Verso, 2006.

Anderson, Jennifer Joline. *Wikipedia: The Company and Its Founders*. Edina, MN: ABDO, 2011.

Anon. Review of Charles Knight, *The English Cyclopædia* (1861). *London Quarterly Review* 113 (April 1863): 183–201.

Anon. Review of Grimm and Grimm, *Deutsches Wörterbuch*; Jakob Grimm, *Deutsche Grammatik*; Jakob Grimm, *Geschichte der deutschen Sprache*. *North American Review* 100, no. 207 (April 1865): 390–422.

Anon. Review of *Schott's Food & Drink Miscellany*. *Publisher's Weekly* 251, no. 24 (June 14, 2004): 52.

[Apperson, G. L.] H., S.J. "Blunders in Our English Dictionaries." *Notes and Queries*, 6th ser., 2 (August 21, 1880): 142.

Appiah, Kwame Anthony, and Henry Louis Gates, Jr., eds. *Africana: The*

Encyclopedia of the African and African American Experience. New York: Basic Books, 1999.

Aristotle's Master-Piece; or, The Secrets of Generation Display'd in All the Parts Thereof. London, 1684.

Aycock, Roy E. "Lord Byron and Bayle's 'Dictionary.'" *Yearbook of English Studies* 5 (1975): 142–52.

Ayers, Phoebe. "If You Liked Britannica, You'll Love Wikipedia." http://www.nytimes.com/roomfordebate/2012/03/14/britannica-define-outdated/if-you-liked-britannica-youll-love-wikipedia.

Baker, Nicholson. "The Charms of Wikipedia." *The New York Review of Books*, March 20, 2008. http://www.nybooks.com/articles/archives/2008/mar/20/the-charms-of-wikipedia/.

——. "Google's Earth." Review of Ken Auletta, *Googled: The End of the World as We Know It. New York Times Book Review*, November 29, 2009, p. 10.

Bakewell, K.G.B. *A Manual of Cataloguing Practice.* Oxford: Pergamon, 1972.

Barbour, Reid. *Sir Thomas Browne: A Life.* Oxford: Oxford University Press, 2013.

Bartlett, John. *A Collection of Familiar Quotations.* Cambridge, MA, 1855.

Bayle, Pierre. *Dictionnaire historique et critique.* Rotterdam, 1697.

Béjoint, Henri. *The Lexicography of English: From Origins to Present.* Oxford: Oxford University Press, 2010.

Berger, Warren. "What's New in Encyclopedias: A Buying Boom Pulls Publishers into the Fold." *New York Times*, May 28, 1989.

Berrera, Francisco. *Abecedario en la lengua que dizen qiche hecho por Mr. Francisco Barrera . . .* Princeton University Library MS Co744 (Garrett-Gates Meso-american Manuscripts, no. 160).

Betham, Matilda. *A Biographical Dictionary of the Celebrated Women of Every Age and Country.* London, 1804.

"The Big Red Book." *St. Petersburg Times* (Florida), November 18, 1991.

Bing, Peter. "The Unruly Tongue: Philitas of Cos as Scholar and Poet." *Classical Philology* 98, no. 4 (2003): 330–48.

Black, Jeremy A., Andrew George, and J. N. Postgate. *A Concise Dictionary of Akkadian.* Wiesbaden: Otto Harrassowitz, 1999.

Blom, Philipp. *Encyclopédie: The Triumph of Reason in an Unreasonable Age*. London: Fourth Estate, 2004.

Blount, Thomas. *Glossographia; or, A Dictionary, Interpreting All Such Hard Words, Whether Hebrew, Greek, Latin, Italian, Spanish, French, Teutonick, Belgick, British or Saxon; as Are Now Used in Our Refined English Tongue*. London, 1656.

——. *A World of Errors Discovered in The New World of Words*. London, 1672.

Bocabularia en lengua Quiche y Castellana. Princeton University Library MS C0744 (Garrett-Gates Mesoamerican Manuscripts, no. 161).

Bol'shaia sovetskaia entsiklopediia. 65 vols. Moscow: Sovetskaia entsiklopediia, 1926–47.

Boswell, James. *Boswell's Life of Samuel Johnson, LL.D.* Edited by G. B. Hill, revised by L. F. Powell. 6 vols. Oxford: Clarendon Press, 1934–64.

——. *Boswell in Holland, 1763–1764*. Edited by Frederick A. Pottle. New York: McGraw-Hill, 1952.

Boyd, Brian. *Vladimir Nabokov: The American Years*. Princeton: Princeton University Press, 1991.

Braudel, Fernand. *Civilization and Capitalism, 15th–18th Century*. Translated by Siân Reynolds. 3 vols. Berkeley: University of California Press, 1982–84.

Brewer, E. C. *Brewer's Dictionary of Phrase and Fable: Centenary Edition*. Edited by Ivor H. Evans. New York: Harper & Row, 1970.

——. *Dictionary of Phrase and Fable*. London: Cassell, 1870.

Briggs, Henry. *Arithmetica logarithmica sive Logarithmorum chiliades triginta*. London, 1624.

Brown, Mark. "Stumped No More: Wisden Almanack Helps British Library Date Pinter Papers." *Guardian*, November 27, 2014.

Brown, Thomas. *Bath: A Satirical Novel*. 4th ed. 3 vols. London, 1818.

Browne, Thomas. *Pseudodoxia Epidemica; or, Enquiries into Very Many Received Tenents, and Commonly Presumed Truths*. London, 1646.

——. *Pseudodoxia Epidemica*. 4th ed. London, 1658.

Bryant, Walter William. *A History of Astronomy*. London, 1907.

Buchwald, Jed Z., and Mordechai Feingold. *Newton and the Origin of Civilization*. Princeton: Princeton University Press, 2013.

Burke, Peter. *A Social History of Knowledge: From Gutenberg to Diderot*. Malden, MA: Polity Press, 2000.

Burns, William E. *Science in the Enlightenment: An Encyclopedia.* Santa Barbara: ABC-CLIO , 2003.

Bush, Vannevar. "As We May Think." *Atlantic Monthly.* July 1945. http://www .theatlantic.com/magazine/print/1945/07/as-we-may-think/303881/.

Calmet, Antoine Augustin. *Dictionnaire historique, critique, chronologique, géographique et littéral de la Bible.* 4 vols. Paris, 1720–21.

Cameron, Malcolm Laurence. *Anglo-Saxon Medicine.* Cambridge: Cambridge University Press, 1993.

Campbell, James W. P., and Will Pryce. *The Library: A World History.* Chicago: University of Chicago Press, 2013.

Campbell-Kelly, M., M. Croarken, R. Flood, and E. Robson, eds. *The History of Mathematical Tables: From Sumer to Spreadsheets.* Oxford: Oxford University Press, 2003.

Campion, Mukti Jain. "Hobson-Jobson: The Words English Owes to India." *BBC News Magazine,* July 11, 2012. http://www.bbc.com/news/ magazine-18796493.

Cannon, Annie Jump. "Classifying the Stars." In *Galileo's Commandment: 2,500 Years of Great Science Writing,* pp. 161–65. Edited by E. B. Bolles. New York: W. H. Freeman, 1997.

Carawan, Edwin. *Rhetoric and the Law of Draco.* Oxford: Oxford University Press, 1998.

Carey, Benedict. "Revising Book on Disorders of the Mind." *New York Times,* February 10, 2010.

Carr, Nicholas. "Is Google Making Us Stupid? What the Internet Is Doing to Our Brains." *Atlantic Monthly,* July–August 2008. http://www.theatlantic .com/magazine/archive/2008/07/is-google-making-us-stupid/306868/.

Carranco, Lynwood. "Let's Stop Worshipping the Dictionary." *Clearing House* 29, no. 2 (October 1954): 72–76.

Carslaw, H. S. "The Discovery of Logarithms by Napier." *Mathematical Gazette* 8, no. 117 (May 1915): 76–84; no. 118 (July 1915): 115–19.

Cartwright, Samuel. "Diseases and Peculiarities of the Negro Race." *Debow's Review* 11 (1851): 331–36.

Cassiodorus. *An Introduction to Divine and Human Readings.* Translated by Leslie Webber Jones. New York: Columbia University Press, 1946.

———. *Institutiones*. Translated by James W. and Barbara Halporn. http://faculty.georgetown.edu/jod/inst-trans.html

Catalogue of Printed Books in the Library of the British Museum. 95 vols. London, 1881–1900.

The Catholic Encyclopedia. Edited by Charles G. Herbermann et al. 16 vols. New York: Appleton, 1907–14.

The Catholic Encyclopedia and Its Makers. New York: Encyclopedia Press, 1917.

Cavendish, Richard. "Publication of the *Guinness Book of Records*: August 27th, 1955." *History Today* 55, no. 8 (August 2005).

Cawdrey, Robert. *A Table Alphabeticall*. London, 1604.

Čermák, F. "Czech Lexicography." In *Encyclopedia of Language & Linguistics*. Edited by Keith Brown. 2nd ed. 14 vols. Amsterdam: Elsevier, 2006.

Chambers, Ephraim. *Cyclopædia; or, An Universal Dictionary of Arts and Sciences*. 2 vols. London, 1728.

Chambers, Robert. *The Book of Days: A Miscellany of Popular Antiquities in Connection with the Calendar, Including Anecdote, Biography, & History, Curiosities of Literature, and Oddities of Human Life and Character*. 2 vols. London and Edinburgh, 1832.

Chang, Kenneth. "How Many Stars? Three Times as Many as We Thought, Report Says." *New York Times*, December 1, 2010.

Chaplin, A. H. *GK: 150 Years of the General Catalogue of Printed Books in the British Museum*. Brookfield, VT: Scolar Press, 1987.

Chemical Rubber Company. *Handbook of Chemistry and Physics: A Ready-Reference Pocket Book of Chemical and Physical Data*. Cleveland: Chemical Rubber Company, 1913.

Clark, Anna. "Female Sexuality." In *The Routledge History of Women in Europe since 1700*, pp. 54–92. Edited by Deborah Simonton. London: Routledge, 2006.

Clark, Randall Baldwin. "Platonic Love in a Colorado Courtroom: Martha Nussbaum, John Finnis, and Plato's *Laws* in *Evans v. Romer*." *Yale Journal of Law & the Humanities* 12, no. 1 (2000).

Clark, Ronald W. *The Huxleys*. New York: McGraw-Hill, 1968.

Classen, Carl Joachim. "*Vita Brevis—Ars Longa*: Pauly's Beginnings and Wissowa–Kroll–Ziegler's Monumental Achievement." *Eikasmos* 21 (2010): 424–31.

Cochrane, Kerry L. "'The Most Famous Book of Its Kind': *Bartlett's Familiar Quotations.*" In Retting, *Distinguished Classics*, pp. 9–17.

Cohen, H. M. "London Letter." *Lancet-Clinic* 102, no. 6 (August 8, 1914): 143–44.

Cohen, Yoram, and Sivan Kedar. "Teacher–Student Relationships: Two Case Studies." In *The Oxford Handbook of Cuneiform Culture*, edited by Karen Radner and Eleanor Robson, pp. 229–47. Oxford: Oxford University Press, 2011.

Colebrooke, Henry Thomas. "Preface to the Author's Edition of the Amara Kosha." In *Miscellaneous Essays.* 2 vols. New ed. London, 1873, 2:46–56.

Colgan, Richard. *Advice to the Healer: On the Art of Caring.* 2nd ed. New York: Springer, 2013.

Collins, Tim. *Are You a Geek? 10^3 Ways to Find Out.* New York: Bantam, 2006.

Collison, Robert. *Encyclopaedias: Their History throughout the Ages.* 2nd ed. New York and London: Hafner Publishing, 1966.

———. *A History of Foreign-Language Dictionaries.* London: Andre Deutsch, 1982.

Commager, Henry Steele. Introduction to *Noah Webster's American Spelling Book.* New York: Columbia University Teachers College, 1958.

Considine, John. *Academy Dictionaries, 1600–1800.* Cambridge: Cambridge University Press, 2014.

———. *Dictionaries in Early Modern Europe: Lexicography and the Making of Heritage.* Cambridge: Cambridge University Press, 2008.

———. "The Lexicographer as Hero: Samuel Johnson and Henri Estienne." *Philological Quarterly* 79, no. 2 (Spring 2000): 205–24.

Cosmas Indicopleustes. *Aigyptiou Monachou Christianike Topographia.* Translated by J. W. McCrindle. London: Hakluyt Society, 1897.

Cottingham, John, ed. *The Cambridge Companion to Descartes.* Cambridge: Cambridge University Press, 1992.

Coughlan, Sean. "Dictionary Reaches Final Definition after Century." *BBC News.* http://www.bbc.com/news/education-28952646.

Cruden, Alexander. *A Complete Concordance to the Holy Scriptures of the Old and New Testament.* London, 1738.

Cullen, L. M. *A History of Japan, 1582–1941: Internal and External Worlds.* Cambridge: Cambridge University Press, 2003.

Cutter, Charles A. "The New Catalogue of Harvard College Library." *North American Review* 108, no. 222 (January 1869): 96–129.

d'Alembert, Jean le Rond. *Preliminary Discourse to the Encyclopedia of Diderot.* Translated by Richard N. Schwab. Indianapolis: Bobbs-Merrill, 1963.

Datta, Amaresh, ed. *The Encyclopaedia of Indian Literature.* 6 vols. New Delhi: Sahitya Akademi, 1988.

Davis, Elisabeth B., and Diane Schmidt. *Guide to Information Sources in the Botanical Sciences.* 2nd ed. Englewood, CO: Libraries Unlimited, 1996.

Davis, L. J. "The Encyclopedia of Insanity: A Psychiatric Handbook Lists a Madness for Everyone." *Harper's* (February 1997): 61–66.

Day, George S. *The Market Driven Organization: Understanding, Attracting, and Keeping Valuable Customers.* New York: Free Press, 1999.

Delitzsch, Friedrich. "Zur juristischen Litteratur Babyloniens." *Beiträge sur Assyriologie* 4 (February 1899): 78–87.

Denlinger, Elizabeth C. "The Garment and the Man: Masculine Desire in *Harris's List of Covent-Garden Ladies*, 1764–1793." *Journal of the History of Sexuality* 11 (2002): 357–94.

DeZelar-Tiedman, Christine. "The Proportion of NUC Pre-56 Titles Represented in the RLIN and OCLC Databases Compared: A Follow-Up to the Beall/Kafadar Study." *College & Research Libraries* 69, no. 5 (2008): 401–6.

Diagnostic & Statistical Manual, Mental Disorders. Washington, D.C.: American Psychiatric Association Mental Hospital Service, 1952.

Dickens, Charles. *David Copperfield.* London, 1850.

Diderot, Denis, and Jean le Rond d'Alembert, eds. *Encyclopédie, ou dictionnaire raisonné des sciences, des arts et des métiers, par une société de gens de lettres.* Paris, 1751–72.

Dilke, O.A.W. "The Culmination of Greek Cartography in Ptolemy." In J. B. Harley and David Woodward, eds., *The History of Cartography,* 6 vols., 1:177–200. Chicago: University of Chicago Press, 1987.

Dille, Catherine. "The *Dictionary* in Abstract." In *Anniversary Essays on Johnson's "Dictionary,"* pp. 198–211. Edited by Jack Lynch and Anne McDermott. Cambridge: Cambridge University Press, 2005.

Disraeli, Isaac. *Curiosities of Literature.* 5th ed. 3 vols. London, 1807.

Dodd, William. *The Beauties of Shakespear: Regularly Selected from Each Play.* 2 vols. London, 1752.

Doody, Aude. "Pliny's Natural History: Enkuklios Paideia and the Ancient Encyclopedia." *Journal of the History of Ideas* 70, no. 1 (2009): 1–21.

Dressman, Michael. "Walt Whitman's Plans for the Perfect Dictionary." *Studies in the American Renaissance* 3 (1979): 457–74.

Du Bois, W. E. B. *The Correspondence of W.E.B. Du Bois.* Edited by Herbert Aptheker. 3 vols. Amherst: University of Massachusetts Press, 1973–78.

Dyson, Freeman. "How We Know" (review of James Gleick, *The Information*). *New York Review of Books* 58, no. 4 (March 10, 2011): 8–12.

Easterling, P. E., and Bernard M. W. Knox, eds. *The Cambridge History of Classical Literature*, vol. 1, *Greek Literature.* Cambridge: Cambridge University Press, 1985.

Edwards, Chilperic. *The Oldest Laws in the World: Being a Complete Translation of the Great Babylonian Inscription Discovered at Susa.* London: Watts & Co., 1906.

Edwards, Edward. *Chapters of the Biographical History of the French Academy.* London, 1864.

Einbinder, Harvey. *The Myth of the Britannica.* London: MacGibbon & Kee, 1964.

Eliot, George. *Middlemarch: A Study of Provincial Life.* London, 1874.

Encyclopædia Britannica; or, A Dictionary of Arts and Sciences, Compiled upon a New Plan. 3 vols. Edinburgh, 1768–71.

Encyclopedia of World Biography. 2nd ed. Detroit: Gale, 2004.

The Englishman in Paris: A Satirical Novel. 3 vols. London, 1819.

Ferlinghetti, Lawrence, and Nancy Joyce Peters. *Literary San Francisco: A Pictorial History from Its Beginnings to the Present Day.* San Francisco: City Lights, 1980.

[Fishlake, J. R.] "Greek-and-English Lexicography" (review of six Greek lexicons). *London Quarterly Review (American Edition)* 150 (March 1845): 157–74.

Fissell, Mary E. "Making a Masterpiece: The Aristotle Texts in Vernacular Medical Culture." In *Right Living: An Anglo-American Tradition of Self-Help Medicine and Hygiene*, pp. 59–87. Edited by Charles E. Rosenberg. Baltimore: Johns Hopkins University Press, 2003.

Flanagan, Padraic. "RIP for OED as World's Finest Dictionary Goes out of Print." *Telegraph*, April 20, 2014.

Folsom, Ed. *Walt Whitman's Native Representations*. Cambridge: Cambridge University Press, 1994.

Franklin, H. Bruce, ed. *Prison Writing in 20th-Century America*. New York: Penguin, 1988.

Freeman, Janet Ing. "Jack Harris and 'Honest Ranger': The Publication and Prosecution of *Harris's List of Covent-Garden Ladies*, 1760–95." *Library* 13, no. 4 (December 2012): 423–56.

Furetière, Antoine. *Nouveau recueil des factums du procez d'entre défunt Mr. l'abé Furetière*. 2 vols. Amsterdam, 1694.

Gagarin, Michael. *Writing Greek Law*. New York: Cambridge University Press, 2008.

Gibbon, Edward. *Decline and Fall of the Roman Empire*. Edited by J. B. Bury. 7 vols. London: Methuen, 1909–14.

Giles, Jim. "Internet Encyclopaedias Go Head to Head." *Nature* 438 (December 15, 2005): 900–901.

Gleick, James. *The Information: A History, a Theory, a Flood*. New York: Pantheon Books, 2011.

———. "The Information Palace." *New York Review Blog*, December 8, 2010.

Goodman, Lenn E. *Avicenna*. London: Routledge, 1992.

Govan, Fiona. "Profile: Saint Isidore—the Patron Saint of the Internet." *Telegraph*, February 18, 2011.

Gove, Philip Babock. "The History of 'Dord'." *American Speech* 29, no. 2 (1954): 136–38.

Grafton, Anthony. "Jumping through the Computer Screen." *New York Review of Books* 57, no. 20 (December 23, 2010): 95–97, 101.

Grattan-Guinness, Ivor. "The Computation Factory: De Prony's Project for Making Tables in the 1790s." In Campbell-Kelly, *The History of Mathematical Tables*, pp. 104–21.

Graves, Charles L. *The Life & Letters of Sir George Grove, C.B.* London: Macmillan, 1903.

Gray, Henry, and Henry Vandyke Cater. *Anatomy Descriptive and Surgical*. London, 1858.

Greene, Edward Lee. *Landmarks of Botanical History*. Washington, D.C.: Smithsonian, 1909.

Grier, David Alan. "Table Making for the Relief of Labour." In Campell-Kelly, *The History of Mathematical Tables*, pp. 265–92.

Grimm, Jacob, and Wilhelm Grimm. *Deutsches Wörterbuch*. 32 vols. Berlin, 1852–1971.

Grotzinger, Laurel. Review of *Merck Index*. *American Reference Books Annual* 38 (2007): 617.

Grove, Sir George. *Beethoven and His Nine Symphonies*. 2nd ed. London, 1796.

——. *A Dictionary of Music and Musicians*. 4 vols. London: Macmillan, 1879–90.

Gutin, JoAnn. "How Big Is a D-Cup? A Trove of Trivia—with Heft." *New York Observer*, September 8, 2003, p. 22.

H., N. *The Ladies Dictionary; Being a General Entertainment for the Fair-Sex*. London, 1694.

Hacking, Ian. "Lost in the Forest." *London Review of Books* 35, no. 15 (August 8, 2013), pp. 7–8.

Hahn, Walther von. *Fachkommunikation: Entwicklung, linguistische Konzepte, betriebliche Beispiele*. Berlin: Walter de Gruyter, 1983.

Haigh, Gideon. *Silent Revolutions: Writings on Cricket History*. London: Aurum, 2006.

Hanson, Bertil L. "Harnessing the Guinness Effect." *Journal of Public Policy* 2, no. 2 (May 1982): 165–77.

Harley, J. B. "The Map and the Development of the History of Cartography." In J. B. Harley and David Woodward, eds., *The History of Cartography*, 6 vols., 1:1–42. Chicago: University of Chicago Press, 1987.

Harris's List of Covent-Garden Ladies. London, 1761.

Hartmann, R.R.K., ed. *The History of Lexicography*. Philadelphia: John Benjamins, 1986.

Harwood, Jeremy. *To the Ends of the Earth: 100 Maps That Changed the World*. Cincinnati: F&W Publications, 2006.

Hausmann, F. J., ed. *Wörterbücher: Ein internationales Handbuch zur Lexikographie*. 3 vols. Berlin: De Gruyter, 1989–91.

Hayman, P.M.C. "E. Cobham Brewer LL.D.: A Brief Memoir by His

Grandson." In *Brewer's Dictionary of Phrase and Fable: Centenary Edition*, pp. vii–xii.

Headrick, Daniel R. *When Information Came of Age: Technologies of Knowledge in the Age of Reason and Revolution, 1700–1850*. Oxford: Oxford University Press, 2000.

Hedrick, Charles W., Jr. *History and Silence: Purge and Rehabilitation of Memory in Late Antiquity*. Austin: University of Texas Press, 2000.

Hill, G. B., ed. *Johnsonian Miscellanies*. 2 vols. Oxford, 1897.

Hirsch, E. D. "Culture and Literacy." *Journal of Basic Literacy* 3, no. 1 (1980): 27–47.

Hogg, Gordon E. "Bolshaia Sovetskaia Entsiklopediia." In *Encyclopedia of Library and Information Science*, edited by Allen Kent, vol. 61, supplement 24 (New York: Marcel Dekker, 1998), pp. 17–61.

Hornblower, Simon, and Antony Spawforth. *The Oxford Classical Dictionary*. 3rd ed. Oxford: Oxford University Press, 1996.

Hoyle, Edmond. *An Essay Towards Making the Doctrine of Chances Easy to Those Who Understand Vulgar Arithmetick Only: To Which Is Added, Some Useful Tables on Annuities for Lives, &c. &c. &c.* London, 1754.

——. *A Short Treatise on the Game of Back-Gammon*. London, 1743.

——. *A Short Treatise on the Game of Whist: Containing the Laws of the Game: And Also, Some Rules*. London, 1742.

——. *Hoyle's Games Improved*. London, 1775.

Hoyle, Norman. "Superlatives and Compromises: The *National Union Catalog, Pre-1956 Imprints*." *RQ* 8, no. 4 (Summer 1969): 235–39.

Hume, David. *Essays, Moral and Political*. Edinburgh, 1741.

The Humours of Whist: A Dramatic Satire. London, 1743.

Index auctorum, et librorum, qui ab officio sanctæ Rom. et Vniuersalis Inquisitionis caueri ab omnibus et singulis in uniuersa Christiana Republica mandantur. Rome, 1559.

Iqbal, Muzaffar. "Avicenna." In *Encyclopedia of Science and Religion*, edited by J. Wentzel Vrede van Huyssteen. 2 vols. New York: Macmillan, 2003.

Isidore. *The Etymologies of Isidore of Seville*. Edited and translated by Stephen A. Barney, W. J. Lewis, J. A. Beach, and Oliver Berghof. Cambridge: Cambridge University Press, 2006.

Jackson, Sidney L. "Towards a History of the Encyclopedia: From Amenemope of Egypt to the Collapse of Greek in Rome." *Journal of Library History* 12, no. 4 (Fall 1977): 342–58.

Jacobs, A. J. "I Read the Encyclopaedia Britannica, and I'll Miss It." http://www.nytimes.com/roomfordebate/2012/03/14/britannica-define-outdated/i-read-the-encyclopaedia-britannica-and-ill-miss-it.

———. *The Know-It-All: One Man's Humble Quest to Become the Smartest Person in the World*. New York: Simon & Schuster, 2004.

Jagger, Graham. "The Making of Logarithm Tables." In Campbell-Kelly, *The History of Mathematical Tables*, pp. 48–77.

James, Robert. *Proposals for Printing a Medicinal Dictionary*. London, 1741.

Jarema, Morgan. "Out-of-Date Encyclopedia Sets Disappearing from Bookshelves." *Grand Rapids Press*, May 5, 2008.

Johnson, Samuel. *A Dictionary of the English Language*. 2 vols. London, 1755.

———. *The Yale Edition of the Works of Samuel Johnson*. 21 vols. to date. New Haven: Yale University Press, 1958–.

Jones, Sir William. *The Works of Sir William Jones*. 6 vols. London, 1799.

Joyce, James. *Ulysses*. Edited by Hans Walter Gabler. New York: Random House, 1986.

K., J. "Catholics and the New 'Encyclopedia Britannica.'" *The Month: A Catholic Magazine* 118 (July–December 1911): 202–03.

Kafker, Frank A. *Notable Encyclopedias of the Seventeenth and Eighteenth Centuries: Nine Predecessors of the Encyclopédie*. Oxford: Voltaire Foundation, 1982.

———. "William Smellie's Edition of the *Encyclopaedia Britannica*." In Kafker, *Notable Encyclopedias*, pp. 145–82.

Kafker, Frank A., and Jeff Loveland, eds. *The Early "Britannica": The Growth of an Outstanding Encyclopedia*. Oxford: Voltaire Foundation, 2009.

Kallendorf, Craig. "The Ancient Book." In *The Book: A Global History*, pp. 39–53. Edited by Michael F. Suarez and H. R. Woudhuysen. Oxford: Oxford University Press, 2013.

Kanas, Nick. *Star Maps: History, Artistry, and Cartography*. Berlin: Springer, 2007.

Katz, Bill, ed. *Cuneiform to Computer: A History of Reference Sources*. History of the Book, ser. 4. Lanham: Scarecrow Press, 1998.

Keller, Mary, and Chester J. Fontenot, Jr., eds. *Re-cognizing W. E. B. DuBois in the Twenty-First Century*. Macon: Mercer University Press, 2007.

Keogil, A. "The 'Encyclopedia Britannica' and the History of the Church." *The Month: A Catholic Magazine* 118 (July–December 1911): 377–88.

Kerr, Robert. *Memoirs of the Life, Writings, & Correspondence of William Smellie*. 2 vols. Edinburgh, 1811.

Khan, Aisha. *Avicenna (Ibn Sina): Muslim Physician and Philosopher of the Eleventh Century*. New York: Rosen, 2006.

Kidd, Patrick. "Don't Stop Now Is the Message: Keep On Accumulating." *Times* (London), April 5, 2013.

———. "150-Year Run and Still Not Out: Nonfiction Patrick Kidd Is Bowled Over by the History of Wisden." *Times* (London), April 13, 2013.

Knight, Amy. *Beria: Stalin's First Lieutenant*. Princeton: Princeton University Press, 1995.

Koeman, C. *The History of Abraham Ortelius and His Theatrum Orbis Terrarum*. New York: American Elsevir, 1964.

Kogan, Herman. *The Great EB: The Story of the Encyclopædia Britannica*. Chicago: University of Chicago Press, 1958.

Kołakowski, Leszek. *Main Currents of Marxism: The Founders, the Golden Age, the Breakdown*. Translated by P. S. Falla. New York: Norton, 2005.

Koning, Hans. "Onward and Upward with the Arts: The Eleventh Edition." *New Yorker*, March 2, 1981, pp. 67–79.

Krafft-Ebing, Richard von. *Psychopathia Sexualis: Mit besonderer Berücksichtigung der conträren Sexualempfindung: Eine klinisch-forensische Studie*. 2nd ed. Stuttgart, 1887.

Kroeger, Alice Bertha. *Guide to the Study and Use of Reference Books: A Manual for Librarians, Teachers and Students*. Chicago: American Library Association, 1904.

LaBelle, G. G. "Salesman [*sic*] Must Say They Are Selling Encyclopedias." Associated Press, 16 March 1982.

Landau, Sidney I. *Dictionaries: The Art & Craft of Lexicography*. New York: Charles Scribner's Sons, 1984.

Lesinski, Jeanne M. *Bill Gates: Entrepreneur and Philanthropist*. Minneapolis: Twenty-First Century Books, 2009.

Lewis, John David. *Early Greek Lawgivers*. Bristol: Bristol Classical Press, 2007.

Liddell, Henry George, and Robert Scott. *A Greek–English Lexicon, Based on the German Work of Francis Passow*. Oxford: Oxford University Press, 1843.

———. *A Greek–English Lexicon*. Rev. Henry Stuart Jones. Oxford: Clarendon Press, 1968.

Liesemer, Dirk. "Scherzeinträge in Lexika: Von Steinläusen und Kurschatten." *Der Spiegel Online*. http://www.spiegel.de/wissenschaft/mensch/scherzeintraege-in-lexika-von-steinlaeusen-und-kurschatten-a-679838.html.

Lih, Andrew. *The Wikipedia Revolution: How a Bunch of Nobodies Created the World's Greatest Encyclopedia*. New York: Hyperion, 2009.

Liptak, Adam. "Dictionary Citations by Justices Rise Sharply." *New York Times*, June 13, 2011.

Livingstone, Josephine. "How We Got Pukka: To Understand India's Influence on English, You Need a Hobson-Jobson." *Prospect*, June 28, 2013. http://www.prospectmagazine.co.uk/arts-and-books/hobson-jobson-henry-yule-kate-teltscher.

Lockman, John. *A New History of Greece: By Way of Question and Answer: In Three Parts*. London, 1750.

Lough, John. *The "Encyclopédie."* London: Longman, 1971.

Luce, Mark. "Vital Irrelevance." *Christian Science Monitor*, August 21, 2003.

Lund, Roger D. "The Eel of Science: Index Learning, Scriblerian Satire, and the Rise of Information Culture." *Eighteenth-Century Life* 22, no. 2 (1998): 18–42.

Manguel, Alberto. *The Library at Night*. New Haven: Yale University Press, 2008.

Maor, Eli. *e: The Story of a Number*. Princeton: Princeton University Press, 1994.

Maritain, Jacques. *The Dream of Descartes, Together with Some Other Essays*. Translated by Mabelle L. Andison. New York: Philosophical Library, 1944.

McArthur, Tom. *Worlds of Reference: Lexicography, Learning and Language from the Clay Tablet to the Computer*. Cambridge: Cambridge University Press, 1986.

McCrimmon, Barbara. *Power, Politics, and Print: The Publication of the British Museum Catalogue, 1881–1900*. Hamden, CT: Linnet Books, 1981.

McCrum, Robert. "God Bless You, Mr Schott, for Your Pointless yet Perfect Miscellany." *Observer*, December 8, 2002.

McWhirter, Norris, and Alan Ross McWhirter. *The Guinness Book of Records*. London: Guinness Superlatives, 1955.

Meaney, Audrey. "Variant Versions of Old English Medical Remedies and the Compilation of Bald's *Leechbook*." *Anglo-Saxon England* 13 (1984): 235–68.

Merbecke [or Marbeck], John. *A Concorda[n]ce, That Is to Saie, a Worke Wherein by the Ordre of the Letters of the A.B.C. Ye Maie Redely Finde Any Worde Conteigned in the Whole Bible, So Often as It Is There Expressed or Mencioned*. London, 1550.

Merck's Index of Fine Chemicals and Drugs for the Materia Medica and the Arts. New York: E. Merck, 1889.

Merck's Manual of the Materia Medica: Together with a Summary of Therapeutic Indications and a Classification of Medicaments: A Ready-Reference Pocket Book for the Practicing Physician. New York: Merck & Co., 1899.

Merryman, John. *The Civil Law Tradition: An Introduction to the Legal Systems of Western Europe and Latin America*. 2nd ed. Stanford: Stanford University Press, 1985.

Metz, Bernhard. "Bibliomania and the Folly of Reading." *Comparative Critical Studies* 5, nos. 2–3 (2008): 249–69.

Michaelis-Jena, Ruth. *The Brothers Grimm*. London: Routledge & Kegan Paul, 1970.

Micklethwait, David. *Noah Webster and the American Dictionary*. Jefferson, NC: McFarland, 2000.

Miller, Edward. *Prince of Librarians: The Life and Times of Antonio Panizzi of the British Museum*. Athens: Ohio University Press, 1967.

Milton, John. *Of True Religion, Haeresie, Schism, Toleration, and What Best Means May Be Us'd against the Growth of Popery*. London, 1673.

Mirashi, Vasudev Vishnu. *Literary and Historical Studies in Indology*. Delhi: Motilal Banarsidass, 1975.

Moore, Matthew. "50 Things That Are Being Killed by the Internet." *Telegraph*, September 4, 2009.

Morozov, Evgeny. "Edit This Page: Is It the End of Wikipedia?" *Boston Review* 34, no. 6 (November–December 2009). http://bostonreview.net/BR34.6/morozov.php.

Morton, Herbert C. *The Story of Webster's Third: Philip Gove's Controversial Dictionary and Its Critics.* Cambridge: Cambridge University Press, 1994.

Murray, K. M. Elisabeth. *Caught in the Web of Words: James A. H. Murray and the "Oxford English Dictionary."* New Haven: Yale University Press, 1977.

Nagashima, Daisuke. "Bilingual Lexicography with Japanese." In Hausmann, *Wörterbücher*, 3:3114–20.

National Union Catalog, Pre-1956 Imprints. 754 vols. London: Mansell, 1968–81.

New International Encyclopedia. 2nd ed. 23 vols. New York: Dodd-Mead, 1914–16.

Newman, Jeremiah Whitaker. *The Lounger's Common-Place Book; or, Alphabetical Arrangement of Miscellaneous Anecdotes: A Biographic, Political, Literary, and Satirical Compilation, in Prose and Verse.* 2 vols. London, 1792–93.

Nienhauser, William H., ed. *The Indiana Companion to Traditional Chinese Literature.* 2 vols. Bloomington: Indiana University Press, 1986–98.

Noorden Graaf, Jan. "In the Shadow of the Language Garden." In *The Emergence of the Modern Language Sciences: Historiographical Perspectives.* Edited by Sheila M. Embleton, John Earl Joseph, and Hans-Josef Niedereh. 2 vols. Philadelphia: Benjamins, 1999.

O'Donnell, James J. *Cassiodorus.* Berkeley: University of California Press, 1979.

Oldenburg, Don. "Consummate Consumer; In Re: Encyclopedias." *Washington Post*, October 17, 1989.

Oliver, Jack. "The Birth of Logarithms." *Mathematics in School* 29, no. 5 (November 2000): 9–13.

Olivier, Edith. *Alexander the Corrector.* New York: Viking Press, 1934.

Olmsted, Larry. *Getting into Guinness: One Man's Longest, Fastest, Highest Journey inside the World's Most Famous Record Book.* New York: HarperCollins, 2008.

Ong, Walter J. *Orality and Literacy: The Technologizing of the Word.* London: Methuen, 1982.

Orr, Mrs. Sutherland. *Life and Letters of Robert Browning.* 2 vols. Boston and New York, 1891.

Osselton, Noel. "Murray and His European Counterparts." In *Lexicography and the OED: Pioneers in the Untrodden Forest.* Edited by Lynda Mugglestone. Oxford: Oxford University Press, 2000, pp. 59–76.

——. "The First English Dictionary? A Sixteenth-Century Compiler at Work." In Hartmann, *History of Lexicography*, pp. 175–84.

Ostler, Nicholas. *Ad Infinitum: A Biography of Latin.* New York: Walker & Company, 2007.

Oxford English Dictionary. 13 vols. London, 1888–1933.

——. 3rd ed. http://www.oed.com.

Panizzi, Anthony. *Catalogue of Printed Books in the British Museum.* London, 1841.

Pauly, August, and Georg Wissowa. *Paulys Realencyclopädie der classischen Altertumswissenschaft: Unter Mitwirkung zahlreicher Fachgenossen.* 98 vols. Stuttgart, 1893–1980.

——. *Der neue Pauly: Enzyklopädie der Antike.* Edited by Hubert Cancik and Helmuth Schneider. Stuttgart: J. B. Metzler, 1996–2003.

Perrot, Jean, ed. *The Palace of Darius at Susa: The Great Royal Residence of Achaemenid Persia.* London: Tauris, 2013.

Phillipps, S. March, and Andrew Amos. *A Treatise on the Law of Evidence.* 8th ed. 2 vols. London, 1838.

Phillips, Edward. *The Mysteries of Love & Eloquence; or, The Arts of Wooing and Complementing; as They Are Manag'd in the Spring Garden, Hide Park; the New Exchange, and Other Eminent Places.* London, 1658.

Pidgeon, Sean. "Rapturous Research." *New York Times,* January 6, 2013, p. SR 9.

Pliny the Elder. *Natural History.* Translated by H. Rackham. Cambridge, MA: Harvard University Press, 1967.

Poole, Joshua. *The English Parnassus; or, A Helpe to English Poesie: Containing a Collection of All Rhyming Monosyllables, the Choicest Epithets, and Phrases.* London, 1657.

Post, Emily. *Etiquette in Society, in Business, in Politics and at Home: Illustrated with Private Photographs and Facsimiles of Social Forms.* London: Funk & Wagnalls, 1922.

——. "How I Came to Write about Etiquette." *Pictorial Review* 38 (October 1936): 4, 56, 64.

Powell, Russell H. *Handbooks and Tables in Science and Technology.* 3rd ed. Phoenix: Oryx Press, 1994.

Pritchard, James B. *Archaeology and the Old Testament.* Princeton: Princeton University Press, 1958.

Ptolemy. *Ptolemy's Geography: An Annotated Translation of the Theoretical Chapters.* Translated by J. Jennard Berggren and Alexander Jones. Princeton: Princeton University Press, 2000.

Read, Allen Walker. "Projected English Dictionaries, 1755–1828." *JEGP, Journal of English and Germanic Philology* 36 (1937): 188–205, 347–66.

Reddy, Sheela. "The Ghazipur and Patna Opium Factories Together Produced the Wealth of Britain." *Outlook,* May 20–28, 2008, pp. 61–64.

Rees, Abraham. *The Cyclopædia; or, Universal Dictionary of Arts, Sciences, and Literature.* 45 vols. London, 1802–20.

Retting, James, ed. *Distinguished Classics of Reference Publishing.* Phoenix: Oryx Press, 1992.

Richardson, Charles. *A New Dictionary of the English Language.* London, 1839.

Richardson, Ruth. *The Making of Mr. Gray's Anatomy: Bodies, Books, Fortune, Fame.* Oxford: Oxford University Press, 2009.

Rickard, Peter. *The French Language in the Seventeenth Century: Contemporary Opinion in France.* Rochester, NY : D. S. Brewer, 1992.

Riggsby, Andrew M. *Roman Law and the Legal World of the Romans.* New York: Cambridge University Press, 2010.

Roan, Shari. "Revising the Book on Mental Illness; Experts Call for Listing Binge Eating and Gambling as Official Disorders, but Not Sex Addiction or Obesity." *Los Angeles Times,* February 10, 2010.

Roberts, Lee M. *Literary Nationalism in German and Japanese Germanistik.* New York: Peter Lang, 2010.

Roegel, Denis. "A Reconstruction of the Tables of Briggs' *Arithmetica logarithmica* (1624)." Research Report, 2010, http://www.researchgate.net/publication/50950173_A_reconstruction_of_the_tables_of_Briggs'_Arithmetica_logarithmica_(1624).

Roffe, David. *Domesday: The Inquest and the Book.* Oxford: Oxford University Press, 2000.

Rosalia, Stephanie. "Students Should Not Abandon Print Research." http://www.nytimes.com/roomfordebate/2012/03/14/britannica-define-outdated/students-should-not-abandon-print-research.

Rosen, Jeffrey. "Disoriented." *New Republic*, October 23, 1995.

Rubenhold, Hallie. *The Covent Garden Ladies: Pimp General Jack and the Extraordinary Story of "Harris' List."* Stroud: Tempus, 2005.

Rushdie, Salman. "Hobson-Jobson." In *Imaginary Homelands: Essays & Criticisms, 1981–1991* (London: Granta, 1991), pp. 81–83.

Ruskin, John. *The Works of John Ruskin*. Edited by E. T. Cook and A. Wedderburn. 39 vols. London: G. Allen, 1903–12.

Sánchez, José. "Evolution of the Spanish Dictionary." *Hispania* 27, no. 2 (May 1944): 131–37.

Sandys, Sir John Edwin. *A History of Classical Scholarship*. 3 vols. Cambridge: Cambridge University Press, 1903–8.

——. Review of Pauly-Wissowa, *Real-Encylopädie*. *Classical Review* 9, no. 2 (March 1895): 113–14.

Sansovino, Francesco. *The Quintesence of Wit: Being a Corrant Comfort of Conceites, Maximies, and Poleticke Deuises*. London, 1590.

Schiff, Stacy. "Know It All: Can Wikipedia Conquer Expertise?" *New Yorker*, July 31, 2006. http://www.newyorker.com/archive/2006/07/31/060731fa_fact.

Schmitt, Charles. "Towards a Reassessment of Renaissance Aristotelianism" (1973). In *Renaissance Thought: A Reader*. Edited by Robert Black. New York: Routledge, 2001, pp. 240–54.

Schott, Ben. *Schott's Original Miscellany*. London: Bloomsbury, 2002.

Schwab, R. N., W. E. Rex, and J. Lough. *Inventory of Diderot's Encyclopédie*. Geneva: Institut et Musée Voltaire, 1971.

Sears, M. U. *The Female's Encyclopædia of Useful and Entertaining Knowledge; Comprising Every Branch of Domestic Economy*. London, 1830.

Segar, Mary. "Dictionary Making in the Early Eighteenth Century." *Review of English Studies* 7 (1931): 210–11.

Shea, Ammon. *The Phone Book: The Curious History of the Book That Everyone Uses but No One Reads*. New York: Perigee, 2010.

———. *Reading the OED: One Man, One Year, 21,730 Pages*. New York: Perigee, 2008.

Shea, Christopher. "The Humanist: Anthony Grafton's Life in the Past and the Present." *Princeton Alumni Weekly* 107 (April 4, 2007): 18–23.

Sheldon, F. "Pierre Bayle." *North American Review* 111, no. 229 (October 1870): 377–402.

Singer, Carol A. *Fundamentals of Managing Reference Collections*. Chicago: American Library Association, 2012.

Skeat, W. W. "Report upon 'Ghost-Words,' or Words Which Have No Real Existence." *Transactions of the Philological Society* 2 (1886): 350–74.

Slade, Joseph W. *Pornography and Sexual Representation: A Reference Guide*. 3 vols. Westport, CT: Greenwood, 2001–.

Smith, Reginald A. *Towards a Living Encyclopædia: A Contribution to Mr. Wells's New Encyclopædism*. London: Andrew Dakers, 1947.

Smith, Scott S. "He Boosted Modern Medicine." *Investor's Business Daily*, January 6, 2009, p. A3.

Smith, William. *A Dictionary of Greek and Roman Antiquities*. London, 1842.

Sonderland, Kenneth W. Review of *The National Union Catalog, Pre-1956 Imprints*. *Library Quarterly* 40, no. 2 (April 1970): 270–71.

Spingarn, J. E., ed. *Critical Essays of the Seventeenth Century*. 5 vols. Bloomington: Indiana University Press, 1957.

Stamper, Kory. "Dear Merriam Webster." https://korystamper.wordpress.com/2012/01/25/dear-merriam-webster/.

Starnes, De Witt T., and Gertrude E. Noyes. *The English Dictionary from Cawdrey to Johnson, 1604–1755*. New ed. Amsterdam: J. Benjamin, 1991.

Stavans, Ilan. *Dictionary Days: A Defining Passion*. St. Paul: Graywolf Press, 2005.

Stein, Gabriele. *The English Dictionary before Cawdrey*. Tübingen: Niemeyer, 1985.

Stern, John, and Marcus Williams, eds. *The Essential Wisden: An Anthology of 150 Years of Wisden Cricketers' Almanack*. London: Bloomsbury, 2013.

Stockwell, Foster. *A History of Information Storage and Retrieval*. Jefferson: McFarland, 2001.

Stray, Christopher, ed. *Classical Dictionaries: Past, Present and Future*. Dorchester: Gerald Duckworth, 2010.

"The Student's Library: A General Notice of the Best Educational Books." *British Medical Journal* 2, no. 456 (September 25, 1869): 349–52.

Suarez, Michael F., S.J., and H. R. Woudhuysen, eds. *The Oxford Companion to the Book*. 2 vols. Oxford: Oxford University Press, 2010.

Tankard, Paul. "Reading Lists." *Prose Studies* 28, no. 3 (2006): 337–60.

Tedlow, Richard S. *Andy Grove: The Life and Times of an American Business Icon*. New York: Penguin, 2006.

Thompson, Alexander John. *Logarithmetica Britannica: Being a Standard Table of Logarithms to Twenty Decimal Places*. 2 vols. Cambridge: Cambridge University Press, 1952.

Thompson, Henry L. *Henry George Liddell, D.D., Dean of Christ Church, Oxford: A Memoir*. New York, 1899.

Thorndike, Lynn. "*L'Encyclopédie* and the History of Science." *Isis* 6, no. 3 (1924): 361–86.

The Traveller's Library, Complete in Twenty-Five Volumes: Vol. 23, Mines and Mining. London, 1856.

Trench, Richard Chenevix. *On Some Deficiencies in Our English Dictionaries: Being the Substance of Two Papers Read before the Philological Society, Nov. 5 and Nov. 19, 1857*. 2nd ed. London, 1860.

Urban, Agricole-Joseph-François Fortia d'. *Nouveau sistêm bibliographique, mis en usage pour la connaissance des enciclopédies, en quelque langue qu'elles soient écrites*. Paris, 1821.

Van Berkel, Klaas, and Arjo Johan Vanderjagt. *The Book of Nature in Early Modern and Modern History*. Groningen: Peeters, 2006.

Van Doren, Charles. "The Idea of an Encyclopedia." *American Behavioral Scientist* 6 (September 1962): 23–26.

Vatsyayana. *The Kama Sutra of Vatsyayana: Translated from the Sanscrit: In Seven Parts, with Preface, Introduction, and Concluding Remarks*. Translated by Richard Burton. London, 1883.

Vitz, Paul C. *Sigmund Freud's Christian Unconscious*. Grand Rapids, MI: Gracewing, 1993.

Von Soden, Wolfram. *The Ancient Orient: An Introduction to the Study of the Ancient Near East*. Grand Rapids, MI: Eerdmans, 1994.

Warburton, William. Preface to Shakespeare. In *The Works of William Shakespeare*. Edited by Samuel Johnson. 8 vols. London, 1765.

Ward, Gilbert O. *The Practical Use of Books and Libraries: An Elementary Manual*. Boston: Boston Book Co., 1911.

Warfel, Harry R. *Noah Webster: Schoolmaster to America*. New York: Macmillan, 1936.

Warren, James P. *Walt Whitman's Language Experiment*. University Park: Pennsylvania State University Press, 1990.

Watson, Alan. *Roman Law and Comparative Law*. Athens: University of Georgia Press, 1991.

Watson, Bruce. "The World's Unlikeliest Bestseller." *Smithsonian Magazine*. August 2005.

Watts, George B. "The *Encyclopédie Méthodique*." *PMLA* 73, no. 4 (September 1958): 348–66.

Webster, Noah. *An American Dictionary of the English Language*. 2 vols. New York, 1828.

———. *A Compendious Dictionary of the English Language*. Hartford and New Haven, 1806.

———. *Letters of Noah Webster*. Edited by Harry R. Warfel. New York: Library Publishers, 1953.

Webster's Third New International Dictionary. Springfield: G. & C. Merriam, 1961.

Wedgeworth, Robert. *World Encyclopedia of Library and Information Sciences*. 3rd ed. Chicago: American Library Association, 1993.

Wells, H. G. *World Brain*. London: Methuen, 1938.

Weinrich, Harald. *Lethe: The Art and Critique of Forgetting*. Ithaca: Cornell University Press, 2004.

Weissenberger, Glen, and James J. Duane. *Federal Rules of Evidence: Rules, Legislative History, Commentary, and Authority*. Cincinnati: Anderson, 1995.

Wellisch, Hans H. *Indexing from A to Z*. Bronx, New York: H. W. Wilson, 1991.

Wentzel Vrede van Huyssteen, J., ed. *Encyclopedia of Science and Religion*. New York: Macmillan Reference, 2003.

Whitmarsh, Tim. *Ancient Greek Literature*. Cambridge: Polity, 2004.

Whittington, Christine C. "Unbeatable: The *Guinness Book of Records*." In Retting, *Distinguished Classics*, pp. 138–46.

"The Wiki Wars Are Under Way." *Los Angeles Times*, September 30, 2007.

Wilkinson, Endymion Porter. *Chinese History: A Manual*. Cambridge, MA: Harvard University Press, 2000.

Willemyns, Roland. *Dutch: Biography of a Language*. Oxford: Oxford University Press, 2013.

Williams, Ann. *The English and the Norman Conquest*. Rochester: Boydell, 1995.

Winder, Robert. *The Little Wonder: The Remarkable History of Wisden*. London: Bloomsbury, 2013.

Wisden, John. *The Cricketer's Almanack, for the Year 1864*. London, 1864.

Witty, Francis J. "Early Indexing Techniques: A Study of Several Book Indexes of the Fourteenth, Fifteenth, and Early Sixteenth Centuries." *Library Quarterly* 35, no. 3 (July 1965): 141–48.

——. "Medieval Encyclopedias: A Librarian's View." *Journal of Library History* 14, no. 3 (Summer 1979: 274–96.

——. "Reference Books of Antiquity." *Journal of Library History* 9, no. 2 (April 1974): 101–19.

Woolsey, T. D. "Greek Lexicography." *Bibliotheca Sacra and Theological Review* 1, no. 4 (November 1844): 613–32.

Woordenboek der Nederlandsche taal. 43 vols. 's-Gravenhage: Martinus Nijhoff & Sdu, 1882–1998.

Wright, G. Frederick, ed. *Records of the Past*. 4 vols. Washington, D.C.: Records of the Past Exploration Society, 1902–14.

Xue Shiqui. "Chinese Lexicography Past and Present." *Dictionaries* 4 (1982): 151–69.

Yeo, Richard R. *Encyclopaedic Visions*. Cambridge: Cambridge University Press, 2001.

——. "Lost Encyclopedias: Before and After the Enlightenment." *Book History* 10 (2007): 47–68.

Yong, Heming, and Jing Peng. *Chinese Lexicography: A History from 1046 BC to AD 1911*. Oxford: Oxford University Press, 2008.

Yule, Amy Frances. *A Memoir of Colonel Sir Henry Yule: With a Bibliography of His Writings*. London: John Murray, 1903.

Yule, Henry, and Arthur Coke Burnell. *Hobson-Jobson: A Glossary of Colloquial*

Anglo-Indian Words and Phrases, and of Kindred Terms, Etymological, Historical, Geographical and Discursive. London, 1886.

Zgusta, Ladislav. *Lexicography Then and Now: Selected Essays.* Edited by Fredric S. F. Dolezal and Thomas B. I. Creamer. Tübingen: Max Niemeyer Verlag, 2006.

NOTES

CHAPTER 0: PROLOGUE

1. Ong, *Orality and Literacy*, p. 31.
2. Landau, *Dictionaries*, p. 4.
3. Ward, *Practical Use*, p. 27.
4. Grafton, "Jumping through the Computer Screen," p. 95.

CHAPTER 1: JUSTICE IN THE EARTH

1. Perrot, *Palace of Darius*, p. xvi.
2. Edwards, *Oldest Laws*, p. 6.
3. Delitzsch, "Zur juristischen Litteratur Babyloniens," p. 80.
4. Pritchard, *Archaeology and the Old Testament*, p. 206.
5. Perrot, *Palace of Darius*, p. xviii.
6. Pritchard, *Archaeology and the Old Testament*, p. 210.
7. Wright, *Records of the Past*, 4:105.
8. Edwards, *Oldest Laws*, p. 13.
9. Pritchard, *Archaeology and the Old Testament*, pp. 213, 215.
10. Edwards, *Oldest Laws*, p. 17.
11. Edwards, *Oldest Laws*, p. 19.
12. Edwards, *Oldest Laws*, p. 26.
13. Edwards, *Oldest Laws*, p. 27.
14. See Lewis, *Early Greek Lawgivers*, p. 12.
15. Gagarin, *Writing Greek Law*, pp. 96–97.
16. Carawan, *Rhetoric and the Law of Draco*, p. 2.
17. Lockman, *New History*, p. 137.
18. Carawan, *Rhetoric and the Law of Draco*, p. 1.
19. Riggsby, *Roman Law*, p. 2.
20. Merryman, *Civil Law Tradition*, p. 7.
21. Watson, *Roman Law and Comparative Law*, pp. 84–85.
22. Riggsby, *Roman Law*, pp. 39–40.
23. Witty, "Reference Books of Antiquity," pp. 114–15.
24. Merryman, *Civil Law Tradition*, p. 9.

CHAPTER 1½: OF MAKING MANY BOOKS

1. Metz, "Bibliomania," p. 252.
2. Stockwell, *History of Information Storage and Retrieval*, p. 47.
3. Anderson, *Imagined Communities*, pp. 33–34.
4. See Gleick, "Information Palace," and Dyson, "How We Know."

5. Burton, *Anatomy of Melancholy*, 1.2.3.15.

16. See Datta, *Encyclopedia of Indian Literature*, s.v. dictionaries (Sanskrit).

CHAPTER 2: IN THE BEGINNING WAS THE WORD

1. Black, George, and Postgate, *Concise Dictionary*.
2. Von Soden, *Ancient Orient*, p. 151.
3. Cohen and Kedar, "Teacher-Student Relationships," p. 235.
4. See Bing, "Unruly Tongue"; Collison, *History*, pp. 26–27; and Stray, *Classical Dictionaries*, p. 5.
5. Yong and Peng, *Chinese Lexicography*, p. 59.
6. Xue, "Chinese Lexicography," p. 152.
7. Nienhauser, *Indiana Companion*, 2:166; Xue, "Chinese Lexicography," pp. 152–53.
8. Xue, "Chinese Lexicography," p. 153.
9. Nienhauser, *Indiana Companion*, 2:166; Xue, "Chinese Lexicography," pp. 153–54.
10. Xue, "Chinese Lexicography," p. 154.
11. Wilkinson, *Chinese History*, p. 62.
12. Mirashi, *Literary and Historical Studies in Indology*, p. 51.
13. Datta, *Encyclopedia of Indian Literature*, s.v. dictionaries (Sanskrit); Mirashi, Literary and Historical Studies, p. 47.
14. Colebrooke, Preface to *Amarakosha*, 2:46.
15. Wilkinson, *Chinese History*, pp. 64–65.

CHAPTER 2½: A FRACTION OF THE TOTAL

1. Furetière, *Nouveau recueil*, 1:4.
2. Stavans, *Dictionary Days*, p. 63.
3. When I first drafted this paragraph, the count stood at 35,650; it has gone up by 3,254 since I started writing the book. No doubt it is higher now.

CHAPTER 3: THE HISTORY OF NATURE

1. Greene, *Landmarks of Botanical History*, p. 58.
2. Hornblower and Spawforth, *Oxford Classical Dictionary*, s.v. Theophrastus.
3. Schmitt, "Towards a Reassessment," p. 250.
4. Pliny, *Natural History*, 1:x–xii.
5. McArthur, *Worlds of Reference*, p. 43.
6. Pliny, *Natural History*, 1:viii–ix.
7. Pliny, *Natural History*, 2.1.1–2, 4 (1:171–73).
8. Pliny, *Natural History*, 2.11 (1:207).
9. Pliny, *Natural History*, 11.16.46–47 (3:461); 14.1.1 (5:187).
10. Stockwell, *History of Information Storage*, p. 19.
11. Pliny, *Natural History*, 14.4.20–14.28.140 (5:199–279).
12. Pliny, *Natural History*, 14.27.132–33 (5:273).

13. Gibbon, *Decline and Fall*, 1:394.

14. Pliny, *Natural History*, 1:13; *Oxford Classical Dictionary*, s.v. Pliny the Elder.

15. See, for instance, Pliny, *Natural History*, 1:ix; Collison, *Encyclopaedias*, pp. 25–26; and Katz, *Cuneiform to Computer*, p. 22.

16. Pliny, *Natural History*, 1:15.

17. Pliny, *Natural History*, 2.40.149 (1:287); 1:13.

18. See Greene, *Landmarks of Botanical History*, p. 158.

CHAPTER 3½: EASY AS ABC

1. See Von Soden, *Ancient Orient*, p. 151.

2. Witty, "Medieval Encyclopedias," pp. 274–75.

3. Gleick, *Information*, p. 58.

4. Cawdrey, *Table Alphabeticall*, sig. A4ᵛ.

5. Burke, *Social History of Knowledge*, p. 110. See also Landau, *Dictionaries*, p. 107.

CHAPTER 4: ROUND EARTH'S IMAGINED CORNERS

1. Harwood, *To the Ends of the Earth*, pp. 11–12.

2. Harley, "Map," 1:1.

3. Ptolemy, *Geography*, p. xi.

4. See Dilke, "Culmination," 1:180.

5. Ptolemy, *Ptolemy's Geography*, p. 63.

6. Dilke, "Culmination," 1:183.

7. Dilke, "Culmination," 1:177.

8. Roffe, *Domesday*, p. 1.

9. Williams, *The English and the Norman Conquest*, p. 198.

CHAPTER 4½: THE INVENTION OF THE CODEX

1. Suarez and Woudhuysen, *Oxford Companion to the Book*, s.v. codex.

2. See Kallendorf, "Ancient Book," p. 49.

CHAPTER 5: THE CIRCLE OF THE SCIENCES

1. See Doody, "Pliny's Natural History," pp. 11–12.

2. Jackson, "Towards a History," pp. 342–43.

3. See *New International Encyclopædia*, s.v. encyclopædia; Collison, *Encyclopaedias*, pp. 21–22; and Collison and Preece, "Encyclopedia."

4. Stockwell, *History of Information Storage and Retrieval*, p. 17.

5. Jackson, "Towards a History," p. 344.

6. Jackson, "Towards a History," pp. 345–46.

7. See Isidore, *Etymologies*, p. 11, and Collison, *Encyclopaedias*, pp. 23–24.

8. Stockwell, *History of Information Storage and Retrieval*, p. 17.

9. Witty, "Reference Books of Antiquity," p. 111.

10. Stockwell, *History of Information Storage and Retrieval*, p. 34.

11. See O'Donnell, *Cassiodorus*,
chapter 9.
12. Stockwell, *History of Information
Storage and Retrieval*, p. 38.
13. Cassiodorus, *Institutiones*, 30.2.
14. Cassiodorus, *Institutiones*, I.ii.3;
Introduction, p. 142.
15. See Collison, *Encyclopaedias*,
pp. 28–29.
16. Witty, "Medieval Encyclopedias,"
p. 275.
17. Isidore, *Etymologies*, I.i.1–3 (p. 39).
18. Isidore, *Etymologies*, I.xxix.2 (p.
55); IV .ii (p. 109).
19. Isidore, *Etymologies*, XII.viii.1
(p. 269).
20. Isidore, *Etymologies*, XVIII.i.2
(p. 359); VI.viii.1–2 (pp. 139–40).
21. Isidore, *Etymologies*, IX.vi.23
(p. 209).
22. Isidore, *Etymologies*, pp. 10–11, 14,
15, 24. See also Witty, "Medieval
Encyclopedias," pp. 275–77, and
Stockwell, *History of Information
Storage and Retrieval*, p. 39.

CHAPTER 5½: THE
DICTIONARY GETS ITS DAY
IN COURT

1. *Hinckley v. U.S.*, 163 F.3d 647,
C.A.D.C., 1999.
2. Liptak, "Dictionary Citations."
3. *Bullock v. BankChampaign, N.A.*,
133 S.Ct. 1754.
4. Liptak, "Dictionary Citations."
5. Weissenberger and Duane, *Federal
Rules of Evidence*, §803.72.

6. Stray, *Classical Dictionaries*, p. 94;
Rosen, "Disoriented"; Clark,
"Platonic Love in a Colorado
Courtroom," esp. p. 10.
7. *U.S. v. Donaghe*, 37 F.3d 477, C.A.9
(Wash.), 1994.
8. Phillipps and Amos, *Treatise*, 8th
ed., 2:580.

CHAPTER 6: LEECHCRAFT

1. Cameron, *Anglo-Saxon Medicine*,
p. 25.
2. Cameron, *Anglo-Saxon Medicine*,
pp. 30, 21, 35.
3. Cameron, *Anglo-Saxon Medicine*,
p. 42.
4. Meaney, "Variant Versions," p. 251.
5. Cameron, *Anglo-Saxon Medicine*,
p. 21.
6. Smith, "He Boosted Modern
Medicine."
7. Iqbal, "Avicenna."
8. Khan, *Avicenna*, p. 65.
9. Goodman, *Avicenna*, p. 33.
10. Colgan, *Advice to the Healer*, p. 37.
11. Goodman, *Avicenna*, p. 35.
12. Cited in Goodman, *Avicenna*,
p. 35.
13. Goodman, *Avicenna*, p. 35.
14. Cohen, "London Letter."

CHAPTER 6½: PLAGIARISM

1. Landau, *Dictionaries*, p. 35.
2. Blount, *World of Errors*, sig. A2^r.
3. Sánchez, "Evolution of the
Spanish Dictionary," p. 134.

4. James, *Proposals for Printing a Medicinal Dictionary*.

5. Landau, *Dictionaries*, p. 35.

CHAPTER 7: NEW WORLDS

1. Cosmas, *Aigyptiou Monachou Christianike Topographia*, pp. xvi–xvii, xix–xx.

2. Harwood, *To the Ends of the Earth*, pp. 93–94.

3. Harwood, *To the Ends of the Earth*, p. 84.

4. Braudel, *Civilization and Capitalism*, 3:143.

5. Harwood, *To the Ends of the Earth*, p. 81.

6. Koeman, *History of Abraham Ortelius*, p. 36.

7. http://wwws.phil.uni-passau.de/histhw/tutcarto/english/4-6-eng.html.

8. See Harwood, *To the Ends of the Earth*, p. 81.

9. Harwood, *To the Ends of the Earth*, p. 81.

10. Adams, *Hitchhiker's Guide*, p. 62.

11. Cannon, "Classifying," p. 165.

12. See Buchwald and Feingold, *Newton and the Origin of Civilization*, pp. 261–62.

13. See Kanas, *Star Maps*, p. 155.

14. Alpha Centauri is not a single star but a binary system, with a third star, Proxima Centauri, invisible to the naked eye. None of this was known in Bayer's day.

15. Kanas, *Star Maps*, p. 156.

16. Katz, *Cuneiform to Computer*, p. 234.

17. See, for instance, Harwood, *To the Ends of the Earth*, p. 93.

18. Chang, "How Many Stars?"

CHAPTER 7½: TELL ME HOW YOU ORGANIZE YOUR BOOKS

1. See Kroeger, *Guides*, p. 3, and Singer, *Fundamentals*, p. 156.

2. Pidgeon, "Rapturous Research."

3. Boyd, *Vladimir Nabokov: The American Years*, p. 376.

4. Stavans, *Dictionary Days*, pp. 16, 19.

5. Shea, "Humanist," p. 20.

CHAPTER 8: ADMIRABLE ARTIFICE

1. Briggs, *Arithmetica logarithmica*, sig. ²Br^r.

2. Campbell-Kelly et al., *History of Mathematical Tables*, p. 3.

3. Thompson, *Logarithmetica Britannica*, 1:xiii.

4. I use modern terminology and base-10 logarithms, even though Napier and Briggs used different terms and unconventional bases; the principles are the same. See Carslaw, "Discovery," p. 77, and Roegel, "Reconstruction."

5. See Maor, *e: The Story of a Number*, p. 6.

6. Oliver, "Birth of Logarithms," p. 9.

7. Maor, *e: The Story of a Number*, p. 4.

8. Oliver, "Birth of Logarithms," p. 9.

9. Maor, *e: The Story of a Number*, p. 3.

10. Campbell-Kelly et al., *History of Mathematical Tables*, p. 52.

11. Jagger, "Making of Logarithm Tables," p. 56.

12. Jagger, "Making of Logarithm Tables," p. 58.

13. Quoted in Bryant, *History of Astronomy*, p. 44.

14. Maor, *e: The Story of a Number*, pp. 14–16.

15. Campbell-Kelly et al., *History of Mathematical Tables*, p. 6.

16. Cited in van Berkel and Vanderjagt, *Book of Nature*, p. 24.

17. "Le Baron de Prony," *Gentleman's Magazine* 166 (1839): 312–13.

18. Grier, "Table Making," p. 273.

CHAPTER 8½: TO BRING PEOPLE TOGETHER

1. Adams, "Dictionary Society," is my source for most of the information here.

CHAPTER 9: THE INFIRMITY OF HUMAN NATURE

1. Anderson, *Imagined Communities*, p. 40.

2. Milton, *Of True Religion*, p. 3.

3. See Barbour, *Sir Thomas Browne*, pp. 296–309.

4. Browne, *Pseudodoxia Epidemica*, pp. 1, 4, 36, a4ʳ, 17.

5. Browne, *Pseudodoxia Epidemica*, 4th ed., p. 327.

6. Browne, *Pseudodoxia Epidemica*, pp. 104, 157, 112.

7. Browne, *Pseudodoxia Epidemica*, p. 342.

8. Browne, *Pseudodoxia Epidemica*, p. 181.

9. Browne, *Pseudodoxia Epidemica*, 4th ed., p. 327.

10. Browne, *Pseudodoxia Epidemica*, p. 20.

CHAPTER 9½: IGNORANCE, PURE IGNORANCE

1. Carranco, "Let's Stop Worshipping the Dictionary," p. 72.

2. Apperson, "Blunders."

3. Chambers, *Cyclopædia*, 1:xxviii.

4. Johnson, *Works*, 18:73.

5. Boswell, *Life*, 1:293.

6. Shea, *Reading the OED*, pp. 139–40.

7. Jacobs, *Know It All*, p. 127.

8. Baker, "Charms of Wikipedia."

9. Giles, "Internet Encyclopaedias," p. 900.

CHAPTER 10: GUARDING THE AVENUES OF LANGUAGE

1. See Sánchez, "Evolution of the Spanish Dictionary," pp. 132, 134.

2. See Considine, *Academy Dictionaries*, pp. 110–19.

3. Hartmann, *History of Lexicography*, p. 13.

4. For the best scholarly overview, see Considine, *Academy Dictionaries*, chapters 3–4.

5. Edwards, *Chapters*, p. 13.

6. Rickard, *French Language*, p. 31.

7. Collison, *History of Foreign-Language Dictionaries*, p. 89.

8. Rickard, *French Language*, p. 31.

9. Considine, *Academy Dictionaries*, p. 51.

10. See Collison, *History of Foreign-Language Dictionaries*, pp. 79–88; Hartmann, *History of Lexicography*, pp. 13–14; and Considine, *Academy Dictionaries*, chap. 3.

11. See Stein, *English Dictionary*; Starnes and Noyes, *English Dictionary*; and Considine, *Dictionaries in Early Modern Europe*, pp. 156–202.

12. See Considine, *Academy Dictionaries*, chap. 6.

13. Spingarn, *Critical Essays*, 2:328 and 311; Hume, "Of Liberty and Despotism," in *Essays*, p. 179; Warburton, preface, 1:clxii.

14. Boswell, *Life*, 1:186.

15. Johnson, *Works*, 18:87–88.

16. Johnson, *Works*, 18:105.

17. Boswell, *Life*, 1:300.

18. Johnson, *Works*, 18:105, 102.

CHAPTER 10½: OF GHOSTS AND MOUNTWEAZELS

1. Skeat, "Report upon 'Ghost-Words,'" p. 352.

2. Skeat, "Report upon 'Ghost-Words,'" pp. 352–53.

3. Gove, "History of 'Dord'," pp. 136–38.

4. Liesemer, "Scherzeinträge in Lexika."

5. Liesemer, "Scherzeinträge in Lexika."

6. Jacobs, *Know It All*, p. 128.

7. Alford, "Not a Word."

8. Nester's Map & Guide Corp. v. Hagstrom Map Co., No. 90 CV 1086, 796 F.Supp. 729 (1992).

CHAPTER 11: THE WAY OF FAITH

1. Cruden, *Complete Concordance*, sig. a1^r.

2. Merbecke, *Concordance*, sig. aii^v.

3. Cruden, *Complete Concordance*, sig. a1^r.

4. Olivier, *Alexander the Corrector*, p. 57.

5. Cruden, *Complete Concordance*, sig. a2^v.

CHAPTER 11½: WHO'S WHO AND WHAT'S WHAT

1. Landau, *Dictionaries*, p. 87.

2. http://www.merriam-webster.com/help/faq/words_in.htm.

3. Stamper, "Dear Merriam Webster."

CHAPTER 12: EROTIC RECREATIONS

1. *Song of Solomon* 4:1–5.

2. "Kama Sutra," episode of the podcast *In Our Time*, February 2, 2012.

3. Phillips, *Mysteries of Love & Eloquence*, sig. A6^v.

4. See Fissell, "Making a Masterpiece," p. 59.

5. *Aristotle's Master-Piece*, sig. A3^r, p. 1.

6. *Aristotle's Master-Piece*, pp. 98–99.

7. *Aristotle's Master-Piece*, sig. A4^v.

8. *Aristotle's Master-Piece*, pp. 6, 10, 9.

9. *Aristotle's Master-Piece*, sig. A4^r, p. 1.

10. *Aristotle's Master-Piece*, pp. 2, 91, 23, 109.

11. Clark, "Female Sexuality," p. 66.

12. Fissell, "Making a Masterpiece," pp. 60–61.

13. Slade, *Pornography and Sexual Representation*, 1:40.

14. Joyce, *Ulysses*, pp. 193, 635.

15. See http://huntingtonblogs.org/2015/04/aristotles-masterpiece/.

16. Rubenhold makes the case for Derrick's involvement, though Freeman replies that "there is no evidence firmly associating Derrick" with the pamphlet ("Jack Harris and 'Honest Ranger,'" p. 431).

17. Denlinger, "Garment and the Man," p. 357.

18. Denlinger, "Garment and the Man," p. 371.

19. Freeman, "Jack Harris and 'Honest Ranger,'" p. 425.

20. Denlinger, "Garment and the Man," p. 358.

21. Freeman, "Jack Harris and 'Honest Ranger,'" pp. 423–33, 446, 455.

22. Freeman, "Jack Harris and 'Honest Ranger,'" p. 423.

23. Krafft-Ebing, *Psychopathia Sexualis*, p. v.

CHAPTER 12½: THE BOYS' CLUB

1. Blount, *Glossographia*, sig. A5^v.

2. N.H., *Ladies Dictionary*, sig. A2^v.

3. N.H., *Ladies Dictionary*, sig. A2^r.

4. Sears, *Female's Encyclopædia*, p. 276.

5. Sears, *Female's Encyclopædia*, p. 213.

6. Betham, *Biographical Dictionary*, p. v.

7. Morozov, "Edit This Page."

CHAPTER 13: COLLECTING KNOWLEDGE INTO THE SMALLEST AREAS

1. Anon, Review of *The English Cyclopædia*, p. 191. Zedler's work influenced the *Encyclopédie*: see Lough, *Encyclopédie*, p. 5.

2. Kafker, *Notable Encyclopedias*, p. 123.

3. Sheldon, "Pierre Bayle," p. 385.

4. See Stockwell, *History of Information Storage and Retrieval*, p. 50.

5. Kafker, *Notable Encyclopedias*, p. 98.

6. Aycock, "Lord Byron and Bayle's 'Dictionary,'" p. 143.

7. Koning, "Onward and Upward with the Arts," p. 67.

8. D'Alembert, *Preliminary Discourse,* pp. xiii, xv.

9. D'Alembert, *Preliminary Discourse,* p. xxv.

10. Manguel, *Library at Night,* p. 84.

11. D'Alembert, *Preliminary Discourse,* p. xxxii.

12. D'Alembert, *Preliminary Discourse,* p. 40.

13. D'Alembert, *Preliminary Discourse,* p. 47.

14. Schwab, *Inventory of Diderot,* pp. 21, 36.

15. Lough, *Encyclopédie,* p. 1.

16. D'Alembert, *Preliminary Discourse,* p. 72.

17. Koning, "Onward and Upward," p. 67.

18. Koning, "Onward and Upward," p. 67. On *droit naturel, autorité politique,* and related entries, see Lough, *Encyclopédie,* chap. 8, and Blom, *Encyclopédie,* pp. 145–46, 171.

19. Kafker, *Notable Encyclopedias,* p. 110.

20. See Kafker and Loveland, *Early "Britannica,"* pp. 6–7; Kogan, *Great EB,* p. 9.

21. Kafker, "Smellie's Edition," p. 148; *Proposals for Printing, by Subscription, a Work, Intitled, Encyclopædia Britannica; or, A New and Complete Dictionary of Arts and Sciences, Composed in the Form of Distinct Treatises or Systems* (Edinburgh, 1768).

22. Kerr, *Memoirs,* 1:362–63; Kogan, *Great EB,* p. 10; Kafker, "Smellie's Edition," p. 150.

23. Kafker, "Smellie's Edition," p. 151.

24. *Encyclopædia Britannica,* 1st ed., p. v.

25. Kerr, *Memoirs of . . . William Smellie,* 1:63.

26. Kafker, "Smellie's Edition," pp. 170–71.

27. Kafker, "Smellie's Edition," p. 175.

28. Kafker, "Smellie's Edition," p. 180.

29. Kogan, *Great EB,* p. 50.

CHAPTER 13½: DICTIONARY OR ENCYCLOPEDIA?

1. Morton, *Story of Webster's Third,* p. 6.

CHAPTER 14: OF REDHEADS AND BABUS

1. Berrera, *Abecedario.*

2. See Burns, *Science in the Enlightenment,* p. 145.

3. Cullen, *History of Japan,* p. 131.

4. Nagashima, "Bilingual Lexicography with Japanese," p. 3114.

5. Cullen, *History of Japan,* p. 132.

6. Yule, *Memoir,* p. 41.

7. See, for instance, *Traveller's Library,* p. 244.

8. *Athenæum* 3062 (July 3, 1886): 7.

9. Campion, "Hobson-Jobson."

10. Reddy, "Ghazipur and Patna Opium Factories," p. 61.

11. Rushdie, "Hobson-Jobson."

12. Livingstone, "How We Got Pukka."

CHAPTER 14½: A SMALL ARMY

1. Van Doren, "Idea of an Encyclopedia," p. 25.
2. Kafker, "William Smellie's Edition of the *Encyclopaedia Britannica*," in Kafker, *Notable Encyclopedias*, p. 149.
3. *New International Encyclopædia*, s.v. encyclopædia.

CHAPTER 15: KILLING TIME

1. Hoyle, *Short Treatise*, p. iii.
2. Hoyle, *Short Treatise*, pp. 4, 11, 16.
3. Hoyle, *Hoyle's Games Improved*, p. 154.
4. Hoyle, *Essay*, p. 46.
5. Hoyle, *Essay*, p. 71.
6. Hoyle, *Essay*, pp. 72–73.
7. Hoyle, *Essay*, p. 73.
8. Hoyle, *Short Treatise*, title page.
9. Hoyle, *Short Treatise on the Game of Back-Gammon*, title page.
10. *Humours of Whist*, p. 5.
11. Fielding, *Tom Jones*, part 13, chap. 5.
12. Johnson, *Works*, 3:81, 85.
13. The phrase appears in *Walker's Hibernian Magazine* for 1786.
14. Brown, *Bath*, 2:187.
15. *Englishman in Paris*, 1:147.
16. Chambers, *Book of Days*, 2:282.
17. Hoyle, *Hoyle's Games Improved*, pp. 211, 215.

18. Winder, *Little Wonder*, p. 32.
19. Quoted in Haigh, *Silent Revolutions*, p. 131.
20. Haigh, *Silent Revolutions*, p. 130.
21. Haigh, *Silent Revolutions*, p. 126.
22. Winder, *Little Wonder*, p. 40.
23. Kidd, "Don't Stop Now Is the Message."
24. Winder, *Little Wonder*, pp. x, xiv.
25. Brown, "Stumped No More."
26. Kidd, "150-Year Run."

CHAPTER 15½: OUT OF PRINT

1. Flanagan, "RIP for *OED*."
2. Jacobs, "I Read the Encyclopaedia Britannica."
3. Rosalia, "Students Should Not Abandon Print Research."
4. Ayers, "If You Liked *Britannica*."

CHAPTER 16: MONUMENTS OF ERUDITION

1. Collison, *History of Foreign-Language Dictionaries*, p. 93; see also Considine, *Academy Dictionaries*, pp. 151–57.
2. See Čermák, "Czech Lexicography."
3. Collison, *History of Foreign-Language Dictionaries*, p. 25.
4. Johnson, *Works*, 18:109.
5. Boswell, *Life*, 2:312.
6. Webster to John Canfield, January 6, 1783, in *Letters*, p. 4.

7. Webster to David Ramsay, October 1807, in *Letters*, p. 291.

8. Cited in Micklethwait, *Noah Webster*, p. 54.

9. See Commager, introduction to Webster, *Noah Webster's American Spelling Book*, and Warfel, *Noah Webster*, p. 3.

10. Webster, *Compendious Dictionary*, p. xxiii.

11. Cited in Micklethwait, *Noah Webster*, p. 161.

12. Morton, *Story of Webster's Third*, p. 43.

13. See Morton, *Story of Webster's Third*, p. 42.

14. Jones, *Works*, 1:26.

15. Anon., review of Grimm, *North American Review*, p. 391.

16. Michaelis-Jena, *Brothers Grimm*, p. 85.

17. Anon., review of Grimm, *North American Review*, p. 400.

18. Anon., review of Grimm, *North American Review*, p. 416.

19. See Michaelis-Jena, *Brothers Grimm*, p. 120.

20. Osselton, "Murray and His European Counterparts," p. 62.

21. Zgusta, *Lexicography Then and Now*, p. 43.

22. Roberts, *Literary Nationalism*, p. 37.

23. Roberts, *Literary Nationalism*, p. 37.

CHAPTER 16½: COUNTING EDITIONS

1. Lih, *Wikipedia Revolution*, p. 19.

CHAPTER 17: GRECIAN GLORY, ROMAN GRANDEUR

1. See Witty, "Reference Books of Antiquity," p. 102, and Sandys, *History of Classical Scholarship*, p. 118.

2. Sandys, *History*, p. 118; Easterling et al., *Cambridge History*, 1:544.

3. For an overview of Latin's history see Ostler, *Ad Infinitum*.

4. Zgusta, *Lexicography Then and Now*, p. 266. See also Considine, *Dictionaries in Early Modern Europe*, chap. 3.

5. See McArthur, *Worlds of Reference*, p. 125.

6. Thompson, *Henry George Liddell*, pp. 2, 5.

7. Thompson, *Henry George Liddell*, p. 10.

8. Thompson, *Henry George Liddell*, p. 54.

9. Stray, *Classical Dictionaries*, p. 97.

10. See Jones's preface in Liddell and Scott, *A Greek–English Lexicon*, revised by Jones, p. iii.

11. Liddell and Scott, *Greek–English Lexicon*, pp. xix, xx, xvii.

12. Woolsey, "Greek Lexicography," p. 630.

13. Fishlake, "Greek-and-English Lexicography," p. 166.

14. Liddell and Scott, *Greek–English Lexicon*, p. xviii.

15. Smith, *Dictionary of Greek and Roman Antiquities*, p. vii.

16. See Classen, "*Ars Longa*," pp. 423–25.

17. Sandys, "Review of Pauly-Wissowa," p. 113.

18. See Classen, "*Ars Longa*," p. 428.

CHAPTER 17½: LOST PROJECTS

1. McArthur, *Worlds of Reference*, p. 78; Witty, "Medieval Encyclopedias," p. 285; Stockwell, *History of Information Storage and Retrieval*, p. 40.

2. See Blom, *Encyclopédie*, pp. 107–8.

3. Wilkinson, *Chinese History*, p. 605; Ding Zhigang, *China*, in Wedgeworth, *World Encyclopedia*.

4. Boswell, *Boswell in Holland*, p. 161.

CHAPTER 18: WORDS TELLING THEIR OWN STORIES

1. See Willemyns, *Dutch*, p. 125.

2. Osselton, "Murray and His European Counterparts," p. 68.

3. Noorden Graaf, "In the Shadow," p. 13.

4. Osselton, "Murray and His European Counterparts," pp. 68–69.

5. See Osselton, "Murray and His European Counterparts," p. 68.

6. Trench, *On Some Deficiencies*, p. 9.

7. Philological Society, *Proposal*, p. 4.

8. Murray, *Caught in the Web of Words*, pp. 11, 32.

9. See Osselton, "Murray and His European Counterparts," p. 73.

10. Trench, *On Some Deficiencies*, p. 29.

11. Trench, *On Some Deficiencies*, p. 31.

12. Osselton, "Murray and His European Counterparts," p. 74.

CHAPTER 18½: OVERLONG AND OVERDUE

1. Dickens, *David Copperfield*, p. 169.

2. Blount, *Glossographia*, sig. A3ʳ.

3. Rees, *Cyclopædia*, 1:vii.

4. Coughlan, "Dictionary Reaches Final Definition."

5. Lough, "*Encyclopédie*," p. 3.

6. Watts, "*Encyclopédie Méthodique*," p. 350.

7. Murray, *Caught in the Web of Words*, pp. 142–43.

8. Headrick, *When Information Came of Age*, p. 155.

9. Osselton, "Murray and His European Counterparts," pp. 61–62.

10. The annual reports from 1991 to 2010 appear at http://oi.uchicago.edu/research/projects/cad/.

CHAPTER 19: AN ALMS-BASKET OF WORDS

1. See Shea, *Phone Book*.

2. Katz, *Cuneiform to Computer*, p. 55.

3. Dodd, *Beauties*, 1:vi, 23.

4. Boswell, *Life*, 3:197.

5. Cochrane, "Most Famous Book of Its Kind," p. 9.

6. Bartlett, *Collection*, p. i.

7. Katz, *Cuneiform to Computer*, p. 79.

8. "Bartlett's Updated," from Gleick's

blog, *Bits in the Ether*, http://www.around.com/bartletts.html.

9. Bunge, "Alms-Basket," p. 24.

10. Hayman, "E. Cobham Brewer," pp. ix–xi.

11. Brewer, *Dictionary of Phrase and Fable*, 1st ed., p. v.

12. Brewer, *Dictionary of Phrase and Fable*, 1st ed., p. v.

13. Hayman, "E. Cobham Brewer," p. x.

14. Brewer, *Dictionary of Phrase and Fable*, 1st ed., p. vii.

CHAPTER 19½: READING THE DICTIONARY

1. Day, *Market Driven Organization*, chapter 6 (no page).

2. Collins, *Are You a Geek?* p. 93.

3. Eliot, *Middlemarch*, p. 52.

4. Disraeli, "Imprisonment of the Learned," in *Curiosities*, 1:56.

5. Quoted in Franklin, *Prison Writing*, p. 153.

6. Hill, ed., *Johnsonian Miscellanies*, 2:352.

7. Orr, *Life and Letters*, 1:75.

8. Folsom, *Walt Whitman's Native Representations*, p. 15.

9. Ferlinghetti and Peters, *Literary San Francisco*, p. 116.

10. Borges, *Seven Nights*, p. 109.

11. Stavans, *Dictionary Days*, p. 31.

12. Clark, *Huxleys*, p. 227.

13. Tedlow, *Andy Grove*, p. 295; Lesinski, *Bill Gates*, p. 9.

14. Anderson, *Wikipedia*, p. 15.

15. Kogan, *Great EB*, pp. 297?98.

16. Jacobs, *Know It All*, p. 5.

17. Jacobs, *Know It All*, p. 120.

18. Jacobs, *Know It All*, p. 9.

19. Shea, *Reading the OED*, pp. ix–x.

CHAPTER 20: MODERN MATERIA MEDICA

1. Gray and Carter, *Anatomy*, p. vii.

2. Richardson, *Making*, p. 14.

3. Richardson, *Making*, p. 144.

4. Richardson, *Making*, p. 6.

5. Richardson, *Making*, p. 166.

6. Gray and Carter, *Anatomy*, p. 675.

7. Richardson, *Making*, p. 168.

8. See Richardson, *Making*, pp. 197–99.

9. "Student's Library," p. 349.

10. Hacking, "Lost in the Forest."

11. Cartwright, *Diseases*, p. 332.

12. Hacking, "Lost in the Forest."

13. Davis, "Encyclopedia of Insanity," p. 64.

14. Carey, "Revising Book on Disorders."

15. Roan, "Revising the Book on Mental Illness."

16. *DSM*, p. 39.

17. Davis, "Encyclopedia of Insanity," pp. 61, 62.

CHAPTER 20½: INCOMPLETE AND ABANDONED PROJECTS

1. Segar, "Dictionary Making," p. 210; Dressman, "Walt Whitman's Plans,"

p. 463; Warren, *Walt Whitman's Language Experiment*, pp. 41–42; and Folsom, *Walt Whitman's Native Representations*, p. 16.

2. Read, "Projected English Dictionaries."

3. Osselton, "First English Dictionary?" pp. 175–76.

4. Stray, *Classical Dictionaries*, p. 59.

5. Sánchez, "Evolution of the Spanish Dictionary," p. 137.

6. Considine, *Academy Dictionaries*, p. 168.

7. Urban, *Nouveau sistême*, p. 54.

8. See Hahn, *Fachkommunikation*, p. 38.

9. Considine, *Academy Dictionaries*, pp. 80–92.

10. Hogg, "Bolshaia Sovetskaia Entsiklopediia," pp. 17–18.

11. See Stockwell, *A History of Information Storage and Retrieval*, p. 109.

12. Appiah and Gates, *Africana*, p. ix.

13. Appiah and Gates, *Africana*, pp. ix–x.

14. Keller and Fontenot, *Re-cognizing W. E. B. DuBois*, p. 73.

CHAPTER 21: THE FOUNDATION STONE

1. See Campbell and Pryce, *Library*, p. 46.

2. See Whitmarsh, *Ancient Greek Literature*, p. 128.

3. Campbell and Pryce, *Library*, pp. 73–74.

4. See Manguel, *Library at Night*, pp. 52–53.

5. Stockwell, *History of Information Storage*, p. 140.

6. See Burke, *Social History of Knowledge*, pp. 92–93.

7. Miller, *Prince of Librarians*, p. 14.

8. Miller, *Prince of Librarians*, p. 143.

9. Cutter, "New Catalogue of Harvard College Library," p. 104.

10. Panizzi, *Catalogue*, 1:v.

11. Panizzi, *Catalogue*, 1:vi.

12. Panizzi, *Catalogue*, 1:vi.

13. Panizzi, *Catalogue*, 1:vii.

14. The best accounts are McCrimmon, *Power, Politics, and Print*, and Chaplin, *GK*.

15. Alston and Jannetta, *Bibliography*, p. 20.

16. Bakewell, *Manual of Cataloguing Practice*, p. 19.

17. Stockwell, *History of Information Storage and Retrieval*, p. 144.

18. Katz, *Cuneiform to Computer*, p. 311.

19. Katz, *Cuneiform to Computer*, p. 311.

20. See Burke, *Social History of Knowledge*, p. 93.

21. See Cutter, "New Catalogue," p. 97.

22. Sonderland, review of *National Union Catalog*, p. 271.

23. Hoyle, "Superlatives and Compromises," p. 235.

24. An up-to-the-minute tally of WorldCat's holdings is at http://

www.oclc.org/worldcat/watch-worldcat-grow.en.html.

25. See DeZelar-Tiedman, "Proportion of NUC Pre-56 Titles."

26. Cutter, "New Catalogue," p. 123.

27. John Overholt (@john_overholt), Twitter posts, July 29, 2014.

28. Cutter, "New Catalogue," p. 129.

CHAPTER 21½: INDEX LEARNING

1. Carr, "Is Google Making Us Stupid?"

2. Witty, "Early Indexing Techniques," p. 141.

3. Pope, *Dunciad*, 1.277–80.

4. *Grub Street Journal* no. 322 (February 26, 1735/36).

5. Richardson, *Correspondence*, 2:229.

6. Tankard, "Reading Lists," p. 349.

7. Plato, *Phaedrus*, in *Works*, 1:610.

CHAPTER 22: THE GOOD LIFE

1. Graves, *Life & Letters*, p. 12.

2. Graves, *Life & Letters*, p. 23.

3. Graves, *Life & Letters*, p. 33.

4. Graves, *Life & Letters*, p. 133.

5. Graves, *Life & Letters*, p. 44.

6. Graves, *Life & Letters*, p. 156.

7. Graves, *Life & Letters*, p. 254.

8. Graves, *Life & Letters*, p. 205.

9. Grove, *Dictionary of Music and Musicians*, 1:v.

10. Graves, *Life & Letters*, p. 228.

11. Graves, *Life & Letters*, p. 285.

12. Graves, *Life & Letters*, p. 293.

13. Graves, *Life & Letters*, pp. 282, 292.

14. Post, "How I Came," p. 64.

15. Post, "How I Came," p. 4.

16. Post, "How I Came," pp. 4, 56.

17. Post, *Etiquette*, pp. xiii–xiv.

18. Post, *Etiquette*, pp. 1, 71, 154, 506.

19. Post, *Etiquette*, p. 4.

20. Post, *Etiquette*, pp. 6, 7.

21. Post, *Etiquette*, pp. 58, 122, 194, 567, 544, 144.

22. Post, *Etiquette*, pp. 152–53, 20, 18–19.

23. Post, *Etiquette*, p. 34.

24. "Emily Price Post," in *Encyclopedia of World Biography*.

25. Poole, *English Parnassus*, sig. a7ᵛ–a8ʳ.

CHAPTER 22½: SOME UNLIKELY REFERENCE BOOKS

1. Stavans, *Dictionary Days*, p. 63.

CHAPTER 23: PRESUMED PURITY

1. Vitz, *Sigmund Freud's Christian Unconscious*, p. 112.

2. Merck, *Merck's Index*, p. iii.

3. Merck, *Merck's Index*, pp. iii–iv, vii–viii.

4. Merck, *Merck's Index*, p. iv.

5. *The American Monthly Microscopical Journal* 10 (April 1889): 94.

6. Merck, *Merck's Index*, p. v.

7. Merck, *Merck's Index*, p. vi.
8. *Annals of Gynecology and Pediatry 3* (1890): 126.
9. Merck, *Merck's Manual*, p. 5.
10. Grotzinger, review of *Merck Index*.
11. Chemical Rubber Company, *Handbook*, p. 3.
12. Chemical Rubber Company, *Handbook*, p. 8.
13. Chemical Rubber Company, *Handbook*, p. 3.
14. Davis and Schmidt, *Guide to Information Sources*, p. 88.
15. Powell, *Handbooks and Tables*.
16. Thorndike, "L'Encyclopédie and the History of Science," p. 361.

CHAPTER 23½: AT NO EXTRA COST!

1. Dille, "The *Dictionary* in Abstract," p. 198.
2. Murray, *Caught in the Web of Words*, p. 251.
3. See Béjoint, *Lexicography of English*, p. 2.
4. Watts, "*Encyclopédie Méthodique*," p. 356.
5. Oldenburg, "Consummate Consumer."
6. Louise Cook, Associated Press story, May 26, 1978; see also Stockwell, *History of Information Storage and Retrieval* p. 133.
7. Kogan, *Great EB*, p. 303.
8. Kogan, *Great EB*, p. 300.
9. Kogan, *Great EB*, p. 306.
10. Kogan, *Great EB*, p. 303.
11. Oldenburg, "Consummate Consumer."
12. LaBelle, "Salesman Must Say."
13. Berger, "What's New in Encyclopedias."
14. "Out of Bounds."

CHAPTER 24: FULL AND AUTHORITATIVE INFORMATION

1. Kafker, "William Smellie's Edition," p. 172.
2. *Catholic Encyclopedia and Its Makers*, p. iii.
3. "J. K.," "Catholics and the New 'Encyclopedia Britannica,'" pp. 202–3; Keogil, "'Encyclopedia Britannica' and the History of the Church," pp. 377, 381.
4. *Catholic Encyclopedia*, 1:v.
5. *Catholic Encyclopedia*, 1:v–vi.
6. *Catholic Encyclopedia and Its Makers*, p. iv.
7. Hogg, "Bolshaia Sovetskaia Entsiklopediia," p. 29.
8. Hogg, "Bolshaia Sovetskaia Entsiklopediia," p. 18.
9. Hogg, "Bolshaia Sovetskaia Entsiklopediia," pp. 23–24.
10. Hogg, "Bolshaia Sovetskaia Entsiklopediia," p. 28.
11. Hogg, "Bolshaia Sovetskaia Entsiklopediia," p. 31.
12. Einbinder, *Myth of the Britannica*, p. 19.

13. Hogg, "Bolshaia Sovetskaia Entsiklopediia," p. 53.
14. Kołakowski, *Main Currents*, p. 903.
15. "Big Red Book."
16. Stockwell, *History of Information Storage and Retrieval*, p. 126.
17. Hirsch, "Culture and Literacy," pp. 36, 45.

CHAPTER 24½: UNPERSONS

1. See Weinrich, *Lethe*, p. 33, and Hedrick, *History and Silence*, pp. 94–95.
2. Weinrich, *Lethe*, p. 33.
3. Knight, *Beria*, p. 3.
4. Hedrick, *History and Silence*, p. 92.

CHAPTER 25: NOTHING SPECIAL

1. Newman, *Lounger's Common-place Book*, 1:iii.
2. Olmsted, *Getting into Guinness*, p. 36.
3. Watson, "World's Unlikeliest Bestseller."
4. Olmsted, *Getting into Guinness*, p. 46.
5. Olmsted, *Getting into Guinness*, p. 47.
6. Whittington, "Unbeatable," p. 139.
7. http://www.book-of-records. info/1950s.html.
8. See Olmsted, *Getting into Guinness*, p. 34.

9. Cavendish, "Publication of the *Guinness Book*."
10. Hanson, "Harnessing the Guinness Effect," p. 165.
11. Watson, "World's Unlikeliest Bestseller."
12. Hanson, "Harnessing the Guinness Effect," p. 165.
13. Watson, "World's Unlikeliest Bestseller."
14. *Schott's Original Miscellany*, p. 5.
15. McCrum, "God Bless You," p. 19.
16. Anon., review of *Schott's Food & Drink Miscellany*.
17. Luce, "Vital Irrelevance."
18. Gutin, "How Big Is a D-Cup?"

EPILOGUE: THE WORLD'S INFORMATION

1. See Maritain, *Dream of Descartes*, pp. 13–26.
2. Cottingham, *Cambridge Companion*, p. 31.
3. Yeo, *Encyclopaedic Visions*, p. 4.
4. Campbell and Pryce, *Library*, p. 39.
5. See Collison, *Encyclopaedias*, p. 2.
6. Stockwell, *History of Information Storage and Retrieval*, p. 21.
7. Burke, *Social History of Knowledge*, p. 175.
8. Yeo, "Lost Encyclopedias," p. 47.
9. Wells, *World Brain*, p. 11.
10. Smith, *Towards a Living Encyclopædia*, p. 28.
11. See Yeo, "Lost Encyclopedias," p. 62.
12. Adams, *Hitchhiker's Guide*, p. 7.

13. Lih, *Wikipedia Revolution*, p. xv.
14. Lih, *Wikipedia Revolution*, p. 14.
15. Lih, *Wikipedia Revolution*, p. 112.
16. Schiff, "Know It All."
17. Baker, "Google's Earth."
18. Baker, "Charms of Wikipedia."
19. Jaschick, "Stand against Wikipedia."
20. Dyson, "How We Know," p. 10.

"The A.B.C." (Le Maire), 50
Académie Française, 138–42, 212, 273
Accademia della Crusca, 138, 141, 212,
    228, 238
Adelung, Johann Christoph, 238
Africana (Appiah and Gates), 310
Alexander the Great, 53
Alexandria, Library of, 244, 311,
    382–83, 389
alphabet, development of, 48–49
alphabetization. *See also* classification
    alternative schemes for, 140–41
    Chinese characters and, 27–28, 48
    early reference works and, 24, 25, 48
    electronic reference works and,
        50–51
    history of, 49–50
    practical issues in, 314–16, 345
Amarakosha, 30–32
Amarasimha, 30–31
Amenemope, 67
*An American Dictionary of the English
    Language* (Webster), 78–79, 231,
    232–34
Anatomy Descriptive and Surgical
    (Gray and Carter), 294–99, 306
*Antiquitates rerum humanarum et
    divinarum* (Varro), 155
Apianus, Petrus, 100

Apollonius the Sophist, 26
*Approaching Elegance. See Erya
    (Erh-ya)*
Aquinas, Thomas, 383–84
Ardens, Radulfus, 383
Aristophanes of Byzantium, 26
Aristotle, 38, 86, 245, 279
Aristotle's Master-Piece, 172–76
Arithmetica logarithmica (Briggs),
    112–14
Ash, John, 133
The Assyrian Dictionary, 275–76
Astronomia instaurata progymnasmata
    (Brahe), 115
astronomy
    history of, 114–15
    logarithm tables in, 113
    star and planetary tables, 115–16
    star maps, 99–103
    stars naming system, 101–2
As We May Think (Bush), 384–85
Átaktoi glôssai (Philitas of Cos),
    26, 244
Atlas (Mercator), 99
Atlas coelestis (Flamsteed), 102
Avicenna, 86–90

Babylonia, legal code of, 11, 12–17
Bacon, Francis, 129, 152

Bailey, Nathan, 182

Baker, Nicholson, 135, 386–88

Balbus, Johannes, 49

Bald, 82–85, 90

Bartlett, John, 281–84, 289

Bartlett's Familiar Quotations, 242

Bartolomeo of San Concordio, 384

The Basilica, 21

Bayer, Johann, 95, 100–102

Bayle, Pierre, 187, 197, 211

Beauties of Shakespear (Dodd), 280–81

Beaver, Sir Hugh, 372–74

Beeton's Dictionary of Universal Information, 379

Bell, Andrew, 193

Betham, Matilda, 183

Bible
 Babylonian law and, 16
 and book, history of, 65
 on information overload, 22, 23
 selection of books for, 122–23
 works on, 70–71, 156–58, 159–65

Bibliotheca universalis (Gesner), 317–18

Biographical Dictionary of the Celebrated Women (Betham), 183

Black's Law Dictionary, 242

Blount, Thomas, 91–92, 181, 273

Bol'shaia sovetskaia entsiklopediia, 362–67, 368–69

book(s), history of, 22–23, 64–66

Book of Healing (Bald), 83–85, 90

Boston Buriensis, 317

Boswell, James, 134, 195, 258–59

Bradshaw's Railway Time Tables, 278

Brahe, Tycho, 100, 115, 116

Brewer, Ebenezer Cobham, 284–89

Briggs, Henry, 111–14

Brockhaus Enzyklopädie, 225–26

Browne, Thomas, 128–32

Brunel, Isambard Kingdom, 327

Bukharin, Nikolai, 363, 364, 369

Burchfield, Robert, 290

Burnell, Arthur Coke, 206–10

Bush, Vannevar, 384–85

Byzantine Empire, law code of, 21

Callimachus, 311–12

Calmet, Antoine Augustin, 156–59

Canon of Medicine (Avicenna), 86–90

Capellanus, Andreas, 170

Carroll, Lewis, 247, 315

Carter, Henry Vandyke, 294, 295–99, 306

Cartwright, Samuel, 301–2

Cassiodorus, Flavius Marcus Aurelius, 69–72, 77, 82, 268

Catalogue of Printed Books in the Library of the British Museum, 313–17

Catalogus scriptorum ecclesiae (Boston Buriensis), 317

Catholic Church. *See Index librorum prohibitorum*

The Catholic Encyclopedia, 356–61

Catholicon (Balbus), 49

Cato the Censor, 68, 257

Cawdrey, Robert, 49–50, 91, 143, 181

Celsus, A. Cornelius, 257

Chambers, Ephraim, 133–34, 186, 188, 193, 197, 384

Chemical Rubber Co., 347, 350

Children's and Household Tales (Grimm and Grimm), 237

China
 early dictionaries, 26–30, 32
 encyclopedias, 257, 258, 383
 libraries in, 312

Chmielowski, Benedykt, 134–35

classification. *See also* alphabetization

in early dictionaries, 27–28, 31, 32
in medicine, 299–306
in natural sciences, 38–40
in reference works, 75–76
Cockeram, Henry, 143, 181
Code Napoléon, 361
Code of Hammurabi, 11, 12–17, 21
codex, history of, 64–66
A Collection of Familiar Quotations
    (Bartlett), 281–84
Comenius, 257–58
Comfort, Alex, 179–80
Commentaire littéral (Calmet), 156
commonplace books, 279–84
Compendious Dictionary (Webster),
    230–32, 232–33
Complete Concordance to the Holy
    Scriptures (Cruden), 159, 160,
    163–64
Comprehensive Pronouncing and
    Explanatory English Dictionary
    (Worcester), 234
computers. *See also* World Wide Web
    and concordances, 166
    early uses of, 117–18
concordances, 159–66
Confucian Classics, 30
Cooper, Thomas, 91, 143
Coote, Edmund, 91
Copernicus, Nicolas, 115, 116, 127, 128
Corneille, Thomas, 140
Coronelli, Vincenzo, 185
Corpus juris civilis, 18–21
Corréard, Marie-Hélène, 184
Crastoni, Giovanni, 245
CRC Handbook of Chemistry and
    Physics, 347–51
Crooke, William, 210
Cruden, Alexander, 159, 160, 163–64

culture
    influence of reference books on,
        5–6, 21, 76, 78–81, 299–306
    reference books as window into,
        4–5, 16–17, 26, 29, 33, 44, 61–62,
        208–9, 210, 284, 345–46, 367
    reference books on, 326–36
Cunningham, Ward, 385–86
Cyclopædia (Chambers), 186, 188, 197,
    384
Cyclopædia (Rees), 273

d'Alembert, Jean le Rond, 188–92,
    196, 363
Damião, Pedro, 214
damnatio memoriae, 368–70
Darwin, Charles, 39, 356
de Byard, Nicholas, 384
Defoe, Daniel, 144
Delitszch, Friedrich, 13–14
de Morgan, Jacques, 12, 14
De Plinii et aliorum in medicina
    erroribus (Leoniceno), 46
de Prony, Gaspard C. F. M. R., 116
Derrick, Samuel, 176
Descartes, René, 382
Deutsche Grammatik (Grimm), 237
Deutsches Wörterbuch (Grimm and
    Grimm), 212, 238–41, 260, 263,
    266, 275
de Vries, Matthias, 261–64, 266, 272
Diagnostic and Statistical Manual of
    Mental Disorders, 6, 80, 299, 300,
    302–6
*Diccionario Griego–Español (*DGE*)*,
    256
dictionaries
    abridged, 352–53
    academies sponsoring, 119

bilingual, 200–210
as business venture, 352–53
of classical languages, 244–51,
    255–56
early, 24–33
editorial decisions in, 167–69
in 18th century, 137–51
vs. encyclopedias, 197–99
errors in, 133–34
ghost words in, 152–53
historical, 260–72
and law, 78–81
of modern languages, 137–38
national dictionary projects, 227–41
and nation building, 228–29, 238,
    240
number of in existence, 34–36
and plagiarism, 91–93, 154
reading through, 290–93
as regulation, 139, 148–51, 228
societies devoted to, 119–21
Dictionary.com, 355
Dictionary of Cultural Literacy
    (Hirsch), 367
Dictionary of Greek and Roman
    Antiquities (Smith), 251–52
Dictionary of Music and Musicians
    (Grove), 328–30
Dictionary of National Biography, 226
Dictionary of Phrase and Fable
    (Brewer), 285–89
Dictionary of the English Language
    (Johnson), 78–79, 142, 145–51,
    152, 211–12, 228, 229–30, 232,
    242–43, 264–65, 278, 291, 352–53
Dictionary of the Russian Academy,
    361–62
Dictionary Society of North America
    (DSNA), 119–21

Dictionnaire de l'Académie françoise,
    138–42, 147, 150, 182, 225, 228, 242,
    273
Dictionnaire des arts et des sciences
    (Corneille), 140
Dictionnaire historique, critique,
    chronologique, géographique et
    littéral de la Bible (Calmet), 156–58
Dictionnaire historique et critique
    (Bayle), 187, 197, 211
Diderot, Denis, 188–92, 196, 356–57,
    363
Dioscorides, Pedanius, 82
Diseases and Peculiarities of the Negro
    Race (Cartwright), 301–2
Dobrovsky, Josef, 229
Dodd, William, 280–81
Doeff, H., 205
The Domesday Book, 58–63, 80–81
Draco, 17–18
Du Bois, W. E. B., 310
Duffy, Richard, 331–33
Dufu Haruma, 205
Duke of Zhou, 27
Dutch dictionaries, 260–64

Edo Haruma (Inamura), 204–5
Elyot, Thomas, 91, 143
Encyclopædia Britannica, 4, 80, 106,
    135–36, 153, 182, 192–95, 212, 213,
    226, 227, 242, 275, 353–55, 357–58,
    359–60
Encyclopedia of Classical Knowledge
    (Pauly et al.), 252–55, 256
encyclopedias
    all-inclusive, as goal, 382–85
    of classical antiquity, 251–55, 256
    vs. dictionaries, 197–99
    early, 67–77

of 18th century, 187–92
errors in, 135–36
history of, 67–69, 76–77
ideology-based, 356–67
importance to science, 351
number of in existence, 34–36
selling of, 353–55
of 17th century, 185–87
Encyclopédie (D'Alembert and
    Diderot), 187–92, 193, 195–96,
    211, 258, 274, 356–57
Encyclopedie methodique
    (Panckoucke), 274
Encyclopedie nouvelle, 361
Entick, John, 232
Entsiklopedicheskii Slovar, 361–62
Epitome astronomiae Copernicanae
    (Kepler), 128
Erasmus, Desiderius, 5, 96, 279, 281
Eratosthenes, 53–54
errors in reference works, 133–36
Erya (Erh-ya), 26–30, 32
Estienne, Henri (H. Stephanus), 140,
    245
Estienne, Robert, 91, 140
Etiquette (Post), 242, 331–36
etymologies, 24, 29–30, 72–77, 140,
    147, 214, 234–35, 239, 264, 286
Etymologies (Isidore), 72–77, 214
Explanation of Names (Liu Xi),
    29–30

The Female Encyclopedia (Sears),
    183
Fihrist (Ibn al-Nadim), 312
Flaccus, Verrius, 257
Flaubert, Gustave, 385
Friend, Joseph, 233–34
Frisius, John, 91

Fügner, Franz, 307
Furetière, Antoine, 34
Furnivall, Frederick, 266

games, reference works on, 214–20
Garden of Delights (Herrad of
    Landsberg), 184
Geographike (Eratosthenes), 54
Geographike hyphegesis (Ptolemy),
    54–57, 63, 94, 95
German Grammar (Grimm), 237
Germany, 19th century nation-
    building efforts in, 235–37, 238,
    240
Gesner, Conrad, 317–18
ghost words, 152–53
Gibson [Gybson], Thomas, 163
Glossarium suiogothicum, 239
Glossographia (Blount), 273
Google, 385, 387, 389–90
*Grammatical Institute of the English
    Language* (Webster), 230
*Grammatisch-kritisches Worterbuch der
    Hochdeutschen Mundart*
    (Adelung), 238
Grand Larousse gastronomique, 242
Gray, Henry, 294, 295–99, 306
Gray's Anatomy, 294–99, 306
Great Soviet Encyclopedia, 362–67,
    368–69
Greece, ancient
    cartography in, 53–54, 94
    dictionaries in, 26, 32–33
    law in, 17–18
    natural science works in, 37–41
A Greek English Lexicon (Liddell and
    Scott), 248, 249–51, 255–56
Grimm, Jacob Ludwig Carl, 212,
    236–41, 260, 266, 275

Grimm, Wilhelm Carl, 212, 236–41,
    260, 266, 275
Grosses vollständiges Universal-
    Lexicon (Zedler), 275
Grove, George, 326–30
Grundy, Valerie, 184
Guiness Book of World Records, 372–77,
    381
Gutenberg, Johannes, 22–23, 66, 123,
    124

Halakhah, 156
Halma, François, 204, 205
Hammurabi, 13, 14, 21
Hammurabi's Code, 11, 12–17
Handbook of Chemistry and Physics,
    347–51
Handbooks and Tables in Science and
    Technology, 351
Handbuch der römischen Alterthümer
    (Mommsen), 254
Handwörterbuch der griechischen
    Sprache (Passow), 246, 249
Handy Tables (Ptolemy), 114
Harley, Edward, 313
Harris, Jack, 176
Harris, John, 192–93, 197
Harris's List of Covent-Garden Ladies,
    176–79
Harris's Pocket Journal, 108
Haruma-wage (Inamura), 204–5
Hebermann, Charles G., 358–59
Herrad of Landsberg, 184, 257
Hesychius, 26
Hildebrand, Rudolf, 240
Hirsch, E. D., Jr., 367
Historia naturalis (History of Plants;
    Pliny the Elder), 42–46, 67, 73

History of Plants (Theophrastus), 38–41
Hobson-Jobson (Yule and Burnell),
    206–10
Hofmann, Johann Jacob, 185
Horne Tooke, John, 264
Hortus deliciarum (Herrad of
    Landsberg), 184, 257
Hoyle, Edmond, 215–20
Huang Ian, 257
Hughes, Robert, 153
Human Genome Project, 351

Ibn al-Nadim, 312
imperialism, and bilingual
    dictionaries, 200
Inamura Sampaku, 204–5
indexes, 65, 323–24
Index librorum prohibitorum, 124–28,
    132, 356–57
Indo-European languages, 234–35
information fatigue, 22–23, 34
Inquisition, Congregation of, 124–25
Institut International de
    Bibliographie, 383
Institutiones divinarum et sæcularium
    litterarum (Cassiodorus), 69–72,
    77
Instruction (Amenemope), 67
International Statistical Classification
    of Diseases, 302
Internet. See World Wide Web
Ishii Shosuke, 204
Isidore, 72–76, 77, 214
Islam, Encyclopedia Britannica on, 195
Islamic world
    cartography in, 57, 94
    early medical texts, 86–90
    libraries in, 312

Jacobs, A. J., 135, 227, 292–93
James, Robert, 92–93, 188
Jamieson, John, 259, 268
Japan
    isolation from West, 200–203
    Japanese-Dutch dictionaries, 203–5
Japanese Explanations of Dutch Botany
    (Noro), 203
Jewett, Charles Coffin, 318
Jewish Encyclopedia, 358
Jiao zhou luo (Zheng Qiao), 312
Johnson, Samuel, 3, 48, 78–79, 92, 93,
    106, 134, 142–51, 152, 211–12, 228,
    229–30, 232, 242–43, 264–65, 268,
    278, 281, 291, 307, 313, 352–53
Jones, Henry Stuart, 251
Jones, William, 234–35
The Joy of Sex (Comfort), 179–80
Judaism, reference books in, 155–56
Jungmann, Josef, 229

Kama Sutra, 170–71
Kepler, Johannes, 111, 115–16, 128
Kersey, John, 134
al-Khwarizmi, Muhammad ibn
    Musa, 57
K'iche'-Spanish Vocabulary, 200
Kinder- und Hausmärchen (Grimm
    and Grimm), 237
Kipling, Rudyard, 210
Kitab al-Qanun fi al-tibb (Avicenna),
    86–90
Knight, W. H., 222
Krafft-Ebing, Richard Freiherr von, 179
*Kritisches griechisch-deutsches
    Handwörterbuch* (Schneider),
    245–46
Krünitz, Johann Georg, 275

The Ladies Dictionary, 182–83
Landau, Sidney, 3, 91, 93, 167
law
    of ancient world, 11–21
    reference works in, 5–6, 11, 21,
        78–81
Leechbook (Bald), 83–85, 90
Le Maire, Louis, 50
Leoniceno, Niccolò, 46
Leonine Index, 128
Leroux, Pierre, 361
Lexeis Homerikai (Apollonius the
    Sophist), 26
Lexicon Livianum (Fügner), 307
Lexicon Technicum (Harris), 192–93,
    197
Lexikon der gesamten Technik
    (Lueger), 351
lex talionis, 16
libraries
    catalogs of, 313–22
    history of, 311–13
Library of Congress, 318, 319–22,
    381
Liddell, Henry George, 247–51,
    255–56
Li Fang, 383
Linguae Bohemicae thesaurus
    (Comenius), 257–58
Littré, Émile, 263
Liu Xi, 29–30
Logarithmorum chilias prima (Briggs),
    111–12
logarithms, 108–11
logarithm tables, 109–14, 117
Lounger's Common-Place Book
    (Newman), 371–72
Lueger, Otto, 351

Macfarquhar, Colin, 193
Mallanaga, Vatsyayana, 171
maps and cartography
  in age of discovery, 94–103
  celestial maps, 99–102
  early works, 52–63
  history of, 52–53, 57, 63, 94, 95
  modern societies promoting, 119
  and plagiarism, 154
Marbecke, John, 163
Marinos of Tyre, 55
Mathematical Tables Project
  (WPA), 117
Mayne, John, 108
McKenzie, Roderick, 251
McWhirter, Norris and A. Ross,
  372–74, 376
medicine
  early works, 82–90
  insurance and, 300–301, 304, 306
  reference works, 294–306
Mercator, Gerardus, 95, 96, 97, 98, 99
Merck & Co., 342–44
Merck Index, 80, 342, 344–47, 351
Merriam-Webster Company, 119,
  234
Merriam-Webster dictionaries, 105,
  106, 108, 120, 167–68, 225, 226
Minamoto no Shitago, 201
*Mirifici logarithmorum canonis
  descriptio* (Napier), 111
Miscellaneous Glosses (Philetas of
  Cos), 244
Mommsen, Theodor, 254
Montagné, Prosper, 336
mountweazels, 153–54
Mundaneum, 383
Muratorian fragment, 122–23

Murray, James A. H., 152, 209,
  266–72, 291
music reference books, 328–30, 336

Nagasaki Haruma, 205
Nâmalingânusâsana. See Amarakosha
Napier, John, 110–11, 116
National Union Catalog, 318–22
natural history, early works in, 37–47
De Nederlandsche taalkunde (de
  Vries), 261–62, 266
Neusner, Jacob, 156
New Characters, 201
New Columbia Encyclopedia, 153–54
*New English Dictionary on Historical
  Principles. See Oxford English
  Dictionary*
*New Grove Dictionary of Music and
  Musicians*, 330
New International Encyclopedia, 213
Newman, Jeremiah Whitaker, 371–72
Nighantu, 30
Niina, 201
Nippo jisho, 201
Nishi Zenzaburo, 203
Noro Genjo, 203
Nosologia methodica (Sauvages), 299
number tables, 107–18, 225. *See also*
  logarithm tables

Oekonomische Encyclopädie (Krünitz),
  275
Online College Library Center
  (OCLC), 322
*On Some Deficiencies in Our English
  Dictionaries* (Trench), 265
Oranda honso wage (Noro), 203
Origines (Isidore), 72–76, 77

Ortelius, Abraham, 95–99, 103
Oudin, César, 92
Oughtred, William, 113
Our Great Books of Song (Li Fang), 383
Overholt, John, 322
Oxford English Dictionary, 23, 79, 119, 131, 135, 152, 167, 209–10, 212–13, 226, 263–71, 274, 277, 290, 291, 293, 353

Panckoucke, Charles Joseph, 274
Panizzi, Antonio, 313–17
Passow, Franz, 246, 249, 251, 265, 268
Patterson, Austin M., 152–53
Pauline Index, 124–26
Pauly, August Friedrich, 252–56
Peiwen yunfu, 32
Peter the Great, 228–29
Philitas of Cos, 26, 244
Phillips, Edward, 92, 133, 171–72
phone books, 278–79
Physician's Desk Reference, 80
Pinakes (Callimachus), 311–12
plagiarism, 91–93, 154
Plantijn, Christophe, 96–97
Plato, 38, 80, 245
The Pleasaunt and Wittie Playe of the Cheasts Renewed (Damião), 214
Pliny the Elder, 41–46, 67, 73, 84
Poole, Joshua, 336
Post, Emily, 242, 331–36
Prokheiroi kanones (Ptolemy), 114
prostitute directories, 176–79
Protestant Reformation, 123–26, 359
Proto-Indo-European languages, 234–35
Pseudodoxia Epidemica (Browne), 128–32

Psychopathia Sexualis (Krafft-Ebing), 179
Ptolemy, Claudius, 54–57, 63, 94, 95, 100, 101, 103, 114

Qinding Gujin tushu jicheng, 383
quotation collections, 279–84

Ratcliffe, Susan, 184
The Ready Guide. See *Erya (Erh-ya)*
Real-Encyclopädie der classischen Altertumswissenschaft (Pauly et al.), 252–55, 256
Rees, Abraham, 273
reference books. See also culture
   abandoned projects, 307–10
   as business venture, 8, 352–55
   definition of, 6
   editions of, 242–43
   editorial decisions in, 167–69
   home libraries of, 104–6
   and information science, 8–9
   intellectual dangers of, 323–24
   lost, 257–59
   number of in existence, 34–36
   prank entries in, 153–54
   public image of, 3–4
   removal of persons from, 368–69
   single-author *vs.* team works, 211–13
   time required to create, 273–77
   on unusual topics, 337–41
   wide range of types, 6–7
   writers' love of, 104
religious reference books, 155–65, 356–61
Reynaud, Jean, 361
Richardson, Charles, 264–65, 268
Robinson, Jancis, 336

Rodrigues, João, 201
Roget, Peter Mark, 32, 212
Roman Empire
  and book, history of, 65
  celestial maps in, 99–100
  encyclopedias in, 68–69
  legal code of, 18–21
  natural history works in, 41–46
  religious reference books in, 155
The Rubber Handbook, 347–48
Rudolphine Tables (Kepler), 115–16
Ruiju myogisho, 201
Russia, reference works in, 228–29, 361
Russian Revolution, 225

Sakoku Edict (1639), 202
Sanger, Larry, 387
Sanskrit, early dictionaries of, 30–32
Sargon (Šarru-kinu), 24
Satrapies, 53
Sauvages de Lacroix, François B. de, 299
Scheil, Jean Vincent, 14
Schneider, Johann G. T., 245–46
Schott, Ben, 378–81
Schott's Food & Drink Miscellany, 380–81
Schott's Original Miscellany, 378–81
science. *See also* medicine
  early natural history works, 37–47
  indexes and handbooks, 342–51
Scott, Robert, 248–51
scrolls, 64
Sears, M. U., 183
Secundus, Gaius P. *See* Pliny the Elder
sex manuals, 170–80
Shea, Ammon, 135, 293

Shimabara Rebellion, 201–2
Shiming (Liu Xi), 29–30
Shinsen Jikyo (Shoju), 201
Shizhou, 26
Shoju, 201
Short Treatise on the Game of Whist (Hoyle), 215–20
Shuowen jiezi (Xu Shen), 27–28
Skeat, W. W., 152
slide rule, 113
Slonimsky, Nicolas, 336
Smellie, William, 193–95, 212, 275
Smith, William, 251–52
Socius Mercatoris (Mayne), 108
Soviet encyclopedia, 362–67, 368–69
Speusippus, 68
sports, reference works on, 214, 220–24
Statistical Manual for the Use of Institutions for the Insane, 302
Stephanus, H. (H. Estienne), 140, 245
Suidas, 32–33
Sumerian language dictionary, 24–26
Sushruta Samhita, 82
Synonymia geographica (Ortelius), 96–97

Table Alphabeticall (Cawdrey), 143, 181
Tabula Rudolphina (Kepler), 115–16
Teuffel, Wilhelm Siegmund, 252–53
Te Winkel, Lamert Allard, 262–63
Text to Dispel Ignorance About Everything (Amenemope), 67
Thackeray, William M., 247
Theatrum orbis terrarum (*Theatre of the World*; Ortelius), 95, 97, 98–99
Theophrastus, 37–41, 46

Thesaurus (Roget), 32, 212
Thesaurus geographicus (Ortelius), 97
Thesaurus linguae graecae (Estienne), 245
Thompson, Alexander John, 108–9
Treasure-House of the Greek Language (Estienne), 245
Trench, Richard Chenevix, 265, 268, 269
Tribonian, 18, 19
Tridentine Index, 126
trivia reference books, 371–81
TV Guide, 7

Uranometria (Bayer), 95, 100–102
Urra=hubullu, 25–26, 48
USNO-BI.o, 103

van Lessing, Jacoba, 263
van Wijk, Gerth, 261
Varro, Marcus Terentius, 68, 155, 257
Vaugelas, Claude F. de, 139–42, 141–42
Veazey, William Reed, 348, 349, 350
Victor, Hierosme, 92
Videnskabernes Selskabs Ordbog, 274
Vocabolario degli Accademici della Crusca, 138, 147, 228, 238
Vocabulario da lingoa de Iapam, 201
von Köchel, Ludwig, 336

Wales, Jimmy, 168–69, 184, 292, 387
Wamyo ruijusho (Minamoto), 201
Warburton, William, 145
Watson, Thomas J., 118
Webster, Noah, 78–79, 92, 229–34, 241, 268, 361

Webster's dictionaries, 78–79, 104, 105, 106, 152–53, 168, 198–99, 226, 229–34, 242, 243, 264–65, 274
Wikipedia, 135–36, 168–69, 184, 211, 243, 323, 355, 385–90
William the Conqueror, 58, 60, 61, 63
Wilson, Halsey William, 320
Winder, Robert, 221
Wisden, John, 220–21
Wisden Cricketers' Almanack, 221–24, 225, 242
Wissowa, Georg O. A., 252–56
women, and reference books, 117, 179, 181–84, 263
Worcester, Joseph Emerson, 92, 234
Works Progress Admin., 116–17, 319
World Book Encyclopedia, 243, 292, 355
WorldCat, 322
World Wide Web, databases on
    access to as issue, 226–27
    and alphabetization, 50–51
    edition concept and, 243
    impact on books, 8, 225–27, 355
    issues and dangers of, 323, 388–90
    library catalogs, 322

Xu Shen, 27–28

Yonglè dàdian, 258, 383
Yule, Henry, 206–10

Zedler, Johann H., 186, 275
Zheng Qiao, 312
Zweck, Anlage, und Ergänzung griechischer Wörterbücher (Passow), 246

A NOTE ON THE AUTHOR

JACK LYNCH is a professor of English at Rutgers University. He specializes in English literature of the eighteenth century and the history of the English language. He is the author of several books, including *The Lexicographer's Dilemma: The Evolution of "Proper" English, from Shakespeare to South Park* and *Samuel Johnson's Insults: A Compendium of Snubs, Sneers, Slights, and Effronteries from the Eighteenth-Century Master.* He lives in New Jersey.